A User's Guide to Design Law

A User's Guide to Design Law

by

Clive Thorne and Simon Bennett

Bloomsbury Professional

Bloomsbury Professional Ltd
Maxwelton House
41–43 Boltro Road
Haywards Heath
West Sussex
RH16 1BJ

© Bloomsbury Professional Ltd 2010

British Library Cataloguing-in-Publication Data
A CIP Catalogue record for this book is available from the British Library.

ISBN 978 1 84766 305 4
Typeset by Columns Design Ltd, Reading, Berkshire
Printed and bound in Great Britain by M & A Thomson Litho Ltd, East Kilbride, Glasgow

Preface

The idea of a separate title in the 'User's Guide' series arose as a result of the chapter in a *User's Guide to Copyright* on the subject of 'The Protection of Designs', and a view that practitioners, and students would benefit from an expanded and separate volume on design law.

In the author's view, there is an undoubted need for such a book, particularly in the light of a significant body of case law and legislative change that has taken place over the past five years.

Moreover, the profound influence of Community Designs law has meant that the choice of remedy for design protection is now a good deal more extensive and convoluted than previously. There are now, at least, six major design protection regimes available: UK registered design, UK unregistered design right, Community unregistered design right, Community registered design, residuary copyright, trademark and passing-off as well as the sui generis protection given to semi-conductor chips.

In the author's view, the two most important developments have been the increased value of the UK unregistered design right and the Community registered design. This book attempts to deal with all design rights existing under English law as at February 2010.

The authors are indebted to Arnold & Porter (UK) LLP for providing us with the facility to prepare this book. We are also grateful to the following: Shelley Blythe, Catherine Young, Flavia Gordon, Melanie Orton and Angela Stagg for their considerable assistance in producing it.

It goes without saying that the views expressed in this book are those of the authors and not their respective firms, Arnold & Porter and Fox Williams, and we take full responsibility for any errors and omissions.

Clive Thorne
Simon Bennett
February 2010

Contents

Preface   v

Table of statutes   xi

Table of statutory instruments   xiii

Table of European legislation   xv

Table of cases   xvii

1 UK registered design   1
  Background   1
  What is a 'registered design'?   2
    Novelty   3
    Individual character   4
    Technical function   13
    Geographical scope   15
    Available to the public   15
    Exclusions from registrability   15
    Protection for parts of products   17
    Designs that are connected to one another: the must fit
      exclusion   18
    Proprietorship   19
    Term   20
    Application process   20
    Infringement of registered designs   21
    Remedies for UK registered design infringement   22
    Defences to an action for infringement   22
    Unjustified threats   23

2 UK national unregistered design right   25
  Background   25
  Definition of design right   26
  Definition of 'design' and infringement   27

Contents

Exceptions to design right   31
  A method or principle of construction   31
  The 'must fit' and 'must match' exceptions   32
  Originality   38
  Commonplace   39
  Qualification for design right protection   42
  Qualifying designer   45
  Computer-generated works   45
  Qualifying country   45
  Qualification through first marketing and commissioned
   designs   45
  Recording of the design   46
  Term of unregistered design right   46
  Licences of right   47
  Rights granted by design right   48
  Infringement   48
  Secondary infringement   50
  Remedies for infringement   50
  Threats   51

3 European registered and unregistered design   53
  Legislation   53
   Availability of rights   53
   The new law after the 2001 Regulations   54
   Definition of 'design'   54
   Definition of 'product'   54
   Complex products   55
   Exclusion of technically functional features ('must fit'
    exclusion)   55
  Novelty   57
   Geographical scope   57
   Available to the public   58
   Individual character   58
   Immaterial differences   59
   Grace period   59
   Operative date establishing novelty and individual character   60
   Proprietorship   61
   The term of protection   62
   Dealings   62
   Infringement of registered designs   62
   Infringement of unregistered Community design right 63
   Remedies for UK registered design infringement   63
   Defences to an action for infringement   64
   Unjustified threats   64

Community unregistered design right 64
Subsistence of Community unregistered design right 65
Duration of Community unregistered design right 65
Infringement of Community unregistered design right 65

4 Copyright in industrially applied artistic works 67
Background 67
Artistic works 68
Sculpture 71
Surface decoration 74
Limitation of copyright protection in case of industrial
application 75

5 Protection of designs by trade marks and passing off 77
Background 77
Trade Marks Act 1994 78
The European Court Decision in *Philips v Remington* 80
Shapes resulting from the nature of the goods themselves 81
Shapes necessary to obtain a technical result 82
Signs that consist exclusively of the shape that gives substantial
value to the goods 82
Passing off 83

6 Semiconductor topographies 87
Introduction 87
What is protected? 87
Protection of a layer 88
Term of protection 89
Infringement 89
Ownership and qualification 90

Appendix 1   IPO Forms 91

Appendix 2   OHIM Application for registered community 113

Appendix 3   Legislation 117
UK
Copyright, Designs and Patents Act 1988 117
Registered Designs Act 1949 142
Copyright (Industrial Process and Excluded Articles)
(No 2) Order 1989 201
Copyright, Designs and Patents Act 1988 (Commencement
No 1) Order 1989 202
Design Right (Semiconductor Topographies) Regulations
1989 203

Contents

Design Right (Proceedings before Comptroller) Rules
  1989   211
Registered Designs Regulations 2001   226
Registered Designs Regulations 2003   251
Regulatory Reform (Registered Designs) Order 2006   253
Registered Designs Rules 2006   257

EU
  Commission Regulation (EC) No 2245/2002 of 21 October
    2002 implementing Council Regulation (EC) No 6/2002
    on Community designs   279
  Council Regulation (EC) No 6/2002 of 12 December 2001
    on Community designs   325
  Directive 98/71/EC of the European Parliament and of the
    Council of 13 October 1998 on the legal protection of
    designs   367
  Council Directive of 16 December 1986 on the legal
    protection of topographies of semiconductor products
    (87/54/EEC)   377

Index   385

Table of statutes

PARA

Copyright Act 1956 .... 1.28, 4.33
Copyright and Design
    Act 1839 .... 1.01
Copyright, Designs and
    Patents Act 1988 ...... 1.04, 1.29,
    2.01, 2.52, 2.83, 4.09, 4.18, 4.19,
    4.24, 4.33, App 3
Pt III 2.02, 2.66
s 4 .... 4.06, **App 3**
    (1) 4.08
       (a) 4.18
    (2) 4.18
  16 .... **App 3**
  51 .... 4.03, 4.04, 4.05,4.30, 4.32,
                           App 3
    (3) 2.36
  52 .... 4.02, 4.33–4.36, **App 3**
  53 .... **App 3**
  62–65 .... **App 3**
  97 .... 2.86
  178 .... 2.63
  213 .... 2.04, **App 3**
    (1) 2.42
    (2) 2.06, 2.14, 6.02
    (3)(a) 2.17, 2.18
       (b) 2.28, 2.34
         (i) 2.22
         (ii) 2.25
       (c) 2.35
    (4) 2.43, 2.44, 2.48, 2.53
    (5) 2.05
    (6) 2.05, 2.69, 2.72
    (7) 2.05
  214 .... **App 3**

PARA

Copyright, Designs and Patents Act 1988
    – *contd*
s 214(1) 2.63
    (2) 2.65
  215 .... 2.67, **App 3**
    (2)–(3) 2.59
    (4) 2.59, 2.68
  216 .... **App 3**
    (1) 2.73
  217 .... 2.59, 2.60, **App 3**
  218 .... 2.04, 2.59, 2.60, **App 3**
  219 .... 2.04, 2.59, 2.60, **App 3**
  220 ... 2.04, 2.59, 2.60, 2.67, **App 3**
    (1) 2.68
  221 ..... 2.04, 2.05, 2.59, 2.60, 2.61,
                           App 3
  222–225 .... **App 3**
  226 .... 2.79
  227 .... 2.85
    (1) 2.85
  229 .... 2.86
  233 .... 2.86
  236 .... **App 3**
  237 .... **App 3**
    (1) 2.74
  238–245 .... **App 3**
  247(4) 2.76
  253 .... **App 3**
    (4) 2.87
  254 .... **App 3**
  255 .... 2.59, 2.66, **App 3**
  256 .... 2.59, 2.66, **App 3**
  257–262 .... **App 3**
  263 .... **App 3**

Table of statutes

PARA

Copyright, Designs and Patents Act 1988
  – *contd*
  s 263(1) 2.70
  264 .... **App 3**

Design Act 1842 .... 1.03
Designing and Printing of
  Linen Act 1787 .... 1.01

Patents and Designs Acts
  1907–1946 .... 1.03

Registered Designs Act 1949 .... 1.04,
  1.14, 1.28, 1.29, 2.01, 2.02, 2.03,
  2.28, 3.02, 2.06, 3.02, 3.08, 3.18,
  3.41, 3.47, 4.33, App 3
  s 1 .... 1.09, **App 3**
  (2) 1.36
  (3) 1.29, 3.11, 3.25
  A .... **App 3**
  B .... 1.13, **App 3**
  (1) 3.26
  (2) 3.40
  (3) 3.35, 3.36
  (4) 3.36
  (6)(a) 1.33, 3.30
  (b) 3.29
  (c) 3.43
  (d) 3.43, 3.48
  (e) 3.44, 3.48
  (8) 1.37, 3.17
  C .... 1.30, **App 3**
  (1) 3.20

PARA

Registered Designs Act 1949 – *contd*
  s 1C(2) 1.40
  (3) 3.21
  D .... 1.34, **App 3**
  2 .... 1.42, **App 3**
  (1)–(4) 3.53
  3–7 .... 1.49, 3.58, **App 3**
  7A .... 3.58, 3.62, **App 3**
  (2) 1.53
  8 .... 3.54, **App 3**
  A–11B .... **App 3**
  12 .... 1.44, 3.57, **App 3**
  13–18 .... **App 3**
  19 .... 3.57, **App 3**
  20–24 .... **App 3**
  24A .... 1.56, **App 3**
  B .... 1.55, 1.56, 3.64, **App 3**
  C–24G .... **App 3**
  25 .... **App 3**
  26 .... 1.57, 3.66, **App 3**
  27 .... **App 3**
  A–49 .... **App 3**
  Sch A1 .... **App 3**
  Sch 1 .... **App 3**
  Sch 2 .... **App 3**

Trade Marks Act 1938 ..... 5.02, 5.04,
  5.05
Trade Marks Act 1994 ...... 5.05–5.11
  s 1 .... 5.11
  (1) 5.07
  3(2) 5.06, 5.07, 5.08, 5.12
  (b) 5.17
  (c) 5.19

Table of statutory instruments

Copyright, Designs and
   Patents Act 1988
   (Commencement No 1)
   Order 1989,
   SI 1989/816 .... 2.69, **App 3**
Copyright (Industrial Process
   and Excluded Articles)
   (No 2) Order 1989,
   SI 1989/1070 .... 4.34, **App 3**

Design Right (Proceedings
   before Comptroller)
   Rules 1989,
   SI 1989/1130 .... **App 3**
Design Right (Semiconductor
   Topographies)
   Regulations 1989,
   SI 1989/1100 .... 6.01, 6.04–6.07,
                      6.12, 6.14, **App 3**
reg 2(1), (2) 6.02
reg 6(1), (2) 6.08
reg 8(4) 6.11
Design Right (Semiconductor
   Topographies)
   (Amendment)
   Regulations 2006,
   SI 2006/1833 .... 6.01

Design Right (Semiconductor
   Topographies)
   (Amendment)
   Regulations 2008,
   SI 2008/1434 .... 6.01

Registered Design Rules 1989,
   SI 1989/1105
r 26 .... 1.34

Registered Design Rules 2006,
   SI 2006/1975 ... 1.48, 4.36, **App 3**

Registered Designs
   Regulations 2001,
   SI 2001/3949 ... 1.04, 1.07, **App 3**
s 1 .... 1.34

Registered Designs
   Regulations 2003,
   SI 2003/550 .... 1.04, **App 3**

Regulatory Reform
   (Registered Designs)
   Order 2006,
   SI 2006/1974 .... 1.04, **App 3**

Table of European legislation

Directive 87/54/EC (Protection
of Topography
Directive) 2.51, 6.01
Directive 89/104 (Trade Marks
Directive)
art 3(1)(e) 5.06
Directive 98/71/EC
(Registered Design
Harmonisation
Directive) 1.06, 3.01, 3.24
Recital 10 .... 3.10
art 1 .... 3.15, **App 3**
2 .... **App 3**
3 .... 3.15, **App 3**
(b) 3.11
(1)(e) 5.12
4 .... 3.15, **App 3**
5 .... 3.26, 3.35, **App 3**
6 .... **App 3**
(1) 3.32
(3) 3.44
7 .... **App 3**
(1) 3.19
(3) 3.21
8 .... 3.20, **App 3**
9 .... **App 3**
10 .... **App 3**
11 .... 3.55, **App 3**
12 .... 3.54, **App 3**
13–21 .... **App 3**

Regulation 6/2002/EC
(Community Design
Regulation)
art 1–6 .... **App 3**
7 .... **App 3**
7(1) 1.33, 3.34
8–111 .... **App 3**

Regulation 2245/2002/EC 3.01,
3.08, 3.17, 3.37, **App 3**
art 1 .... **App 3**
(3)(d) 3.13
(6) 3.11
2 .... **App 3**
3 .... **App 3**
(a) 3.08, 3.09
(b) 3.08
4 .... **App 3**
5 .... 3.08, **App 3**
6 .... 3.08, 3.35, **App 3**
7 .... **App 3**
8 .... 3.08, **App 3**
(3) 3.21
9 .... 3.08, **App 3**
10 .... **App 3**
11 .... 3.72, **App 3**
(2) 3.50
12–87 .... **App 3**

Table of cases

A

PARA

AMP Inc v Utilux Pty Ltd [1971] FSR 572, [1972] RPC 103 ..... 1.27, 3.22, 4.01, 4.17

B

Baby Dan AS v Brevi SRL [1999] FSR 377 .... 2.07, 2.84
Bonz Group (Pty) Ltd v Cooke [1994] 3 NZLR 216, (1994) 6 TCLR 23 .... 4.12
Bosch Security Systems BV v Taiden Industrial (Shenzen) Co Ltd Case
    R 1437/2006–3 .... 1.23, 3.60
Brain v Ingledew Brown Bennison and Garrett (a firm) (No 3) [1997] FSR
    511, (1997) 20(5) IPD 20047 .... 2.89
British Leyland Motor Corpn Ltd v Armstrong Patents Co Ltd [1986] AC
    577, [1986] 1 All ER 850, [1986] 2 WLR 400, [1986] ECC 534,
    [1986] FSR 221, [1986] RPC 279, 130 Sol Jo 203, [1986] 2 FTLR 8,
    [1986] LS Gaz R 974, [1986] NLJ Rep 211 ..... 2.03, 2.21, 2.32, 2.34, 4.01, 5.04
British Northrop Ltd v Texteam Blackburrn Ltd [1974] RPC 57/[1976] RPC
    344 .... 2.57

C

C & H Engineering v F Kulcznik & Sons Ltd [1992] FSR 421 .... 2.81
Canon Kabushiki Kaisha v Green Cartridge Co (Hong Kong) Ltd [1997] AC
    728, [1997] 3 WLR 13, [1997] FSR 817, 141 Sol Jo LB 112 .... 2.34
Coca-Cola Co's Applications, Re [1986] 2 All ER 274, [1986] 1 WLR 695,
    [1986] FSR 472, [1986] RPC 421, 130 Sol Jo 429,
    [1986] LS Gaz R 2090, [1986] NLJ Rep 463 .... 5.02, 5.05

D

Davis (J & S) (Holdings) Ltd v Wright Health Group Ltd [1988] RPC 403 .... 4.21
Dualit Ltd's (Toaster Shapes) Trade Mark Applications, Re [1999] RPC 304,
    (1999) 22(1) IPD 22010 .... 5.20

Table of cases

PARA

Dyson Ltd v Qualtex (UK) Ltd [2004] EWHC 2981 (Ch), [2004] EWHC
2981 (Ch), [2005] RPC 395, [2005] IP & T 656, [2004] All ER (D)
375 (Dec) 2.11, 2.12, 2.24, 2.26, 2.30, 2.38, 2.47, 2.55, 2.57

F

Farmers Build Ltd (in liquidation) v Carier Bulk Materials Handling Ltd
[2000] ECDR 42, [1999] RPC 461, [2000] IP & T 49, [1998] All ER
(D) 681 . . . . 2.45, 2.50, 2.53, 2.54, 2.57
Ford Motor Co Ltd's Design Applications, Re [1995] 1 WLR 18,
[1995] RTR 68, [1995] RPC 167, [1995] 08 LS Gaz R 39 . . . . 2.28, 2.29
Frayling Furniture v Premier Upholstery Ltd (1999) 22(5) IPD 22051 . . . . 2.83
Fulton (A) Co Ltd v Grant Barnett Ltd [2001] RPC 16, (2001) 24(1) IPD
24003 . . . . 2.16
Fulton (A) Co Ltd v Totes Isotoner (UK) Ltd [2003] EWCA Civ 1514,
[2004] RPC 301, (2003) Times, 19 November, 147 Sol Jo LB 1306,
[2003] All ER (D) 33 (Nov) 2.08, 2.11, 2.12, 2.16, 6.05
Fundacion Espanola para la Innovacion de la Artesania (FEIA) v Cul de Sac
Espacio Creativo SL Case C-32/08 [2009] ECDR 19, [2009] All ER
(D) 53 (Jul) 1.43

G

Gardex Ltd v Sorata Ltd [1986] RPC 623 . . . . 1.29
Green Lane Products v PMS International Group plc [2008] EWCA Civ
358, [2008] FSR 701, [2009] IP & T 233, [2008] All ER (D) 313
(Apr) 1.33, 3.34

H

Hensher (George) Ltd v Restawhile Upholstery (Lancs) Ltd [1976] AC 64,
[1974] 2 All ER 420, [1974] 2 WLR 700, [1974] FSR 173,
[1975] RPC 31, 118 Sol Jo 329 . . . . 4.09, 4.10, 4.12, 4.15, 4.16, 4.17
Hodgkinson and Corby Ltd v Wards Mobility Services Ltd (No 1)
[1994] 1 WLR 1564, [1995] FSR 169 . . . . 5.26, 5.27

I

Interlego AG v Tyco Industries Inc [1989] AC 217, [1988] 3 All ER 949,
[1988] 3 WLR 678, [1988] RPC 343, 132 Sol Jo 698 . . . . 1.28, 2.46, 4.19

J

Jif Lemon. *See* Reckitt & Colman Products Ltd v Borden Inc (No 3)
Jimmy Choo (Jersey) Ltd v Towerstone Ltd [2008] EWHC 346 (Ch), [2008]
FSR 485, [2008] IP & T 866, [2008] All ER (D) 35 (Jan) 1.55

PARA

K

Karen Millen Ltd v Dunnes Stores [2007] IEHC 449 .... 1.21
Koninklijke Philips Electronics NV v Remington Consumer Products Ltd
    (No 2) [2004] EWHC 2327 (Ch), [2005] FSR 325, (2004) Times,
    2 November, [2004] All ER (D) 301 (Oct); rvsd in part [2006] EWCA
    Civ 16, [2006] FSR 537, [2007] IP & T 206, [2006] All ER (D) 188
    (Jan) 5.17
Koninklijke Philips Electronics NV v Remington Products Australia Pty Ltd
    [2000] FCA 876 .... 3.22, 5.10, 5.11

L

Lambretta Clothing Co Ltd v Teddy Smith (UK) Ltd [2004] EWCA Civ
    886, [2005] RPC 88, [2005] IP & T 609, (2004) Times, 28 September,
    148 Sol Jo LB 911, [2004] All ER (D) 269 (Jul) 2.55, 2.56
Landor & Hawa International Ltd v Azure Designs Ltd [2006] EWCA Civ
    1285, [2007] FSR 181, [2006] All ER (D) 17 (Aug) 2.16, 2.17
LB (Plastics) Ltd v Swish Products Ltd [1979] FSR 145, [1979] RPC 551 .... 2.03,
                                                                            2.32, 4.01
Lloyd Schuhfabrik Meyer & Co GmbH v Klijsen Handel BV Case C-342/97
    [1999] ECR I-3819, [1999] All ER (EC) 587, [1999] IP & T 11 .... 1.19
Lucasfilm Ltd v Ainsworth [2008] EWHC 1878 (Ch), [2009] FSR 103,
    [2009] IP & T 401, [2008] 33 LS Gaz R 24, [2008] All ER (D) 07
    (Aug); rvsd in part [2009] EWCA Civ 1328, (2010) Times, 4 January,
    [2009] All ER (D) 166 (Dec) 1.34, 4.11, 4.15, 4.19, 4.20, 4.26–4.29

M

Mars UK Ltd v Paragon Products BV Case R 1291/2006–3 .... 1.24
Masterman's Design [1991] RPC 89 .... 1.34
Mattel Inc v Woolbro (Distributors) Ltd [2003] EWHC 2412 (Ch), [2004]
    FSR 217 .... 3.75
Metix (UK) Ltd v G H Maughan (Plastics) Ltd [1997] FSR 718 .... 4.23

O

Oakley Inc v Animal Ltd [2005] EWHC 210 (Ch), [2005] RPC 713, (2005)
    Times, 10 March, [2005] All ER (D) 301 (Feb) 4.25
Ocular Sciences Ltd v Aspect Vision Care Ltd (No 2) [1997] RPC 289,
    (1997) 20(3) IPD 20022 .... 1.39, 2.10, 2.24, 2.50, 2.51, 2.82, 3.25

P

Philips Electronics BV v Remington Consumer Products Ltd [1999] ETMR
    816, [1999] RPC 809, [1999] All ER (D) 465 .... 5.18

Table of cases

PARA

Philips Electronics NV v Remington Consumer Products Ltd Case C-299/99
 [2003] Ch 159, [2002] ECR I-5475, [2002] All ER (EC) 634,
 [2003] 1 WLR 294, [2002] 2 CMLR 1329, [2002] IP & T 683, (2002)
 Times, 20 June, [2002] All ER (D) 110 (Jun) 5.08–5.13, 5.15
Procter & Gamble Co v Reckitt Benckiser (UK) Ltd [2007] EWCA Civ 936,
 [2008] Bus LR 801, [2008] FSR 208, [2008] IP & T 704, (2007)
 Times, 17 October, [2007] All ER (D) 133 (Oct) 1.18, 3.26, 3.39

R

R v Registered Designs Appeal Tribunal, ex p Ford Motor Co Ltd
 [1995] 1 WLR 18, [1995] RTR 68, [1995] RPC 167,
 [1995] 08 LS Gaz R 39 . . . . 1.34
Reckitt & Colman Products Ltd v Borden Inc (No 3) [1990] 1 All ER 873,
 [1990] 1 WLR 491, [1990] RPC 341, 134 Sol Jo 784,
 [1990] 16 LS Gaz R 42 . . . . 5.22–5.27
Rolawn Ltd v Turfmech Machinery Ltd [2008] EWHC 989 (Pat),
 [2008] RPC 663, [2008] All ER (D) 77 (May) 1.22, 1.31, 2.06s

S

Sifam Electrical Instrument Co Ltd v Sangamo Weston Ltd [1971] 2 All ER
 1074, [1971] FSR 337, [1973] RPC 899 . . . . 1.08
Stafford Engineering Services Ltd's Licence of Right (Copyright)
 Application Patent Office No 0/454/99, [2000] RPC 797 . . . . 2.78

V

Vermaat (t/a Cotton Productions) v Boncrest Ltd [2001] FSR 5, [2000] All
 ER (D) 737, (2000) 23(8) IPD 23062 . . . . 4.14
Virgin Atlantic Airways Ltd v Premium Aircrafts Interiors Group Ltd
 [2009] EWHC 26 (Pat), [2009] All ER (D) 166 (Jan) 2.82
Volumatic Ltd v Myriad Technologies Ltd (10 April 1995, unreported) 2.13

W

Wham-O Manufacturing Co v Lincoln Industries Ltd [1985] RPC 127,
 [1984] 1 NZLR 641, 3 IPR 115 . . . . 4.19–4.22
Woodhouse UK v Architectural Lighting Systems [2006] ECDR 11,
 [2006] RPC 1 . . . . 1.16

Chapter 1

UK registered design

Background

1.01 Although the protection of designs first became possible in the eighteenth century[1] primarily to protect the designing and printing of linens and cottons, it was not until 1839 that the concept of registration of designs was first introduced. Under the Copyright and Design Act 1839,[2] a registration system was implemented and, unless a design was registered before it had been published, design protection could not be obtained.

1.02 The same Act extended protection far beyond textiles and gave protection to every new or original design including textiles. It also allowed protection for the ornamentation and for the shape and configuration of any article of manufacture.

1.03 The Design Act 1842 divided the possible articles of manufacture and substances into classes. In 1843 this was amended to extend protection of the Act to designs to industrial items. This meant that designs such as springs for a bicycle, an oil can and gas pilot light were capable of registration. From 1911–49 design registration was governed by the designs portion of the Patents and Designs Acts 1907–1946.

1.04 The Registered Designs Act 1949 (RDA 1949) followed and is the current law which provides for the registration of designs and the protection of registered designs in the United Kingdom. It has been amended several times including by the Copyright, Designs and Patents Act 1988, Registered Designs Regulations 2001, Registered Designs Regulations 2003 and the Regulatory Reform (Registered Designs) Order 2006.

---

1   The Designing and Printing of Linen Act in 1787 extended protection to those who engaged in the 'arts of designing and printing linens, cottons, calicos and muslin'.
2   The Copyright and Design Act 1839 also considerably increased the protection given to fabrics by extending the law to fabrics composed of wool, silk or hair and to mixed fabrics.

1.05 The Registered Designs Rules 2006 sets out the procedural rules that the Designs Registry applies when accepting items for inclusion on the register.

1.06 The most far-reaching amendments were made following the Registered Design Regulations 2001 that implemented European Directive 98/71/EC and was intended to harmonise registered design law throughout Europe. The new law applies to UK registered designs which are applied for on or after 9 December 2001. In this chapter we intend to concentrate principally on the new law as the number of UK design registrations that are covered by the old law are diminishing, although we have referred to the old law in order to highlight major differences and where the old law is helpful in interpreting the new law or otherwise remains unchanged by the new law.

What is a 'registered design'?

1.07 Before the amendments that were made following the Registered Designs Regulations 2001, 'a design' was defined as meaning:

> 'Features of shape, configuration, pattern or ornament applied to an article by any industrial process, being features which in the finished article appeal to and are judged by the eye.'

This definition applied to both three-dimensional products (shape and configuration) and two-dimensional products (pattern and ornament).

1.08 What was registered is not the design itself but the article incorporating the design. The design must therefore have been registered separately for various kinds of articles incorporating the same design. In *Sifam Electrical Instrument Co Ltd v Sangamo Weston Ltd*[3] 'an article' was held to be 'anything intended to be sold separately'.

1.09 The definition of 'design' has now changed to:

> 'the appearance of the whole or a part of a product resulting from the features of, in particular, the lines, contours, colours, shape, texture or materials of the product or its ornamentation'.[4]

1.10 The requirement for 'eye appeal', formerly an issue that caused much debate, has disappeared as part of the legislative framework but the concept is still helpful as a reference point when considering the registrability of purely functional items. We will come back to this issue in para **1.25** et seq below.

---

3   [1971] 2 All ER 1074, [1973] RPC 899.
4   RDA 1949 s 1.

1.11 The issue of the protection of parts of products is considered in para **1.35** et seq below.

1.12 The essential elements are now:

- novelty;
- individual character;
- the appearance of the item not being dictated by technical function.

Novelty

1.13 Section 1B of the RDA 1949, headed 'Requirement of novelty and individual character', defines novelty as follows:

'(1) A design shall be protected by a right in a registered design to the extent that the design is new and has individual character.

(2) For the purposes of subsection (1) above, a design is new if no identical design or no design whose features differ only in immaterial details has been made available to the public before the relevant date.

(3) For the purposes of subsection (1) above, a design has individual character if the overall impression it produces on the informed user differs from the overall impression produced on such a user by any design which has been made available to the public before the relevant date.

(4) In determining the extent to which a design has individual character, the degree of freedom of the author in creating the design shall be taken into consideration.

(5) For the purposes of this section, a design has been made available to the public before the relevant date if:-

(a)　it has been published (whether following registration or otherwise), exhibited, used in trade or otherwise disclosed before that date; and

(b)　the disclosure does not fall within subsection (6) below.

(6) A disclosure falls within this subsection if:-

(a)　it could not reasonably have become known before the relevant date in the normal course of business to persons carrying on business in the European Economic Area and specialising in the sector concerned;

(b)　it was made to a person other than the designer, or any successor in title of his, under conditions of confidentiality (whether express or implied);

(c)　it was made by the designer, or any successor in title of his, during the period of 12 months immediately preceding the relevant date;

    (d)   it was made by a person other than the designer, or any successor in title of his, during the period of 12 months immediately preceding the relevant date in consequence of information provided or other action taken by the designer or any successor in title of his; or

    (e)   it was made during the period of 12 months immediately preceding the relevant date as a consequence of an abuse in relation to the designer or any successor in title of his.'

1.14 The design must be new in order to qualify for protection. This is generally expressed by the term 'novelty' in the RDA 1949. It should be noted that novelty is different from 'originality' which applies to copyright and unregistered designs and which is explained in Chapter **2**. Originality requires the element of independent creation, whereas novelty does not. Two people may have arrived at the same design independently, in which case both designs cannot be novel, whereas they could be original. The concept of novelty also applies to community unregistered design right, which produces curious result that an object could acquire UK unregistered design right but be deprived of community unregistered design right if it is not novel. The date when the assessment of novelty is made is when the application is filed or if priority is claimed from an earlier application.[5]

Individual character

1.15 A design has individual character if the overall impression it produces on the informed user differs from the overall impression produced on such a user by any design that has been made available to the public before the relevant date.

1.16 In *Woodhouse UK v Architectural Lighting Systems,*[6] the court interpreted the concept of 'informed user' as meaning the person who is more familiar about what was relevant than one might expect of the average consumer, so that he had some awareness of product trends and what was available in the recent past, but did not have an archival mind (or eye) or more than an average memory. It had to be a regular user of articles of the sort that were the subject of the registered design – a consumer or buyer or someone otherwise familiar with the subject matter – but neither the manufacturer of the articles or 'the man in the street'. The individual in question would typically also have some knowledge of basic technical considerations.

---

5   The Paris Convention allows an applicant in a Paris Convention country to claim priority of the application if made within six months of the first application.

6   [2006] ECDR 11, [2006] RPC1.

1.17   His Honour Judge Fysh said:

'First, this notional person must obviously be a user of articles of the
sort which is subject of the registered design–and I would think, a
regular user at that. He could thus be a consumer or buyer or be
otherwise familiar with the subject matter say, through use at work.
The quality smacks of practical considerations. In my view the
informed user is first, a person to whom the design is directed.
Evidently he is not a manufacturer of the articles and both counsel
roundly rejected the candidature of "the man in the street". "
Informed" to my mind adds a notion of familiarity with the relevant
rather more than what one might expect of the average consumer; it
imports the notion of "what's about in the market?" and "what has
been about in the recent past?". I do not think it requires an archival
mind (or eye) or more than an average memory but it does I think
demand some awareness of product trend and availability and some
knowledge of basic technical considerations (if any). In connection
with the latter, one must not forget that we are in the territory of
designs and thus what matters most is the appearance of things; as
Mr Davis reminded me, these are not petty patents. Therefore, focus
on eye appeal seems more pertinent than familiarity with the under-
lying operational or manufacturing technology (if any)'.

1.18   This issue was also considered in *Procter & Gamble Co v
Reckitt Benckiser (UK) Ltd*.[7] This was a dispute concerning air freshen-
ers. Procter & Gamble had a registered community design for a
'sprayer', which was marketed as 'Febreze', and Reckitt marketed a
product called Air Wick (see photo, p 6 below). P&G claimed that the
Air Wick product infringed its design and Reckitt counterclaimed that
P&G's design was invalid. The two designs in question are set out at pp
6–7 below with the design of the Procter & Gamble product compared
to the Reckitt Air Wick product.

1.19   The court held that the 'informed user' was not the same person
as the 'average consumer' in trade mark law.[8] The 'informed user' has
greater experience and a greater power of recollection. In particular the
'informed user' was to be taken to be aware of the similar designs that
formed part of the 'design corpus'. Here, design corpus related to
sprayers in general, not only sprayers for air-fresheners.

---

7   [2007] EWCA Civ 936, [2008] Bus. LR 801.
8   See *Lloyd Schuhfabrik Meyer v Klijsen Handel Case* C-342/97 [1999] ECR 1–3819.

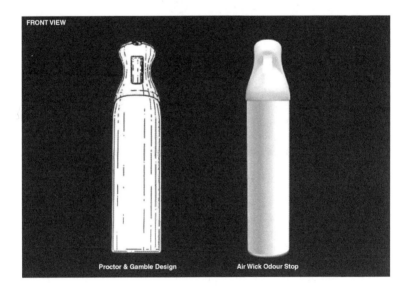

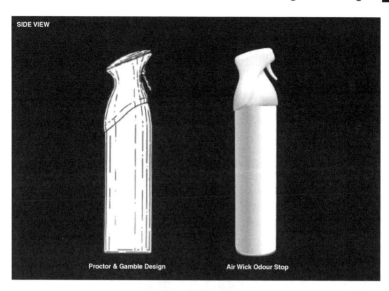

SIDE VIEW

Proctor & Gamble Design   Air Wick Odour Stop

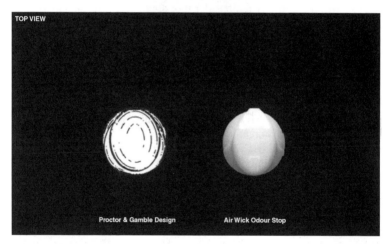

TOP VIEW

Proctor & Gamble Design   Air Wick Odour Stop

1.20 In particular Jacob LJ said:

'25. The informed user of design law is more discriminating. Whilst
I do not say that imperfect recollection has no part to play in judging
what the overall impression of design is, it cannot be decisive. The
Judge placed more emphasis than I think is right on an "imperfect
recollection" test or something like it. He accepted Mr Wyand's
submission that "the overall impression of a design is what sticks in

the mind after [my emphasis] it has been carefully viewed" [57]. I would say that what matters is what strikes the mind of the informed user when it is carefully viewed.

26. I think the Higher Provisional Court in Vienna, in holding that P&G's design is not infringed by the Air-Wick product (decision of 6th December 2006, overruling a lower court decision granting an interim injunction) was right when it said: "The 'informed user' will, in the view of the Appeals Court, have more extensive knowledge than an 'average consumer in possession of average information, awareness and understanding" (see 4 Ob 239/04g), in particular he will be open to design issues and will be fairly familiar with them (*Bulling/Langöhrig/Hellwig, Gemeinschaftsgeschmackmuster* [Community designs], Rz 56).

27. Policy considerations point the same way. The main point of protection of a trade mark is to prevent consumer confusion or deception. The possibility of imperfect recollection plays a significant part in that. The point of protecting a design is to protect that design as a design. So what matters is the overall impression created by it: will the user buy it, consider it or appreciate it for its individual design? That involves the user looking at the article, not half-remembering it. The motivation is different from purchasing or otherwise relying on a trade mark as a guarantee of origin.'

1.21 In the Republic of Ireland in *Karen Millen Ltd v Dunnes Stores*,[9] the court followed this analysis. In particular, Finlay Geoghegan J noted with approval Jacob LJ's conclusion that the 'informed user' is an end user of the products who is alert to design issues, who is better informed than the 'average consumer' in trade mark law, yet is less so than a designer would be. She said:

'the notional informed user for the designs at issue is a woman with a keen sense of fashion, a good knowledge of designs of women's tops and shirts previously made available to the public, alert to design and with a basic understanding of any functional or technical limitations on designs for women's tops and shirts'.

1.22 More recently in *Rolawn Ltd v Turfmech Machinery Ltd*[10] Mann J applied Jacob LJ's consideration of the informed user to be someone who used machines in the turf-growing industry and 'so the design corpus encompasses wide area mowers and other agricultural machinery towed or mounted on the back of tractors for cultivating wide areas'. In this instance clear and manifest differences were identified between Rolawn's

9   Irish High Court, 21 December 2007, [2007] IEHC 449.
10   [2008] EWHC 989 (Pat), [2008] RPC 663.

mower and earlier mowers and non-mowers. Rolawn's mower created a different overall impression and Turfmech's invalidity claim failed.

1.23   The designer's degree of freedom is taken into account when assessing whether a design has 'individual character'. In *Bosch Security Systems BV v Taiden Industrial (Shenzen) Co Ltd*[11] this issue was considered in the context of units for conference systems. In particular the designer's freedom was not limited by the functionality of the units. The designer had a relatively wide degree of freedom and therefore it was difficult to see why the design was so close to the previous design. The differences between the designs, while not immaterial, were not sufficient to create a different overall impression on the user.

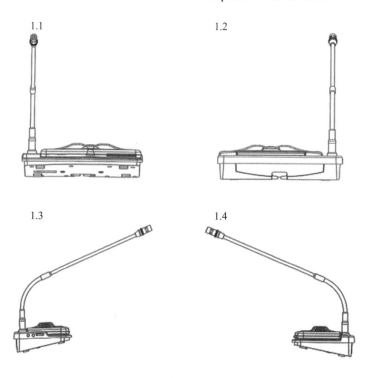

1.1   1.2

1.3   1.4

11   Case R 1437/2006–3.

1.5

1.6

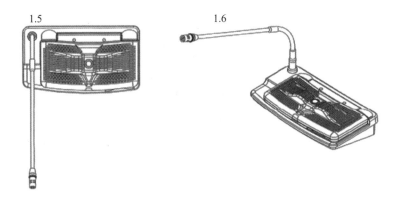

1.7

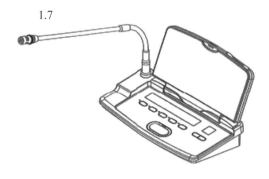

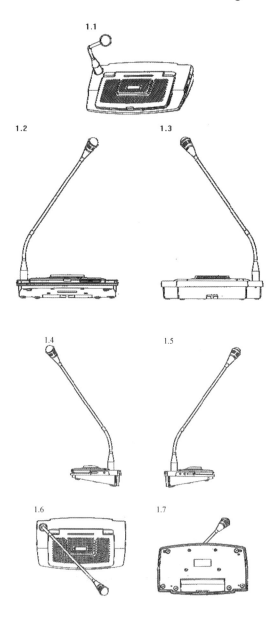

1.1

1.2   1.3

1.4   1.5

1.6   1.7

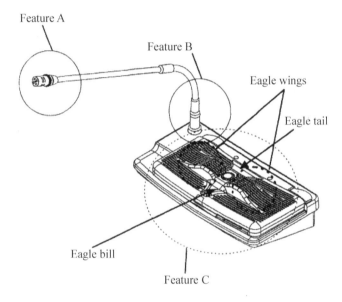

Feature A

Feature B

Eagle wings

Eagle tail

Eagle bill

Feature C

1.24 This issue was also considered in *Mars UK Ltd v Paragon Products BV*[12] which held that the design of a dog chew was invalid. In this case the applicant had an almost unlimited degree of freedom and could have distanced itself much more from the earlier design than simply adding a prong to the design.

12   Case R1291/2006–3.

I.25 It has been held that the whole design need not be new to qualify for registration. It should be noted that the concept of 'new' is not the same concept as 'originality' in copyright. The design will not be new if it differs only in immaterial respects or by way of common trade variants from a prior design.

Technical function

I.26 The issue of the registration of functional items or items dictated solely by their technical function has been an issue that has been the subject of much dispute.

I.27 Under the old law the issue often arose when considering whether an object had 'eye appeal'. In particular, in *AMP Inc v Utilux Pty Ltd,*[13] the House of Lords held that an electrical terminal clip for use inside a washing machine was a (solely) functional design which did not 'appeal to' nor was 'judged by the eye'. The House of Lords set out a number of general propositions, including the following:

(1) the eye to be considered is the 'eye of the customer' and not the 'eye of the judge';
(2) an article may still appeal to the eye even though it is not of aesthetic quality or a work of art;
(3) the intention of the designer is of value but it is not conclusive; and
(4) a solely functional article does not possess features judged solely by the eye since the only issue of interest to purchasers is whether the article will meet its intended function.

I.28 The issue was considered extensively by the Privy Council in *Interlego AG v Tyco Industries Inc.*[14] The case involved the design of children's building blocks. It was argued by Interlego that the designs of the blocks were dictated (solely) by function, which, under the 1956 Copyright Act, would have entitled the design to copyright protection for a period of life plus 50 years rather than the shorter 15-year period from the date of first marketing if it could be shown that the design of the bricks was capable of registration under the RDA 1949. The Privy Council held that an article qualified as a design under the RDA 1949 if its features or configurations, taken as a whole, had 'eye-appeal' even though there were some features that were dictated by purely functional requirements. The shape of the bricks was found to have not only eye-appeal but also significant features of outline and proportion which were not dictated by any mechanical function which the brick had to

---

13 [1971] FSR 572, [1972] RPC 103.
14 [1989] AC 217, [1988] RPC 343.

perform as part of the construction set. In summary, therefore, unless every feature of the design is dictated by the function which the article is to perform, the design of the article is in principle capable of registration as a registered design under the RDA 1949 Act.

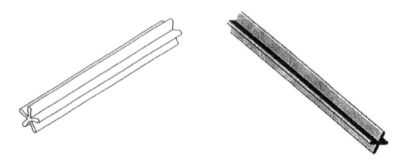

1.29   A further amendment was made by the Copyright, Designs and Patents Act 1988 (CDPA) to RDA s 1(3) to the effect that a design shall not be registered if the 'appearance of the article is not material, that is, if aesthetic considerations are not normally taken into account to a material extent by persons acquiring or using articles of that description, and would not be so taken into account if the designs were applied to the article'. This amendment has the effect of removing from protection under the RDA 1949 many household articles which might otherwise be registrable on the basis that their design is not dictated by function. For example, the case of *Gardex Ltd v Sorata Ltd,*[15] where the design of the underside of a shower tray was held to be registrable, would now be decided differently.

1.30   Section 1C of the RDA 1949 deals with technical function which is as follows:

'(1) A right in a registered design shall not subsist in features of appearance of a product which are solely dictated by the product's technical function.

(2) A right in a registered design shall not subsist in features of appearance of a product which must necessarily be reproduced in their exact form and dimensions so as to permit the product in which the design is incorporated or to which it is applied to be mechanically connected to, or placed in, around or against, another product so that either product may perform its function.

15   [1986] RPC 623.

(3) Subsection (2) above does not prevent a right in a registered design subsisting in a design serving the purpose of allowing multiple assembly or connection of mutually interchangeable products within a modular system.'

1.31   The issue of technical function was referred to in *Rolawn Ltd v Turfmech Machinery Ltd.*[16] In this case, Turfmech claimed that Rolawn's mower design consisted of features of appearance that were dictated solely by the machine's technical function. The issue was abandoned shortly before trial, a fact that Mann J noted with approval in his decision.

Geographical scope

1.32   A UK registered design is new if no identical (or similar) design has been published or is disclosed publicly in the United Kingdom or the European Economic Area (EEA). For example, a design would not be considered new if it had been 'published' on the internet on a site viewable in the EEA before the date it was filed.

Available to the public

1.33   The concept of making available to the public differs from prior art disclosures in patents. In *Green Lane Products v PMS International Group plc*[17] the Court of Appeal confirmed the interpretation of the High Court's interpretation of art 7(1) of the Community Design Regulation[18] – the relevant sector for the purposes of the article included the sector of the prior art and was not limited to the sector for which the design was registered. Prior art available for attacking novelty extends to all kinds of goods, subject to the limited exception of prior art that was obscure even in the sector from which it came (see p 16).

Exclusions from registrability

1.34   Prior to the 2001 Regulations, the old law expressly excluded the following from registration.[19]

(1) Methods or principles of construction, ie the process that gives the article its appearance. For example, weaving of a basket has been held to be a method of construction, whilst the surface ribbing on a hot water bottle has been held to be a design feature rather than a production feature.

---

16   [2008] EWHC 989 (Pat), [2008] RPC 663.
17   [2008] EWCA Civ 358, [2008] FSR 28.
18   6/2002/EC. Article 7(1) is reproduced as s 1B(6)(a) of the RDA 1949.
19   At s 1.

(2) Features of shape or configuration that are dependent upon the appearance of another article of which the article is intended by the author of the design to form an integral part. The effect of this exception is that designs for spare parts, such as car body panels that must fit both with the rest of the body structure and with the design of the car body as a whole, are not normally capable of registration. This should be contrasted with car accessories such as mirrors or alloy wheels, which are likely to be sold separately and registrable in their own right. This so-called 'must match' exception was therefore introduced to prevent the registration of a design whose purpose was to enable the article to which the design has been applied to fit with some other article. This section was

considered by the House of Lords in *R v Registered Designs Appeal Tribunal, ex p Ford Motor Co Ltd*[20] in which their Lordships excluded from registration articles which had 'no independent life as an article of commerce'.

(3) Designs contrary to law or morality. Section 1D of the RDA 1949 excludes designs from registration which would be 'contrary to public policy or to accepted principles of morality'. This issue was considered in *Masterman's Design,*[21] where the court on appeal from the Registrar held that the design of a model doll of a Scotsman wearing and raising a kilt did not offend against morality.

(4) Designs excluded under r 26 of the Registered Design Rules 1989, including sculptures, wall plaques, medallions and printed matter primarily of a literary or artistic character. The issue of sculpture was considered in *Lucasfilm Ltd v Ainsworth.*[22] The case considered the helmets and armour of the stormtroopers from the film *Star Wars* and held that they were not sculptures but a mixture of costume and prop, the primary focus being utilitarian. The concept of sculpture should not go far beyond what an ordinary member of the public would think it meant. There had to be something which 'of its nature is capable of appealing to artistic sensibilities, which must to some extent be the purpose of the article. Mann J, whose views were largely approved by the Court of Appeal,[23] gave the following example:

> 'If the pile of bricks sat in the Tate Modern for two weeks on display as an exhibit, it could be a sculpture. However, if it was left outside a part of a building project, it would clearly not be a sculpture. The difference lay in the purpose of the creator of the pile.'

1.35 To the extent that a design was registered before 2001 these exclusions still apply.

Protection for parts of products

1.36 Registered designs are expressly defined to include 'parts of products'.[24] Formerly the design could only be registered if it was a specific article that could be made or sold separately. This means that it is possible now to register and obtain protection for parts of larger products even if these parts are not sold separately. For example the design of a table leg, which formerly could only be protected as part of

20 [1995] 1 WLR 18, [1995] RPC 167.
21 [1991] RPC 89.
22 [2008] EWHC 1878 (Ch), [2009] FSR 2.
23 [2009] EWCA Civ 1328.
24 The definition of 'design' is: '... the whole *or a part of* a product ...' (RDA 1949 s 1(2)).

the whole table, can now be protected as a separate item, provided it is not considered a functional item. Therefore if only part of a product is novel and has individual character it may be more sensible to register the part only.

1.37 As regards component parts of complex products s 1B(8) of the RDA 1949 states the following:

'(8) For the purposes of this section, a design applied to or incorporated in a product which constitutes a component part of a complex product shall only be considered to be new and to have individual character:

(a)   if the component part, once it has been incorporated into the complex product, remains visible during normal use of the complex product; and

(b)   to the extent that those visible features of the component part are in themselves new and have individual character.

(9) In subsection (8) above "normal use" means use by the end user; but does not include any maintenance, servicing or repair work in relation to the product.'

1.38 In summary, therefore, if the design that is claimed is for a product that is part of a larger product it is not registrable if the product cannot be seen during normal use and the parts themselves that are visible have to be novel and have individual character. Therefore parts of the internal mechanism of an engine may not be registrable or the internal parts of a telephone although under the Semiconductor Topography Regulations it is possible to protect semiconductor circuit boards, which may be hidden from view. This issue is considered in greater detail in Chapter **6**.

Designs that are connected to one another: the must fit exclusion

1.39 The 'must fit' exclusion to design protection is not a new concept and has existed in UK unregistered design right for some time. For example, the sorts of items that would fall within the exception in unregistered design right are contact lenses (because they have to be shaped in a particular way to fit the curvature of the eyeball[25]). The issue is discussed in more detail at paras **2.22–2.24**. The new law is primarily concerned with industrial items to permit products made by different manufacturers to interoperate. Therefore the provision is not

---

25   *Ocular Sciences Ltd v Aspect Vision Care Ltd (No 2)* [1997] RPC 289, (1997) 20(3) IPD 20022.

as broad in scope as that under unregistered design (eg it would not apply to human eyeballs) but the concept is the same.

1.40 Section 1C(2) of the RDA 1949 is set out below:

'(2) A right in a registered design shall not subsist in features of appearance of a product which must necessarily be reproduced in their exact form and dimensions so as to permit the product in which the design is incorporated or to which it is applied to be mechanically connected to, or placed in, around or against, another product so that either product may perform its function.'

1.41 The issue of 'must fit' can be contrasted with the 'must match' exclusion under the old law which is considered in more detail at para **2.25**.

Proprietorship

1.42 Section 2 of the RDA 1949 sets out the ownership criteria of a UK registered design as follows:

'(1) The author of a design shall be treated for the purposes of this Act as the original proprietor of the design, subject to the following provisions.

(1A) Where a design is created in pursuance of a commission for money or money's worth, the person commissioning the design shall be treated as the original proprietor of the design;

(1B) Where, in a case not falling within subsection (1A), a design is created by an employee in the course of his employment, his employer shall be treated as the original proprietor of the design.

(2) Where a design becomes vested, whether by assignment, transmission or operation of law, in any person other than the original proprietor, either alone or jointly with the original proprietor, that other person, or as the case may be the original proprietor and that other person, shall be treated for the purposes of this Act as the proprietor of the design.

(3) In this Act the "author" of a design means the person who creates it.

(4) In the case of a design generated by computer in such that there is no human author, the person by whom the arrangements necessary for the creation of the design are made shall be taken to be the author.'

1.43 In effect this means that the author of the design shall be treated as the original proprietor save that:

(1) where a design is created in pursuance of the commission, the person commissioning the design shall be treated as the original proprietor;

(2) where the design is created by an employee in the course of his employment, his employer is treated as the original proprietor (in *Fundacion Espanola para la Innovacion de la Artesania (FEIA) v Cul de Sac Espacio Creativo SL*,[26] the right of a registered design belongs to the employer where the design has been produced by an employed designer in execution of his duties under the employment contract); and

(3) when a design is computer-generated (where there is no human author) the person who makes the arrangements which are necessary for the creation of the design is the author. The author of the design is defined as the person who creates it.

1.44 Also, registered designs can be assigned, mortgaged and licensed. Dealings with registered UK designs must be registered in the same way as patents.[27] Licences of right of registered designs are no longer available but crown licences are available under RDA s 12, in a similar manner to patents.

Term

1.45 The term of protection is initially five years from the date of the registration of the design. The period for which the right subsists may be extended for a second, third, fourth and fifth period of five years, by applying to the registrar for an extension and paying the prescribed renewal fee. This means that provided the renewal fees are paid (currently on a sliding scale as follows):[27a]

- 2nd period renewal £130.00
- 3rd period renewal £210.00
- 4th period renewal £310.00
- 5th period renewal £450.00

the registration will last for 25 years. Conversely, if the first, second, third or fourth period expires without such application and payment being made, the right shall cease to have effect.

Application process

1.46 Applications for registration are made by submitting Form DF2A and the relevant fee (which is currently £60) to the Patent Office

---

26 [2009] ECDR 19.
27 RDA s 19.
27a Fees correct as of February 2010.

and are examined by the Registrar. Information on how to apply for a design is given on the IPO website.[28]

1.47   In summary the application is only examined to determine that the design:

- is not dictated only by how it works;
- is not offensive; or
- does not involve using certain protected flags and international emblems.

1.48   No prior art search or any substantive considerations as to registrability are undertaken unlike those done to the patent examination process. The examination process normally takes about two months. If the application is rejected the applicant has the right to a hearing to try to persuade the examiner that the registration is registrable. Provided there are no objections the design is registered in three months. The application procedure and how to deal with objections or proceedings before the Registrar is governed by the Registered Design Rules 2006.[29]

Infringement of registered designs

1.49   Community registered designs and registered UK designs[30] give exclusive rights to the use of the design in the respective territorial scope of the design. Infringement arises when the registered design or any design 'which does not produce a different overall impression on the informed user' is used within that territory.

1.50   When considering the 'different overall impression on the informed user' the degree of freedom of the author in creating the design shall be taken into consideration. See paras **1.16–1.20** for more discussion of this issue, and the extent to which a product made to the design is capable of infringing the design registration in question.

1.51   To prove infringement of a design the proprietor must prove that:

- there was an act of infringement; and
- the infringing design is the same or sufficiently similar to fall within the scope of the monopoly protection.

1.52   Use of the design is taken to 'include' a reference to:

---

28   See www.ipo.gov.uk/d-howtoapply.pdf.
29   See www.opsi.gov.uk/si/si2006/20061975.htm.
30   RDA(E) s 7.

- the making, offering, putting on the market, importing, exporting or using of a product in which the design is incorporated or to which it is applied; or
- stocking such a product for these purposes.

Any acts that are done without the permission of the owners of the registered design but fall into the categories set out above will constitute infringement.

1.53 It is not an infringement to do acts privately and for non-commercial purposes or for experimental or teaching purposes.[31]

1.54 Proceedings may not be brought for infringement before the certificate of registration is granted.

Remedies for UK registered design infringement

1.55 Actions for UK registered design right infringement may be brought in the High Court of Justice (Patents Court) or the Patents county court. A successful claimant would normally be entitled to:

- an injunction restraining further infringement;
- an order for the delivery-up or destruction of articles that infringe the design;
- damages for infringement (which would probably be assessed at a separate damages inquiry). However, no damages can be awarded against a defendant who was unaware and had no reasonable ground for supporting that the design was registered;[32] and/or
- an account of the profits made by the infringing defendant.

Defences to an action for infringement

1.56 A defendant to a claim for infringement would normally wish to consider defending the action on the basis that:

- the articles complained of did not infringe the design. The defendant would have to prove that the items in question gave a different overall impression to the informed consumer; and/or
- to counterclaim that the registered design was invalid because it lacked novelty and/or individual character, so that the register should be rectified by removal of the design and marked with an indication of its invalidity (or a declaration that there is no relevant Community unregistered design); and/or

---

31 RDA 1949 s 7A(2).
32 RDA s 24B. However see *Jimmy Choo (Jersey) Ltd v Towerstone Ltd* [2008] EWHC 346 (Ch) where it was held that the defence of innocent infringement only applied to UK Registered Designs and not Community registered designs.

- a limited defence is available for 'innocent infringement'.[33] However, this is not available when the infringer is deemed to have been aware or it is reasonable to expect that the design was registered, such as the article is marked as being protected by a registered design.

Unjustified threats

1.57 Section 26 of the RDA 1949 provides remedies for groundless threats of registered design infringement. Extreme care should be taken to ensure that an act of infringement is not threatened. 'Mere notification' of the design does not constitute a threat. A person threatened can:

- claim against the proprietor or any person (including professional advisers) making the threat, that the threats are unjustified;
- seek an injunction to restrain continued threats; and
- seek damages to compensate for any loss suffered.

1.58 The UK courts have construed widely what constitutes a threat. The writer of a letter, even if acting in a professional capacity (eg a solicitor), may also have a personal liability in addition to the client. It is normally prudent therefore to do no more in open correspondence addressed to the infringer than notify of the existence of the registration.

33 RDA ss 24A and 24B.

Chapter 2

UK national unregistered design right

Background

2.01 Unregistered design right or 'design right' as it is more commonly known, was introduced in the Copyright, Designs and Patents Act 1988 (CDPA 1988) as a means of providing residual protection for functional designs that would not qualify for protection under the RDA 1949. The scope of design right, however, is sufficiently wide so as to encompass designs that might also be registered under the RDA.

2.02 The right is something of a hybrid, incorporating elements from copyright, registered design and patent law. Overall, the monopoly protection given by a registered design creates a stronger right. The main differences between registered design protection under the RDA and unregistered design protection are as follows:

	Registered design	Unregistered design right
1.	Subject to official examination at Designs Registry.	Arises automatically subject to qualification.
2.	Registrable at Designs Registry.	Not registrable.
3.	Must be novel.	Need not be novel but a requirement of 'original' creation; must be created independently and not be 'commonplace'.
4.	Infringement does not require copying.	Infringement requires copying.
5.	Maximum term 25 years.	Maximum term 15 years.
6.	Governed by RDA 1949 as amended.	Governed by Part III of CDPA 1988.
7.	In general the rights granted can overlap with unregistered rights.	

2.03 The introduction of design right was also intended to represent a commercial compromise from the prior law of design copyright, which reached its apotheosis in *LB (Plastics) Ltd v Swish Products Ltd*[1] with the unnecessarily long 50 year plus life term of protection for purely functional designs and the then 15 years from the date of first marketing term of protection for aesthetic designs capable of registration under the RDA. The intention behind the new right was threefold: to provide a relatively easy means of design protection; to provide for a term of protection not exceeding 15 years from the date of first marketing; and to reach a compromise in respect of the protection of spare parts following *British Leyland Motor Corpn Ltd v Armstrong Patents Co Ltd.*[2]

Definition of design right

2.04 Section 213 of the CDPA 1988 provides as follows:

'(1) Design right is a property right which subsists in accordance with this Part in an original design.

(2) In this Part "design" means the design of any aspect of the shape or configuration (whether internal or external) of the whole or part of an article.

(3) Design right does not subsist in—

(a) a method or principle of construction,
(b) features of shape or configuration of an article which—

(i) enable the article to be connected to, or placed in, around or against, another article so that either article may perform its function, or
(ii) are dependent upon the appearance of another article of which the article is intended by the designer to form an integral part, or

(c) surface decoration.

(4) A design is not "original" for the purposes of this Part if it is commonplace in the design field in question at the time of its creation.

(5) Design right subsists in a design only if the design qualifies for design right protection by reference to—

1   [1979] RPC 511.
2   [1986] AC 577, [1986] RPC 279.

(a)   the designer or the person by whom the design was commissioned or the designer employed (see sections 218 and 219), or

(b)   the person by whom and country in which articles made to the design were first marketed (see section 220),

or in accordance with any Order under section 221 (power to make further provision with respect to qualification).

(6) Design right does not subsist unless and until the design has been recorded in a design document or an article has been made to the design.

(7) Design right does not subsist in a design which was so recorded, or to which an article was made, before the commencement of this Part.'

2.05   It should be noted that 'design right' is merely described as 'a property right which subsists in accordance with this Part in an original design'. It should also be noted that in order to qualify for protection, the design right subsists:

(1)   only if the design qualifies for design right protection by reference to the designer or the person by whom the design was commissioned or the designer employed; or of the person by whom and the country in which articles made to the design were first marketed; or in accordance with any order under s 221 (power to make further provision with respect to qualification);[3]

(2)   unless and until the design has been recorded in a design document, or an article has been made to the design;[4]

(3)   the design was so recorded or an article was made to the design, before the commencement of this Part, ie 1 August 1989[5]

Definition of 'design' and infringement

2.06   CDPA 1988 s 213(2) states that 'design' means 'the design of any aspect of the shape or configuration (whether internal or external) of the whole or part of an article'. Helpful interpretation of the meaning of this section is given by Mann J in *Rolawn Ltd v Turfmech Machinery*[6] who pointed out that the right cannot exist until there is an embodiment of the design in an article or in a design document.

2.07   This definition has given considerable difficulty in practice. This is because the proprietor of the design can choose to assert design right

---

3   CDPA 1988 s 213(5).
4   CDPA s 213(6).
5   CDPA s 213(7).
6   [2008] RPC 27.

in 'the whole or in any part of his product'. Thus in *Baby Dan AS v Brevi SRL*,[7] Jacob J referred to the analogy of a teapot so that the right vests in the teapot as a whole as well as in parts such as the spout, handle, or lid or even part of the lid. It was argued that even if the part in relation to which protection was claimed lacked 'visual significance' it would still be protected.

2.08 An unfortunate side effect of the definition, which was surprisingly approved by the Court of Appeal in *A Fulton Co Ltd v Totes Isotoner (UK) Ltd* [8] is that infringement may be established in part only of the design, even though the infringing article, when looked at as a whole, could not be regarded as a reproduction of the protected design. That case related to the design of a fabric umbrella case with a slit at the top of one corner of the case.

7   [1999] FSR 377.
8   [2003] EWCA Civ 1514, [2004] RPC 16.

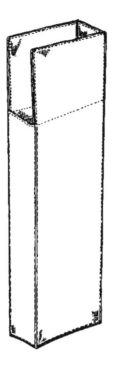

2.09 The Court of Appeal approved the concept of infringement of part only of the design even though, at first instance, Judge Fysh in the Patents county court had found that the infringing umbrella case, when taken as a whole, did not infringe the claimant's registered design of the whole umbrella case.

2.10 The practice had grown up (following Laddie J in *Ocular Sciences v Aspect Vision Care*[9]) of pleading unregistered design infringement, not merely in the design as a whole but in 'cropped' or 'trimmed' parts of the design. This, undoubtedly, had the unjust effect of a defendant not being able to evaluate the merits of the claim against it nor of establishing whether the defendant's design infringes until the claim against it is fully pleaded or at the least fully set out in an initial demand letter.

9   [1997] RPC 289 at 422.

2.11 The point was considered again by the Court of Appeal in *Dyson Ltd v Qualtex (UK) Ltd*[10] where the court followed *A Fulton v Totes Isotoner (UK) Ltd* but stressed there must be a 'limit.'

2.12 Jacob LJ gave the leading judgment in both appeals and stated in *Dyson*:

'So I turn to the individual points argued, of which this was the first. UDR can subsist in the "design of any aspect of the shape or configuration (whether internal or external) of the whole or part of an article". This is extremely wide – it means that a particular article may and generally will embody a multitude of "designs" – as many aspects of the whole or part of the article as can be. What the point was of defining "design" in this way, I do not know. The same approach is not adopted for ordinary copyright where the work is treated as a whole. But even if with this wide definition, there is a limit: there must be an "aspect" of at least a part of the article. What are the limits of that? I put it this way in *Fulton v Totes* (2004) RPC 16:

"The notion conveyed by 'aspect' in the composite phrase ... is 'discernible' or 'recognisable'.'"

2.13 In response to counsel's argument that the limit was more extensive, and following a reference to the unreported case of *Volumatic Ltd v Myriad Ltd*[11] where the judge adopted a copyright type case of 'visual significance', Jacob LJ continued:

'That is alright for features of shape provided one remembers that UDR can subsist in an aspect of part of an article. The test does not mean that one can simply forget an aspect of the design or the whole article on the grounds that it is a visually insignificant feature of the design of the whole article. If one focuses on that aspect consisting of the alleged "twiddle" alone, it is difficult to see how it can be visually insignificant. That is why I prefer my formulation.'

2.14 Jacob LJ also recognised that design right can subsist in aspects of detail because they are 'aspects of part of an article' and so qualify within CDPA 1988 s 213(2). He justified that view by saying that it 'hardly lies in the mouth of an exact copyist to say that the exactitude with which he has copied does not matter visually'. With respect that may be the position with regard to 'exact copies' but arguably does not justify the position when a particular 'aspect' of an article only has been taken.

---

10   [2006] EWCA Civ 166, [2006] RPC 31.
11   Sir John Vinelott, 10 April 1995.

Exceptions to design right

2.15   Unregistered design right does not subsist in the following.

A method or principle of construction[12]

2.16   This was considered in *A Fulton Co Ltd v Grant Barnett Ltd*[13] where Park J considered that the design (of an umbrella case) was based on the shape or configuration produced by methods of construction of the design. Park J (whose remarks were approved by the Court of Appeal in *Landor & Hawa International Ltd v Azure Designs Ltd*[14]) stated:

> 'The fact that a special method or principle of construction may have been used in order to create an article with a particular shape or configuration, does not mean that there is no design right in the shape or configuration. The law of design right will not prevent competitors using that method or principle of construction to create competing designs ... as long as the competing designs do not have the same shape or configuration as the design right owner's design has.'

2.17   Behind the Court of Appeal's reasoning in *Landor & Hawa* was the view that CDPA 1988 s 213(3)(a) should be construed narrowly and that it did not apply merely because a design served a functional purpose. It would not apply unless it could be shown that the functional purpose could not be achieved by any other means.

2.18   In giving the leading judgment, Neuberger LJ stated:

> 'In my opinion, the Judge's interpretation of section 213(3)(a) is correct. First the section does not, as a matter of ordinary language, preclude a design being protected merely because it has a functional purpose. The language is perhaps a little opaque, but the words "method or principle" are important, and serve, in my view, to emphasize that mere functionality is quite insufficient to exclude a design from protection. Tempting though it may be to seek to redefine or expand on those words, I think it would normally be unhelpful in practice, and arguably wrong in principle, to do so, save to explain in a particular case why they do or do not apply.'

2.19   That case arose as a result of a dispute about the design of a type of suitcase having an 'expander' section. The main issue was whether design right protection was excluded because the expander section constituted 'a method or principle of construction'.

---

12   CDPA 1988 s 213(3)(a).
13   [2001] RPC 16, (2001) 24(1) IPD 24003.
14   [2006] EWCA Civ 1285, [2007] FSR 9.

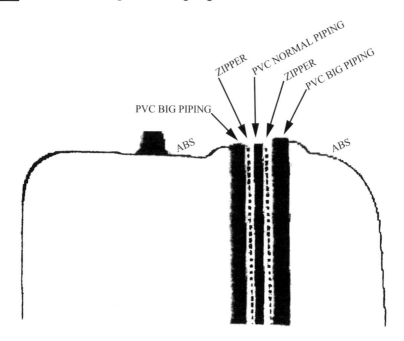

The 'must fit' and 'must match' exceptions

2.20 Features of the shape or configuration of an article that enable the article to be connected to or placed in, around or against another article so that either article may perform its function, or which are dependent upon the appearance of another article of which the article is intended by the design to form an integral part, constitute the so-called well-known 'must fit' and 'must match' exceptions.[15]

2.21 Features of articles that are dictated by the need to fit or interface with each other so that the two together can perform their intended function, e g car mechanical parts such as an exhaust pipe, or which are dictated by the appearance of another part with which it is required to form an integral whole, such as car body parts, are excluded from design right protection. These exceptions were influenced by the 'spare parts exception' as expounded by the House of Lords in *British Leyland Motor Corpn Ltd v Armstrong Patents Co Ltd*[16] and in an attempt to reach a compromise in respect of spare part protection with the new right, the unregistered design right.

15 CDPA 1988 s 213(3).
16 [1986] AC 577, [1986] RPC 279.

THE 'MUST FIT' EXCEPTION[17]

2.22   CDPA 1988 s 213(3)(b)(i) provides that:

'Design right does not subsist in—

(b)   features of shape or configuration of an article which—

(i)   enable the article to be connected to, or placed in, around or against, another article so that either article may perform its function, …'

2.23   This subsection sets out the so-called 'must fit' exception even though the section does not specifically refer to a concept of 'must fit'.

2.24   The leading authority is the Court of Appeal decision in *Dyson Ltd v Qualtex (UK) Ltd.*[18] The Court of Appeal accepted propositions set out in the judgment of the trial judge, Mann J.[19] These are as follows:

(1)   It does not matter if there are two ways of achieving the necessary fit or connection between the subject article and the article to which it fits or with which it interfaces. If the design chosen by the design right owner is a way of achieving that fit or interface, then it does not attract design right no matter how many alternative ways of achieving the same 'fit' might be available. The article with which the subject article is interfacing can be part of the human body.

   In that case, triggers and a catch were designed to interface with the human finger or thumb. (The judge relied upon the earlier decision of Laddie LJ in *Ocular Sciences Ltd v Aspect Vision Care Ltd*[20] who had held that the design of contact lenses was excluded from protection because they were designed to fit with the eyeball which was an 'article', albeit living.)

(2)   The exception excludes design right even if the relevant part of the design performs some function other than the function described in CDPA 1998 s 213(3)(b)(i).

   The subject matter of *Dyson v Qualtex* were spare parts for Dyson vacuum cleaners and in particular spare parts known as 'pattern parts'. These are replicas of the original parts made deliberately so to look as close as possible to the original parts.

17   CDPA 1988 s 213(3)(b)(i).
18   [2006] EWCA Civ 166, [2006] RPC 31.
19   [2004] EWHC 2981 (Ch), [2005] RPC 19.
20   [1997] RPC 289, (1997) 20(3) IPD 20022.

THE 'MUST MATCH' EXCEPTION[21]

2.25 CDPA 1988 s 213(3)(b)(ii) provides that:

'Design right does not subsist in—

(b)   features of shape or configuration of an article which—

(ii)   are dependent upon the appearance of another article of which the article is intended by the designer to form an integral part ...'

2.26 It can be seen that the crucial word within the subsection is 'dependent' and whether there is dependency upon the appearance of another article of which the first article is intended by the designer to form an integral part. In *Dyson v Qualtex*, the trial judge applied the test by considering whether there is dependency of the kind, or to the extent, which would make the overall article in question (art 2) radically different in appearance if (art 1) it were not the shape it is. He held that this was a test of fact and degree and of impression. He recognised that, in many cases, it would be a difficult test to apply and raised the possibility of 'saleability' of the item as a cross-check in particular cases.

2.27 This view was rejected by the Court of Appeal on the basis that the concept of 'dependency' is concerned with the relationship between the appearance of the part and the appearance of the whole.

2.28 The Court of Appeal considered the earlier House of Lords decision in *Ford Motor Co Ltd's Design Application*,[22] which was a case concerned with registrability under the RDA 1949 of design parts for Ford vehicles. The RDA, as it had been amended in 1988, excluded from registration the features of shape or configuration defined in the same way as under CDPA 1988 s 213(3)(b). Jacob LJ commented that carrying over the provision into s 213 was 'an odd thing to do'. This was because registered designs are limited to articles, whereas unregistered design right can subsist in an aspect of a design.

2.29 *Ford's Design Application* concerned an application for registration of a range of parts. At first instance, Mr Julian Jeffs QC rejected the argument that you consider the article with the part missing, eg. a car minus a door as one 'article' and the 'part' as the other article. He stressed that the designer of the door did not intend it to form an integral part of a vehicle with the door missing but rather an integral part of the complete vehicle. In applying the test, Mr Jeffs found that

21   CDPA 1988 s 213(3)(b)(ii).
22   [1995] 1 WLR 18, [1995] RPC 167.

there was design dependency in relation to body panels but in relation to accessories, such as wheels, steering wheels and wing mirrors, he held there was no dependence and therefore the application for the registered design could proceed . He said:

'I come now to the second group of components, such items as wing mirrors, wheels, seats and the steering wheel. All of them are visible on the car as sold but substitutions can be made without radically affecting the appearance or identity of the vehicle. It is such standard practice that I can take judicial notice of the fact that alternatives may be offered for items such as these and an owner may choose to substitute proprietary items in order to give his vehicle a sportier appearance, or (where a seat is concerned) greater comfort, or for a variety of other reasons. Although if any substitution is made, the owner may wish it to blend in the general style of the vehicle, I am of the view that such items are not 'dependent upon the appearance of another article'.'

2.30   In the Divisional Court, McCowan LJ relied upon the concept of 'design freedom' so that if the question is whether the manufacturer of the spare part has design freedom, then he is a candidate for registration, but if he has not, he is not such a candidate. This view was accepted by Jacob LJ in the Court of Appeal in *Dyson Ltd v Qualtex* when he stated:

'The Judge's "radically different in appearance" test is much the same as Mr Jeffs' "substitutions can be made without radically affecting the appearance or identity of the vehicle" test. It is another way of looking at dependency. If there is, as a technical matter, design freedom for the part, then there is no dependency ...

I accept this latter proposition. One has to approach the provision bearing in mind that Parliament did not intend to exclude all spare parts, or even all externally visible portions of spare parts, yet such was the substance of Mr Arnold's submission. "Dependency" must be viewed practically. In some cases, the answer is obvious – the paradigm example being body parts for cars. In others it may be necessary to examine the position more carefully. But unless the spare parts dealer can show that as a practical matter there is a real need to copy a feature of shape or configuration because of some design consideration of the whole article, he is not within the exclusion. It is not enough to assert that the public "prefers" an exact copy for it will always do so for the reason I gave above. The more there is design freedom the less is there room for the exclusion. In the end it is a question of degree – the sort of thing where a judge is called upon to make a value judgment. Unless wrong in principle, his evaluation will not be interfered with on appeal.'

2.31 It is submitted that the test of 'design freedom' represents the only practical test that will be workable in practice. Moreover, it has the merit of providing protection for designs that have been created with the necessary degree of design freedom. Those designs that have been dictated by the need to 'match' and inherently cannot be the subject of design freedom are rightly excluded from design right protection.

THE BRITISH LEYLAND EXCEPTION

2.32 The background to *British Leyland Motor Corpn Ltd v Armstrong Patents Co Ltd*[23] was the interpretation of the Design Copyright Act 1968 as ultimately approved by the House of Lords in *LB (Plastics) Ltd v Swish Products Ltd*,[24] which accepted that copyright law could be used to prevent the copying of most industrial articles on the basis of three-dimensional copying of the two-dimensional design drawings. This was coupled with the inevitable commercial desire on the part of original designers and manufacturers of consumer items (OEMs – original equipment manufacturers) to control the trade in spare parts for their machines. The practice grew up of reserving the market in spare parts to the manufacturer of the original item, eg a motor car, and therefore controlling or licensing spare parts such as the exhaust pipe, the subject of the *British Leyland* case.

2.33 There was a strong view in the House of Lords against the exercise of intellectual property monopoly rights to control the sale of spare parts that led, particularly in the speeches of Lord Bridge of Harwich and Lord Templeman, to the development of an implied right of repair and non-derogation of grant to prevent the use of copyright law to prevent the sale of spare parts. The decision has been described by Jacob LJ as 'truly remarkable':

> 'All the appellants' arguments were rejected but the House of Lords found a new one of its own. And it did so without hearing argument on the point or giving the respondents an opportunity of commenting on the argument or the authorities used to justify it. If a lower court had done that, it would have been rightly castigated.'[25]

2.34 It is unclear as to the extent to which the spare parts exception remains available by way of defence in intellectual property cases. It has been much criticised. In particular, the Privy Council in *Canon v*

---

23 [1986] AC 577, [1986] RPC 279.
24 [1979] FSR 145, [1979] RPC 551.
25 See *The Judicial House of Lords* (OUP, 2009) 721.

Green Cartridge[26] rejected the applicability of the exception to economic circumstances in Hong Kong on the basis, as was put by Lord Hoffmann, that the doctrine was limited to clear cases of anticompetitiveness, or those where the ordinary man would 'unquestionably assume that he could do for himself (or commission someone else to do'). Nevertheless, it is submitted that the exception remains law and the decision of the House of Lords in *British Leyland* remains binding on lower courts. In practice, there appears to be a recognition that it is something of an aberration designed to deal with the design law protection pre-CDPA and where defences, such as CDPA 1988 s 213(3)(b) in respect of design right infringement and defences available to European registered design protection, did not exist. It has not, though, been put fully to bed as an available defence.

SURFACE DECORATION[27]

2.35   Surface decoration is excluded from unregistered design right by CDPA 1988 s 213(3)(c).

2.36   It should be noted that this corresponds with CDPA 1988 s 51(3) in respect of copyright protection where 'design' is defined as:

'means the design of any aspect of the shape or configuration (whether internal or external) of the whole or part of an article, *other* than surface decoration'.

2.37   The effect, therefore, is that surface decoration is not excluded from ordinary copyright protection, but is excluded from unregistered design right protection.

2.38   The meaning of surface decoration was considered by the Court of Appeal in *Dyson Ltd v Qualtex (UK) Ltd*[28] where the trial judge took the view that the distinction between surface decoration and the overall shape and configuration of the design of the product overall may well be 'a matter of fact and impression, or a value judgment'. The Court of Appeal considered that surface decoration should not necessarily be limited to a surface that is already there, but that it was a matter for the 'ordinary reasonable consumer or designer' to decide whether they were looking at a decorated surface.

2.39   Jacob LJ, who gave the leading judgment, went on by saying:

'I do not see why design law should see things differently: that law already sometimes seems to be a particularly abstruse branch of

26   [1997] AC 728, [1997] FSR 817.
27   CDPA s 213(3)(c).
28   [2006] EWCA Civ 166, [2006] RPC 31.

metaphysics. There is no need to make things worse by finding things to be surface decoration which would not ordinarily be so perceived.'

2.40 The Court of Appeal rejected any limitation of surface decoration to the decoration of a surface that was already present and pointed out that there was no reason why the decoration should not come into existence with the surface.

2.41 The court was also asked to consider whether surface features that have a function could be regarded as surface decoration. The Court of Appeal took the view that surface decoration would not include 'surface features which have significant function'. The court approved the example of ribbing on a handle that provided a grip as a finding of fact. Such ribbing was therefore not surface decoration.

Originality

2.42 CDPA 1988 s 213(1) provides that the:

'design right is a property right which subsists in accordance with this Part in an original design'.

2.43 'Original design' is not defined. However, CDPA 1988 s 213(4) provides that:

'a design is not "original" for the purposes of this Part if it is commonplace in the design field in question at the time of its creation'.'

2.44 An early question to be decided by the courts was whether 'original' for the purposes of s 213(4) was akin to 'novelty' in the sense used by patent law or 'originality' in the sense used by copyright law.

2.45 The Court of Appeal in *Farmers Build Ltd* (*in liquidation*) *v Carier Bulk Materials Handling Ltd*[29] considered it in a copyright sense. Mummery LJ put it on the following basis:

'The Court must be satisfied that the design for which protection is claimed has not simply been copied (e g lack of photocopy) from the design of an earlier article. It must not forget that, in the field of designs of functional articles, one design may be very similar to, or even identical with another design and yet not be a copy: it may be an original and independent shape and configuration coincidentally the same or similar. If, however, the Court is satisfied that it has been slavishly copied from an earlier design, it is not an "original" design in the "copyright sense".'

29   [2000] ECDR 42, [1999] RPC 461.

2.46   The leading copyright decision on originality in the context of industrial designs remains *Interlego AG v Tyco*[30] where the Privy Council adopted a test of 'visual significance' (but on the basis that there had been a prior act of copying). The case involved design drawings for Lego bricks in which later drawings were produced by a redrawing process equivalent to photocopying or tracing the earlier drawing and making small alterations or emendations to it. Lord Oliver put it this way:

> 'the post 1972 drawings do demonstrate some very minor visual deviations from the original pre-1973 drawings from which they are derived, but they are visually insignificant, with the possible exception of the omission of the radii on the outer diameters of the tubes'.

2.47   A good example of the test in operation is *Dyson Ltd v Qualtex (UK) Ltd* where the Court of Appeal gave the caveat that '… adding an old thing onto something else, even if that is new, is not enough to create an original new design. Thus on the facts of the case, adding an "old winder" to a "new handle" did not constitute "originality".'

Commonplace

2.48   CDPA 1988 s 213(4) provides that:

> 'A design is not 'original' for the purposes of this Part (of the CDPA) if it is commonplace in the design field in question at the time of its creation.'

2.49   The purpose of excluding commonplace designs from unregistered design right protection appears to be an attempt to prevent designers monopolising designs that competitors could produce in the normal course of trade to prevent a designer from monopolising design contents that are well-known in the trade.

2.50   The concept of 'commonplace' was first considered in depth by Laddie J in *Ocular Sciences v Aspect Vision*[31] and subsequently by the Court of Appeal in *Farmers Build Ltd v Carrier Bulk Materials (Handling) Ltd.*[32]

2.51   In *Ocular Sciences* Laddie J noted that the origin of the word 'commonplace' came from the Semi-Conductor Topography Directive, Directive No 87/54/EC, which provided that:

---

30   [1989] AC 217, [1988] RPC 343.
31   [1997] RPC 289, (1997) 20(3) IPD 20022.
32   [2000] ECDR 42, [1999] RPC 461.

'Any new combination of well-known features was intended to be the subject of a monopoly, all semi-conductor topographies would be protected and the commonplace exclusion would be no exclusion at all.'

2.52 He went on as follows:

'It is always undesirable to replace one ambiguous expression by another, and for that reason it is not right to redefine the word "commonplace" in the 1988 Act but it seems to me that the flavour of the word is much along the lines suggested by … Any design which is trite, trivial, common-or-garden, hackneyed or the type which would excite no peculiar attention in the relevant art.'

2.53 The Court of Appeal in *Farmers Build* appeared to accept that concept and considered that in practice construction of the commonplace exclusion should be narrow. Mummery LJ stated:

'The shorter life of the design right (rather than registered designs), the narrower scope of protection against copying and the prima facie protection given by the design's functional articles are indications that the reference to "commonplace" designs in section 213(4) should be interpreted narrowly rather than broadly.'

2.54 In *Farmers Build* the Court of Appeal suggested five steps that would lead to defining whether in any particular case a design is commonplace. These are as follows:

(1) The court should compare a design of the article in which the design right is claimed with the design of other articles in the same field, including the alleged infringing article, as at the time of its creation.

(2) The court must be satisfied that the design for which the protection is claimed has not simply been copied (e g like a photocopier) from the design of an earlier article.

(3) If the court is satisfied that the design has not been copied from an earlier design, then it is 'original' in the 'copyright' sense. The court then has to decide whether it is 'commonplace'. For that purpose it is necessary to ascertain how similar that design is to the design of similar articles in the same field of design made by persons other than the parties or persons unconnected with the parties.

(4) This comparative exercise must be conducted objectively in the light of the evidence, including evidence from experts in the relevant field pointing out the similarities and the differences and explaining the significance of them.

(5) If there are aspects of the plaintiff's design of the article that are not to be found in any other design in the field in question and

those aspects are found in the defendant's design the court would be entitled to conclude that the design in question is not commonplace. That would be so even though the design in question would not begin to satisfy any requirements of novelty in the registered design's registration.

The five tests set out by Mummery LJ have been much criticised.[33].

2.55 An alternative view has been taken by Jacob LJ in two appeal decisions: *Lambretta Clothing Co Ltd v Teddy Smith (UK) Ltd*[34] and *Dyson Ltd v Qualtex (UK) Ltd.*[35]

2.56 In *Lambretta* Jacob LJ stated:

'What really matters is what prior designs the experts are able to identify and how much those designs are shown to be current in the thinking of designers in the field at the time of creation of the designs.'

2.57 In *Dyson Ltd v Qualtex UK Ltd* Jacob LJ stated:

'I am not sure that the differences of opinion have any significance. For it is difficult to think of an example where it matters. It is important here to focus on exactly the context in which the question "commonplace or not" arises. That context is this: a particular aspect of the shape or configuration of an article or part of an article has been identified and has been found "original in the copyright sense". One then asked whether that aspect is commonplace. Clearly there will be cases where the answer is yes – for instance every aspects of the washers whose design drawings were held original in *British Northrop*. To that extent, at least, the criticism of *Farmers Build* in Laddie et al paragraph 53.25, namely it can be read as "giving the commonplace exclusion of vanishing small scope" must be an error. If all you have done is to design a common object, you have merely made your own design of that which is commonplace.'

2.58 Jacob LJ then went on to consider the case where the designer started with 'something old, very well-known but unique to a particular manufacturer'. He used the example of a Coca-Cola bottle. He stated:

'If a man just copies it his work will not be "original". So there is no need for the commonplace exception there. If he copies it but makes visual variants which can properly be called "aspects of part of his

33 See, for example, Laddie Prescott and Vitoria *Modern Law of Copyright and Design* (3rd edn, 2000) para 53.25.
34 [2004] EWCA Civ 886, [2005] RPC 6.
35 [2006] EWCA Civ 166, [2006] RPC 31.

design" then those variants will get UDR unless they themselves are either not original or are commonplace. But that is unlikely. The example shows that what one is focusing on is the ultimate "design": whether the designer started with some well-known prior art or not. Only if the designer make an "original" (because not copied) design of a bottle which happens to be the same as that of a Coca-Cola bottle does the problem arise of whether that design is to be regarded as commonplace. But that is improbable.'

Qualification for design right protection

2.59   CDPA 1988 ss 217–221 provide as follows:

'217 Qualifying individuals and qualifying persons

(1) In this Part—

"qualifying individual" means a citizen or subject of, or an individual habitually resident in, a qualifying country; and
"qualifying person" means a qualifying individual or a body corporate or other body having legal personality which—

> (a)   is formed under the law of a part of the United Kingdom or another qualifying country, and
> (b)   has in any qualifying country a place of business at which substantial business activity is carried on.

(2) References in this Part to a qualifying person include the Crown and the government of any other qualifying country.

(3) In this section "qualifying country" means—

(a)   the United Kingdom,
(b)   a country to which this Part extends by virtue of an Order under section 255,
(c)   another member State of the European Economic Community, or
(d)   to the extent that an Order under section 256 so provides, a country designated under that section as enjoying reciprocal protection.

(4) The reference in the definition of "qualifying individual" to a person's being a citizen or subject of a qualifying country shall be construed—

(a)   in relation to the United Kingdom, as a reference to his being a British citizen, and
(b)   in relation to a colony of the United Kingdom, as a reference to his being a British Dependent Territories' citizen by connection with that colony.

(5) In determining for the purpose of the definition of "qualifying person" whether substantial business activity is carried on at a place of business in any country, no account shall be taken of dealings in goods which are at all material times outside that country.

218 Qualification by reference to designer

(1) This section applies to a design which is not created in pursuance of a commission or in the course of employment.

(2) A design to which this section applies qualifies for design right protection if the designer is a qualifying individual or, in the case of a computer-generated design, a qualifying person.

(3) A joint design to which this section applies qualifies for design right protection if any of the designers is a qualifying individual or, as the case may be, a qualifying person.

(4) Where a joint design qualifies for design right protection under this section, only those designers who are qualifying individuals or qualifying persons are entitled to design right under section 215(1) (first ownership of design right: entitlement of designer).

219 Qualification by reference to commissioner or employer

(1) A design qualifies for design right protection if it is created in pursuance of a commission from, or in the course of employment with, a qualifying person.

(2) In the case of a joint commission or joint employment a design qualifies for design right protection if any of the commissioners or employers is a qualifying person.

(3) Where a design which is jointly commissioned or created in the course of joint employment qualifies for design right protection under this section, only those commissioners or employers who are qualifying persons are entitled to design right under section 215(2) or (3) (first ownership of design right: entitlement of commissioner or employer).

220 Qualification by reference to first marketing

(1) A design which does not qualify for design right protection under section 218 or 219 (qualification by reference to designer, commissioner or employer) qualifies for design right protection if the first marketing of articles made to the design—

(a)   is by a qualifying person who is exclusively authorised to put such articles on the market in the United Kingdom, and

(b) takes place in the United Kingdom, another country to which this Part extends by virtue of an Order under section 255, or another member State of the European Economic Community.

(2) If the first marketing of articles made to the design is done jointly by two or more persons, the design qualifies for design right protection if any of those persons meets the requirements specified in subsection (1)(a).

(3) In such a case only the persons who meet those requirements are entitled to design right under section 215(4) (first ownership of design right: entitlement of first marketer of articles made to the design).

(4) In subsection (1)(a) "exclusively authorised" refers—

(a) to authorisation by the person who would have been first owner of design right as designer, commissioner of the design or employer of the designer if he had been a qualifying person, or by a person lawfully claiming under such a person, and

(b) to exclusivity capable of being enforced by legal proceedings in the United Kingdom.

221 Power to make further provision as to qualification

(1) Her Majesty may, with a view to fulfilling an international obligation of the United Kingdom, by Order in Council provide that a design qualifies for design right protection if such requirements as are specified in the Order are met.

(2) An Order may make different provision for different descriptions of design or article; and may make such consequential modifications of the operation of sections 215 (ownership of design right) and sections 218 to 220 (other means of qualification) as appear to Her Majesty to be appropriate.

(3) A statutory instrument containing an Order in Council under this section shall be subject to annulment in pursuance of a resolution of either House of Parliament.'

2.60 Complicated provisions contained in CDPA 1988 ss 217–221 govern the qualification for design right protection. Generally, only designs created in the United Kingdom, the EU and certain limited designated countries (mainly British dependent territories) are entitled to protection. In particular, designs created in nations such as the United States, Japan and the EEA nations, such as Norway, would not normally qualify for design right protection. For a design to be protected:

(1) the designer must be a qualifying person;

(2) the design must have been created by an employee of or commissioned by persons who are qualifying persons.

(3) the first marketing of articles made to the design must have been undertaken by a qualifying person and in a qualifying country.

2.61 There is power under s 221 to add to these methods of qualification by order-in-council where it is necessary to do so to meet any international obligation.

Qualifying designer

2.62 CDPA 1988 s 214(1) provides that:

'In this Part the "designer", in relation to a design, means the person who creates it.'

2.63 CDPA 1988 s 214(1) defines the designer as the person who creates the design. In the case of computer-generated designs, it is deemed to be the person by whom the arrangements necessary for the creation of the design are undertaken. (This accords with a similar definition in respect of copyright works under CDPA 1988 s 178.)

2.64 The designer must be a citizen or subject or an individual habitually resident in a qualifying country.

Computer-generated works

2.65 CDPA 1988 s 214(2) provides that:

'In the case of a computer-generated design the person by whom the arrangements necessary for the creation of the design are undertaken shall be taken to be the designer.'

Qualifying country

2.66 This is defined as meaning:

(1) the United Kingdom;

(2) a country to which Part III of the Act extends by virtue of an order under s 255;

(3) another member state of the European Economic Area; or

(4) a country designated under s 256 as enjoying reciprocal protection.

Qualification through first marketing and commissioned designs

2.67 CDPA 1988 s 215 provides that:

'215. Ownership of design right

(1) The designer is the first owner of any design right in a design which is not created in pursuance of a commission or in the course of employment.

(2) Where a design is created in pursuance of a commission, the person commissioning the design is the first owner of any design right in it.

(3) Where, in a case not falling within subsection (2) a design is created by an employee in the course of his employment, his employer is the first owner of any design right in the design.

(4) If a design qualifies for design right protection by virtue of section 220 (qualification by reference to first marketing of articles made to the design), the above rules do not apply and the person by whom the articles in question are marketed is the first owner of the design right.'

2.68 First marketing may provide an alternative method of qualification for design right, in which case the first owner of the design right is deemed to be the person who performs the act of first marketing under CDPA 1988 s 215(4). Section 220(1) provides four requirements for qualification by first marketing. These are:

(1) 'articles made to the design' have been marketed;
(2) the marketing of such articles takes place first in one of a number of qualifying countries;
(3) such first marketing is by a 'qualifying person';
(4) the qualifying person is exclusively authorised to put the articles on the market in the United Kingdom.

Recording of the design

2.69 Under CDPA 1988 s 213(6), design right does not subsist until the design has been recorded in a design document or, alternatively, an article has been made to the design under the transitional provisions contained in SI 1989/816. The recording of a design must have taken place after 1 August 1989.

2.70 CDPA 1988 s 263(1) provides that a design document is any record of a design whether in the form of a drawing, a written description, a photograph, data stored in a computer or otherwise.

2.71 The basis of this requirement is that a record exists of the design that can be identified and provides the basis of design right. This is essential given the fact that unregistered design right is not a registered right.

Term of unregistered design right

2.72 Design right is expressed to last for 15 years from the recording of the design document pursuant to CDPA 1988 s 213(6) or, more commonly, 10 years from the date on which articles made for the design were placed on the market in the United Kingdom.

2.73 This is governed by CDPA 1988 s 216(1) which provides:

'Design right expires—

(a) fifteen years from the end of the calendar year in which the design was first recorded in a design document or an article was first made to the design, whichever first occurred, or

(b) if articles made to the design are made available for sale or hire within five years from the end of that calendar year, ten years from the end of the calendar year in which that first occurred.'

Licences of right

2.74 During the final five years of the term of design right, any person is entitled, as of right, to a licence of right. This is governed by CDPA 1988 s 237(1) which provides:

'Any person is entitled as of right to a licence to do in the last five years of the design right term anything which would otherwise infringe the design right.'

2.75 The basis of the licence of right is to make the design available for exploitation by third parties during the last five years of the term of design right in circumstances when such exploitation would otherwise constitute infringement.

2.76 Application for a licence of right, in the absence of grant by the design right owner, should be made to the Comptroller-General. CDPA 1988 s 247(4) provides that in fixing the terms of a licence, the Comptroller shall have regard to such factors as may be prescribed by the Secretary of State. To date, no such factors have been prescribed.

2.77 A licence settled by the Comptroller reverts back to the date of the application or, if the application was made before the last five-year period of design right, to the beginning of the five-year period.

2.78 There is little case law on the subject of design right licences of right. An example is *Stafford Engineering Services Ltd's Application.*[36] In that case, the design right owner failed to disclose drawings of the design pursuant to an order of the Comptroller. The Comptroller ordered that the applicant for the licence should be given a royalty-free licence in respect of all drawings, if any, which should have been but were not disclosed. A term was also inserted in the licence requiring the

36 Patent Office No 0/454/99.

design right owner to indemnify the applicant in the event that the rights licensed were not owned by him. A royalty of 4% on sales was fixed in respect of the licence for the design subject of those drawings which had been disclosed.

Rights granted by design right

2.79 The owner of the design right is granted the exclusive right (without territorial limitation) to reproduce the design for commercial purposes by making articles to the design or by making a design document recording the design for the purpose of enabling such articles to be made. It follows that infringement occurs when a person without the licence of a design right owner does or authorises another to do anything which is one of the owner's exclusive rights. This infringement is set out in CDPA 1988 s 226:

'(1) The owner of design right in a design has the exclusive right to reproduce the design for commercial purposes—

(a)   by making articles to that design, or
(b)   by making a design document recording the design for the purpose of enabling such articles to be made.

(2) Reproduction of a design by making articles to the design means copying the design so as to produce articles exactly or substantially to that design, and references in this Part to making articles to a design shall be construed accordingly.

(3) Design right is infringed by a person who without the licence of the design right owner does, or authorises another to do, anything which by virtue of this section is the exclusive right of the design right owner.

(4) For the purposes of this section reproduction may be direct or indirect, and it is immaterial whether any intervening acts themselves infringe the design right.

(5) This section has effect subject to the provisions of Chapter III (exceptions to rights of design right owner).'

Infringement

2.80 Pursuant to CDPA 1988 s 226(2), infringement consists of copying the design so as to reproduce articles exactly or substantially to the design. An infringer makes an article to a design if he incorporates or has applied to it those aspects of shape or configuration that constitute the design.

2.81 The test for infringement was considered by Aldous J in *C & H Engineering v F Kulcznik & Sons Ltd*,[37] a case involving pig fenders for use in pig-feeding. The judge compared the alleged infringement in its entirety with the design and held that because the infringement embodied other features, there was, on the evidence, no infringement. There must be a copying of the design so as to reproduce articles exactly or substantially to a design. He held that substantiality was an objective test to be decided through the eyes of the person to whom the design was directed, ie the intended customer. In deciding whether the infringement was sufficiently close, it was legitimate to look at the offending articles with the design right claim and consider the differences between them as to whether they not only attracted the customer's eye but would also be seen as being functionally significant. The test means that it is open to a court to consider whether, on the evidence, a customer is likely to consider that certain features of the alleged infringement are of greater significance because of their function and therefore attract visual attention.

2.82 This should be contrasted with *Ocular Sciences Ltd v Aspect Vision Care*,[38] a case involving contact lenses where the differences were not capable of being considered by the eye alone. In that case, the court accepted expert evidence as to the differences. In considering infringement the test is for the court. The role of expert evidence is limited to pointing out to the court the similarities and differences between the design and infringement and their significance. A good example is Lewison J in *Virgin Atlantic Airways Ltd v Premium Aircrafts Interiors Group Ltd*[39] a case involving flat seats in aircraft.

2.83 There are a number of cases where the defendant has relied upon the similarity of the infringing design with prior art that exists. It is argued that bringing in a concept of 'novelty' is unjustified in the field of unregistered design right and that this is an issue which goes to 'commonplace' rather than infringement. Thus in *Frayling Furniture v Premier Upholstery Ltd*[40] the defendant relied upon drawings of prior designs that were close to the allegedly infringing designs and argued that the scope of the design right should be narrow. The judge stated:

'The squeeze argument had a lot of force where one item of prior art can destroy the registration. It has far less force in the field of unregistered design right under the 1988 Act, where the identical or

---

37 [1992] FSR 421.
38 [1997] RPC 289, (1997) 20(3) IPD 20022.
39 [2009] EWCHC 26.
40 (1999) 22(5) IPD 22051.

closely similar prior art have to exist in sufficient numbers and be sufficiently well known to make the design commonplace.'

2.84 Similarly in *Baby Dan AS v Brevi SRL*,[41], Jacob J stated:

'Where differences between the design in question and earlier designs not relied upon are small so that the degree of originality is small, the claimant can only succeed if the differences between the defendant's design and the design complained of is closer than that of the earlier design.'

Secondary infringement

2.85 Secondary infringement provisions exist under CDPA 1988 s 227. Section 227(1) provides:

'(1) Design right is infringed by a person who, without the licence of the design right owner—

(a)   imports into the United Kingdom for commercial purposes, or
(b)   has in his possession for commercial purposes, or
(c)   ells, lets for hire, or offers or exposes for sale or hire, in the course of a business,

an article which is, and which he knows or has reason to believe is, an infringing article.'

Remedies for infringement

2.86 The usual remedies for infringement of intellectual property rights are available, including damages, injunctions and accounts of profit. In addition, in cases of flagrant infringement of design right, the court has jurisdiction to award additional damages on a basis similar to CDPA 1988 s 97. The equivalent provisions are set out in s 229:

'(1) An infringement of design right is actionable by the design right owner.

(2) In an action for infringement of design right all such relief by way of damages, injunctions, accounts or otherwise is available to the plaintiff as is available in respect of the infringement of any other property right.

(3) The court may in an action for infringement of design right, having regard to all the circumstances and in particular to—

41   [1999] FSR 377, (1998) 21(12) IPD 21134.

(a) the flagrancy of the infringement, and
(b) any benefit accruing to the defendant by reason of the infringement,

award such additional damages as the justice of the case may require.

(4) This section has effect subject to section 233 (innocent infringement).'

Threats

2.87 It is an actionable tort to make threats of unjustified unregistered design infringement under CDPA 1988 s 253(4). It should be noted that it is not actionable merely to notify a third party that a design is protected by design right,[42] nor is it actual for threat to bring infringement proceedings in respect of the manufacture or importation of articles and design documents.[43] These provisions are similar to those relating to unjustified threats of patent infringement and registered design infringement.

'(1) Where a person threatens another person with proceedings for infringement of design right, a person aggrieved by the threats may bring an action against him claiming—

(a) a declaration to the effect that the threats are unjustifiable;
(b) an injunction against the continuance of the threats;
(c) damages in respect of any loss which he has sustained by the threats.

(2) If the plaintiff proves that the threats were made and that he is a person aggrieved by them, he is entitled to the relief claimed unless the defendant shows that the acts in respect of which proceedings were threatened did constitute, or if done would have constituted, an infringement of the design right concerned.

(3) Proceedings may not be brought under this section in respect of a threat to bring proceedings for an infringement alleged to consist of making or importing anything.

(4) Mere notification that a design is protected by design right does not constitute a threat of proceedings for the purposes of this section.'

42 CDPA 1988 s 253(4).
43 CDPA 1988 s 253(3).

2.88   It has been argued strongly[44] that the incorporation of a threats provision into design right law is ill-conceived. The original justification for unjustified threats was to attempt to prevent unscrupulous owners of registered rights from using threats of infringement proceedings as a basis of stifling competition. In the case of registered rights such as patents, trade marks and registered designs, there may be greater justification for threats remedies on the basis that the rights in question are registered and publicly available. In the case of an unregistered right such as design right, it should arguably be necessary for the design right owner to write fully to the alleged infringer pointing out the basis and scope of the right.

2.89   A good example of the harshness of the threats provisions can be seen in *Brain v Ingledew Brown Bennison and Garrett (a firm) (No 3)*.[45]

2.90   In *Grimme Landmaschinenfabrik GmbH & Co KG v Scott*[46] a successful claim for unjustified threats of unregistered design infringement arose in relation to a letter in which the defendant had stated:

'Please note that our client does not intend to commence proceedings against you … but of course our client reserves all its rights in this matter.'

Floyd J accepted that it was well established that a threat could be implied as well as being expressed. The test was what effect the letter would have on the ordinary recipient. In the circumstances, the letter constituted 'a veiled threat of infringement proceedings' so that the ordinary recipient of the letter reading the sentence referred to above would take the view that the claimant did not at present intend to commence proceedings against the recipient of the letter but would be likely to do so in the future.

---

44   See, for example, Laddie Prescott and Vitoria *Modern Law of Copyright and Design* (3rd edn, 2000), para 556.41.
45   [1997] FSR 511, (1997) 20(5) IPD 20047.
46   [2010] FSR 11.

Chapter 3

European registered and unregistered design

Legislation

3.01 Commission Regulation 2245/2002/EC of 12 December 2001 (the 'Regulation') which implemented Council Directive (EC) 6/2002 introduced a system of European registered and unregistered rights. This is binding in its entirety and directly applicable in all member states. There is therefore no national implementing legislation in respect of the Community rights. The Regulation creates directly enforceable rights. The Regulation is in key aspects identically worded to the Registered Design Harmonisation Directive 98/71/EEC.

3.02 The UK's RDA 1949 was substantially amended to ensure the UK's law on registered designs was harmonised with the rest of the Community. As some pre-Community amendment designs and law are still relevant we refer to the RDA 1949 amended to reflect the Community legislation as the 'RDA'.

3.03 This section discusses the law as it applies to both Community registered design and Community unregistered design right, as well as UK registered design right. Where there are differences between the individual rights, these are set out at the end of each section.

Availability of rights

3.04 The Community Registry at the Office of Harmonization for the Internal Market (OHIM) began accepting applications for Community registered designs from 1 April 2003.

3.05 The Community unregistered design right applies to designs which were first made publicly available within the Community or put on the market from 6 March 2002.

3.06 The RDA applies to UK registered designs applied for from 9 December 2001.

3.07 The Community and UK registered design rights are largely similar, but they differ in geographic coverage and application procedure

The new law after the 2001 Regulations[1]

3.08 In order to be protectable as either a Community design (registered and unregistered) or a UK registered design under the RDA the following requirements must be satisfied:

- the definition of 'design' must be satisfied (art 3(a));
- the 'design' must relate to a 'product' (art 3(b));
- the 'design' must not relate to functional features (art 8);
- the 'design' must be 'new' (art 5);
- the 'design' must have 'individual character' (art 6);
- the 'design' must not be contrary to public policy or morality.[2]

Definition of 'design'

3.09 Under art 3(a) 'design' is defined as 'the *appearance* of the whole or part of a product resulting from the features of, in particular, the lines, contours, colours, shape, texture and/or materials of the product itself and/or its ornamentation'.

3.10 Recital 10 of the Directive makes it clear that the 'appearance' of the product is of paramount concern.

Definition of 'product'

3.11 A 'product' is defined as 'any industrial or handicraft item other than a computer program; and, in particular, includes packaging, get-up, graphic symbols, typographic typefaces and parts intended to be assembled into a complex product'.[3]

3.12 The inclusion of typographic typefaces reflects old-style printing plates, even though typefaces are now generally electronic.

3.13 Although a design relates to a specific product, the scope of protection is not limited to that product, but applies to any product in which the design is used.[4] This is a very different position to the pre-RDA position, under which the protection applied only to the application of the design to that type of product.

---

1   Commission Regulation 2245/2002/EC of 12 December 2001.
2   Regulation art 9 (RDA s 1D).
3   Directive art 3(b), Regulation art 1(6) and RDA s 1(3).
4   Regulation art 1(3)(d).

Complex products

3.14 The definition of 'product' is widely worded and includes parts intended to be assembled into a complex product, eg packaged kit-form kitchen units.

3.15 A 'complex product' is defined as 'a product that is composed of at least two replaceable component parts permitting disassembly and reassembly of the product'.[5] There are special rules relating to design for component parts of 'complex products'.[6]

3.16 Component parts must remain visible when the complex product is in normal use by the end user of the 'complex product' and the design only applies to the extent that the visible features of the component part fulfil the requirements for novelty and individual character.

3.17 This concept was introduced into UK law[7] by the Community Regulation and differs from the previous UK position that a design had to apply to a specific article, which could be made and sold separately.

3.18 Consequently, spare and replacement parts can generally now be registered (unlike the position under previous incarnations of the UK's RDA 1949). Although, this should be contrasted with para **3.20** below, which provides that articles that 'must fit' or connect to another article are not registrable.

Exclusion of technically functional features ('must fit' exclusion)[8]

3.19 In general, a design can now be registered irrespective of any aesthetic merit, ie designs with an element of functionality may be registrable, though designs 'dictated solely by the product's technical function' may not be registered.

3.20 This 'must fit' exclusion is contained in Directive art 8.[9] In other words, features which must be reproduced in their exact form and dimensions so as to permit the product incorporating the design, or products to which the design is applied, to be connected to another product so either can perform its function, eg auditorium seating with interlocking features that provide for multiple assembly, cannot be registered.

5   Directive art 1.
6   Directive arts 3 and 4.
7   RDA s 1B(8).
8   Also see Directive art 7(1).
9   RDA s 1C(1).

3.21 There is an exemption to the 'must fit' exclusion for 'modular products'. This is where designs serve 'the purpose of allowing multiple assembly or connection of mutually interchangeable products within a modular system'.[10] This is what's known as the 'Lego Bricks' clause since Lego bricks would be covered. However, this exception does not permit designs dictated by technical function of the product.

3.22 The new 'must fit' exclusion is a similar exclusion to that arising in pre-1988 UK design copyright law. Thus the electric terminal considered by the House of Lords in *AMP Inc v Utilux Pty Ltd*[11] would not attract protection. A similar interpretation was accorded by the ECJ in the trade mark case of *Philips v Remington,*[12] where the court held that:

> 'the grounds for refusal of [trade mark] registration ... is to prevent trade mark protection from granting its proprietor a monopoly on technical solutions or characteristics of a product ...'

3.23 Although functional features are not protected, the definition of 'design' includes 'texture' and 'ornamentation' (e g surface decoration'), so some features that have largely functional purposes or two dimensional objects (see para **3.24** below) may be registrable.

3.24 The wide scope of the Directive also permits two-dimensional objects to be registered: some examples of two-dimensional designs that have been registered are:

3.25 In the UK case of *Ocular Sciences Ltd v Aspect Vision Care Ltd*[13] it was held that a human eyeball is an 'article' and therefore the registered design for a contact lens fell within this exemption. However, it is difficult to see how an eyeball could be considered a

---

10 Directive art 7(3), Regulation art 8(3) and RDA s 1C(3).
11 [1971] FSR 572, [1972] RPC 103.
12 [2000] FCA 876.
13 [1997] RPC 289 at line 425–35, (1997) 20(3) IPD 20022.

'product' under the wording of the RDA s 1(3), which refers to 'any industrial or handicraft item'; so the contact lens would probably be registerable under the new law.

Novelty

3.26   Directive art 5 requires a design to be 'new' and have 'individual character'[14] These requirements apply to both registered and unregistered Community designs: and UK registered design under the RDA. This issue has been discussed at length in **Chapter 1** concerning the *Reckitt Benckiser* case and can be contrasted with UK unregistered designs where the originality requirement is still necessary. When applying for a design registration the Designs Registry does not examine the application to test if it is new or compare it to other entries on the register.

3.27   The onus is therefore placed on the applicant to consider the novelty and individual character of their design before applying to register it. Otherwise the design may subsequently be challenged by a third party who believes that the design is not novel and this may lead to invalidation of the registration.

3.28   If an applicant is in doubt about the validity of their design they can ask the UK-IPO or a trade mark or patent agent to carry out a search of prior registered designs. This may help the applicant to decide if their design is novel.

3.29   Registered design protection is not lost if the design is disclosed under express or implied conditions of confidentiality (s 1B(6)(b)).

Geographical scope

3.30   The novelty of a registered or unregistered Community Design will now be defeated by prior disclosure anywhere in the world where it could reasonably have come to the attention of someone carrying on business in the European Economic Area (s 1B(6)(a)).

3.31   Previously registered UK design right would only be defeated by such disclosure in the United Kingdom. It is not clear whether the geographical scope for prior disclosure in relation to a new UK registered design is worldwide or limited to the United Kingdom. Given the global nature of the markets, however, it would appear logical for the disclosure to be on a worldwide basis, but the courts may chose to treat this on a case-by-case basis.

14   RDA s 1B(1).

Available to the public

3.32   Article 6(1) of the Directive defines the concept of making a design *available to the public*, ie publishing the design.

3.33   This definition extends to UK and Community registered design and Community unregistered design. The concept of making available to the public differs from the old UK law on designs and the law relating to prior art disclosures in patents. The definition gives rise to several grey areas including:

- whether the disclosure of the design should be in relation to a particular product;
- how many people should the publication be made towards and whether you have to prove that those people were actually aware of the publication; and
- what is meant by the 'sector concerned'. Does it relate to the sector to which the prior art is relevant or the sector to which the registered or unregistered design in issue is relevant, or both?

3.34   Those issues have been partly resolved now following *Green Lane Products v PMS International Group plc*[15] in which the Court of Appeal confirmed the interpretation of the High Court's interpretation of art 7(1) of the Community Design Regulation (6/2002/EC)[16] – the relevant sector for the purposes of the article included the sector of the prior art and was not limited to the sector for which the design was registered. Prior art available for attacking novelty extends to all kinds of goods, subject to the limited exception of prior art that was obscure even in the sector from which it came.

Individual character

3.35   Article 6 of the Regulation provides that a design shall be considered to have individual character:

> 'if the overall impression it produces on the informed user differs from the overall impression produced on such a user by any design which has been made available to the public.'[17]

3.36   The designer's degree of freedom is taken into account when assessing whether a design has 'individual character'.[18]

---

15 [2008] EWCA Civ 358, [2008] FSR 28.
16 Article 7(1) is reproduced as RDA s 1B(6)(a).
17 This wording is derived from Directive art 5 and is reflected in RDA s 1B(3).
18 RDA s 1B(3) and (4).

3.37   The Regulation's recitals also require consideration to be given to the product to which the design applies and the industrial sector to which the design belongs.

3.38   It should be noted that 'overall impression' is the key issue to be decided by an 'informed user'. This is not the same as the patent law concept of a 'person skilled in the art' and the court, in considering the validity of the design, should consider an individual who is aware of similar designs that form part of the 'design corpus'.

3.39   This issue was considered at length in *Procter & Gamble Co v Reckitt Benckiser*. We have covered this issue in paras **1.15–1.27**.

Immaterial differences

3.40   The prior disclosure need not be of an identical design. A similar design differing in 'immaterial details' may be effective prior art, destroying the novelty.[19]

3.41   Under the UK's pre-RDA 1949 'immaterial details' were assessed by comparing the designs both side by side and apart and a little distance away. It is not clear whether the test under the Community legislation is the same as under the UK's pre-RDA position, as the new legislation contains the additional requirement of the design having an 'individual character' which produces a different overall impression on the informed user from any prior design. This requirement for individual character appears to impose a higher threshold before a design will be registered. However, it should be noted that on an application the design is only examined on limited grounds and no prior art search is undertaken by the Registry to compare the application with those applications already on the register. The factors that are taken into account are set out in para **1.47**.

3.42   European Registered Design, unlike the UK Registered Design, permits designs to differ by 'trade variants', ie variants in design commonly used in the trade. This means that some new designs will be registrable as a Community Design that would not have been registered unlike the RDA.

Grace period

3.43   Although prior publication of a third party's design will render later designs invalid a design owner has a 12-month 'grace period' following the first publication of their own design in which to apply for a Community or UK registered design. This is to allow a designer to

19   RDA s 1B(2); Directive art 4.

market a design and ascertain its commercial value, before incurring the cost of registration.[20] This grace period covers disclosures of the designer's design, such as photographs of the designer's product by third parties.

3.44 The 12-month grace period also applies where a design is published as a result of 'an abuse in relation to the designer or his successor in title'.[21] This is similar to, but not exactly the same as, the concept of 'bad faith' in trade mark law.

3.45 It may, nevertheless, be prudent to apply for registration as soon as the design is in a state which is capable of registration in order to obtain priority against a possible third party application for registration of a conflicting design. A note of caution, given that the design application is not compared to existing designs on the register, it should not therefore be assumed that once a design is registered that it is not vulnerable to challenges to its validity on the basis of existing designs that are the same or similar. A third party who has pre-existing right can challenge a registration and have it declared invalid on the grounds that the design registration lacks novelty.

3.46 If the designer subsequently makes an application for a design that is different from that which he has marketed, eg following amendments as a result of customer feedback, it is not clear how far the grace period will apply. Such a grace period may be broken down into parts of the design or be held to apply to the design as a whole, notwithstanding the changes. Of course, if such amendments were sufficient to alter the overall impression of the product the later design would be valid in its own right as a new design and the designer would not require a grace period.

3.47 The UK's RDA also has provisions that exclude the operation of the prior publication rule in certain circumstances including:

- disclosure in breach of a duty of confidentiality or in breach of good faith;
- disclosure with the proprietor's consent at an exhibition certified by the Secretary of State for Trade; or
- communication of the design to a government department to allow its merits to be assessed.

Operative date establishing novelty and individual character

3.48 The operative date for establishing novelty and individual character in respect of Community registered and UK designs is the date of

---

20 RDA s 1B (6)(c) and (d).
21 Directive art 6(3) and RDA s 1B(6)(e).

filing the application. This applies even if the designer/applicant wishes to take advantage of the 12 month grace period referred to in para **3.43** above. This has a potential downside in that if, during the grace period, a third party either makes or registers an article to the design this could destroy the novelty of the design if its date of filing post-dates the earlier article. Also there may have been developments in the design field in question such that the design is now not novel. There is, however, a saving provision in that registered design protection is not lost if the design was made public during the period of 12 months immediately preceding the relevant date by someone acting on information provided by the designer, or by abusing trust placed in them by the designer[21a].

3.49 A saving provision that could help reduce this risk is that an applicant for a UK registered design may be able to take advantage of an earlier priority date if priority is claimed from an earlier application. However, it is possible to amend an application for a UK registered design after these dates, so if there is a significant modification individual character is assessed as at the date of modification.

3.50 By contrast, if an applicant for an Community registered design wishes to amend the design significantly he must submit a new application as art 11(2) of the Regulation states that applications can only be amended if the 'identity of the design is retained'.

3.51 Unregistered Community design is assessed on the date the design was first made available to the public.

3.52 As with patent law there are special provisions under both the UK and Community registration procedures for when an application conflicts with an earlier registration, even if the earlier registration has not been published.

Proprietorship

3.53 The author of the design shall be treated as the original proprietor save that:

- where a design is created in pursuance of a commission, the person commissioning the design shall be treated as the original proprietor;
- where the design is created by an employee in the course of his employment, his employer is treated as the original proprietor; and
- when a design is computer-generated (where there is no human author) the person who makes the arrangements that are necessary

---

21a RDA s 1B(6)(d) and (e).

for the creation of the design is the author. The author of the design is defined as the person who creates it.[22]

The term of protection

3.54 Both Community registered design and UK registered design last initially for five years from the date of application, but can be renewed for a maximum of four further periods of five years, to a maximum term of 25 years.[23] Further fees are payable on each extension, which means that the majority of designs are not renewed after the end of the second five-year period.

3.55 Unregistered Community design has a three-year term, beginning from the date when it was first made available to the public within the Community.[24]

Dealings

3.56 Registered designs can be assigned, mortgaged and licensed. Any assignment or mortgage will not be effective unless it is in writing, signed by or on behalf of the assessor.

3.57 Dealings with registered UK designs must be registered in the same way as patents.[25] This means that any person who becomes entitled by assignment, licence transmission or operation of law must apply to the registrar for the change in title to be registered. Similarly, licences of right and crown licences are available under RDA s 12, in a similar manner to patents.

Infringement of Community registered designs

3.58 Community registered design right and registered UK design right[26] give exclusive rights to the design in the respective territorial scope of the design right. Infringement arises when the registered design or any design 'which does not produce a different overall impression on the informed user' is used within that territory.

3.59 To prove infringement of a design the proprietor must prove that:

22 RDA s 2(1)–(4).
23 DIR art 12 and RDA s 8.
24 DIR art 11.
25 RDA s 19.
26 RDA ss 7 and 7A.

- there was an act of infringement; and
- the infringing design is the same or sufficiently similar to fall within the scope of the monopoly protection.

3.60 When considering the 'different overall impression on the informed user' the degree of freedom of the author in creating the design shall be taken into consideration. This issue is considered further at para **1.23** following the decision in *Bosch Security Systems BV v Taiden Industrial (Shenzen) Co Ltd*.[27]

3.61 Use of the design is taken to 'include':

- the making, offering, putting on the market, importing, exporting or using of a product in which the design is incorporated or to which it is applied; or
- stocking such a product for these purposes.

3.62 Under UK law it is not an infringement to do acts privately and for non-commercial purposes or for experimental or teaching purposes.[28]

3.63 Proceedings may not be brought for infringement before the certificate of registration is granted, but damages can be backdated to the date of application.

Remedies for Community registered design infringement

3.64 Actions for Community registered design right infringement may be brought in the High Court (Patents Court) or the Patents County Court. A successful claimant would normally be entitled to:

- an injunction restraining further infringement;
- an order for the delivery-up or destruction of articles that infringe the design; and
- damages for infringement (which would probably be assessed at a separate damages inquiry). However, no damages can be awarded against a defendant who was unaware and had no reasonable ground for supporting that the design was registered;[29] or
- an account of the profits made by the infringing defendant.

Defences to an action for infringement

3.65 A defendant to a claim for infringement would normally wish to consider defending the action on the basis that:

---

27 Case R 1437/2006–3.
28 RDA s 7A.
29 RDA s 24B.

- the articles complained of did not infringe the design. The defendant would have to prove that the items in question gave a different overall impression to the informed consumer; and
- to counterclaim that the registered design was invalid because it lacked novelty and/or individual character, so that the register should be rectified by removal of the design and marked with an indication of its invalidity (or a declaration that there is no relevant Community unregistered design); and/or
- a limited defence is available for 'innocent infringement'. However, if the defendant was 'reckless' as to the existence of such rights it is likely that such a defence would fail. An example of a situation where the defence would fail is where the design is marked 'protected by registered design'.

Unjustified threats

3.66 Section 26 of the RDA 1949 provides remedies for groundless threats of registered design infringement. Extreme care should be taken to ensure that an act of infringement is not threatened. 'Mere notification' of the design does not constitute a threat. A person threatened can:

- claim against the proprietor or any person (including professional advisers) making the threat, that the threats are unjustified;
- seek an injunction to restrain continued threats; and
- seek damages to compensate for any loss suffered.

3.67 The UK courts have construed widely what constitutes a threat. The writer of a letter, even if acting in a professional capacity (eg a solicitor), may also have a personal liability in addition to the client. It is normally prudent therefore to do no more in open correspondence addressed to the infringer than notify of the existence of the registration.

Community unregistered design right

3.68 This right was created as an adjunct to the Community registered design. However, the Community unregistered design right is an unusual combination between the principles of registered design rights and unregistered design rights.

Subsistence of Community unregistered design right

3.69 Unlike other unregistered rights, such as copyright and the UK's unregistered design right, the subsistence of the Community unregistered design right is based on whether the design is novel and the overall impression of the design ('individual character') being different from that of the prior art, rather than the workmanship of the author.

3.70   The date for assessing such criteria is the date which the design was first made available to the public.[30] This can include exhibiting the item at a trade fair or publishing the article in a look book.

3.71   This requirement for novelty rather than 'originality' (which is the test under UK unregistered design and copyright) means that community unregistered design may be denied in circumstances when a UK unregistered design or copyright would survive.

Duration of Community unregistered design right

3.72   This right only lasts three years from the date when it was first made available to the public within the Community.[31] This is much shorter than UK registered design right, which can last for up to 15 years; community unregistered design is therefore more transitory in nature. This is presumably to reflect the fact that in many cases fashions change and protection is not necessary for longer periods. If protection is desired for a longer period the designer can apply for protection through registration

Infringement of Community unregistered design right

3.73   Unregistered Community design right also conveys an exclusive right to use the design within the Community. However, in addition to the 'overall impression' requirements described above, there is an additional requirement of 'copying', ie that the contested use results from copying the protected design. Copying will not arise if the 'contested use' results 'from an independent work of creation by a designer who may be reasonably thought not to be familiar with the design'.

3.74   If it can be shown that the alleged infringer attended a relevant trade fair or received copies of the design prior to the creation of the infringing design, he or she will have to demonstrate that the design was created before receipt of such information.[32] In practice if two articles are identical, copying will be assumed and the burden of proof will pass to the alleged infringer to show that there has not been copying. It will then be for the alleged infringer to show that their work has been independently created. This would normally be achieved by the alleged infringer producing original design drawings where their date of creation can be verified.

30   Regulation art 6/5(1)(a).
31   Regulation art 11.
32   See below para **3.71**.

3.75 This suggests that the UK courts will approach infringement of unregistered Community design in similar terms to their approach to copyright and unregistered (national) design right: ie independent creation will provide a defence. Although in practice where the design complained of is identical to the alleged infringing design, the burden of proof will shift to the defendant to prove that there has not been copying. Laddie J gave some assistance towards determining the UK courts' view in *Mattel Inc v Woolbro (Distributors) Ltd*[33] where in a case of Community unregistered design infringement the court admitted evidence of 'similar fact' evidence of copying, eg where there was a pattern of copying by the defendant.

---

33 [2003] EWHC 2412 (Ch), [2004] FSR 12.

Chapter 4

Copyright in industrially applied artistic works

Background

4.01 The much criticised use of copyright in two-dimensional design drawings to protect three-dimensional articles, as approved by the House of Lords in *LB (Plastics) Ltd v Swish Products Ltd*[1] led to a considerable political and judicial backlash. In summary, it was pointed out by critics that such protection for the then maximum copyright term of 50 years plus life was undeserved for most industrial articles, which lacked aesthetic merit or eye-appeal; certainly in respect of items such as electric terminal blocks,[2] washers and parts for car exhausts.[3] In *British Leyland Motor Corpn Ltd v Armstrong Patents Co Ltd*,[4] the House of Lords wrestled with the possibility of limiting protection by reversing *LB Plastics* under the Practice Direction of 1966. In the event the House of Lords accepted *LB Plastics* as settled law on the basis that it had established 'existing rights'. Instead the House of Lords developed an unsatisfactory solution for spare parts; the so-called 'spare parts exception'.

4.02 It was against this background that s 52 of the Copyright, Designs and Patents Act 1988 (CDPA 1988) was implemented to restrict copyright in circumstances where there had been industrial exploitation.

4.03 The legislative process was two-fold. Firstly, CDPA 1988 s 51 dealt with the reproduction of a drawing by means of a three-dimensional object by removing copyright protection.

4.04 So far as material, CDPA 1988 s 51 reads:

1   [1979] FSR 145, [1979] RPC 551.
2   See *AMP Inc v Utilux Pty Ltd* [1971] FSR 572, [1972] RPC 103.
3   See *British Leyland Motor Corp v Armstrong Patents Co Ltd* [1986] AC 577, [1986] RPC 279.
4   [1986] AC 577, [1986] RPC 279.

'51 Design Documents and Models

(1) It is not an infringement of any copyright in a design document or model or recording or embodying a design for anything other than an artistic work or a typeface to a make an article to the design or to copy an article made to the design

(3) In this section—

'design means the design of any aspect of the shape or configuration or (whether internal or external) of the whole or part of an article, other than surface decoration'.

'design document' means any record of a design, whether in the form of a drawing, a written description, a photograph, data stored in a computer or otherwise.'

4.05 CDPA 1988 s 51 therefore bars a copyright infringement claim in relation to the design document if it is for 'anything other than an artistic work'. If the items in question are not artistic works s 51 prevents the works copied from being infringements.

4.06 In considering whether or not copyright protection exists it is therefore necessary in all cases to consider whether the works in question constitute 'an artistic work' as defined by CDPA 1988 s 4.

4.07 The matter is complicated because it has been held[5] that a 'sculpture' is an artistic work. This means it is necessary to consider separately whether the work in question is a 'sculpture' or 'an artistic work'.

Artistic works

4.08 CDPA 1988 s 4(1) defines, as an 'artistic work' afforded copyright protection, '4(1)(c) a work of artistic craftsmanship'.

4.09 It should be noted that no definition or elaboration of that term is provided for within the CDPA 1988. The leading authority as to what constitutes 'a work of artistic craftsmanship' remains the House of Lords decision in *George Hensher Ltd v Restawhile Upholstery Lancs Ltd*[6] involving a set of designer chairs. Although the case was decided before the coming into effect of the CDPA 1988 it remains good law.[7]

---

5 See the latest authority, *Lucasfilm Ltd v Ainsworth* [2008] EWHC 1878 (Ch), [2009] FSR 2.
6 [1976] AC 64, [1975] RPC 31.
7 See the comments of Mann J in *Lucasfilm Ltd v Ainsworth* [2008] EWHC 1878 (Ch), [2009] FSR 2.

4.10   Each of the judges in *Hensher* gave separate speeches so that it is not easy to establish a common ratio decidendi. All the judges, however, considered the intention of the designer as material. Lords Reid and Simon of Glaisdale pointed out that the origin of the phrase 'a work of artistic craftsmanship', arose for the purpose of giving copyright protection to the products of the Arts and Crafts movement with emphasis on the applied or decorative arts. Lord Reid stated:

> 'It is I think of importance that the maker or designer of the thing should have intended that it should have an artistic appeal but I would not regard that as either necessary or conclusive. If any substantial section of the public genuinely admires and values a thing for its appearance and gets pleasure or satisfaction, whether emotional or intellectual, from looking at it, I would accept that it is artistic although many others may think it meaningless or common or vulgar. ... During the last century there was a movement to bring art to the people. I doubt whether the craftsman who set out with that intention would have regarded all their products as works of art, but they were certainly works of artistic craftsmanship, whether or not they were useful as well as having an artistic appeal.'

4.11   Lords Morris of Borth-y-Gest and Simon of Glaisdale both considered that the phrase should bear its natural and ordinary meaning so that there was a combination of a work which was 'artistic' as well as 'craftsmanship'. All the judges stressed that the artistic merit of the work is irrelevant not least because the courts were ill-fitted to consider the 'metaphysics of art'. In *Lucasfilm Ltd v Ainsworth*,[8] Mann J summarised the conclusions that should be drawn from the case:

(1)   The intention of the creator has some real relevance.

(2)   The composite phrase 'a work of artistic craftsmanship' is important and has to be borne in mind.

(3)   He noted that some of the judges, but not all, contemplated that expert evidence would be necessary. He (Mann J) found that it was not necessary and as was shown in subsequent cases the question was determined without it.

4.12   Mann J found particularly helpful the decision of the New Zealand High Court in *Bonz Group (Pty) Ltd v Cooke*[9] where the court had to consider artistic craftsmanship in the context of woollen sweaters. Having considered *Hensher*, the judge, Tipping J, concluded that:

> '... for a work to regarded as one of artistic craftsmanship it must be possible fairly to say that the author was both a craftsman and an

---

8   [2008] EWHC 1878 (Ch), [2009] FSR 2.
9   [1994] 3 NZLR 216.

artist. A craftsman is a person who makes something in a skilful way and takes justified pride in their workmanship. An artist is a person with creative ability who produces something which has aesthetic appeal.'

4.13 On the facts of the case, the judge was prepared to combine the artistry of the designer and the craftsmanship of the knitters and conclude that the sweaters fell within the description. He rejected authorities that tended to suggest that they had to be one and the same person. Mann J commented 'that that appeared to be a sensible approach'. He went on:

'If William Morris conceived a design, but it was actually given form by others working (as he intended) from those designs, I do not see why it should be disqualified from being a work of artistic craftsmanship when, if he had made it himself, it would have qualified.'

4.14 The analysis undertaken by Tipping J was also accepted by Evans-Lombe J in *Vermaat (t/a Cotton Productions) v Boncrest Ltd (No 1)*[10] in relation to bedspread designs. The judge found that on the evidence the designs were not sufficiently artistic to fall within the description. He held it was always a matter of 'judicial judgment'.

4.15 The latest authority is *Lucasfilm Ltd v Ainsworth*.[11] In this case the question arose as to whether helmets and armour created for *Star Wars* characters were works of artistic craftsmanship. Reviewing the authorities, including *Hensher*, the judge went on to consider whether the articles were works of artistic craftsmanship. In doing so he applied a two-fold test: firstly, to decide whether they were works of craftsmanship and, secondly, whether they were works of artistic craftsmanship. Dealing with the first, he was prepared to accept that the ultimate production of the articles was 'an act of craftsmanship'. He accepted that, on the facts, the designer 'can fairly be called a craftsman – he produces high quality products and has a justifiable pride in his work. He is not a slavish copier, or a jobbing tradesman. The production of the helmets and armour required the activity of a craftsman to realise the vision of the creators of the film in this respect.'

4.16 He then went on to consider the second limb of the test; were the works of craftsmanship works of 'artistic craftsmanship'? He decided that in considering their conception they plainly were not. Their purpose was not to appeal to the aesthetic at all but rather to give a particular impression in a film. That was sufficient to deny the works

10 [2001] FSR 5, (2000) 23(8) IPD 23062.
11 [2008] EWHC 1878 (Ch), [2009] FSR 2.

artistic quality. In reaching that decision he adopted to the William Morris Arts and Crafts analogy referred to by Lord Reid in *Hensher* as follows:

'If one takes products of the Arts and Crafts movement as an exemplar, the helmet and armour share nothing of the conceptual purpose of such products. A work of artistic craftsmanship does not have to be something of which William Morris would have been proud, but it is a not wholly irrelevant test in a case like the present to consider whether he would recognise it as having anything at all with what his movement was seeking to do. I do not think he would (I stress that I do not propose that is a general test. It is I who has to decide this case, not the ghost of William Morris. It is merely a way of making a point in a case as striking as the present). That was not changed when the conception was put into operation. The purpose remained the same. Unlike a work of artistic craftsmanship, they were not intended to sustain close scrutiny. They carry their own acts of deception – what looked like corrugations of a gas tube are in fact painted on, as are some apparent event.'

4.17   It is submitted that the approach of Mann J is not inconsistent with the majority speeches in *Hensher*. Moreover it is consistent with the theme of aestheticism and the intention of the designer that has run through English design law.[12]

Sculpture

4.18   A sculpture falls within the definition of an 'artistic work' under the CDPA 1988 even though there is no statutory definition of 'sculpture' within the Act. There is nevertheless a somewhat oblique definition of what is included. CDPA 1988 s 4(2) refers to a 'sculpture' as including 'a cast or model made for the purposes of sculpture'. Section 4(1)(a) also provides that an article can be a sculpture 'irrespective of its artistic quality'.

4.19   The high point in affording protection to an industrially applied work as a 'sculpture' is the New Zealand Court of Appeal decision in *Wham-O Manufacturing Co v Lincoln Industries Ltd*.[13] Prior to the CDPA the practice grew up of pleading infringement based upon a substantial reproduction of the three-dimensional sculpture. An example of this was *Interlego AG v Tyco Industries Inc*.[14] The claimant, Interlego, argued that the Lego brick was a sculpture copyright in which

---

12   See for example *AMP Inc v Utilux Pty Ltd* [1971] FSR 572, [1972] RPC 103.
13   [1985] RPC 127.
14   [1989] AC 217, [1988] RPC 343.

had been infringed by the reproduction of a near identical plastic brick by the defendant, Tyco Industries. The issue was argued in the Privy Council but not pursued. In the event the case was decided largely on the basis of 'originality'. Nevertheless the doctrine still appears current and was the subject of argument in *Lucasfilm Ltd v Ainsworth*.

4.20 In *Wham-O* the New Zealand Court of Appeal considered whether a preparatory mould for 'frisbee' was a sculpture. A frisbee is a form of plastic flying disc manufactured as a toy by an injection-moulding process. The court took the view that 'sculpture' should be given its 'ordinary' meaning. It held that the wooden models of the frisbee prepared for manufacture fell within the definition of 'sculpture' and were therefore 'properly the subject of copyright protection' whereas the frisbee itself was not. *Wham-O* was considered by Mann J in *Lucafilm Ltd v Ainsworth*, and he summarised the conclusions to be reached from *Wham-O* as follows:

(1) The Court should start with the 'normal understanding of the expression "sculpture".'
(2) Not every three-dimensional object produced as a result of a human design is capable of being a sculpture.

4.21 *Wham-O* was followed by the decision of Whitford J in *J&S Davis (Holdings) Ltd v Wright Health Group Ltd,*[15] a case involving a model of a dental impression tray made out of modelling material. The judge rejected the claim that the model was a sculpture and took the view that the models were no more than steps in the production of the prototype and for the manufacture of the tooling from which the production was secured. He considered that they were not made for the purposes of sculpture and it was never intended that they should have any continuing existence.

4.22 He distinguished the wooden model in *Wham-O* by saying:

'A carved wooden model is one thing. A model fashioned in plasticine or some other suitable modelling material, which never intended to have had any permanent existence, being no more than a stage in production, is another. The claim based on either the models or the casts as being sculptures must, in my judgment, fail.'

4.23 *Metix (UK) Ltd v G H Maughan (Plastics) Ltd*[16] was another unsuccessful attempt to claim copyright in relation to a mould industrial article as a sculpture. The case involved moulds made for making

15 [1988] RPC 403.
16 [1997] FSR 718.

industrial products ie twin cartridges for a double-barrelled syringe. The claimant unsuccessfully argued that the moulds were works of sculpture.

4.24 Laddie J rejected the argument and in an attempt to close the 'sculpture' line of argument once and for all stated:

'The law has been bedevilled by attempts to widen out the field covered by the Copyright Acts. It is not possible to say with precision what is and what is not sculpture, but I think Mr Meade is close to the heart of the issue. He suggested that a sculpture is a three dimensional work made by an artist's hand. It seems to me that there is no reason why the words "sculpture" in the 1988 Act should be extended far beyond the meaning which that word has to ordinary members of the public. There is nothing in the particulars in this case which suggest that the manufacturers of these moulds considered themselves, or were considered by anybody else to be artists when they designed the moulds or that they were concerned in any way with the shape or appearance of what they were making, save for the purpose of achieving a precise functional effect.'

4.25 Laddie J's comments should be contrasted with obiter remarks of Mr Peter Prescott QC (sitting as a Deputy High Court Judge) in *Oakley Inc v Animal Ltd*.[17] He referred to the example of the author of a sculpture (an artistic work) licensing and reproducing the sculpture as mass-produced garden gnomes. He considered it probable that the design of the gnome would, following the views of both Laddie J and the New Zealand Court of Appeal, constitute what an ordinary member of the public would consider to be sculpture.

4.26 Full argument as to the meaning of 'sculpture' took place in *Lucasfilm Ltd v Ainsworth*[18] where Mann J attempted to pull together the following guidelines from the cases. He stressed that in his view the cases did not lay down hard and fast rules 'in an area where subjective considerations are likely to intrude'. He summarised the position as follows:

'(i) Some regard has to be had to the normal use of the word sculpture;

(ii) The concept can be applicable to things going beyond what one would normally expect to be art in the sense they are the sort of things that one would expect to find in art galleries;

17   [2005] EWHC 210 (Pat), [2005] RPC 30.
18   [2008] EWHC 1878 (Ch), [2009] FSR 2.

(iii) It is inappropriate to stray too far from what would normally be regarded as sculpture;

(iv) No judgment is to be made about artistic worth;

(v) Not every three dimensional representation of a concept can be regarded as a sculpture. Otherwise every three dimensional construction or fabrication would be a sculpture.

(vi) It is of the essence of a sculpture that it should have as part of its purpose a visual appeal in the sense that it might be enjoyed for that purpose alone.

(vii) The fact that the object has some other use does not necessarily disqualify it from being a sculpture but it still has to have an intrinsic quality of being intended to be enjoyed as a visual thing.'

4.27 Mann J's approach was accepted by Jacob LJ in the Court of Appeal[19] where he stated:

'The result of this analysis is that it is not possible or wise to attempt to devise a comprehensive or exclusive definition of "sculpture" sufficient to determine the issue in any given case. Although this may be close to adopting the elephant test of knowing when you see one, it is almost inevitable in this field. We therefore consider that the judge was right to adopt the multi-factorial approach which he did.'

4.28 He used the colourful example of a pile of books temporarily on display at the Tate Modern for two weeks. He said that it was plainly capable of being a sculpture. However, an identical pile of books dumped at the end of His Lordship's driveway for two weeks preparatory to a building project is equally plainly not. If one asks why there is that difference, it lies in its purpose: 'One is created by the hand of an artist for artistic purposes, and the other is created by a builder for building purposes.'

4.29 On the facts of the case the judge rejected the argument that the helmet and the armour the subject of the claim were sculpture: 'The ordinary perception of what is a sculpture would be overstretched by including this helmet within it.'

Surface decoration

4.30 The definition of 'design' in CDPA 1988 s 51 excludes surface decoration. The consequence of this is that where an artistic work is used as surface decoration for an article the copyright in the surface decoration is enforceable and not barred by s 51.

---

19 [2009] EWCA Civ 1328, (2010) Times, 4 January.

4.31 The fact that the decoration should be applied to the surface of the article suggests that it excludes decoration that affects the shape of the article. In practice the distinction will depend upon the facts.

4.32 An example would be a set of disposable picnic plates to which is applied a cartoon of a media character. The cartoon would be protectable by copyright as an artistic work whereas copyright in respect of the plates would be excluded by CDPA 1988 s 51.

Limitation of copyright protection in case of industrial application[20]

4.33 CDPA 1988 s 52 in limiting the term of copyright to 25 years from the date of first marketing follows upon the Copyright Act 1956, which provided that the term of copyright for designs capable of registration was limited to the term of registered design protection under the RDA 1949. CDPA 1988 s 52 is consistent with the CDPA amending the RDA 1949 to a maximum term of registered design protection of 25 years.

4.34 CDPA 1988 s 52 essentially provides that where artistic copyright has been exploited, by an industrial process, the copyright term is reduced to 25 years from the end of the calendar year in which the articles were first marketed. The provisions of the Copyright (Industrial Process and Excluded Articles) (No 2) Order 1989[21] provides that an article, for the purposes of CDPA 1988 s 52, is made by an industrial process if it is one of more than 50 articles that fall to be treated as copies of a particular artistic work but do not constitute a single set of articles, or consists of goods manufactured in lengths or pieces, not being handmade goods.

4.35 The Order specifically provides that the following are excluded from the operation of CDPA 1988 s 52:

(1) works of sculpture, other than casts or models used or intended to be used as models or patterns to be multiplied by any industrial process;
(2) wall plaques, medals and medallions;
(3) printed matter, primarily of a literary or artistic character, including books jackets, calendars, certificates, coupons, dress-making patterns, greeting cards, labels, leaflets, maps, plans, playing cards, postcards, stamps, trade advertisements, trade forms and cards, transfers and similar articles.

---

20 CDPA 1988 s 52.
21 SI 1989/1070.

4.36 It should be noted that the list is identical to the list of exclusions from design registration contained in the Registered Designs Rules 2006.[22] The listed articles would have the full term of copyright protection and not be limited to the 25 years from the date of first marketing within CDPA 1988 s 52.

22 SI 2006/1975.

Chapter 5

Protection of designs by trade marks and passing off

Background

5.01　There is a long history of companies attempting to use the law of trade marks and passing off to protect the shapes or designs of the products.

5.02　A good example is *Re Coca-Cola Co's Applications*,[1] a decision under the Trade Marks Act 1938, where the House of Lords held that the distinctive shape of a Coca Cola bottle was not a mark for the purposes of the 1938 Act.

5.03　In that case, Lord Templeman who gave the leading judgment, deprecated the use of trade mark law for the protection of designs which, at that time, were more properly the concern of copyright law and registered design law.

5.04　He stated:

'This is another attempt to expand the boundaries of intellectual property and to convert a protective law into a source of monopoly. The attempt to use the Copyright Act 1956 for this purpose failed recently in *British Leyland Motor Corporation Ltd v Armstrong Patents Co Ltd* [1986] 2 WLR 400. The present attempt is based on the Trade Marks Act 1938 ...

It is not sufficient for the Coca-Cola bottle to be distinctive. The Coca-Cola Co must succeed in the startling proposition that a bottle is a trade mark. If so, then any other container or any article of a distinctive shape is capable of being a trade mark. This raises the spectre of a total and perpetual monopoly in containers and articles achieved by means of the Act of 1938. Once the container or article

---

1　[1986] 1 WLR 695, [1986] FSR 472.

has become associated with the manufacturer and distinctiveness has been established, with or without the help of the monopolies created by the Patents Act, the Registered Designs Act or the Copyright Act, the perpetual trade mark monopoly in the container or article can be achieved. In my opinion the Act of 1938 was not intended to confer on the manufacturer of a container or on the manufacturer of an article a statutory monopoly on the ground that the manufacturer has in the eyes of the public established a connection between the shape of the container or article and the manufacturer. A rival manufacturer must be free to sell any container or article of similar shape provided the container or article is labelled or packaged in a manner which avoids confusion as to the origin of the goods in the container or the origin of the article.'

5.05 *Re Coca-Cola* is no longer authoritative law as a result of the Trade Marks Act 1994 (TMA 1994). However, it should be noted that there is nothing in the Trade Mark Act 1938, nor in the TMA 1994, to the effect that anything capable of protection under design law is excluded from registration as a trade mark.

Trade Marks Act 1994

5.06 TMA 1994 s 3(2), which is identical to the wording of art 3(1)(e) of the Trade Marks Directive 89/104, provides as follows:

'A sign shall not be registered as a trade mark if it consists exclusively of—

(a)   the shape which results from the nature of the goods themselves,

(b)   the shape of goods which is necessary to obtain a technical result, or

(c)   the shape which gives substantial value to the goods'

5.07 TMA 1994 s 1(1) states that a trade mark may consist of the shape of goods or their packaging. Thus before registration of a trade mark for a shape and subject to the requirements of representation as a sign, and distinctiveness, the shape must comply with the three prohibitions set out in s 3(2).

5.08 The leading interpretation of TMA 1994 s 3(2) is the decision of the European Court in *Philips Electronics NV v Remington Consumer Products Ltd*.[2]

---

2   [2002] ECR 1–5475.

5.09   The registered trade mark, the subject of the case, was a pictorial representation in two dimensions, of the face of the claimant's three-headed rotary shaver and the registration was for 'Electric Shavers'. The case began as an infringement action in the Chancery Division, whilst the defendant, Remington, counterclaimed for a declaration of invalidity.

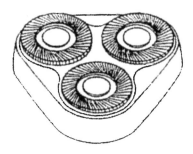

5.10   At first instance, the court considered the issue of whether the mark, ie the pictorial representation, was capable of distinguishing the claimant's goods. Jacob J took the view that it could not:

> 'I think that this is the case here; Philips can never get away from the fact that the sign primarily denotes function. More use could not make a difference. The sign can never only denote shavers made by Philips and no-one else because it primarily says "here is a three-headed rotary shaver". It is not "capable" of denoting only Philips goods.'

5.11   In the Court of Appeal, Aldous LJ took the view that the public associated the shape of the shaver head with a Philips rotary shaver and nobody else. This reflected the fact that Philips had a de facto monopoly in the United Kingdom in relation to rotary shavers and the public's perception reflected that. However, he went on to express the view that he did not consider the fact that a trade mark has by use become such as to denote goods of a particular trader necessarily means that it is capable of distinguishing as required by TMA 1994 s 1. He went on:

> 'Shapes such as shown in the trade mark are pictorial descriptions of products. The test of registrability is the same for such shapes as that for word marks. The trade mark shows the head of a particular three-headed rotary shaver and it would be recognised by the trade and public as such, albeit as one made by Philips. Even though there were a number of other designs of three-headed rotary shavers that could be produced, the shape shown in the trade mark is a shape

which, absent patent, registered design, copyright or unfair trading protection another trader is entitled to make. It is not capable of distinguishing Philips shavers of that shape from those of other traders who could use shavers with a similar shaped head. An application to register a picture of a reel for cotton or a flag for coffee would succeed as they are not descriptive of the goods for which registration is sought; but that does not mean that a shape of an article is registrable in respect of the article shown in the application. To so hold would enable a few traders to obtain registrations of all the best designs in an article and thereby monopolize those designs. In my view, a shape of an article cannot be registered in respect of goods of that shape unless it contains some addition to the shape of the article which has trade mark significance.'

He concluded that Jacob J was right in finding that the mark did not constitute a registrable trade mark.

The European Court Decision in *Philips v Remington*

5.12   The court explained the reasoning for the restrictions on registration of a shape contained in TMA 1994 s 3(2) on the grounds that the purpose of art 3(1)(e) of the Directive is to prevent trade mark protection from granting the proprietor of the mark a monopoly on technical solutions or functional characteristics of a product which a user is likely to seek in the products of competitors. It is intended to prevent the protection conferred by trade mark law from being extended beyond signs that serve to distinguish a product or service from those offered by competitors to forming an obstacle preventing competitors from freely offering for sale products incorporating 'technical solutions or functional characteristics' in competition with the proprietor of the trade mark.

5.13   In summary, the decision of the court results in the following conclusions:

(1)   Shapes resulting from the nature of the goods themselves cannot be considered distinctive and therefore reserved to one undertaking.
(2)   Shapes necessary to achieve a technical result are protected by other intellectual property rights with a more limited duration, e g patents and designs.
(3)   Shapes that add substantial value to the goods are protected by other essential property rights of limited duration, such as design rights. In the absence of such rights, the competitors should be at liberty to use such shapes.

5.14 *Philips v Remington* was considered by the Court of First Instance in Case T-270/06 *Lego Juris v OHIM*.[2] The court considered that the rationale of art 3(1)(e) of the Directive was to prevent trade mark protection from granting to the trade mark proprietor a monopoly on technical solutions or functional characteristics of a product. The article was intended to preclude the registration of shapes whose essential characteristics perform a technical function with the result that the exclusivity inherent in the trade mark right would limit the possibility of competitors supplying a product incorporating such a function.

In *Lego*, Lego and its main competitor, Mega Brands, disputed whether it is possible to register as a trade mark a photographic representation of a typical Lego brick or whether its design contained 'essential characteristics of the shape of the brick' which, because of their functionality, must remain available to any toy manufacturer and are therefore prohibited from registration. The court accepted that registration was precluded where the essential characteristics of the shape combine the characteristics which are technically causal of and sufficient to obtain the intended technical result and are therefore attributable to that technical result. The court also found that the functionality of the shape must be assessed independently of whether other shapes exist.

Lego Juris appealed to the Full Court. The Opinion of the Advocate-General was delivered on 26 January 2010.

The Advocate-General followed *Philips v Remington* in finding that the existence of other shapes that could achieve the same technical result cannot overcome the ground for refusal or invalidity contained in art 3(1)(e), which precluded from registration 'signs composed exclusively of the shape necessary to obtain the technical result'. On the evidence the Lego brick design was shown to be purely functional. Thus Lego Juris could not rely on the nuances in the judgment in *Philips v Remington* that suggested that art 3(1)(e) was limited to essential characteristics. All the characteristics of the Lego brick, essential or otherwise, were functional. The trade mark that would be granted would always monopolise the shape. It remains to be seen whether the Full Court of Justice dismisses Lego Juris's appeal.

Shapes resulting from the nature of the goods themselves[3]

5.15 This exclusion from trade mark registration is designed to prevent the registration of shapes resulting from the nature of the goods

---

3   TMA 1994 s 3(2)(a).

themselves. In *Philips Electronics NV v Remington Consumer Products Ltd (No 1)*[4] Aldous LJ used the example of natural shapes such as that of a banana. A sign consisting of the shape of a banana or bananas would be a shape that results from the nature of the goods themselves.

5.16 This does not deal with the issue of what is meant by 'the goods.' Aldous LJ, in the Court of Appeal suggested that 'the goods' referred to the description of goods in the specification, so that a representation of a banana for fruit would be incapable of registration as would a picture of a banana for registration of bananas. This may, in practice, have little consequence because if goods are themselves the subject of a design, they are unlikely to result from the 'nature of the goods themselves'.

Shapes necessary to obtain a technical result[5]

5.17 This was considered by Rimer J in *Philips Electronics NV v Remington Consumer Products Ltd (No 2)*[6] where he set out the test as follows:

(1) In every case it is a question of fact as to whether the shape in issue falls foul of the prohibition in TMA 1994 s 3(2)(b).
(2) The shape in issue must be assessed in order to identify its essential characteristics or features.
(3) If those essential characteristics or features are solely attributable to achieving the intended technical result, the prohibition applies. It would make no difference if the shape includes non-essential features that are not so attributable.
(4) The test is an objective one and does not depend upon the subjective intentions and the design of the shape.
(5) Such a conclusion is not prevented by finding that a different shape can also achieve the same technical result.

Signs that consist exclusively of the shape that gives substantial value to the goods[7]

5.18 In *Philips Electronics NV v Remington Consumer Products Ltd (No 1)*[8] Jacob J suggested that this provision referred to an exclusion of

---

4   [1999] ETMR 816, [1999] RPC 809.
5   TMA 1994 s 3(2)(b).
6   [2004] EWHC 2327 (Ch), [2005] FSR 17.
7   TMA 1994 s 3(2)(c).
8   [1998] ETMR 124, [1998] RPC 283.

shapes that exclusively add some sort of value (design or functional appearance or perhaps something else) to the goods disregarding any value attributable to trade mark (ie source identification) function. He raised the example of a Rolls-Royce radiator grille adding value to a Rolls Royce, but suggested that this was because it signified Rolls-Royce and not because of the inherent shape of the grille.

5.19 The Court of Appeal took a different view, that the purpose of TMA 1994 s 3(2)(c) was to exclude aesthetic type shapes that had an element of eye appeal. If a shape had, in relevant terms, 'substantial value', it would be excluded from registration.

5.20 An example in practice is *Dualit Ltd's Toaster Shapes Trade Mark Application*[9] where the Trade Marks Registry in considering the shape of two models of toaster as the subject of an application for registration held that the shapes were such that they did give substantial value to the goods.

Passing off

5.21 The law of passing off has long been used as the basis to attempt to protect the design of the get-up of a product where the get-up of the product is the shape or appearance of the product itself.

5.22 The fundamentals of the common law tort of passing off were re-affirmed by the House of Lords in *Reckitt & Colman Products Ltd v Borden Inc (No 3)*.[10] In this case (better known as *Jif Lemon*) Lord Oliver outlined the matters a successful claimant must prove as follows:

(1) a goodwill or reputation attached to the goods or services that the claimant supplies in the mind of the purchasing public by association with the identifying 'get up';
(2) a misrepresentation by the defendant to the public (whether or not intentional) leading or likely to lead the public to believe that the goods or services offered are those of or associated with those of the claimant;
(3) the claimant suffers or is likely to suffer damage by reason of the defendant's misrepresentation.

5.23 *Jif Lemon* was a claim by the manufacturers of lemon juice sold in distinctive lemon-shaped containers against the defendants who also supplied lemon juice in similar shaped plastic containers. The case largely turned upon the lemon-shape design of the containers.

9   [1999] RPC 304. (1999) 22(1) IPD 22010.
10   [1990] 1 WLR 491, [1990] RPC 341.

5.24 The claimants argued that the defendant had not taken sufficient steps to distinguish their products. Evidence was given of customer confusion between the two lemon-shaped products and this was held sufficient to justify the finding of passing-off.

5.25 In the House of Lords, Lord Jauncey[11] held that the shape and configuration of the article could be protected against deception and confusion. He stated:

'This principle [that no man may sell his goods under the pretence that they are the goods of another] applies as well to the goods themselves as to their get-up. A markets a ratchet screwdriver with a distinctively shaped handle. The screwdriver has acquired a reputation for reliability and utility and is generally recognised by the public as being the produce of A because of the handle. A would be entitled to protection against B if the latter sought to market a ratchet screwdriver with a similarly shaped handle without taking sufficient steps to see that the public was not misled into thinking that his product was that of A.'

5.26 The decision in *Jif Lemon* was subsequently relied upon by the claimant in *Hodgkinson and Corby Ltd v Wards Mobility Services Ltd (No 1)*[12] (better known as the 'Roho' case). The subject matter of the case was a cushion, known as the 'Roho' cushion, for use on a wheelchair that was made by the claimant. The defendant proposed to sell a 'look alike' cushion under the mark 'Flo'Tair'. The claimant alleged that the sales of the defendant's cushion would constitute passing-off of the goodwill attached to the Roho cushion. The claim did not include a claim for design infringement but was solely brought on the basis of passing-off.

5.27 The court held that the claimant had failed to prove its claim for passing-off on the basis that the claimant had failed to prove that the shape of the Roho cushion was the 'crucial point of reference' for those who specifically wanted a Roho cushion. The fact that the defendant's cushion appeared to be a copy of the claimant's cushion was insufficient to satisfy the *Jif Lemon* case. Jacob J stated:

'I turn to consider the law and begin by identifying what is not the law. There is no tort of copying. There is no tort of taking a man's market or customers. Neither the market nor the customers are the Plaintiffs to own. There is no tort of making use of another's goodwill as such. There is no tort of competition. I say this because at times the Plaintiffs seem close to relying on such torts ... At the

11 [1990] 1 WLR 491 at 518.
12 [1994] 1 WLR 1564, [1995] FSR 169.

heart of passing-off lies deception or its likelihood, deception of the ultimate consumer in particular. Over the years, passing off has developed from the classic case of the Defendant selling his goods as and for those of the Plaintiff to cover other kinds of deception, eg that the Defendant's goods are the same as those of the Plaintiff when they are not. ... never has the tort shown even a slight tendency to stray beyond cases of deception. Were it to so, it would enter the field of honest competition, declared unlawful for some reason other than deceptiveness. Why there should be any such reason, I cannot imagine. It would serve only to stifle competition.'

Chapter 6

Semiconductor topographies

Introduction

6.01 The semiconductor topography right is an additional element to unregistered design law that is intended to protect a specific industrial article, namely the electronic circuit board and the arrangement of semiconductors. It was implemented into English law under the Protection of Topography Directive 87/54/EC and by the Design Right (Semiconductor Topographies) Regulations 1989 (the Regulations).[1] These Regulations have since been amended by the Design Right (Semiconductor Topographies) (Amendment) Regulations 2006[2] and 2008[3] which essentially extend protection of the right to designs from countries such as Vietnam, Ukraine and Madagascar.

What is protected?

6.02 The Regulations provide as follows:

(1) ' "Semiconductor product" means an article the purpose, or one of the purposes, of which is the performance of an electronic function and which consists of two or more layers, at least one of which is composed of semi conducting material and in or upon one or more of which is a pattern appertaining to that or another function.'

(2) ' "Semiconductor topography" means a design within the meaning of section 213(2) of the [Copyright, Designs and Patents] Act which is a design of either of the following:

(a) a pattern fixed, or intended to be fixed, in or upon:

---

1   SI 1989/1100.
2   SI 2006/1833.
3   SI 2008/1434.

      (i) a layer of semiconductor products; or

      (ii) a layer of material in the course of and for the purpose of the manufacture of a semiconductor product, or

    (b) the arrangement of two patterns fixed, or intended to be fixed, in or upon the layers of a semiconductor product in relation to one another.'

6.03 In essence the semiconductor topography right is treated in the same or in a very similar way to unregistered design right. In fact, the term of protection is 10 years but the right is based upon the special characteristics of a semiconductor design. No licences of right are available and protection of designs originating in a large number of countries are protected.

Protection of a layer

6.04 The Semiconductor Topography Regulations make explicit reference to the protection of layers in a semiconductor design; therefore protection is given not only to the whole semiconductor board but also the layers or parts within it. This means that the pattern of metal conductors on the circuit board are protected one by one.

6.05 The layering issue was referred to in the case of *A Fulton Co Ltd v Totes Isotoner (UK) Ltd*[4] on appeal where Jacob LJ referenced the Semiconductor Topography Regulations to support the finding in the case that one aspect or part of a design can be protected under design copyright law. He said:

'The design of even a single layer of a whole chip is taken and constituted as a "design"... Incidentally, the reference to a design including even the arrangement of patterns within a layer in relation to other layers further makes it clear that Mr Thorley's "aspect" argument must be wrong. Such an arrangement can't be described as "way of looking at" the chip as part of it.'

6.06 The Semiconductor Topography Regulations explicitly cover 'patterns' and will therefore apply to two-dimensional designs of semiconductor topographies. This is normally not protected as a design right because often a 'pattern' will be ' surface decoration' or could be 'features of shape or configuration', both of which are excluded from protection under CDPA 1988 s 213(3)(c).

6.07 An interestingly additional factor of the Semiconductor Topography Regulation is that the Regulations cover not only patterns 'on',

---

4   [2003] EWCA Civ 1514, [2004] RPC 16, CA.

but also patterns 'in' a circuit board. Arguably this could extend to features that are not visible but that are contained within the circuit. Again, this is an aspect of protection that does not arise under design right.

Term of protection

6.08 The term of protection for a semiconductor topography under the Regulations is as follows:

(1) 10 years from the end of the calendar year in which the topography or articles under the topography were first made available for sale or hire anywhere in the world by or with the licence of the design right owner; or

(2) if neither the topography nor articles made to the topography are so made available within a period of 15 years commencing with the earlier of the time when the topography was first recorded in a design document or the time when an article was first made to the topography, at the end of such period.

6.09 This means that, in theory, if an article is not made until the last day of the 14th year following the first record of the topography, it will then continue to have a further 10 years' protection, thereby extending protection to about 25 years.

6.10 If the product is made available for sale or hire or is first marketed and the semiconductor topography in question is subject to an obligation of confidence the time period does not start running. The exceptions to this are if the semiconductor topography has been sold or hired previously or if the obligation of confidence has been imposed by the UK government or any other government for the protection of security or for the production of arms, munitions or war material.

Infringement

6.11 Infringement of a semiconductor topography right is treated in the same way as an infringement of a design right, which means that it is an infringement to make articles to that design or to make a design document recording the design for the purposes of enabling such articles to be made to the design. However, unlike design law, there is an exception in that special provision is made that permits reverse engineering:

'it is not an infringement of design right in a semiconductor topography to:

(a) create another original semiconductor topography as a result of an analogous or evaluation of the first topography or of the concepts, processes, systems or techniques embodied in it, or

(b) reproduce that other topography.'[5]

6.12 The concept of exhaustion of rights and parallel imports is also covered in the Semiconductor Topography Regulations, which in common with other IP rights provides that it is not an infringement if the article in question has been sold or hired within the United Kingdom or in the EU by or with the permission of the semiconductor topography design owner or with the consent of the person who is entitled to import it into or sell it within the EU. Presumably the same concepts of what constitutes 'consent' as applied to other intellectual property rights will apply (see *Zino Davidoff SA v A&G Imports Ltd (C-414/99)* [2002] All ER(EC) 55).

Ownership and qualification

6.13 Ownership of the semiconductor topography design right is treated in the same way as ordinary design right in that, provided the design is not created in pursuance of a commission or in the course of employment, it belongs to the designer. If it is created during the course of employment semiconductor topography design rights are owned by the employer unless there is any written agreement to the contrary. This is different from the design right provision, which does not explicitly permit agreements between employers and employees that provide that the employee retains ownership.

6.14 If the semiconductor topography design right is protected by a designer in one of the countries listed in the Regulations it qualifies for protection. The list of countries is long and this is a significant difference from design right where protection is limited to designs from the EU and a very limited number of other countries.

5 Design Right (Semiconductor Topographies) Regulations 1989, SI 1989/1100, reg 8(4).

Appendix 1

IPO forms

 **INTELLECTUAL**
PROPERTY OFFICE

Designs Form DF2A
Official fee due with this form

Application to register one or more designs

Concept House
Cardiff Road
Newport
South Wales
NP10 8QQ

Please read the guidance note below about filling in this form.

1.	Your reference:	
2.	If you are applying for more than one design, please state the total number.	
	How many of these designs do you wish to have published and registered immediately?	
3.	**Full name and address (including postcode) of the applicant.**	
	Designs ADP number (if you know it).	
	If you are applying in the name of a company, where is it incorporated?	
	If incorporated in the USA, in which state is it incorporated?	
4.	Full name and address (including postcode) of your agent or your contact address if not the same as in section 3 above.	
	Designs ADP number (if you know it).	
5.	**Fees enclosed.**	
6.	**Signature of the applicant or their representative.**	
	Name in BLOCK CAPITALS.	
	Date.	
7	**Name and daytime phone number of the person we should contact in case of query. You may also provide your e-mail address.**	
	How many pages are you sending us?	**This is sheet 1 of**

Note:

Section 5: If this application contains more than one design, attach a Designs Ready Reckoner sheet.

(REV AUG07)   Intellectual Property Office is an operating name of the Patent Office   **Form DF2A**

Appendix 1 IPO forms

This is the _____ (for example, first) design out of a total of _____ designs

You must answer these questions for each design in a multiple application, so copy this sheet as many times as you need.

A.	**Name of the applicant.**	
B.	**Which product or products is the design for?**	
C.	**How many illustration sheets are there for this design?**	
D.	Write "RSP" if this is the design of a pattern which repeats across the surface of a product, for example, wallpaper.	
E.	If you wish, you may give a brief description of the design shown in the illustration or sample.	
F.	List any limitations or disclaimers you want to record.	
G.	**Do you agree that we should publish this design as soon as possible? Please state yes or no.**	
H.	If you are claiming priority from an earlier application to register this design, give these details.	Priority date Country Application number
I.	If the earlier application was made in a different name, say how the current applicant has a right to apply. If, for example, by assignment of the earlier application, give the date of the transaction.	

Notes: **You MUST answer all of the questions above which are shown in BOLD print.**

Please phone us on 08459 500 505 if you need help to fill in this form.

Checklist   Tick the box if you have included priority documents with this application ☐

(REV AUG07)   Form DF2A

Illustration sheet

This is the _____ (for example, first) design out of a total of _____ designs

INTELLECTUAL
PROPERTY OFFICE

Filling in the application form DF2A

If there is not enough space for any of your answers on the form, please use separate sheets. Number each sheet and write in section 7 of the form how many extra sheets you have used. If you need any more help to fill in this form, contact our Enquiry Unit on 08459 500 505.

What to put in each section of the form

First page

Section 1   Please include your reference. You don't have to provide one, but if you do we will use it whenever we contact you.

Section 2   Say how many different designs you are applying for in this application if there is more than one. Remember that you will need to pay for each design. See the "Designs Ready Reckoner" sheet attached to help you to calculate the total fee payable. In the case of a multiple application, you also need to tell us how many designs in the application are to be published immediately. For example, if this is a multiple application of three designs and you want all three to proceed to publication and registration as soon as possible, state "3". If however this is a multiple application of three designs and you want to defer the publication of one of the designs then state "2".

Section 3   This section must contain the details of the owner of the design. So only give your own details if you are either the owner or a joint owner with another person or company. Do not automatically name yourself as the designer if you are applying in the name of a company. If you are applying as a partnership, the name of the partnership must be provided. It would be helpful if the names of all the partners are listed also, but this is not essential. If your address is outside the UK, you must provide an address either within the European Economic Area or the Channel Islands as your contact address in section 4. You will only have an ADP number (which means Automatic Data Processing) if you have previously applied to us to register a design, but if you do not know it then leave this space blank.

Section 4   If you appoint someone (for example, a patent attorney or a trade mark attorney) to deal with your application, give details here. If, as the applicant your address at section 3 is outside the UK, you must provide a contact address within the European Economic Area or the Channel Islands. We will send all our letters to this contact address (which we call an "address for service"). If you leave this section blank, we will write to you at the address given in section 3 as long as it is within the UK or elsewhere in the European Economic Area or the Channel Islands. You can change or appoint an agent or change a contact address at any time after making your application by sending us Form DF1A. You can get this form from us.

Section 5   Before working out how much your application will cost, you will need to count the total number of designs and decide if you want to defer publication of any or all of the designs that you include. Please complete the "Designs Ready Reckoner" sheet attached.

If you have requested deferment of publication of any design within your application, you must send us a Form DF2C requesting publication within 12 months of the date of application. Otherwise your design will <u>not</u> be registered. When you send us Form DF2C to ask us to publish each design, you will need to pay the £20 publication fee for each design as well as a deferral fee of £20 for each design. So, for example, a single design on which you defer publication will eventually cost you £80 (£40 for the application, £20 for the publication and £20 for the deferral) instead of £60. And any other design in a multiple application on which you defer publication will eventually cost you £60 (£20 for the application, £20 for the publication and £20 for the deferral) instead of £40. You can choose to defer publication of any design for up to12 months from the date of the application. This period cannot be extended. On all designs where you have not requested deferred publication we will publish these as soon as possible, once the application is in order.

Section 6   You or your agent must sign and date the form.

Section 7   It will help us to sort out any queries more quickly if you can provide the name and daytime phone number of someone we can contact. You can also provide your e mail address if you would like us to contact you in this way. In this section you should also say the total number of sheets of paper that make up this form so that we can account for everything. You do not have to attach samples of the products which show your design, as lined drawings, photographs or computer generated images should be perfectly adequate. But if you are unable to clearly show the design with paper illustrations then you may attach a sample of each design and say how many are attached.

(REV OCT06)   Intellectual Property Office is an operating name of the Patent Office   **Form DF2A Notes**

Second page

You should use this sheet to give information that is special to the single design or to each design in a multiple application. So, you should copy the sheet as many times as you need. You should identify the number of designs in the illustrations, and say at the top of the second page which design each sheet refers to.

Section A This must be the same applicant as in section 3. You cannot include designs owned by other people with this application.

Section B Say the product that you have designed, or which product or products the design is normally applied to, for example a watch or a teapot. If the design is surface decoration, say the products that the decoration is most likely to be applied to e.g. textiles, wallpaper or clothing. And if the design is the shape of something, say the product or products that the shape is applied to e.g. a table or a vase. Please avoid long descriptions. We want to know which products the design is applied to or used for so that we can accurately classify the design for our public search database. This is so that when anyone searches our website for designs of various products they will see your design registration in the product types where you are most likely to use it. We will restrict the classifications of each design to a maximum of four different product types, and may change the product descriptions that you give to ensure correct classification. These product classifications will not restrict the design registration in any way at all. It is the design itself that will be protected, regardless of which products you say are the most likely to be used.

Section C Your illustrations should show enough different views of the design so that there is no doubt about exactly what you want to register. So tell us how many views of the design you have included.

Section D Designs of a repeating surface pattern (RSP) should show the complete pattern and be surrounded by enough of the repeat to fully illustrate the entire pattern. So if you are, for example, applying for the design of wallpaper or textile materials that are intended to cover a large area, make sure that your design illustration covers more than the whole pattern, and say "RSP" in section D. Otherwise we will treat the design exactly as it appears in the illustrations, without any repeat.

Section E You may give a brief description of any design features that you feel may not be adequately shown in the illustrations, such as lines, contours, colours, shape, texture and materials used.

Section F In some cases you may want to protect the design that is applied to only part of a product. In these cases, you must clearly identify the design features on the part or parts of the product you want to protect. You can do this by (i) colouring the part or parts in question, (ii) drawing the part or parts in question in solid lines and the other parts in dotted lines, or, (iii) carefully circling the part or parts in red ink. You must do this on all the views of the product in your illustrations. You should then include a "partial disclaimer" in section F worded something like "The features of the design for which protection is sought are the [lines, contours, colours, shape, texture or materials as appropriate] of the part or parts of the product shaded in blue in the illustrations". Limitations and disclaimers will restrict the scope of the registered design.

Section G If you wish you may defer publication and therefore registration of the design for up to 12 months. The period for deferment cannot be extended. If you do not want us to proceed to publication and registration as soon as possible, please say "No" and make sure that you have filled in a "Designs Ready Reckoner" sheet to pay only the application fee at this stage. You will need to fill in a Form DF2C and pay us the publication fee and an extra fee for deferral when you want to have the design published. You must not forget to do this as the design application will be automatically deemed abandoned after 12 months and you will not then gain a registration at all. See the notes at section 5 for more information about the fees you must send with a Form DF2C.

Section H If you are claiming priority from an earlier design application made in another country, provide details in this section. You must apply within 6 months of your earlier application.

Section I Only fill in this section if you are not the person or company named in the priority application in section H.

Third page

You should use this sheet for illustrations of your design. If you need to copy the sheet to show the different views of the design then please do so, and show the continuation of the design number, for example, design number 4 continued out of a total of 7.

Your illustrations should show enough of the design so that there is no doubt about exactly what you want to register. If your design is for the shape of a product, the best views are often those which show the product in perspective. Perspective views show how the design looks from different angles and can reveal important details that do not always show up in a single sided view. Your illustrations can be drawings or photographs or, (in cases where the design is on a flat surface) samples. They should be presented on A4 size paper. Use only one side of the sheet of paper and, where possible, show the product in an upright position. You should label each different view in your set of illustrations, for example "front view" "view of one side" and so on. If colour is meant to form part of the design features then you should show the exact colour or colours in the illustrations or sample of the design. If colour is not meant to form part of the design features, or, if you want to protect the design in any colour, you can disclaim the colour by adding words such as "No claim is made for the colour or colours shown".

If you are having difficulty in showing your design on paper, then you may send us samples of the designs that are not harmful or perishable and which can be held by hand. We regret that we cannot return such samples. If you wish to make an application by using samples of products instead of paper illustrations then you should say so in a covering letter, or phone our Enquiry Line on 08459 500 505 and ask to meet with a Designs Examiner who will help you with your application.

(REV OCT06)   **Form DF2A Notes**

 **INTELLECTUAL**
PROPERTY OFFICE

Designs Form DF2B
Official fee due with this form

Application to register one or more designs
divided from an earlier application

Please read the guidance note below about filling in this form.

Concept House
Cardiff Road
Newport
South Wales
NP10 8QQ

1.	Your reference:	
2.	**Design number of earlier application.**	
3.	If you are applying for more than one design, please state the total number.	
	How many of these designs do you wish to have published and registered immediately?	
4.	**Full name of the applicant.**	
	Designs ADP number (if you know it).	
	If you are applying in the name of a company, where is it incorporated?	
	If incorporated in the USA, in which state is it incorporated?	
5.	Full name and address (including postcode) of your agent or your contact address (including postcode) if not the same as in section 4 above.	
	Designs ADP number (if you know it).	
6.	**Fees enclosed.**	
7.	**Signature of the applicant or their representative.**	
	Name in BLOCK CAPITALS.	
	Date.	
8.	**Name and daytime phone number of the person we should contact in case of query. You may also provide your e-mail address.**	
	How many pages are you sending us?	This is sheet 1 of

Note:

Section 6: If this application contains more than one design, attach a Designs Ready Reckoner sheet.

(REV AUG06)   Intellectual Property Office is an operating name of the Patent Office   **Form DF2B**

97

Appendix I IPO forms

This is the _____ (for example, first) design out of a total of _____ designs

You must answer these questions for each design in a multiple application, so copy this sheet as many times as you need.

A. Name of the applicant.	
B. Which product or products is the design for?	
C. How many illustration sheets are there for this design?	
D. Write "RSP" if this is the design of a pattern which repeats across the surface of a product, for example, wallpaper.	
E. If you wish, you may give a brief description of the design shown in the illustration or sample.	
F. List any limitations or disclaimers you want to record.	
G. Do you agree that we should publish this design as soon as possible? Please state yes or no.	
H. If you are claiming priority from an earlier application to register this design, give these details.	Priority date Country Application number
I. If the earlier application was made in a different name, say how the current applicant has a right to apply. If, for example, by assignment of the earlier application, give the date of the transaction.	

Notes: **You MUST answer all of the questions above which are shown in BOLD print.**

Please phone us on 08459 500 505 if you need help to fill in this form.

Checklist   Tick the box if you have included priority documents with this application ☐

(REV AUG06)   **Form DF2B**

Illustration sheet

This is the   (for example, first) design out of a total of   designs

---

Form DF2B

INTELLECTUAL
PROPERTY OFFICE

Filling in the application form DF2B

Filling in the application form DF2B to register one or more designs divided from an earlier application

If there is not enough space for any of your answers on the form, please use separate sheets. Number each sheet and write in section 8 of the form how many extra sheets you have used. If you need any more help to fill in this form, contact our Enquiry Unit on 08459 500 505.

What to put in each section of the form

First page

Section 1   Please include your reference. You don't have to provide one, but if you do we will use it whenever we contact you.

Section 2   Tell us the number that has been allocated to your original application that contained the design or designs that you are now applying for.

Section 3   Say how many different designs you are applying for in this application if there is more than one. Remember that you will need to pay for each design. See the "Designs Ready Reckoner" sheet attached. In the case of a multiple application you also need to tell us how many designs in the application are to be published immediately. For example, if this is a multiple application of three designs and you want all three to proceed to publication and registration as soon as possible, state "3". If however this is a multiple application of three designs and you want to defer the publication of one of the designs then state "2".

Section 4   This section must contain the details of the owner of the design. So only give your own details if you are either the owner or joint owner with another person or company. Do not automatically name yourself as the designer if you are applying in the name of a company. If you are applying as a partnership, the name of the partnership must be provided. It would be helpful if the names of all of the partners are listed also, but this is not essential. If your address is outside the UK, you must provide an address either within the European Economic Area or the Channel Islands as your contact address in section 5. You will only have an ADP number (which means Automatic Data Processing) if you have previously applied to us to register a design, but if you do not know it then leave this space blank.

Section 5   If you appoint someone (for example, a patent attorney or a trade mark attorney) to deal with your application, give details here. If, as the applicant, your address at section 3 is outside the UK, you must provide a contact address within the European Economic Area or the Channel Islands. We will send all our letters to this contact address (which we call an "address for service"). If you leave this section blank, we will write to you at the address given in section 3 as long as it is within the UK or elsewhere in the European Economic Area or the Channel Islands. You can change or appoint an agent or change a contact address at any time after making your application by sending us Form DF1A. You can get this form from us.

Section 6   Before working out how much your application will cost, you will need to count the total number of designs and decide if you want to defer publication of any or all of the designs that you include. Please complete the "Designs Ready Reckoner" sheet attached.

If you have requested deferment of publication of any design within your application, you must send us a Form DF2C requesting publication within 12 months of the date of application. Otherwise your design will not be registered. When you send us Form DF2C to ask us to publish each design, you will need to pay the £20 publication fee for each design as well as a deferral fee of £20 for each design. So, for example, a single design on which you defer publication will eventually cost you £80 (£40 for the application, £20 for the publication and £20 for the deferral) instead of £60. And any other design in a multiple application on which you defer publication will eventually cost you £60 (£20 for the application, £20 for the publication and £20 for the deferral) instead of £40. You can choose to defer publication of any design for up to12 months from the date of the application. This period cannot be extended.

On all designs where you have not requested deferred publication we will publish these as soon as possible, once the application is in order.

Section 7   You or your agent must sign and date the form.

(REV OCT06)   Intellectual Property Office is an operating name of the Patent Office   **Form DF2B Notes**

Section 8 It will help us to sort out any queries more quickly if you can provide the name and daytime phone number of someone we can contact. You can also provide your e mail address if you would like us to contact you in this way. In this section you should also say the total number of sheets of paper that make up this form so that we can account for everything. You do not have to attach samples of the products which show your design, as lined drawings, photographs or computer generated images should be perfectly adequate. But if you are unable to clearly show the design with paper illustrations then you may attach a sample of each design and say how many are attached.

Second page

You should use this sheet to give information that is special to the single design or to each design included in a multiple application. So, you should copy the sheet as many times as you need. You should identify the number of designs in the illustrations, and say at the top of the second page which design each sheet refers to.

Section A This must be the same applicant as in section 4. You cannot include designs owned by other people with this application.

Section B Say the product that you have designed or which product or products the design is normally applied to, for example a watch or a teapot. If the design is surface decoration, say the products that the decoration is most likely to be applied to e.g textiles, wallpaper or clothing. And if the design is the shape of something, say the product or products that the shape is applied to e.g. a table or a vase. Please avoid long descriptions. We want to know which products the design is applied to or used for so that we can accurately classify the design for our public search database. This is so that when anyone searches our website for designs of various products they will see your design registration in the product types where you are most likely to use it. We will restrict the classifications of each design to a maximum of four different product types, and may change the product descriptions that you give to ensure correct classification. These product classifications will not restrict the design registration in any way at all. It is the design itself that will be protected, regardless of which product or products you say are the most likely to be used.

Section C Your illustrations should show enough different views of the design so that there is no doubt about exactly what you want to register. So tell us how many views of the design you have included.

Section D Designs of a repeating surface pattern (RSP) should show the complete pattern and be surrounded by enough of the repeat to fully illustrate the entire pattern. So if you are, for example, applying for the design of wallpaper or textile materials that are intended to cover a large area, make sure that your design illustration covers more than the whole pattern, and say "RSP" in section D. Otherwise we will treat the design exactly as it appears in the illustrations, without any repeat.

Section E You may give a brief description of any design features that you feel may not be adequately shown in the illustrations, such as lines, contours, colours, shape, texture and materials used.

Section F   In some cases you may want to protect the design that is applied to only part of a product. In these cases, you must clearly identify the design features on the part or parts of the product you want to protect. You can do this by (i) colouring the part or parts in question, (ii) drawing the part or parts in question in solid lines and the other parts in dotted lines, or, (iii) carefully circling the part or parts in red ink. You must do this on all the views of the product in your illustrations. You should then include a "partial disclaimer" in section F worded something like "The features of the design for which protection is sought are the [lines, contours, colours, shape, texture or materials as appropriate] of the part or parts of the product shaded in blue in the illustrations". Limitations and disclaimers will restrict the scope of the registered design.

Section G If you wish you may defer publication and therefore registration of the design for up to 12 months. The period for deferment cannot be extended. If you do not want us to proceed to publication and registration as soon as possible, please say "No" and make sure that you have filled in a "Designs Ready Reckoner" sheet to pay only the application fee at this stage. You will need to fill in a Form DF2C and pay us the publication fee and an extra fee for deferral when you want to have the design published. You must not forget to do this as the design application will be automatically deemed abandoned after 12 months and you will not then gain a registration at all. See the notes at section 6 for more information about the fees you must send with a Form DF2C.

Section H If you are claiming priority from an earlier design application made in another country, provide details in this section. You must apply within 6 months of your earlier application.

Section I Only fill in this section if you are not the person or company named in the priority application in section H.

Appendix 1 IPO forms

Third page

You should use this sheet for illustrations of your design. If you need to copy the sheet to show the different views of the design then please do so, and show the continuation of the design number, for example, design number 4 continued out of a total of 7.

Your illustrations should show enough of the design so that there is no doubt about exactly what you want to register. If your design is for the shape of a product, the best views are often those which show the product in perspective. Perspective views show how the design looks from different angles and can reveal important details that do not always show up in a single sided view. Your illustrations can be drawings or photographs or, (in cases where the design is on a flat surface) samples. They should be presented on A4 size paper. Use only one side of the sheet of paper and, where possible, show the product in an upright position. You should label each different view in your set of illustrations, for example "front view" "view of one side" and so on. If colour is meant to form part of the design features then you should show the exact colour or colours in the illustrations or sample of the design. If colour is not meant to form part of the design features or, if you want to protect the design in any colour, you can disclaim the colour by adding words such as "No claim is made for the colour or colours shown".

If you are having difficulty in showing your design on paper, then you may send us samples of the designs that are not harmful or perishable and which can be held by hand. We regret that we cannot return such samples. If you wish to make an application by using samples of products instead of paper illustrations then you should say so in a covering letter, or phone our Enquiry Line on 08459 500 505 and ask to meet with a Designs Examiner who will help you with your application.

INTELLECTUAL
PROPERTY OFFICE

Designs Ready Reckoner

Concept House
Cardiff Road
Newport
South Wales
NP10 8QQ

Please return this sheet with your application form **DF2A** *or* **DF2B**

Write in this box how many
designs you are applying for.

Write in this box how many designs
you want to be published immediately.

Add the two numbers.

(That is, multiply the sum of the two numbers
by 20, add 20, and write the answer in the box.
Then write this number in section 5 of form
DF2A or section 6 of form DF2B).

X 20 + 20 =

(REV OCT06)   Intellectual Property Office is an operating name of the Patent Office   **Designs Ready Reckoner**

103

Appendix I IPO forms

 **INTELLECTUAL**
PROPERTY OFFICE

Designs Form DF2C
Official fee for each design due with this

Application to publish one or more designs

Concept House
Cardiff Road
Newport
South Wales
NP10 8QQ

Please read the guidance notes below about filling in this form

1. Your reference:	
2. Design application number or numbers.	
3. Filing date of application.	
4. Full name of the applicant. Designs ADP number (if you know it).	
5. Full name and address (including postcode) of your agent (if any). Designs ADP number (if you know it).	
6. Fees enclosed.	£
7. Signature of the applicant or their representative.	
Name in BLOCK CAPITALS. Date.	
8. Name and daytime phone number of the person we should contact in case of query. You may also provide your e-mail address.	

Notes:

You must apply for your design to be published within one year of applying to register the design. If you do not do so, we will treat your application as abandoned.

(REV OCT06)   Intellectual Property Office is an operating name of the Patent Office   **Form DF2C**

You need only complete this form if you did not consent to publication in the original application form.

(REV OCT06)   Intellectual Property Office is an operating name of the Patent Office   **Form DF2C**

105

INTELLECTUAL
PROPERTY OFFICE

Designs Form DF9A
Official fee due with this form

Renewal of design registration

Concept House
Cardiff Road
Newport
South Wales
NP10 8QQ

1. Your reference:	
2. Design number.	
3. Full name of the registered proprietor.	
4. Renewal date.	

5. Fees:	Amount of renewal fee.	£
	Amount of late renewal fee. (You must pay this if you are renewing up to six months after the renewal date.)	£
	Total fees.	£

6. If you would like confirmation of renewal sent to an address that is not the address of the registered proprietor, please give details here. Designs ADP number (if you know it).	
7. Signature.	
Name in BLOCK CAPITALS.	
Date.	
8. Name and daytime phone number of the person we should contact in case of query. You may also provide your e-mail address.	

INTELLECTUAL
PROPERTY OFFICE

Designs Form DF21
Official fee due with this form

Request for a search of the UK designs register

Concept House
Cardiff Road
Newport
South Wales
NP10 8QQ

Please read the guidance notes below about filling in this form.

1.	Your reference:	
2.	Full name and address (including postcode) where we should send the result of the search.	
3.	In relation to which product or products (up to a maximum of three) do you want us to carry out a search for the attached design?	
4.	Signature.	
	Name in BLOCK CAPITALS.	
	Date.	
5.	Name and daytime phone number of the person we should contact in case of query. You may also provide your e-mail address.	

Notes:

You must tell us which product or products you want us to search for and send us an illustration of the design you want us to look for.

You must use a separate form and pay a separate fee for each different design that you want us to look for.

Appendix 1 IPO forms

INTELLECTUAL
PROPERTY OFFICE

Form FS2

Fee sheet for: UK Designs, Patents, Trade Marks Patent,
Co-operation Treaty (PCT) and Company Names Tribunal Forms.
Please read the guidance notes on the next page about filling in this form.

Your Account Number (if you have one).	**Details of the person we should contact in case of query.** Name:
Your name and full address (including postcode).	Daytime phone number: Fax Number:
Your reference	E-mail:

How do you wish to pay?   **Tick only one box**

Deduction from Deposit Account quoted ☐

Cheque, made payable to 'Intellectual Property Office ☐   **Fax Filing 01633 817777**

Credit or debit card, details as filled in below ☐   If you fax us your forms, say how many sheets (including this one) you are sending

Bank transfer (see details on next page) ☐

List of forms included   **Date:**

	Form Type & Number	Name, Number or Other Identifier	Fee (£)
1			
2			
3			
4			
5			
		Total	

Faxback   If you fax us your forms, we will fax them back for you to check if you tick here ☐ and add £25 to the fees.

- -

Credit or Debit Card Details

Card Type: Visa Credit ☐   Visa Debit ☐   MasterCard ☐
                   AmEx ☐   Solo ☐   Maestro ☐
                   (Tick the one that does apply.)

Card number:

Valid From: \   Expiry Date: \   Issue No. (Solo / Maestro):

Cardholder name: (exactly as shown on card)   Cardholder Signature:

Intellectual Property Office is an operating name of The Patent Office

How to fill in this form

Fill in your reference. We will print this on the fee acknowledgement that we send you, so you can link the transactions with your own papers.

Arrange the forms that you send in the same order that you list them on this form.

How to pay

Note that we cannot accept card payments for PCT fees, but we can accept card payments for entry to the National Phase.

If you want to pay by bank transfer, our bank account details are as follows.

Bank sort code:	20-18-15
Bank name:	Barclays Bank PLC 121 Queen Street CARDIFF CF10 2XU
Account number:	80531766
Account name:	Intellectual Property Office
Reference:	Quote your account number (as shown on the front of this form) or some other identifier.
SWIFT code:	BARCGB22
IBAN number:	GB31 BARC 2018 1580 5317 66

How to send us your forms

Fax them to:	01633 817777
or post them to:	Intellectual Property Office Concept House Cardiff Road Newport South Wales NP10 8QQ

DDU/F100/04-09

Appendix 1 IPO forms

INTELLECTUAL
PROPERTY OFFICE

Form FS3

Fee sheet for: Handling OHIM Design and Trade Mark applications
made through the Intellectual Property Office.
Please read the guidance notes on the next page about filling in this form.

Your Account Number
(if you have one).

Your name and full
address
(including postcode).

Your reference

Details of the person we should contact in case of query.

Name:

Daytime phone number:

Fax Number:

E-mail:

How do you wish to pay?   Tick only one box

Deduction from Deposit Account quoted   ☐

Cheque, made payable to 'Intellectual Property Office'   ☐

Credit or debit card, details as filled in below   ☐

Bank transfer (see details on next page)   ☐

List of forms included   **Date:**

	Application Type (D or T)	Application reference (exactly as shown on page 1 of your application form)	Number of pages including attachments	Handling Fee (£)
1				
2				
3				
4				
5				
			Total	

Credit or Debit Card Details

Card Type: Visa Credit ☐   Visa Debit ☐   MasterCard ☐
             AmEx ☐   Solo ☐   Maestro ☐
             (Tick the one that does apply.)

Card number:

Valid From: \   Expiry Date: \   Issue No. (Solo / Maestro):

Cardholder name:
(exactly as shown on
card)   Cardholder Signature:

Intellectual Property Office is an operating name of The Patent Office

How to fill in this form

Fill in your reference. We will print this on the fee acknowledgement that we send you, so you can link the transactions with your own papers.

Arrange the forms that you send in the same order that you list them on this form.

Application Type: Write 'D' for design applications or 'T' for trademark applications. Do not send us any other OHIM forms apart from applications. Please list designs and trademarks on separate fee sheets.

Application reference: Write the same reference that you put in the first page of your OHIM application form.

Number of pages: Write the total number of sides in your application form and attachments. Do not count any blank pages.

How to pay

Note that we cannot accept payment for any application fees. You must pay these in Euros straight to OHIM. If you send us any OHIM fees, we will return them to you.

If you want to pay our handling fee by bank transfer, our bank account details are as follows.

Bank sort code: 20-18-15

Bank name: Barclays Bank PLC
121 Queen Street
CARDIFF
CF10 2XU

Account number: 80531766

Account name: Intellectual Property Office

Reference: Quote your account number (as shown on the front of this form) or some other identifier.

SWIFT code: BARCGB22

IBAN number: GB31 BARC 2018 1580 5317 66

How to send us your forms

Post them to: Intellectual Property Office
Concept House
Cardiff Road
Newport
South Wales
NP10 8QQ

You can also apply on-line at www.oami.europa.eu. There is a reduced fee for using the on-line service.

Appendix 2

OHIM Application for registered Community design

OFFICE FOR HARMONIZATION IN THE INTERNAL MARKET (OHIM)

APPLICATION FOR REGISTERED COMMUNITY DESIGN

	Date of receipt (DD/MM/YYYY)	Number of pages (including this one)	
For receiving office	/ /		Mod. 001
For OHIM	/ /		

Application Type		Applicant/representative reference (not more than 20 characters)	
Multiple application Number of designs		*Language	
Deferment[1]		Language of the application or ISO code	
Specimen[2]			ES DE EN FR IT
		Second language	

Applicant[3]   ID number   ☐ legal entity ☐ natural person

*Name of legal entity or first name and surname	
Tel, fax, e-mail	
*Address Street and number	
City and postal code	
Country	
Postal address (if different)	
Nationality / State of incorporation	

Representative[3]   ID number

Name	
Tel, fax, e-mail	
Address Street and number	
City and postal code	
Country	
Postal address (if different)	

Type of representative ☐ legal practitioner ☐ professional representative ☐ association of representatives ☐ employee

Fee check-list		TOTAL	*Payment of fees
Registration fee (1st design)		230 €	Current account with OHIM
for 2nd to 10th design	(115 € x . . .)	0 €	
from 11th onwards	(50 € x .0.)	0 €	☐ Account No
Publication fee (1st design)	120 €	120 €	☐ Do not use my current account with OHIM
for 2nd to 10th design	(60 € x . . .)	0 €	
from 11th onwards	(30 € x . .0)	0 €	Transfer to account of OHIM
Fee for deferment of publication (1st design) 40 €		€	☐ Banco Bilbao Vizcaya Argentaria
for 2nd to 10th design	(20 € x . . .)	0 €	☐ La Caixa
from 11th onwards	(10 € x . .0)	0 €	Date of transfer (DD/MM/YYYY) / /
TOTAL AMOUNT PAID		350 €	

Signature			
Name		*Signature	

* Mandatory details
[1] Please tick the box if the application contains at least one design of which publication is deferred
[2] Please tick the box if the application contains at least one specimen of a two-dimensional design
[3] If more than one or if space provided is not sufficient, please continue on the attachment sheet

RESET FORM

page number
1 of

#DS001EN

APPLICATION FOR REGISTERED COMMUNITY DESIGN
(continuation)
Reproduce this sheet in case of more than 1 design (use 1 sheet per design)

Mod 002

Tick the box if the following data is the same for all designs contained in the application

Design number	out of total of	Applicant name

*Indication of product(s)¹	☐ Same indication of product for all designs	Locarno classification

Convention priority²
☐ Same priority for all designs   ☐ Document attached

Country of first filing or ISO

Date of first filing³ / /

Filing number

Exhibition priority²
☐ Same priority for all designs   ☐ Document attached

Name of the exhibition

Date and place³ / /

Date of first disclosure³ / /

Designer²
☐ Same designer for all designs   ☐ Waiver

Name

Address

Miscellaneous
☐ Request for deferment of publication   ☐ Number of views
☐ Design filed with a specimen⁴

Brief description of the representation/specimen⁵

---

* Mandatory details

¹ Indicate the usual generic name of the product(s) in which the design is intended to be incorporated or to which it is intended to be applied, preferably using the term(s) included in the EuroLocamo Database. If the space provided is not sufficient, please continue on the attachment sheet

² If more than one, please continue on the attachment sheet

³ (DD/MM/YYYY)

⁴ Filing with a specimen is only allowed in the case of deferment (see explanatory notes)

⁵ Please continue on the attachment sheet if the space provided is not sufficient

RESET FORM   page number [ ] of [ ]

REPRESENTATION/SPECIMEN SHEET

Mod. 003

Number of views	Design number(s)	out of total of	Applicant name

Reproduce this sheet if space is not sufficient
A representation / specimen per design is mandatory

page number
of

RESET FORM

Appendix 2 OHIM Application for registered Community design

ATTACHMENT SHEET

Applicant name	Mod. 004

This sheet should be used for any additional information relating to :

additional applicant, additional representative, additional priority, additional designer, indication of product, brief description.

Please specify the field name(s) for each additional information

RESET FORM

page number

| | of | |

Appendix 3
Legislation

UK

Copyright, Designs and Patents Act 1988

Part I
Copyright

4—Artistic works

(1) In this Part "artistic work" means—

    (a)   a graphic work, photograph, sculpture or collage, irrespective of artistic quality,

    (b)   a work of architecture being a building or a model for a building, or

    (c)   a work of artistic craftsmanship.

(2) In this Part—

"building" includes any fixed structure, and a part of a building or fixed structure;

"graphic work" includes—

    (a)   any painting, drawing, diagram, map, chart or plan, and

    (b)   any engraving, etching, lithograph, woodcut or similar work;

"photograph" means a recording of light or other radiation on any medium on which an image is produced or from which an image may by any means be produced, and which is not part of a film;

"sculpture" includes a cast or model made for purposes of sculpture.

NOTES

    Act amended by Broadcasting Act 1990 (c 42), s 176, Sch 17 para 7(1).

    Part I modified by S I 1989/988, art 2(3); extended by S I 1989/1293, arts 2(3), 3, 4(4)(5)(6).

16—The acts restricted by copyright in a work.

(1) The owner of the copyright in a work has, in accordance with the following provisions of this Chapter, the exclusive right to do the following acts in the United Kingdom—

  (a) to copy the work (see section 17);
  (b) to issue copies of the work to the public (see section 18);
  [(ba) to rent or lend the work to the public (see section 18A);][1]
  (c) to perform, show or play the work in public (see section 19);
  [(d) to communicate the work to the public (see section 20);][2]
  (e) to make an adaptation of the work or do any of the above in relation to an adaptation (see section 21);

and those acts are referred to in this Part as the " acts restricted by the copyright".

(2) Copyright in a work is infringed by a person who without the licence of the copyright owner does, or authorises another to do, any of the acts restricted by the copyright.

(3) References in this Part to the doing of an act restricted by the copyright in a work are to the doing of it—

  (a) in relation to the work as a whole or any substantial part of it, and
  (b) either directly or indirectly;

and it is immaterial whether any intervening acts themselves infringe copyright.

(4) This Chapter has effect subject to—

  (a) the provisions of Chapter III (acts permitted in relation to copyright works), and (b) the provisions of Chapter VII (provisions with respect to copyright licensing).

NOTES
  1 Added by Copyright and Related Rights Regulations 1996/2967 Pt II reg 10(1) (December 1, 1996).
  2 Substituted subject to the savings specified in SI 2003/2498 reg 32 by Copyright and Related Rights Regulations 2003/2498 Pt 2 reg.6(2) (October 31, 2003: substitution has effect subject to the savings specified in SI 2003/2498 reg 32).

51—Design documents and models

(1) It is not an infringement of any copyright in a design document or model recording or embodying a design for anything other than an artistic work or a typeface to make an article to the design or to copy an article made to the design.

(2) Nor is it an infringement of the copyright to issue to the public, or include in a film [or communicate to the public][1], anything the making of which was, by virtue of subsection (1), not an infringement of that copyright.

(3) In this section—

"design" means the design of any aspect of the shape or configuration (whether internal or external) of the whole or part of an article, other than surface decoration; and

"design document" means any record of a design, whether in the form of a drawing, a written description, a photograph, data stored in a computer or otherwise.

NOTES
1 Words substituted subject to the savings specified in SI 2003/2498 reg 32 by Copyright and Related Rights Regulations 2003/2498 Sch 1(1) para 8(3) (October 31, 2003: substitution has effect subject to the savings specified in SI 2003/2498 reg 32)

52—Effect of exploitation of design derived from artistic work

(1) This section applies where an artistic work has been exploited, by or with the licence of the copyright owner, by—

(a) making by an industrial process articles falling to be treated for the purposes of this Part as copies of the work, and

(b) marketing such articles, in the United Kingdom or elsewhere.

(2) After the end of the period of 25 years from the end of the calendar year in which such articles are first marketed, the work may be copied by making articles of any description, or doing anything for the purpose of making articles of any description, and anything may be done in relation to articles so made, without infringing copyright in the work.

(3) Where only part of an artistic work is exploited as mentioned in subsection (1), subsection (2) applies only in relation to that part.

(4) The Secretary of State may by order make provision—

(a) as to the circumstances in which an article, or any description of article, is to be regarded for the purposes of this section as made by an industrial process;

(b) excluding from the operation of this section such articles of a primarily literary or artistic character as he thinks fit.

(5) An order shall be made by statutory instrument which shall be subject to annulment in pursuance of a resolution of either House of Parliament.

(6) In this section—

(a) references to articles do not include films; and

(b) references to the marketing of an article are to its being sold or let for hire or offered or exposed for sale or hire.

NOTES
Act amended by Broadcasting Act 1990 (c 42), s 176, Sch 17 para 7(1).
Part I modified by SI 1989/988, art 2(3); extended by SI 1989/1293, arts 2(3), 3, 4(4)(5)(6).
Amended by Broadcasting Act 1990 (c 42), s 176, Sch 17 para 7(1).
S 52 excluded by SI 1989/1070, art 3.

53—Things done in reliance on registration of design

(1) The copyright in an artistic work is not infringed by anything done—

- (a) in pursuance of an assignment or licence made or granted by a person registered under the Registered Designs Act 1949 as the proprietor of a corresponding design, and
- (b) in good faith in reliance on the registration and without notice of any proceedings for the cancellation [or invalidation] of the registration or for rectifying the relevant entry in the register of designs;

and this is so notwithstanding that the person registered as the proprietor was not the proprietor of the design for the purposes of the 1949 Act.

(2) In subsection (1) a "corresponding design", in relation to an artistic work, means a design within the meaning of the 1949 Act which if applied to an article would produce something which would be treated for the purposes of this Part as a copy of the artistic work.

NOTES
Words inserted by Registered Designs Regulations 2001/3949 Sch 1 para 16 (December 9, 2001).

Miscellaneous: literary, dramatic, musical and artistic works

62 Representation of certain artistic works on public display

(1) This section applies to—

- (a) buildings, and
- (b) sculptures, models for buildings and works of artistic craftsmanship, if permanently situated in public place or in premises open to the public.

(2) The copyright in such a work is not infringed by—

- (a) making a graphic work representing it,
- (b) making a photograph or film of it, or
- (c) [making a broadcast of] a visual image of it.

(3) Nor is the copyright infringed by the issue to the public of copies, or the [communication to the public] , of anything whose making was, by virtue of this section, not an infringement of the copyright.

NOTES
1 Words substituted subject to the savings specified in SI 2003/2498 reg 32 by Copyright and Related Rights Regulations 2003/2498 Sch 1(1) para 14 (31 October 2003: substitution has effect subject to the savings specified in SI 2003/2498 reg 32).
2 Words substituted subject to the savings specified in SI 2003/2498 reg 32 by Copyright and Related Rights Regulations 2003/2498 Sch 1(1) para 5(c) (31 October 2003: substitution has effect subject to the savings specified in SI 2003/2498 reg 32).

63 Advertisement of sale of artistic work

(1) It is not an infringement of copyright in an artistic work to copy it, or to issue copies to the public, for the purpose of advertising the sale of the work.

(2) Where a copy which would otherwise be an infringing copy is made in accordance with this section but is subsequently dealt with for any other purpose, it shall be treated as an infringing copy for the purposes of that dealing, and if that dealing infringes copyright for all subsequent purposes.

For this purpose "dealt with" means sold or let for hire, offered or exposed for sale or hire, exhibited in public [, distributed or communicated to the public] .

NOTES
1   Words substituted subject to the savings specified in SI 2003/2498 reg 32 by Copyright and Related Rights Regulations 2003/2498 Pt 2 reg 17 (31 October 2003: substitution has effect subject to the savings specified in SI 2003/2498 reg 32).

64 Making of subsequent works by same artist

Where the author of an artistic work is not the copyright owner, he does not infringe the copyright by copying the work in making another artistic work, provided he does not repeat or imitate the main design of the earlier work.

NOTES
1   Act amended by Broadcasting Act 1990 s 176 Sch 17 para 7(1).
2   Part I modified by SI 1989/988 art 2(3); extended by SI1989/1293 arts 2(3), 3, 4(4)(5)(6).
3   Amended by Broadcasting Act 1990 s 176 Sch 17 para 7(1).

65 Reconstruction of buildings

Anything done for the purposes of reconstructing a building does not infringe any copyright—

   (a)   in the building, or
   (b)   in any drawings or plans in accordance with which the building was, by or with the licence of the copyright owner, constructed.

NOTES
1   Act amended by Broadcasting Act 1990 s 176 Sch 17 para 7(1).
2   Part I modified by SI 1989/988 art 2(3); extended by SI 1989/1293 arts 2(3), 3, 4(4)(5)(6).
3   Amended by Broadcasting Act 1990 s 176 Sch 17 para 7(1).

Adaptations

76 Adaptations

An act which by virtue of this Chapter may be done without infringing copyright in a literary, dramatic or musical work does not, where that work is an adaptation, infringe any copyright in the work from which the adaptation was made.

NOTES
1 Act amended by Broadcasting Act 1990 s 176 Sch 17 para 7(1) 2
2 Part I modified by SI 1989/988 art 2(3); extended by SI 1989/1293 arts 2(3), 3, 4(4)(5)(6) 2
3 Amended by Broadcasting Act 1990 s 176 Sch 17 para 7(1) 2

Part III
DESIGN RIGHT

Chapter I
DESIGN RIGHT IN ORIGINAL DESIGNS

Introductory

213 Design right

(1) Design right is a property right which subsists in accordance with this Part in an original design.

(2) In this Part "design" means the design of any aspect of the shape or configuration (whether internal or external) of the whole or part of an article.

(3) Design right does not subsist in—

(a) a method or principle of construction,
(b) features of shape or configuration of an article which—

(i) enable the article to be connected to, or placed in, around or against, another article so that either article may perform its function, or
(ii) are dependent upon the appearance of another article of which the article is intended by the designer to form an integral part, or

(c) surface decoration.

(4) A design is not "original" for the purposes of this Part if it is commonplace in the design field in question at the time of its creation.

(5) Design right subsists in a design only if the design qualifies for design right protection by reference to—

(a) the designer or the person by whom the design was commissioned or the designer employed (see sections 218 and 219), or
(b) the person by whom and country in which articles made to the design were first marketed (see section 220),

or in accordance with any Order under section 221 (power to make further provision with respect to qualification).

[(5A) Design right does not subsist in a design which consists of or contains a controlled representation within the meaning of the Olympic Symbol etc (Protection) Act 1995.]

(6) Design right does not subsist unless and until the design has been recorded in a design document or an article has been made to the design.

(7) Design right does not subsist in a design which was so recorded, or to which an article was made, before the commencement of this Part.

NOTES
    1   Added by Olympic Symbol etc. (Protection) Act 1995 s 14(1) (20 September 1995).

214 The designer

(1) In this Part the "designer", in relation to a design, means the person who creates it.

(2) In the case of a computer-generated design the person by whom the arrangements necessary for the creation of the design are undertaken shall be taken to be the designer.

NOTES
    1   Act amended by Broadcasting Act 1990 s 176 Sch 17 para 7(1).
    2   Pt III (ss 213–264) modified by SI 1989/1100 art 3.

215 Ownership of design right

(1) The designer is the first owner of any design right in a design which is not created in pursuance of a commission or in the course of employment.

(2) Where a design is created in pursuance of a commission, the person commissioning the design is the first owner of any design right in it.

(3) Where, in a case not falling within subsection (2) a design is created by an employee in the course of his employment, his employer is the first owner of any design right in the design.

(4) If a design qualifies for design right protection by virtue of section 220 (qualification by reference to first marketing of articles made to the design), the above rules do not apply and the person by whom the articles in question are marketed is the first owner of the design right.

NOTES
    1   Act amended by Broadcasting Act 1990 s 176 Sch 17 para 7(1).
    2   Pt III (ss 213–264) modified by SI 1989/1100 art 3.

216 Duration of design right

(1) Design right expires—

    (a)   fifteen years from the end of the calendar year in which the design was first recorded in a design document or an article was first made to the design, whichever first occurred, or

    (b)   if articles made to the design are made available for sale or hire within five years from the end of that calendar year, ten years from the end of the calendar year in which that first occurred.

(2) The reference in subsection (1) to articles being made available for sale or hire is to their being made so available anywhere in the world by or with the licence of the design right owner.

NOTES
1   Act amended by Broadcasting Act 1990 s 176 Sch 17 para 7(1).
2   Pt III (ss 213–264) modified by SI 1989/1100 art 3.

Qualification for design right protection

217   Qualifying individuals and qualifying persons

(1) In this Part—

> "qualifying individual" means a citizen or subject of, or an individual habitually resident in, a qualifying country; and
> "qualifying person" means a qualifying individual or a body corporate or other body having legal personality which—
> (a)   is formed under the law of a part of the United Kingdom or another qualifying country, and
> (b)   has in any qualifying country a place of business at which substantial business activity is carried on.

(2) References in this Part to a qualifying person include the Crown and the government of any other qualifying country.

(3) In this section "qualifying country" means —

(a)   the United Kingdom,
(b)   a country to which this Part extends by virtue of an Order under section 255,
(c)   another member State of the European Economic Community, or
(d)   to the extent that an Order under section 256 so provides, a country designated under that section as enjoying reciprocal protection.

(4) The reference in the definition of "qualifying individual" to a person's being a citizen or subject of a qualifying country shall be construed —

(a)   in relation to the United Kingdom, as a reference to his being a British citizen, and
(b)   in relation to a colony of the United Kingdom, as a reference to his being a British Dependent Territories' citizen by connection with that colony.

(5) In determining for the purpose of the definition of "qualifying person" whether substantial business activity is carried on at a place of business in any country, no account shall be taken of dealings in goods which are at all material times outside that country.

NOTES
1   Act amended by Broadcasting Act 1990 s 176 Sch 17 para 7(1).
2   Pt III (ss 213–264) modified by SI 1989/1100 art 3.

218 Qualification by reference to designer

(1) This section applies to a design which is not created in pursuance of a commission or in the course of employment.

(2) A design to which this section applies qualifies for design right protection if the designer is a qualifying individual or, in the case of a computer-generated design, a qualifying person.

(3) A joint design to which this section applies qualifies for design right protection if any of the designers is a qualifying individual or, as the case may be, a qualifying person.

(4) Where a joint design qualifies for design right protection under this section, only those designers who are qualifying individuals or qualifying persons are entitled to design right under section 215(1) (first ownership of design right: entitlement of designer).

NOTES
 1   Act amended by Broadcasting Act 1990 s 176 Sch 17 para 7(1).
 2   Pt III (ss 213–264) modified by SI 1989/1100 art 3.

219 Qualification by reference to commissioner or employer

(1) A design qualifies for design right protection if it is created in pursuance of a commission from, or in the course of employment with, a qualifying person.

(2) In the case of a joint commission or joint employment a design qualifies for design right protection if any of the commissioners or employers is a qualifying person.

(3) Where a design which is jointly commissioned or created in the course of joint employment qualifies for design right protection under this section, only those commissioners or employers who are qualifying persons are entitled to design right under section 215(2) or (3) (first ownership of design right: entitlement of commissioner or employer).

NOTES
 1   Act amended by Broadcasting Act 1990 s 176 Sch 17 para 7(1)
 2   Pt III (ss 213–264) modified by SI 1989/1100 art 3

220 Qualification by reference to first marketing

(1) A design which does not qualify for design right protection under section 218 or 219 (qualification by reference to designer, commissioner or employer) qualifies for design right protection if the first marketing of articles made to the design—

  (a) is by a qualifying person who is exclusively authorised to put such articles on the market in the United Kingdom, and
  (b) takes place in the United Kingdom, another country to which this Part extends by virtue of an Order under section 255, or another member State of the European Economic Community.

(2) If the first marketing of articles made to the design is done jointly by two or more persons, the design qualifies for design right protection if any of those persons meets the requirements specified in subsection (1)(a).

(3) In such a case only the persons who meet those requirements are entitled to design right under section 215(4) (first ownership of design right: entitlement of first marketer of articles made to the design).

(4) In subsection (1)(a) "exclusively authorised" refers—

  (a) to authorisation by the person who would have been first owner of design right as designer, commissioner of the design or employer of the designer if he had been a qualifying person, or by a person lawfully claiming under such a person, and
  (b) to exclusivity capable of being enforced by legal proceedings in the United Kingdom.

NOTES
  1   Act amended by Broadcasting Act 1990 s 176 Sch 17 para 7(1).
  2   Pt III (ss 213–264) modified by SI 1989/1100 art 3.

221 Power to make further provision as to qualification

(1) Her Majesty may, with a view to fulfilling an international obligation of the United Kingdom, by Order in Council provide that a design qualifies for design right protection if such requirements as are specified in the Order are met.

(2) An Order may make different provision for different descriptions of design or article; and may make such consequential modifications of the operation of sections 215 (ownership of design right) and sections 218 to 220 (other means of qualification) as appear to Her Majesty to be appropriate.

(3) A statutory instrument containing an Order in Council under this section shall be subject to annulment in pursuance of a resolution of either House of Parliament.

NOTES
  1   Act amended by Broadcasting Act 1990 s 176 Sch 17 para 7(1).
  2   Pt III (ss 213–264) modified by SI 1989/1100 art 3.

Dealings with design right

222 Assignment and licences

(1) Design right is transmissible by assignment, by testamentary disposition or by operation of law, as personal or moveable property.

(2) An assignment or other transmission of design right may be partial, that is, limited so as to apply—

  (a) to one or more, but not all, of the things the design right owner has the exclusive right to do;
  (b) to part, but not the whole, of the period for which the right is to subsist.

(3) An assignment of design right is not effective unless it is in writing signed by or on behalf of the assignor.

(4) A licence granted by the owner of design right is binding on every successor in title to his interest in the right, except a purchaser in good faith for valuable consideration and without notice (actual or constructive) of the licence or a person deriving title from such a purchaser; and references in this Part to doing anything with, or without, the licence of the design right owner shall be construed accordingly.

NOTES
    1   Act amended by Broadcasting Act 1990 s 176 Sch 17 para 7(1).
    2   Pt III (ss 213–264) modified by SI 1989/1100 art 3.

223   Prospective ownership of design right

(1) Where by an agreement made in relation to future design right, and signed by or on behalf of the prospective owner of the design right, the prospective owner purports to assign the future design right (wholly or partially) to another person, then if, on the right coming into existence, the assignee or another person claiming under him would be entitled as against all other persons to require the right to be vested in him, the right shall vest in him by virtue of this section.

(2) In this section—

> "future design right" means design right which will or may come into existence in respect of a future design or class of designs or on the occurrence of a future event; and
> "prospective owner" shall be construed accordingly, and includes a person who is prospectively entitled to design right by virtue of such an agreement as is mentioned in subsection (1).

(3) A licence granted by a prospective owner of design right is binding on every successor in title to his interest (or prospective interest) in the right, except a purchaser in good faith for valuable consideration and without notice (actual or constructive) of the licence or a person deriving title from such a purchaser; and references in this Part to doing anything with, or without, the licence of the design right owner shall be construed accordingly.

NOTES
    1   Act amended by Broadcasting Act 1990 s 176 Sch 17 para 7(1).
    2   Pt III (ss 213–264) modified by SI 1989/1100 art 3.

224   Assignment of right in registered design presumed to carry with it design right

Where a design consisting of a design in which design right subsists is registered under the Registered Designs Act 1949 and the proprietor of the registered design is also the design right owner, an assignment of the right in the registered design shall be taken to be also an assignment of the design right, unless a contrary intention appears.

NOTES
1   Act amended by Broadcasting Act 1990 s 176 Sch 17 para 7(1).
2   Pt III (ss 213–264) modified by SI 1989/1100 art 3.

225   Exclusive licences

(1) In this Part an "exclusive licence" means a licence in writing signed by or on behalf of the design right owner authorising the licensee to the exclusion of all other persons, including the person granting the licence, to exercise a right which would otherwise be exercisable exclusively by the design right owner.

(2) The licensee under an exclusive licence has the same rights against any successor in title who is bound by the licence as he has against the person granting the licence.

NOTES
1   Act amended by Broadcasting Act 1990 s 176 Sch 17 para 7(1).
2   Pt III (ss 213–264) modified by SI 1989/1100 art 3.

Chapter III
Exceptions to Rights of Design Right Owners

Infringement of copyright

236.   Infringement of copyright

Where copyright subsists in a work which consists of or includes a design in which design right subsists, it is not an infringement of design right in the design to do anything which is an infringement of the copyright in that work.

NOTES
1   Act amended by Broadcasting Act 1990 s 176 Sch 17 para 7(1).
2   Pt III (ss 213–264) modified by SI 1989/1100 art 3.

Availability of licences of right

237   Licences available in last five years of design right

(1) Any person is entitled as of right to a licence to do in the last five years of the design right term anything which would otherwise infringe the design right.

(2) The terms of the licence shall, in default of agreement, be settled by the comptroller.

(3) The Secretary of State may if it appears to him necessary in order to—

    (a)   comply with an international obligation of the United Kingdom, or
    (b)   secure or maintain reciprocal protection for British designs in other countries,

by order exclude from the operation of subsection (1) designs of a description specified in the order or designs applied to articles of a description so specified.

(4) An order shall be made by statutory instrument; and no order shall be made unless a draft of it has been laid before and approved by a resolution of each House of Parliament.

NOTES
1   Act amended by Broadcasting Act 1990 s 176 Sch 17 para 7(1).
2   Pt III (ss 213–264) modified by SI 1989/1100 art 3.

238   Powers exercisable for protection of the public interest

[(1) Subsection (1A) applies where whatever needs to be remedied, mitigated or prevented by the Secretary of State, the Competition Commission or (as the case may be) the Office of Fair Trading under section 12(5) of the Competition Act 1980 or section 41(2), 55(2), 66(6), 75(2), 83(2), 138(2), 147(2) or 160(2) of, or paragraph 5(2) or 10(2) of Schedule 7 to, the Enterprise Act 2002 (powers to take remedial action following references to the Commission in connection with public bodies and certain other persons, mergers or market investigations etc.) consists of or includes—

(a)   conditions in licences granted by a design right owner restricting the use of the design by the licensee or the right of the design right owner to grant other licences, or

(b)   a refusal of a design right owner to grant licences on reasonable terms.

(1A) The powers conferred by Schedule 8 to the Enterprise Act 2002 include power to cancel or modify those conditions and, instead or in addition, to provide that licences in respect of the design right shall be available as of right.

(2) The references to anything permitted by Schedule 8 to the Enterprise Act 2002 in section 12(5A) of the Competition Act 1980 and in sections 75(4)(a), 83(4)(a), 84(2)(a), 89(1), 160(4)(a), 161(3)(a) and 164(1) of, and paragraphs 5, 10 and 11 of Schedule 7 to, the Act of 2002 shall be construed accordingly.]

(3) The terms of a licence available by virtue of this section shall, in default of agreement, be settled by the comptroller.

NOTES
1   Section238(1), (1A) and (2) substituted for s 238(1)–(2) by Enterprise Act 2002 c. 40 Sch 25 para 18(4) (20 June 2003: substitution has effect subject to SI 2003/1397 arts 3(1) and 8 and SI 2004/3233 art 2 and Sch 1).

239   Undertaking to take licence of right in infringement proceedings

(1) If in proceedings for infringement of design right in a design in respect of which a licence is available as of right under section 237 or 238 the defendant undertakes to take a licence on such terms as may be agreed or, in default of agreement, settled by the comptroller under that section—

(a)   no injunction shall be granted against him,
(b)   no order for delivery up shall be made under section 230, and

(c)   the amount recoverable against him by way of damages or on an account of profits shall not exceed double the amount which would have been payable by him as licensee if such a licence on those terms had been granted before the earliest infringement.

(2) An undertaking may be given at any time before final order in the proceedings, without any admission of liability.

(3) Nothing in this section affects the remedies available in respect of an infringement committed before licences of right were available.

NOTES
1   Act amended by Broadcasting Act 1990 s 176 Sch 17 para 7(1).
2   Pt III (ss 213–264) modified by SI 1989/1100 art 3.

Crown use of designs

240   Crown use of designs

(1) A government department, or a person authorised in writing by a government department, may without the licence of the design right owner—

(a)   do anything for the purpose of supplying articles for the services of the Crown, or
(b)   dispose of articles no longer required for the services of the Crown;

and nothing done by virtue of this section infringes the design right.

(2) References in this Part to "the services of the Crown" are to—

(a)   the defence of the realm,
(b)   foreign defence purposes, and
(c)   health service purposes.

(3) The reference to the supply of articles for "foreign defence purposes" is to their supply—

(a)   for the defence of a country outside the realm in pursuance of an agreement or arrangement to which the government of that country and Her Majesty's Government in the United Kingdom are parties; or
(b)   for use by armed forces operating in pursuance of a resolution of the United Nations or one of its organs.

(4) The reference to the supply of articles for "health service purposes" are to their supply for the purpose of providing—

[(za) primary medical services or primary dental services under [the National Health Service Act 2006 or the National Health Service (Wales) Act 2006] [or primary medical services under Part 1 of the National Health Service (Scotland) Act 1978]
[(a)   pharmaceutical services, general medical services or general dental services under— [

        (i)   Chapter 1 of Part 7 of the National Health Service Act 2006, or

Chapter 1 of Part 7 of the National Health Service (Wales) Act 2006 (in the case of pharmaceutical services),]

(ii) Part II of the National Health Service (Scotland) Act 1978 [(in the case of pharmaceutical services or general dental services)], or

(iii) the corresponding provisions of the law in force in Northern Ireland; or

(b) personal medical services [or personal dental services] in accordance with arrangements made under—

[…]

(ii) section 17C of the 1978 Act [(in the case of personal dental services)] , […]

(iii) the corresponding provisions of the law in force in Northern Ireland [, or]]

[(c) local pharmaceutical services provided under [the National Health Service Act 2006 or the National Health Service (Wales) Act 2006.]

[…]]

(5) In this Part—

"Crown use", in relation to a design, means the doing of anything by virtue of this section which would otherwise be an infringement of design right in the design; and

"the government department concerned", in relation to such use, means the government department by whom or on whose authority the act was done.

(6) The authority of a government department in respect of Crown use of a design may be given to a person either before or after the use and whether or not he is authorised, directly or indirectly, by the design right owner to do anything in relation to the design.

(7) A person acquiring anything sold in the exercise of powers conferred by this section, and any person claiming under him, may deal with it in the same manner as if the design right were held on behalf of the Crown. […]

NOTES

1   Modified by Health and Social Care (Community Health and Standards) Act 2003 Sch 11 para 52 (1 April 2004 as SI 2004/480).

2   Words substituted by National Health Service (Consequential Provisions) Act 2006 Sch 1 para 113(a) (1 March 2007).

3   Words inserted by Primary Medical Services (Scotland) Act 2004 (Consequential Modifications) Order 2004/957 Sch 1 para 5(a) (1 April 2004).

4   Substituted by National Health Service (Primary Care) Act 1997 Sch 2(I) para 63 (1 April 1998 as specified in SI 1998/631 art 2(1); 13 August 1998 otherwise).

5   Substituted by National Health Service (Consequential Provisions) Act 2006 Sch 1 para 113(b) (1 March 2007).

6   Words inserted by Primary Medical Services (Scotland) Act 2004 (Consequential Modifications) Order 2004/957 Sch 1 para 5(b) (1 April 2004).

7   Words inserted by National Health Service (Primary Care) Act 1997 Sch 2(I) para 63 (August 13, 1998 as SI 1998/1998).

8 Words inserted by Primary Medical Services (Scotland) Act 2004 (Consequential Modifications) Order 2004/957 Sch 1 para 5(c) (1 April 2004).
9 Added by Health and Social Care Act 2001 Sch 5(1) para 7 (1 January 2003 as SI 2003/53).
10 Words substituted for existing s 240(4)(c)(i) and (ii) by National Health Service (Consequential Provisions) Act 2006 c. 43 Sch 1 para 113(c) (1 March 2007).

241 Settlement of terms for Crown use

(1) Where Crown use is made of a design, the government department concerned shall—

(a) notify the design right owner as soon as practicable, and
(b) give him such information as to the extent of the use as he may from time to time require,

unless it appears to the department that it would be contrary to the public interest to do so or the identity of the design right owner cannot be ascertained on reasonable inquiry.

(2) Crown use of a design shall be on such terms as, either before or after the use, are agreed between the government department concerned and the design right owner with the approval of the Treasury or, in default of agreement, are determined by the court.

In the application of this subsection to Northern Ireland the reference to the Treasury shall, where the government department referred to in that subsection is a Northern Ireland department, be construed as a reference to the Department of Finance and Personnel.

[In the application of this subsection to Scotland, where the government department referred to in that subsection is any part of the Scottish Administration, the words "with the approval of the Treasury" are omitted.]

(3) Where the identity of the design right owner cannot be ascertained on reasonable inquiry, the government department concerned may apply to the court who may order that no royalty or other sum shall be payable in respect of Crown use of the design until the owner agrees terms with the department or refers the matter to the court for determination.

NOTES
1 Words inserted by Scotland Act 1998 (Consequential Modifications) (No 2) Order 1999/1820 Sch 2(I) para 93(2) (1 July 1999 the principal appointed day for 1998 c 46).

242 Rights of third parties in case of Crown use

(1) The provisions of any licence, assignment or agreement made between the design right owner (or anyone deriving title from him or from whom he derives title) and any person other than a government department are of no effect in relation to Crown use of a design, or any act incidental to Crown use, so far as they—

(a) restrict or regulate anything done in relation to the design, or the use of any model, document or other information relating to it, or

(b) provide for the making of payments in respect of, or calculated by reference to such use;

and the copying or issuing to the public of copies of any such model or document in connection with the thing done, or any such use, shall be deemed not to be an infringement of any copyright in the model or document.

(2) Subsection (1) shall not be construed as authorising the disclosure of any such model, document or information in contravention of the licence, assignment or agreement.

(3) Where an exclusive licence is in force in respect of the design—

(a) if the licence was granted for royalties—

    (i) any agreement between the design right owner and a government department under section 241 (settlement of terms for Crown use) requires the consent of the licensee, and

    (ii) the licensee is entitled to recover from the design right owner such part of the payment for Crown use as may be agreed between them or, in default of agreement, determined by the court;

(b) if the licence was granted otherwise than for royalties—

    (i) section 241 applies in relation to anything done which but for section 240 (Crown use) and subsection (1) above would be an infringement of the rights of the licensee with the substitution for references to the design right owner of references to the licensee, and

    (ii) section 241 does not apply in relation to anything done by the licensee by virtue of an authority given under section 240. (4) Where the design right has been assigned to the design right owner in consideration of royalties—

    (a) section 241 applies in relation to Crown use of the design as if the references to the design right owner included the assignor, and any payment for Crown use shall be divided between them in such proportion as may be agreed or, in default of agreement, determined by the court; and

    (b) section 241 applies in relation to any act incidental to Crown use as it applies in relation to Crown use of the design.

(5) Where any model, document or other information relating to a design is used in connection with Crown use of the design, or any act incidental to Crown use, section 241 applies to the use of the model, document or other information with the substitution for the references to the design right owner of references to the person entitled to the benefit of any provision of an agreement rendered inoperative by subsection (1) above.

Appendix 3 Legislation

(6) In this section—

"act incidental to Crown use" means anything done for the services of the Crown to the order of a government department by the design right owner in respect of a design;

"payment for Crown use" means such amount as is payable by the government department concerned by virtue of section 241; and

"royalties" includes any benefit determined by reference to the use of the design.

NOTES
1   Act amended by Broadcasting Act 1990 s 176 Sch 17 para 7(1).
2   Pt III (ss 213–264) modified by SI 1989/1100 art 3.

243   Crown use: compensation for loss of profit

(1) Where Crown use is made of a design, the government department concerned shall pay—

(a)   to the design right owner, or

(b)   if there is an exclusive licence in force in respect of the design, to the exclusive licensee,

compensation for any loss resulting from his not being awarded a contract to supply the articles made to the design.

(2) Compensation is payable only to the extent that such a contract could have been fulfilled from his existing manufacturing capacity; but is payable notwithstanding the existence of circumstances rendering him ineligible for the award of such a contract.

(3) In determining the loss, regard shall be had to the profit which would have been made on such a contract and to the extent to which any manufacturing capacity was under-used.

(4) No compensation is payable in respect of any failure to secure contracts for the supply of articles made to the design otherwise than for the services of the Crown.

(5) The amount payable shall, if not agreed between the design right owner or licensee and the government department concerned with the approval of the Treasury, be determined by the court on a reference under section 252; and it is in addition to any amount payable under section 241 or 242.

(6) In the application of this section to Northern Ireland, the reference in subsection (5) to the Treasury shall, where the government department concerned is a Northern Ireland department, be construed as a reference to the Department of Finance and Personnel.

[(7) In the application of this section to Scotland, where the government department referred to in subsection (5) is any part of the Scottish Administration, the words "with the approval of the Treasury" in that subsection are omitted.]

NOTES
1   Added by Scotland Act 1998 (Consequential Modifications) (No 2) Order 1999/1820 Sch 2(I) para 93(3) (1 July 1999, the principal appointed day for 1998 c 46).

244   Special provision for Crown use during emergency

(1) During a period of emergency the powers exercisable in relation to a design by virtue of section 240 (Crown use) include power to do any act which would otherwise be an infringement of design right for any purpose which appears to the government department concerned necessary or expedient—

(a)   for the efficient prosecution of any war in which Her Majesty may be engaged;

(b)   for the maintenance of supplies and services essential to the life of the community;

(c)   for securing a sufficiency of supplies and services essential to the well-being of the community;

(d)   for promoting the productivity of industry, commerce and agriculture;

(e)   for fostering and directing exports and reducing imports, or imports of any classes, from all or any countries and for redressing the balance of trade;

(f)   generally for ensuring that the whole resources of the community are available for use, and are used, in a manner best calculated to serve the interests of the community; or

(g)   for assisting the relief of suffering and the restoration and distribution of essential supplies and services in any country outside the United Kingdom which is in grave distress as the result of war.

(2) References in this Part to the services of the Crown include, as respects a period of emergency, those purposes; and references to "Crown use" include any act which would apart from this section be an infringement of design right.

(3) In this section "period of emergency" means a period beginning with such date as may be declared by Order in Council to be the beginning, and ending with such date as may be so declared to be the end, of a period of emergency for the purposes of this section.

(4) No Order in Council under this section shall be submitted to Her Majesty unless a draft of it has been laid before and approved by a resolution of each House of Parliament.

NOTES
1   Act amended by Broadcasting Act 1990 s 176 Sch 17 para 7(1).
2   Pt III (ss 213–264) modified by SI 1989/1100 art 3.

General

245   Power to provide for further exceptions

(1) The Secretary of State may if it appears to him necessary in order to—

    (a)   comply with an international obligation of the United Kingdom, or

    (b)   secure or maintain reciprocal protection for British designs in other countries,

by order provide that acts of a description specified in the order do not infringe design right.

(2) An order may make different provision for different descriptions of design or article.

(3) An order shall be made by statutory instrument and no order shall be made unless a draft of it has been laid before and approved by a resolution of each House of Parliament.

NOTES
    1   Act amended by Broadcasting Act 1990 s 176 Sch 17 para 7(1).
    2   Pt III (ss 213–264) modified by SI 1989/1100 art 3.

Miscellaneous

253 Remedy for groundless threats of infringement proceedings

(1) Where a person threatens another person with proceedings for infringement of design right, a person aggrieved by the threats may bring an action against him claiming—

    (a)   a declaration to the effect that the threats are unjustifiable;

    (b)   an injunction against the continuance of the threats;

    (c)   damages in respect of any loss which he has sustained by the threats.

(2) If the plaintiff proves that the threats were made and that he is a person aggrieved by them, he is entitled to the relief claimed unless the defendant shows that the acts in respect of which proceedings were threatened did constitute, or if done would have constituted, an infringement of the design right concerned.

(3) Proceedings may not be brought under this section in respect of a threat to bring proceedings for an infringement alleged to consist of making or importing anything.

(4) Mere notification that a design is protected by design right does not constitute a threat of proceedings for the purposes of this section.

NOTES
    1   Act amended by Broadcasting Act 1990 s 176 Sch 17 para 7(1).
    2   Pt III (ss 213–264) modified by SI 1989/1100 art 3.

254 Licensee under licence of right not to claim connection with design right owner

(1) A person who has a licence in respect of a design by virtue of section 237 or 238 (licences of right) shall not, without the consent of the design right owner—

(a) apply to goods which he is marketing, or proposes to market, in reliance on that licence a trade description indicating that he is the licensee of the design right owner, or

(b) use any such trade description in an advertisement in relation to such goods.

(2) A contravention of subsection (1) is actionable by the design right owner.

(3) In this section "trade description", the reference to applying a trade description to goods and "advertisement" have the same meaning as in the Trade Descriptions Act 1968.

NOTES
   1   Act amended by Broadcasting Act 1990 s 176 Sch 17 para 7(1).
   2   Pt III (ss 213–264) modified by SI 1989/1100 art 3.

Extent of operation of this Part

255 Countries to which this Part extends

(1) This Part extends to England and Wales, Scotland and Northern Ireland.

(2) Her Majesty may by Order in Council direct that this Part shall extend, subject to such exceptions and modifications as may be specified in the Order, to—

(a) any of the Channel Islands,
(b) the Isle of Man, or
(c) any colony.

(3) That power includes power to extend, subject to such exceptions and modifications as may be specified in the Order, any Order in Council made under section 221 (further provision as to qualification for design right protection) or section 256 (countries enjoying reciprocal protection).

(4) The legislature of a country to which this Part has been extended may modify or add to the provisions of this Part, in their operation as part of the law of that country, as the legislature may consider necessary to adapt the provisions to the circumstances of that country; but not so as to deny design right protection in a case where it would otherwise exist.

(5) Where a country to which this Part extends ceases to be a colony of the United Kingdom, it shall continue to be treated as such a country for the purposes of this Part until—

(a) an Order in Council is made under section 256 designating it as a country enjoying reciprocal protection, or
(b) an Order in Council is made declaring that it shall cease to be so treated by reason of the fact that the provisions of this Part as part of the law of that country have been amended or repealed.

(6) A statutory instrument containing an Order in Council under subsection (5)(b) shall be subject to annulment in pursuance of a resolution of either House of Parliament.

NOTES
1 Act amended by Broadcasting Act 1990 s 176 Sch 17 para 7(1).
2 Pt III (ss 213–264) modified by SI 1989/1100 art 3.

256 Countries enjoying reciprocal protection

(1) Her Majesty may, if it appears to Her that the law of a country provides adequate protection for British designs, by Order in Council designate that country as one enjoying reciprocal protection under this Part.

(2) If the law of a country provides adequate protection only for certain classes of British design, or only for designs applied to certain classes of article, any Order designating that country shall contain provision limiting, to a corresponding extent, the protection afforded by this Part in relation to designs connected with that country.

(3) An Order under this section shall be subject to annulment in pursuance of a resolution of either House of Parliament.

NOTES
1 Act amended by Broadcasting Act 1990 s 176 Sch 17 para 7(1).
2 Pt III (ss 213–264) modified by SI 1989/1100 art 3.

257 Territorial waters and the continental shelf

(1) For the purposes of this Part the territorial waters of the United Kingdom shall be treated as part of the United Kingdom.

(2) This Part applies to things done in the United Kingdom sector of the continental shelf on a structure or vessel which is present there for purposes directly connected with the exploration of the sea bed or subsoil or the exploitation of their natural resources as it applies to things done in the United Kingdom.

(3) The United Kingdom sector of the continental shelf means the areas designated by order under section 1(7) of the Continental Shelf Act 1964.

NOTES
1 Act amended by Broadcasting Act 1990 s 176 Sch 17 para 7(1).
2 Pt III (ss 213–264) modified by SI 1989/1100 art 3.

Interpretation

258 Construction of references to design right owner

(1) Where different persons are (whether in consequence of a partial assignment or otherwise) entitled to different aspects of design right in a work, the design right owner for any purpose of this Part is the person who is entitled to the right in the respect relevant for that purpose.

(2) Where design right (or any aspect of design right) is owned by more than one person jointly, references in this Part to the design right owner are to all the owners, so that, in particular, any requirement of the licence of the design right owner requires the licence of all of them.

NOTES
1 Act amended by Broadcasting Act 1990 s 176 Sch 17 para 7(1).
2 Pt III (ss 213–264) modified by SI 1989/1100 art 3.
3 Modified by SI 1989/1100 art 3.

259 Joint designs

(1) In this Part a "joint design" means a design produced by the collaboration of two or more designers in which the contribution of each is not distinct from that of the other or others.

(2) References in this Part to the designer of a design shall, except as otherwise provided, be construed in relation to a joint design as references to all the designers of the design.

NOTES
1 Act amended by Broadcasting Act 1990 s 176 Sch 17 para 7(1).
2 Pt III (ss 213–264) modified by SI 1989/1100 art 3.
3 Modified by SI 1989/1100 art 3.

260 Application of provisions to articles in kit form

(1) The provisions of this Part apply in relation to a kit, that is, a complete or substantially complete set of components intended to be assembled into an article, as they apply in relation to the assembled article.

(2) Subsection (1) does not affect the question whether design right subsists in any aspect of the design of the components of a kit as opposed to the design of the assembled article.

NOTES
1 Act amended by Broadcasting Act 1990 s 176 Sch 17 para 7(1).
2 Pt III (ss 213–264) modified by SI 1989/1100 art 3.
3 Modified by SI 1989/1100 art 3.

261 Requirement of signature: application in relation to body corporate

The requirement in the following provisions that an instrument be signed by or on behalf of a person is also satisfied in the case of a body corporate by the affixing of its seal—

section 222(3) (assignment of design right),
section 223(1) (assignment of future design right),
section 225(1) (grant of exclusive licence).

NOTES
1 Act amended by Broadcasting Act 1990 s 176 Sch 17 para 7(1).
2 Pt III (ss 213–264) modified by SI 1989/1100 art 3.
3 Modified by SI 1989/1100 art 3.

262 Adaptation of expressions in relation to Scotland

In the application of this Part to Scotland—

"account of profits" means accounting and payment of profits;
"accounts" means count, reckoning and payment;
"assignment" means assignation;
"costs" means expenses;
"defendant" means defender;
"delivery up" means delivery;
"injunction" means interdict;
"interlocutory relief" means interim remedy; and
"plaintiff" means pursuer.

NOTES
1   Act amended by Broadcasting Act 1990 s 176 Sch 17 para 7(1).
2   Pt III (ss 213–264) modified by SI 1989/1100 art 3.
3   Modified by SI 1989/1100 art 3.

263 Minor definitions

(1) In this Part—

"British design" means a design which qualifies for design right protection by reason of a connection with the United Kingdom of the designer or the person by whom the design is commissioned or the designer is employed;
"business" includes a trade or profession;
"commission" means a commission for money or money's worth;
"the comptroller" means the Comptroller-General of Patents, Designs and Trade Marks;
"computer-generated", in relation to a design, means that the design is generated by computer in circumstances such that there is no human designer,
"country" includes any territory;
"the Crown" includes the Crown in right of Her Majesty's Government in Northern Ireland [and the Crown in right of the Scottish Administration] [and the Crown in right of the Welsh Assembly Government] ;
"design document" means any record of a design, whether in the form of a drawing, a written description, a photograph, data stored in a computer or otherwise;
"employee", "employment" and "employer" refer to employment under a contract of service or of apprenticeship;
"government department" includes a Northern Ireland department [and any part of the Scottish Administration] [and any part of the Welsh Assembly Government] .

(2) References in this Part to "marketing", in relation to an article, are to its being sold or let for hire, or offered or exposed for sale or hire, in the course of a business, and related expressions shall be construed accordingly; but no

account shall be taken for the purposes of this Part of marketing which is merely colourable and not intended to satisfy the reasonable requirements of the public.

(3) References in this Part to an act being done in relation to an article for "commercial purposes" are to its being done with a view to the article in question being sold or hired in the course of a business.

NOTES
1 Words inserted by Scotland Act 1998 (Consequential Modifications) (No 2) Order 1999/1820 Sch 2(I) para 93(4)(a) (1 July 1999 the principal appointed day for 1998 c 46).
2 Words inserted by Government of Wales Act 2006 Sch 10 para 31(2) (3 May 2007 immediately after the ordinary election as specified in 2006 c.32 s 161(1); 25 May 2007 immediately after the end of the initial period for purposes of functions of the Welsh Ministers, the First Minister, the Counsel General and the Assembly Commission and in relation to the Auditor General and the Comptroller and Auditor General as specified in 2006 s 161(4)–(5)).
3 Words inserted by Scotland Act 1998 (Consequential Modifications) (No 2) Order 1999/1820 Sch 2(I) para 93(4)(b) (1 July 1999 the principal appointed day for 1998 c 46).
4 Words inserted by Government of Wales Act 2006 c 32 Sch 10 para 31(3) (3 May 2007 immediately after the ordinary election as specified in 2006 c 32 s 161(1); 25 May 2007 immediately after the end of the initial period for purposes of functions of the Welsh Ministers, the First Minister, the Counsel General and the Assembly Commission and in relation to the Auditor General and the Comptroller and Auditor General as specified in s 161(4)–(5)).

264   Index of defined expressions

The following Table shows provisions defining or otherwise explaining expressions used in this Part (other than provisions defining or explaining an expression used only in the same section)—

account of profits and accounts (in Scotland)	section 262
assignment (in Scotland)	section 262
British designs	section 263(1)
business	section 263(1)
commercial purposes	section 263(3)
commission	section 263(1)
the comptroller	section 263(1)
computer-generated	section 263(1)
costs (in Scotland)	section 262
country	section 263(1)
the Crown	section 263(1)
Crown use	sections 240(5) and 244(2)

defendant (in Scotland)	section 262
delivery up (in Scotland)	section 262
design	section 213(2)
design document	section 263(1)
designer	sections 214 and 259(2)
design right	section 213(1)
design right owner	sections 234(2) and 258
employee, employment and employer	section 263(1)
exclusive licence	section 225(1)
government department	section 263(1)
government department concerned (in relation to Crown use)	section 240(5)
infringing article	section 228
injunction (in Scotland)	section 262
interlocutory relief (in Scotland)	section 262
joint design	section 259(1)
licence (of the design right owner)	sections 222(4), 223(3) and 258
making articles to a design	section 226(2)
marketing (and related expressions)	section 263(2)
original	section 213(4)
plaintiff (in Scotland)	section 262
qualifying individual	section 217(1)
qualifying person	sections 217(1) and (2)
signed	section 261

NOTES
1   Act amended by Broadcasting Act 1990 s 176 Sch 17 para 7(1).
2   Pt III (ss 213–264) modified by SI 1989/1100 art 3.
3   Modified by SI 1989/1100 art 3.

Registered Designs Act 1949

An Act to consolidate certain enactments relating to registered designs.

[16th December 1949]

NOTES
1   Functions of Board of Trade and of President of Board of Trade now exercisable concurrently by Secretary of State: SI 1970/1537 art 2(1).

Registrable designs and proceedings for registration

[1 Registration of designs

(1) A design may, subject to the following provisions of this Act, be registered under this Act on the making of an application for registration.

(2) In this Act "design" means the appearance of the whole or a part of a product resulting from the features of, in particular, the lines, contours, colours, shape, texture or materials of the product or its ornamentation.

(3) In this Act—

"complex product" means a product which is composed of at least two replaceable component parts permitting disassembly and reassembly of the product; and

"product" means any industrial or handicraft item other than a computer program; and, in particular, includes packaging, get-up, graphic symbols, typographic type-faces and parts intended to be assembled into a complex product.][1]

NOTES
1 Sections 1, 1A, 1B, 1C and 1D are substituted for s 1 by Registered Designs Regulations 2001/3949 reg 2 (9 December 2001).

[…]

NOTES
1 Repealed by Regulatory Reform (Registered Designs) Order 2006/1974 art 3 (1 October 2006).

[1B Requirement of novelty and individual character

(1) A design shall be protected by a right in a registered design to the extent that the design is new and has individual character.

(2) For the purposes of subsection (1) above, a design is new if no identical design or no design whose features differ only in immaterial details has been made available to the public before the relevant date.

(3) For the purposes of subsection (1) above, a design has individual character if the overall impression it produces on the informed user differs from the overall impression produced on such a user by any design which has been made available to the public before the relevant date.

(4) In determining the extent to which a design has individual character, the degree of freedom of the author in creating the design shall be taken into consideration.

(5) For the purposes of this section, a design has been made available to the public before the relevant date if—

(a) it has been published (whether following registration or otherwise), exhibited, used in trade or otherwise disclosed before that date; and

(b)   the disclosure does not fall within subsection (6) below.

(6) A disclosure falls within this subsection if—

(a)   it could not reasonably have become known before the relevant date in the normal course of business to persons carrying on business in the European Economic Area and specialising in the sector concerned;

(b)   it was made to a person other than the designer, or any successor in title of his, under conditions of confidentiality (whether express or implied);

(c)   it was made by the designer, or any successor in title of his, during the period of 12 months immediately preceding the relevant date;

(d)   it was made by a person other than the designer, or any successor in title of his, during the period of 12 months immediately preceding the relevant date in consequence of information provided or other action taken by the designer or any successor in title of his; or

(e)   it was made during the period of 12 months immediately preceding the relevant date as a consequence of an abuse in relation to the designer or any successor in title of his. (7) In subsections (2), (3), (5) and (6) above "the relevant date" means the date on which the application for the registration of the design was made or is treated by virtue of section 3B(2), (3) or (5) or 14(2) of this Act as having been made.

(8) For the purposes of this section, a design applied to or incorporated in a product which constitutes a component part of a complex product shall only be considered to be new and to have individual character—

(a)   if the component part, once it has been incorporated into the complex product, remains visible during normal use of the complex product; and

(b)   to the extent that those visible features of the component part are in themselves new and have individual character.

(9) In subsection (8) above "normal use" means use by the end user; but does not include any maintenance, servicing or repair work in relation to the product.]

NOTES

1   Sections 1, 1A, 1B, 1C and 1D are substituted for s 1 by Registered Designs Regulations 2001/3949 reg 2 (9 December 2001).

2   Functions of Board of Trade and of President of Board of Trade now exercisable concurrently by Secretary of State: SI 1970/1537 art 2(1).

[1C   Designs dictated by their technical function

(1) A right in a registered design shall not subsist in features of appearance of a product which are solely dictated by the product's technical function.

(2) A right in a registered design shall not subsist in features of appearance of a product which must necessarily be reproduced in their exact form and dimensions so as to permit the product in which the design is incorporated or to which

it is applied to be mechanically connected to, or placed in, around or against, another product so that either product may perform its function.

(3) Subsection (2) above does not prevent a right in a registered design subsisting in a design serving the purpose of allowing multiple assembly or connection of mutually interchangeable products within a modular system.]

NOTES
1   Sections 1, 1A, 1B, 1C and 1D are substituted for s 1 by Registered Designs Regulations 2001/3949 reg 2 (9 December 2001).
2   Functions of Board of Trade and of President of Board of Trade now exercisable concurrently by Secretary of State: SI 1970/1537 art 2(1).

[1D   Designs contrary to public policy or morality

A right in a registered design shall not subsist in a design which is contrary to public policy or to accepted principles of morality.]

NOTES
1   Sections 1, 1A, 1B, 1C and 1D are substituted for s 1 by Registered Designs Regulations 2001/3949 reg2 (9 December 2001).
2   Functions of Board of Trade and of President of Board of Trade now exercisable concurrently by Secretary of State: SI 1970/1537 art 2(1).

2   Proprietorship of designs

[(1) The author of a design shall be treated for the purposes of this Act as the original proprietor of the design, subject to the following provisions.

(1A) Where a design is created in pursuance of a commission for money or money's worth, the person commissioning the design shall be treated as the original proprietor of the design.

(1B) Where, in a case not falling within subsection (1A), a design is created by an employee in the course of his employment, his employer shall be treated as the original proprietor of the design.]

(2) Where a design […] becomes vested, whether by assignment, transmission or operation of law, in any person other than the original proprietor, either alone or jointly with the original proprietor, that other person, or as the case may be the original proprietor and that other person, shall be treated for the purposes of this Act as the proprietor of the design […] .

[(3) In this Act the 'author' of a design means the person who creates it.

(4) In the case of a design generated by computer in circumstances such that there is no human author, the person by whom the arrangements necessary for the creation of the design are made shall be taken to be the author.]

NOTES
1   Section 2(1) substituted by Copyright, Designs and Patents Act 1988 s 267(2).
2   Words repealed by Registered Designs Regulations 2001/3949 Sch 2 para 1 (9 December 2001).
3   Section 2(3)(4) inserted by Copyright, Designs and Patents Act 1988 s 267(3)(4).

[3 Applications for registration

(1) An application for the registration of a design [or designs] shall be made in the prescribed form and shall be filed at the Patent Office in the prescribed manner.

(2) An application for the registration of a design [or designs] shall be made by the person claiming to be the proprietor of the design [or designs] .

(3) An application for the registration of a design [or designs] in which national unregistered design right subsists shall be made by the person claiming to be the design right owner.

(4) [...]

(5) An application for the registration of a design which, owing to any default or neglect on the part of the applicant, has not been completed so as to enable registration to be effected within such time as may be prescribed shall be deemed to be abandoned.]

NOTES
1 Sections 3, 3A, 3B, 3C and 3D substituted for s 3 by Registered Designs Regulations 2001/3949 reg 4 (9 December 2001).
2 Words inserted by Regulatory Reform (Registered Designs) Order 2006/1974 art 11(2) (1 October 2006).
3 Words inserted by Regulatory Reform (Registered Designs) Order 2006/1974 art 11(3) (1 October 2006).
4 Words inserted by Regulatory Reform (Registered Designs) Order 2006/1974 art 11(4) (1 October 2006).
5 Repealed by Regulatory Reform (Registered Designs) Order 2006/1974 art 4 (1 October 2006).

[3A Determination of applications for registration

(1) Subject as follows, the registrar shall not refuse [to register a design included in an application under this Act] .

(2) If it appears to the registrar that an application for the registration of a design [or designs] has not been made in accordance with any rules made under this Act, he may refuse [to register any design included in it] .

(3) If it appears to the registrar that [the applicant is not under section 3(2) or (3) or 14 entitled to apply for the registration of a design included in the application, he shall refuse to register that design.]

[(4) If it appears to the registrar that the application for registration includes—

(a) something which does not fulfil the requirements of section 1(2) of this Act;
(b) a design that does not fulfil the requirements of section 1C or 1D of this Act; or
(c) a design to which a ground of refusal mentioned in Schedule A1 to this Act applies,

he shall refuse to register that thing or that design.]]

NOTES
1 Sections 3, 3A, 3B, 3C and 3D substituted for s 3 by Registered Designs Regulations 2001/3949 reg 4 (9 December 2001).
2 Words substituted by Regulatory Reform (Registered Designs) Order 2006/1974 art 12(2) (1 October 2006).
3 Words inserted by Regulatory Reform (Registered Designs) Order 2006/1974 art 12(3)(a) (1 October 2006).
4 Words substituted by Regulatory Reform (Registered Designs) Order 2006/1974 art 12(3)(b) (1 October 2006).
5 Words substituted by Regulatory Reform (Registered Designs) Order 2006/1974 art 12(4) (1 October 2006).
6 Substituted by Regulatory Reform (Registered Designs) Order 2006/1974 art 5 (1 October 2006).

[3B Modification of applications for registration

(1) The registrar may, at any time before an application for the registration of a design [or designs] is determined, permit the applicant to make such modifications of the application as the registrar thinks fit.

(2) Where an application for the registration of a design [or designs] has been modified before it has been determined in such a way that [any design included in the application] has been altered significantly, the registrar may, for the purposes of deciding whether and to what extent the design is new or has individual character, direct that the application [so far as relating to that design] shall be treated as having been made on the date on which it was so modified.

(3) Where—

(a) an application for the registration of [more than one design] has been modified before it has been determined to exclude one or more designs from the application; and

(b) a subsequent application for the registration of a design so excluded has, within such period (if any) as has been prescribed for such applications, been made by the person who made the earlier application or his successor in title,

the registrar may, for the purpose of deciding whether and to what extent the design is new or has individual character, direct that the subsequent application shall be treated as having been made on the date on which the earlier application was, or is treated as having been, made.

(4) Where […] the registration of a design has been refused on any ground mentioned in [section 3A(4)(b) or (c)] of this Act, the application [for the design] may be modified by the applicant if it appears to the registrar that—

(a) the identity of the design is retained; and

(b) the modifications have been made in accordance with any rules made under this Act.

(5) An application modified under subsection (4) above shall be treated as the original application and, in particular, as made on the date on which the original application was made or is treated as having been made.

(6) Any modification under this section may, in particular, be effected by making a partial disclaimer in relation to the application.]

NOTES

1 Sections 3, 3A, 3B, 3C and 3D substituted for s 3 by Registered Designs Regulations 2001/3949 reg 4 (9 December 2001).

2 Words inserted by Regulatory Reform (Registered Designs) Order 2006/1974 art 13(2) (1 October 2006).

3 Words inserted by Regulatory Reform (Registered Designs) Order 2006/1974 art 13(3)(a) (1 October 2006).

4 Words substituted by Regulatory Reform (Registered Designs) Order 2006/1974 art 13(3)(b) (1 October 2006).

5 Words inserted by Regulatory Reform (Registered Designs) Order 2006/1974 art 13(3)(c) (1 October 2006).

6 Words substituted by Regulatory Reform (Registered Designs) Order 2006/1974 art 13(4) (1 October 2006).

7 Words repealed by Regulatory Reform (Registered Designs) Order 2006/1974 art 13(5)(a) (1 October 2006).

8 Words substituted by Regulatory Reform (Registered Designs) Order 2006/1974 art 6 (1 October 2006).

9 Words inserted by Regulatory Reform (Registered Designs) Order 2006/1974 art 13(5)(b) (1 October 2006).

[3C Date of registration of designs

(1) Subject as follows, a design, when registered, shall be registered as of the date on which the application was made or is treated as having been made.

(2) Subsection (1) above shall not apply to an application which is treated as having been made on a particular date by section 14(2) of this Act or by virtue of the operation of section 3B(3) or (5) of this Act by reference to section 14(2) of this Act.

(3) A design, when registered, shall be registered as of—

(a) in the case of an application which is treated as having been made on a particular date by section 14(2) of this Act, the date on which the application was made;

(b) in the case of an application which is treated as having been made on a particular date by virtue of the operation of section 3B(3) of this Act by reference to section 14(2) of this Act, the date on which the earlier application was made;

(c) in the case of an application which is treated as having been made on a particular date by virtue of the operation of section 3B(5) of this Act by reference to section 14(2) of this Act, the date on which the original application was made.]

NOTES

1 Sections 3, 3A, 3B, 3C and 3D substituted for s 3 by Registered Designs Regulations 2001/3949 reg 4 (9 December 2001).

2 Functions of Board of Trade and of President of Board of Trade now exercisable concurrently by Secretary of State: SI 1970/1537 art 2(1).

[3D Appeals in relation to applications for registration

An appeal lies from any decision of the registrar under section 3A or 3B of this Act.]

NOTES
1   Sections 3, 3A, 3B, 3C and 3D substituted for s 3 by Registered Designs Regulations 2001/3949 reg 4 (9 December 2001).
2   Functions of Board of Trade and of President of Board of Trade now exercisable concurrently by Secretary of State: SI 1970/1537 art 2(1).

[…]

NOTES
1   Repealed by Registered Designs Regulations 2001/3949 Sch 2 para 1 (9 December 2001).

5   Provisions for secrecy of certain designs

(1) Where, either before or after the commencement of this Act, an application for the registration of a design has been made, and it appears to the registrar that the design is one of a class notified to him by [the Secretary of State] as relevant for defence purposes, he may give directions for prohibiting or restricting the publication of information with respect to the design, or the communication of such information to any person or class of persons specified in the directions.

[(2) The Secretary of State shall by rules make provision for securing that where such directions are given—

(a)   the representation or specimen of the design, […]

[…]

shall not be open to public inspection at the Patent Office during the continuance in force of the directions.]

(3) Where the registrar gives any such directions as aforesaid, he shall give notice of the application and of the directions to [the Secretary of State], and thereupon the following provisions shall have effect, that is to say:—

(a)   [the Secretary of State] shall, upon receipt of such notice, consider whether the publication of the design would be prejudicial to the defence of the realm and unless a notice under paragraph (c) of this subsection has previously been given by that authority to the registrar, shall reconsider that question before the expiration of nine months from the date of filing of the application for registration of the design and at least once in every subsequent year;

(b)   for the purpose aforesaid, [the Secretary of State] may, at any time after the design has been registered or, with the consent of the applicant, at any time before the design has been registered, inspect the representation or specimen of the design […] filed in pursuance of the application;

(c)   if upon consideration of the design at any time it appears to [the Secretary of State] that the publication of the design would not, or would no longer, be prejudicial to the defence of the realm, [he] shall give notice to the registrar to that effect;

(d) on the receipt of any such notice the registrar shall revoke the directions and may, subject to such conditions, if any, as he thinks fit, extend the time for doing anything required or authorised to be done by or under this Act in connection with the application or registration, whether or not that time has previously expired.

(4) No person resident in the United Kingdom shall, except under the authority of a written permit granted by or on behalf of the registrar, make or cause to be made any application outside the United Kingdom for the registration of a design of any class prescribed for the purposes of this subsection unless—

(a) an application for registration of the same design has been made in the United Kingdom not less than six weeks before the application outside the United Kingdom; and

(b) either no directions have been given under subsection (1) of this section in relation to the application in the United Kingdom or all such directions have been revoked:

Provided that this subsection shall not apply in relation to a design for which an application for protection has first been filed in a country outside the United Kingdom by a person resident outside the United Kingdom.

[…]

NOTES
1 Words substituted by Copyright, Designs and Patents Act 1988 s 272 Sch 3 para 3(2).
2 Section 5(2) substituted by Copyright, Designs and Patents Act 1988 s 272 Sch 3 para 3(3).
3 And the word "and" immediately preceding it is repealed by Registered Designs Regulations 2001/3949 Sch 2 para 1 (9 December 2001).
4 Words repealed by Registered Designs Regulations 2001/3949 Sch 2 para 1 (9 December 2001).
5 Word substituted by Copyright, Designs and Patents Act 1988 s 272 Sch 3 para 3(2).
6 Repealed by Copyright, Designs and Patents Act 1988 ss 272, 303(2) Sch 3 para 3(5) Sch 8.

[…]

NOTES
1 Repealed subject to savings specified in SI 2006/1975 Sch 2, para 12 by Registered Designs Regulations 2001/3949 Sch 2 para 1 (9 December 2001)

Effect of registration, etc

[7 Right given by registration

(1) The registration of a design under this Act gives the registered proprietor the exclusive right to use the design and any design which does not produce on the informed user a different overall impression.

(2) For the purposes of subsection (1) above and section 7A of this Act any reference to the use of a design includes a reference to—

(a)   the making, offering, putting on the market, importing, exporting or using of a product in which the design is incorporated or to which it is applied; or

(b)   stocking such a product for those purposes.

(3) In determining for the purposes of subsection (1) above whether a design produces a different overall impression on the informed user, the degree of freedom of the author in creating his design shall be taken into consideration.

(4) The right conferred by subsection (1) above is subject to any limitation attaching to the registration in question (including, in particular, any partial disclaimer or any declaration by the registrar or a court of partial invalidity).]

NOTES
  1 Sections 7 and 7A substituted for s 7 by Registered Designs Regulations 2001/3949 reg 5 (9 December 2001).

[7A   Infringements of rights in registered designs

(1) Subject as follows, the right in a registered design is infringed by a person who, without the consent of the registered proprietor, does anything which by virtue of section 7 of this Act is the exclusive right of the registered proprietor.

(2) The right in a registered design is not infringed by—

(a)   an act which is done privately and for purposes which are not commercial;

(b)   an act which is done for experimental purposes;

(c)   an act of reproduction for teaching purposes or for the purposes of making citations provided that the conditions mentioned in subsection (3) below are satisfied;

(d)   the use of equipment on ships or aircraft which are registered in another country but which are temporarily in the United Kingdom;

(e)   the importation into the United Kingdom of spare parts or accessories for the purposes of repairing such ships or aircraft; or

(f)   the carrying out of repairs on such ships or aircraft.

(3) The conditions mentioned in this subsection are—

(a)   the act of reproduction is compatible with fair trade practice and does not unduly prejudice the normal exploitation of the design; and

(b)   mention is made of the source.

(4) The right in a registered design is not infringed by an act which relates to a product in which any design protected by the registration is incorporated or to which it is applied if the product has been put on the market in the European Economic Area by the registered proprietor or with his consent.

(5) The right in a registered design of a component part which may be used for the purpose of the repair of a complex product so as to restore its original appearance is not infringed by the use for that purpose of any design protected by the registration.

(6) No proceedings shall be taken in respect of an infringement of the right in a registered design committed before the date on which the certificate of registration of the design under this Act is granted.]

NOTES
1 Sections 7 and 7A substituted for s 7 by Registered Designs Regulations 2001/3949 reg 5 (9 December 2001).
2 Functions of Board of Trade and of President of Board of Trade now exercisable concurrently by Secretary of State: SI 1970/1537 art 2(1).

[8 Duration of right in registered design

(1) The right in a registered design subsists in the first instance for a period of five years from the date of the registration of the design.

(2) The period for which the right subsists may be extended for a second, third, fourth and fifth period of five years, by applying to the registrar for an extension and paying the prescribed renewal fee.

(3) If the first, second, third or fourth period expires without such application and payment being made, the right shall cease to have effect; and the registrar shall, in accordance with rules made by the Secretary of State, notify the proprietor of that fact.

(4) If during the period of six months immediately following the end of that period an application for extension is made and the prescribed renewal fee and any prescribed additional fee is paid, the right shall be treated as if it had never expired, with the result that—

(a) anything done under or in relation to the right during that further period shall be treated as valid,

(b) an act which would have constituted an infringement of the right if it has not expired shall be treated as an infringement, and

(c) an act which would have constituted use of the design for the services of the Crown if the right had not expired shall be treated as such use.

[…]]

NOTES
1 Section 8, 8A and 8B substituted for s 8 by Copyright,Designs and Patents Act 1988 s 269(1)(2).
2 Repealed by Registered Designs Regulations 2001/3949 Sch 2 para 1 (9 December 2001).

[8A Restoration of lapsed right in design

(1) Where the right in a registered design has expired by reason of a failure to extend, in accordance with section 8(2) or (4), the period for which the right subsists, an application for the restoration of the right in the design may be made to the registrar within the prescribed period.

(2) The application may be made by the person who was the registered proprietor of the design or by any other person who would have been entitled to

the right in the design if it had not expired; and where the design was held by two or more persons jointly, the application may, with the leave of the registrar, be made by one or more of them without joining the others.

(3) Notice of the application shall be published by the registrar in the prescribed manner.

(4) If the registrar is satisfied that the [failure of the proprietor] to see that the period for which the right subsisted was extended in accordance with section 8(2) or (4) [was unintentional], he shall, on payment of any unpaid renewal fee and any prescribed additional fee, order the restoration of the right in the design.

(5) The order may be made subject to such conditions as the registrar thinks fit, and if the proprietor of the design does not comply with any condition the registrar may revoke the order and give such consequential directions as he thinks fit.

(6) Rules altering the period prescribed for the purposes of subsection (1) may contain such transitional provisions and savings as appear to the Secretary of State to be necessary or expedient.]

NOTES
1   Section 8, 8A and 8B substituted for s 8 by Copyright, Designs and Patents Act 1988 s 269(1)(2).
2   Words substituted by Regulatory Reform (Registered Designs) Order 2006/1974 art 17(a) (1 October 2006).
3   Words inserted by Regulatory Reform (Registered Designs) Order 2006/1974 art 17(b) (1 October 2006).

[8B   Effect of order for restoration of right

(1) The effect of an order under section 8A for the restoration of the right in a registered design is as follows.

(2) Anything done under or in relation to the right during the period between expiry and restoration shall be treated as valid.

(3) Anything done during that period which would have constituted an infringement if the right had not expired shall be treated as an infringement—

(a)   if done at a time when it was possible for an application for extension to be made under section 8(4); or

(b)   if it was a continuation or repetition of an earlier infringing act.

(4) If, after it was no longer possible for such an application for extension to be made and before publication of notice of the application for restoration, a person—

(a)   began in good faith to do an act which would have constituted an infringement of the right in the design if it had not expired, or

(b)   made in good faith effective and serious preparations to do such an act, he has the right to continue to do the act or, as the case may be, to do the act, notwithstanding the restoration of the right in the design; but this does not extend to granting a licence to another person to do the act.

(5) If the act was done, or the preparations were made, in the course of a business, the person entitled to the right conferred by subsection (4) may—

(a) authorise the doing of that act by any partners of his for the time being in that business, and

(b) assign that right, or transmit it on death (or in the case of a body corporate on its dissolution), to any person who acquires that part of the business in the course of which the act was done or the preparations were made.

(6) Where [a product] is disposed of to another in exercise of the rights conferred by subsection (4) or subsection (5), that other and any person claiming through him may deal with [the product] in the same way as if it had been disposed of by the registered proprietor of the design.

(7) The above provisions apply in relation to the use of a registered design for the services of the Crown as they apply in relation to infringement of the right in the design.]

NOTES
1   Section 8, 8A and 8B substituted for s 8 by Copyright, Designs and Patents Act 1988 s 269(1)(2).
2   Words substituted by Registered Designs Regulations 2001/3949 Sch 1 para 2(a) (9 December 2001).
3   Words substituted by Registered Designs Regulations 2001/3949 Sch 1 para 2(b) (9 December 2001).

[…]

NOTES
1   Repealed by Intellectual Property (Enforcement, etc.) Regulations 2006/1028 Sch 4 para 1 (29 April 2006).

[…]

NOTES
1   Repealed by Registered Designs Regulations 2001/3949 Sch 2 para 1 (9 December 2001).

[11   Cancellation of registration

The registrar may, upon a request made in the prescribed manner by the registered proprietor, cancel the registration of a design.]

NOTES
1   Sections 11–11ZF are substituted for s 11 subject to savings specified in SI 2006/1975 Sch 2, para 13 by Registered Designs Regulations 2001/3949 reg 7 (9 December 2001).

[11ZA Grounds for invalidity of registration

(1)

[The registration of a design may be declared invalid

- (a) on the ground that it does not fulfil the requirements of section 1(2) of this Act;
- (b) on the ground that it does not fulfil the requirements of sections 1B to 1D of this Act; or
- (c) where any ground of refusal mentioned in Schedule A1 to this Act applies.]

[(1A) The registration of a design ("the later design") may be declared invalid if it is not new or does not have individual character when compared to a design which—

- (a) has been made available to the public on or after the relevant date; but
- [(b) is protected as from a date prior to the relevant date—
  - (i) by virtue of registration under this Act or the Community Design Regulation or an application for such registration, or
  - (ii) by virtue of an international registration (within the meaning of Articles 106a to 106f of that Regulation) designating the Community.]

(1B) In subsection (1A) "the relevant date" means the date on which the application for the registration of the later design was made or is treated by virtue of section 3B(2), (3) or (5) or 14(2) of this Act as having been made.]

(2) The registration of a design may be declared invalid on the ground of the registered proprietor not being the proprietor of the design and the proprietor of the design objecting.

(3) The registration of a design involving the use of an earlier distinctive sign may be declared invalid on the ground of an objection by the holder of rights to the sign which include the right to prohibit in the United Kingdom such use of the sign. (4) The registration of a design constituting an unauthorised use of a work protected by the law of copyright in the United Kingdom may be declared invalid on the ground of an objection by the owner of the copyright.

(5) In this section and sections 11ZB, 11ZC and 11ZE of this Act (other than section 11ZE(1)) references to the registration of a design include references to the former registration of a design; and these sections shall apply, with necessary modifications, in relation to such former registrations.]

NOTES
1 Sections 11–11ZF are substituted for s 11 subject to savings specified in SI 2006/1975 Sch 2, para 13 by Registered Designs Regulations 2001/3949 reg 7 (9 December 2001).
2 Section11ZA(1)(a)-(c) substituted for words subject to transitional provisions specified in SI 2006/1974 art 18 by Regulatory Reform (Registered Designs) Order 2006/1974 art 7(2) (1 October 2006: substitution has effect subject to transitional provisions specified in SI 2006/1974 art 18).
3 Inserted subject to transitional provisions specified in SI 2006/1974 art 18 by

Regulatory Reform (Registered Designs) Order 2006/1974 art 7(3) (1 October 2006: insertion has effect subject to transitional provisions specified in SI 2006/1974 art 18).

4 Substituted by Designs (International Registrations Designating the European Community) Regulations 2007/3378 reg 2 (1 January 2008).

[11ZB Applications for declaration of invalidity

(1) Any person interested may make an application to the registrar for a declaration of invalidity [under section 11ZA(1)(a) or (b)] of this Act.

(2) Any person concerned by the use in question may make an application to the registrar for a declaration of invalidity [under section 11ZA(1)(c)] of this Act.

(3) The relevant person may make an application to the registrar for a declaration of invalidity [under section 11ZA(1A)] of this Act.

(4) In subsection (3) above "the relevant person" means , in relation to an earlier design protected by virtue of registration under this Act [or the Community Design Regulation] or an application for such registration, the registered proprietor of the design [, the holder of the registered Community design] or (as the case may be) the applicant .

(5) The person able to make an objection under subsection (2), (3) or (4) of section 11ZA of this Act may make an application to the registrar for a declaration of invalidity [under] that subsection.

(6) An application may be made under this section in relation to a design at any time after the design has been registered.]

NOTES
1 Sections 11–11ZF are substituted for s 11 subject to savings specified in SI 2006/1975 Sch 2, para 13 by Registered Designs Regulations 2001/3949 reg 7 (9 December 2001).
2 Words substituted subject to transitional provisions specified in SI 2006/1974 art 18 by Regulatory Reform (Registered Designs) Order 2006/1974 art 8(2) (1 October 2006: substitution has effect subject to transitional provisions specified in SI 2006/1974 art 18).
3 Words substituted subject to transitional provisions specified in SI 2006/1974 art 18 by Regulatory Reform (Registered Designs) Order 2006/1974 art 8(3) (1 October 2006: substitution has effect subject to transitional provisions specified in SI 2006/1974 art 18).
4 Words substituted subject to transitional provisions specified in SI 2006/1974 art 18 by Regulatory Reform (Registered Designs) Order 2006/1974 art 8(4) (1 October 2006: substitution has effect subject to transitional provisions specified in SI 2006/1974 art 18).
5 Words inserted by Registered Designs Regulations 2003/550 reg2(3)(a) (1 April 2003: insertion has effect subject to transitional provisions specified in SI 2003/550 regs 3–5).
6 Words inserted by Registered Designs Regulations 2003/550 reg2(3)(b) (1 April 2003: insertion has effect subject to transitional provisions specified in SI 2003/550 regs 3–5).
7 Words substituted subject to transitional provisions specified in SI 2006/1974

art 18 by Regulatory Reform (Registered Designs) Order 2006/1974 art 8(5)
(1 October 2006: substitution has effect subject to transitional provisions specified
in SI 2006/1974 art 18).

[11ZC   Determination of applications for declaration of invalidity

(1) This section applies where an application has been made to the registrar for
a declaration of invalidity in relation to a registration.

(2) If it appears to the registrar that the application has not been made in
accordance with any rules made under this Act, he may refuse the application.

(3) If it appears to the registrar that the application has not been made in
accordance with section 11ZB of this Act, he shall refuse the application.

(4) Subject to subsections (2) and (3) above, the registrar shall make a
declaration of invalidity if it appears to him that the ground of invalidity
specified in the application has been established in relation to the registration.

(5) Otherwise the registrar shall refuse the application.

(6) A declaration of invalidity may be a declaration of partial invalidity.]

NOTES
1   Sections 11–11ZF are substituted for s 11 subject to savings specified in
    SI 2006/1975 Sch 2, para 13 by Registered Designs Regulations 2001/3949 reg 7
    (9 December 2001).
2   Functions of Board of Trade and of President of Board of Trade now exercisable
    concurrently by Secretary of State: SI 1970/1537 art 2(1).

[11ZD   Modification of registration

(1) Subsections (2) and (3) below apply where the registrar intends to declare
the registration of a design invalid [under section 11ZA(1)(b) or (c), (1A), (3) or
(4)] of this Act.

(2) The registrar shall inform the registered proprietor of that fact.

(3) The registered proprietor may make an application to the registrar for the
registrar to make such modifications to the registration of the design as the
registered proprietor specifies in his application.

(4) Such modifications may, in particular, include the inclusion on the register
of a partial disclaimer by the registered proprietor.

(5) If it appears to the registrar that the application has not been made in
accordance with any rules made under this Act, the registrar may refuse the
application.

(6) If it appears to the registrar that the identity of the design is not retained or
the modified registration would be invalid by virtue of section 11ZA of this Act,
the registrar shall refuse the application.

(7) Otherwise the registrar shall make the specified modifications.

(8) A modification of a registration made under this section shall have effect,
and be treated always to have had effect, from the grant of registration.]

NOTES

1   Sections 11–11ZF are substituted for s 11 subject to savings specified in SI 2006/1975 Sch 2, para 13 by Registered Designs Regulations 2001/3949 reg 7 (9 December 2001).

2   Words substituted subject to transitional provisions specified in SI 2006/1974 art 18 by Regulatory Reform (Registered Designs) Order 2006/1974 art 9 (1 October 2006: substitution has effect subject to transitional provisions specified in SI 2006/1974 art 18).

[11ZE   Effect of cancellation or invalidation of registration

(1) A cancellation of registration under section 11 of this Act takes effect from the date of the registrar's decision or from such other date as the registrar may direct.

(2) Where the registrar declares the registration of a design invalid to any extent, the registration shall to that extent be treated as having been invalid from the date of registration or from such other date as the registrar may direct.]

NOTES

1   Sections 11–11ZF are substituted for s 11 subject to savings specified in SI 2006/1975 Sch 2, para 13 by Registered Designs Regulations 2001/3949 reg 7 (9 December 2001).

2   Functions of Board of Trade and of President of Board of Trade now exercisable concurrently by Secretary of State: SI 1970/1537 art 2(1).

[11ZF   Appeals in relation to cancellation or invalidation

An appeal lies from any decision of the registrar under section 11 to 11ZE of this Act.]

NOTES

1   Sections 11–11ZF are substituted for s 11 subject to savings specified in SI 2006/1975 Sch 2, para 13 by Registered Designs Regulations 2001/3949 reg 7 (9 December 2001).

2   Functions of Board of Trade and of President of Board of Trade now exercisable concurrently by Secretary of State: SI 1970/1537 art 2(1).

[11A   Powers exercisable for protection of the public interest

(1) Where a report of the [Competition Commission] has been laid before Parliament containing conclusions to the effect—

(a)   [...]

(b)   [...]

(c)   on a competition reference, that a person was engaged in an anti-competitive practice which operated or may be expected to operate against the public interest, or

(d)   on a reference under section 11 of the Competition Act 1980 (reference of public bodies and certain other persons), that a person is pursuing a course of conduct which operates against the public interest, the appropriate Minister or Ministers may apply to the registrar to take action under this section.

(2) Before making an application the appropriate Minister or Ministers shall publish, in such a manner as he or they think appropriate, a notice describing the nature of the proposed application and shall consider any representations which may be made within 30 days of such publication by persons whose interests appear to him or them to be affected.

(3) If on an application under this section it appears to the registrar that the matters specified in the Commission's report as being those which in the Commission's opinion operate or operated or may be expected to operate against the public interest include—

    (a)   conditions in licences granted in respect of a registered design by its proprietor restricting the use of the design by the licensee or the right of the proprietor to grant other licences, [...]

    (b)   [...]

he may by order cancel or modify any such condition [...] .

[...]

(6) An appeal lies from any order of the registrar under this section.

(7) In this section "the appropriate Minister or Ministers" means the Minister or Ministers to whom the report of the [Competition Commission] was made.]

NOTES
1   Sections 11A and 11B inserted by Copyright, Designs and Patents Act 1988 ss 266(5), 270.
2   Words substituted by Competition Act 1998 (Competition Commission) Transitional, Consequential and Supplemental Provisions Order 1999/506 Pt II art 9 (1 April 1999).
3   Repealed by Enterprise Act 2002 Sch 26 para 1 (June 20, 2003 as SI 2003/1397).
4   Repealed subject SI 2003/1397 arts.3(1) and 8 and SI 2004/3233 art 2 and Sch 1 by Enterprise Act 2002 c. 40 Sch 26 para 1 (June 20, 2003: repeal has effect subject to SI 2003/1397 arts.3(1) and 8 and SI 2004/3233 art 2 and Sch 1).
5   And the word "or" immediately preceding it is repealed by Registered Designs Regulations 2001/3949 Sch 2 para 1 (9 December 2001).
6   Words repealed by Registered Designs Regulations 2001/3949 Sch 2 para 1 (9 December 2001).
7   Repealed by Registered Designs Regulations 2001/3949 Sch 2 para 1 (9 December 2001).

[11AB   Powers exercisable following merger and market investigations

(1) Subsection (2) below applies where—

    (a)   section 41(2), 55(2), 66(6), 75(2), 83(2), 138(2), 147(2) or 160(2) of, or paragraph 5(2) or 10(2) of Schedule 7 to, the Enterprise Act 2002 (powers to take remedial action following merger or market investigations) applies;

    (b)   the Competition Commission or (as the case may be) the Secretary of

State considers that it would be appropriate to make an application under this section for the purpose of remedying, mitigating or preventing a matter which cannot be dealt with under the enactment concerned; and

(c) the matter concerned involves conditions in licences granted in respect of a registered design by its proprietor restricting the use of the design by the licensee or the right of the proprietor to grant other licences.

(2) The Competition Commission or (as the case may be) the Secretary of State may apply to the registrar to take action under this section.

(3) Before making an application the Competition Commission or (as the case may be) the Secretary of State shall publish, in such manner as it or he thinks appropriate, a notice describing the nature of the proposed application and shall consider any representations which may be made within 30 days of such publication by persons whose interests appear to it or him to be affected.

(4) The registrar may, if it appears to him on an application under this section that the application is made in accordance with this section, by order cancel or modify any condition concerned of the kind mentioned in subsection (1)(c) above.

(5) An appeal lies from any order of the registrar under this section.

(6) References in this section to the Competition Commission shall, in cases where section 75(2) of the Enterprise Act 2002 applies, be read as references to the Office of Fair Trading.

(7) References in section 35, 36, 47, 63, 134 or 141 of the Enterprise Act 2002 (questions to be decided by the Competition Commission in its reports) to taking action under section 41(2), 55, 66, 138 or 147 shall include references to taking action under subsection (2) above.

(8) An order made by virtue of this section in consequence of action under subsection (2) above where an enactment mentioned in subsection (1)(a) above applies shall be treated, for the purposes of sections 91(3), 92(1)(a), 162(1) and 166(3) of the Enterprise Act 2002 (duties to register and keep under review enforcement orders etc.), as if it were made under the relevant power in Part 3 or (as the case may be) 4 of that Act to make an enforcement order (within the meaning of the Part concerned).]

NOTES

1 Inserted subject to savings specified in SI 2003/1397 art 12 by Enterprise Act 2002 Sch 25 para 1(3) (20 June 2003: insertion has effect subject to savings specified in SI 2003/1397 art 12).

2 Functions of Board of Trade and of President of Board of Trade now exercisable concurrently by Secretary of State: SI 1970/1537 art 2(1).

[…][1]

NOTES

1 Repealed by Registered Designs Regulations 2001/3949 Sch 2 para 1 (9 December 2001).

12 Use for services of the Crown

The provisions of the First Schedule to this Act shall have effect with respect to the use of registered designs for the services of the Crown and the rights of third parties in respect of such use.

NOTES
1   Functions of Board of Trade and of President of Board of Trade now exercisable concurrently by Secretary of State: SI 1970/1537 art 2(1).
2   Section 12 extended by SI 1965/1536 Sch 3.

International Arrangements

13 Orders in Council as to convention countries

(1) His Majesty may, with a view to the fulfilment of a treaty, convention, arrangement or engagement, by Order in Council declare that any country specified in the Order is a convention country for the purposes of this Act:

Provided that a declaration may be made as aforesaid for the purposes either of all or of some only of the provisions of this Act, and a country in the case of which a declaration made for the purposes of some only of the provisions of this Act is in force shall be deemed to be a convention country for the purposes of those provisions only.

(2) His Majesty may by Order in Council direct that any of the Channel Islands, any colony, […]shall be deemed to be a convention country for the purposes of all or any of the provisions of this Act; and an Order made under this subsection may direct that any such provisions shall have effect, in relation to the territory in question, subject to such conditions or limitations, if any, as may be specified in the Order.

(3) For the purposes of subsection (1) of this section, every colony, protectorate, territory subject to the authority or under the suzerainty of another country, and territory administered by another country […] under the trusteeship system of the United Nations, shall be deemed to be a country in the case of which a declaration may be made under that subsection.

NOTES
1   Words repealed by Statute Law (Repeals) Act 1986 s 1(1) Sch 1 Pt VI.
2   Functions of Board of Trade and of President of Board of Trade now exercisable concurrently by Secretary of State: SI 1970/1537 art 2(1).

14 Registration of design where application for protection in convention country has been made

(1) An application for registration of a design [or designs] in respect of which protection has been applied for in a convention country may be made in accordance with the provisions of this Act by the person by whom the application for protection was made or his personal representative or assignee:

Provided that no application shall be made by virtue of this section after the expiration of six months from the date of the application for protection in a convention country or, where more than one such application for protection has been made, from the date of the first application.[

(2) Where an application for registration of a design [or designs] is made by virtue of this section, the application shall be treated, for the purpose of determining whether [(and to what extent)] that or any other design is new [or has individual character] , as made on the date of the application for protection in the convention country or, if more than one such application was made, on the date of the first such application.

(3) Subsection (2) shall not be construed as excluding the power to give directions under [section 3B(2) or (3)] of this Act in relation to an application made by virtue of this section.]

(4) Where a person has applied for protection for a design by an application which—

    (a) in accordance with the terms of a treaty subsisting between two or more convention countries, is equivalent to an application duly made in any one of those convention countries; or

    (b) in accordance with the law of any convention country, is equivalent to an application duly made in that convention country.

he shall be deemed for the purposes of this section to have applied in that convention country.

NOTES

1   Words inserted by Regulatory Reform (Registered Designs) Order 2006/1974 art 14(2) (1 October 2006).

2   Section 14(2)(3) substituted by Copyright, Designs and Patents Act 1988 s 272 Sch 3. para 7.

3   Words inserted by Regulatory Reform (Registered Designs) Order 2006/1974 art 14(3) (1 October 2006).

4   Words inserted by Registered Designs Regulations 2001/3949 Sch 1 para 4(2)(a) (9 December 2001).

5   Words inserted by Registered Designs Regulations 2001/3949 Sch 1 para 4(2)(b) (9 December 2001).

6   Words substituted by Registered Designs Regulations 2001/3949 Sch 1 para 4(3) (9 December 2001).

15 Extension of time for applications under s 14 in certain cases

(1) If [the Secretary of State is satisfied] that provision substantially equivalent to the provision to be made by or under this section has been or will be made under the law of any convention country, [he] may make rules empowering the registrar to extend the time for making application under subsection (1) of section fourteen of this Act for registration of a design in respect of which protection has been applied for in that country in any case where the period specified in the proviso to that subsection expires during a period prescribed by the rules.

(2) Rules made under this section—

(a)   may, where any agreement or arrangement has been made between His Majesty's Government in the United Kingdom and the government of the convention country for the supply or mutual exchange of information or [products] , provide, either generally or in any class of case specified in the rules, that an extension of time shall not be granted under this section unless the design has been communicated in accordance with the agreement or arrangement;

(b)   may, either generally or in any class of case specified in the rules, fix the maximum extension which may be granted under this section;

(c)   may prescribe or allow any special procedure in connection with applications made by virtue of this section;

(d)   may empower the registrar to extend, in relation to an application made by virtue of this section, the time limited by or under the foregoing provisions of this Act for doing any act, subject to such conditions, if any, as may be imposed by or under the rules;

(e)   may provide for securing that the rights conferred by registration on an application made by virtue of this section shall be subject to such restrictions or conditions as may be specified by or under the rules and in particular to restrictions and conditions for the protection of persons (including persons acting on behalf of His Majesty) who, otherwise than as the result of a communication made in accordance with such an agreement or arrangement as is mentioned in paragraph (a) of this subsection, and before the date of the application in question or such later date as may be allowed by the rules, may have imported or made [products] to which the design is applied [or in which it is incorporated] or may have made an application for registration of the design.

NOTES
1   Words substituted by Copyright, Designs and Patents Act 1988 s 272 Sch 3 para 8.
2   Word substituted by Copyright, Designs and Patents Act 1988 s 272 Sch 3 para 8.
3   Word substituted by Registered Designs Regulations 2001/3949 Sch 1 para 5(a) (9 December 2001).
4   Word substituted by Registered Designs Regulations 2001/3949 Sch 1 para 5(b)(i) (9 December 2001).
5   Words inserted by Registered Designs Regulations 2001/3949 Sch 1 para 5(b)(ii) (9 December 2001).

[…]

NOTES
1   Repealed by Registered Designs Regulations 2001/3949 Sch 2 para 1 (9 December 2001).

Property in and dealing with registered designs and applications

[15A   The nature of registered designs

A registered design or an application for a registered design is personal property (in Scotland, incorporeal moveable property).]

NOTES
  1   Added by Intellectual Property (Enforcement, etc.) Regulations 2006/1028 Sch 1
      para 2 (29 April 2006).
  2   Functions of Board of Trade and of President of Board of Trade now exercisable
      concurrently by Secretary of State: SI 1970/1537 art 2(1).

[15B   Assignment, &c of registered designs and applications for registered designs

(1) A registered design or an application for a registered design is transmissible by assignment, testamentary disposition or operation of law in the same way as other personal or moveable property, subject to the following provisions of this section.

(2) Any transmission of a registered design or an application for a registered design is subject to any rights vested in any other person of which notice is entered in the register of designs, or in the case of applications, notice is given to the registrar.

(3) An assignment of, or an assent relating to, a registered design or application for a registered design is not effective unless it is in writing signed by or on behalf of the assignor or, as the case may be, a personal representative.

(4) Except in Scotland, the requirement in subsection (3) may be satisfied in a case where the assignor or personal representative is a body corporate by the affixing of its seal.

(5) Subsections (3) and (4) apply to assignment by way of security as in relation to any other assignment.

(6) A registered design or application for a registered design may be the subject of a charge (in Scotland, security) in the same way as other personal or moveable property.

(7) The proprietor of a registered design may grant a licence to use that registered design.

(8) Any equities (in Scotland, rights) in respect of a registered design or an application for a registered design may be enforced in like manner as in respect of any other personal or moveable property.]

NOTES
  1   Added by Intellectual Property (Enforcement, etc.) Regulations 2006/1028 Sch 1
      para 2 (29 April 2006).
  2   Functions of Board of Trade and of President of Board of Trade now exercisable
      concurrently by Secretary of State: SI 1970/1537 art 2(1).

[15C   Exclusive licences

(1) In this Act an "exclusive licence" means a licence in writing signed by or on behalf of the proprietor of the registered design authorising the licensee to the exclusion of all other persons, including the person granting the licence, to exercise a right which would otherwise be exercisable exclusively by the proprietor of the registered design.

(2) The licensee under an exclusive licence has the same rights against any successor in title who is bound by the licence as he has against the person granting the licence.]

NOTES
1   Added by Intellectual Property (Enforcement, etc.) Regulations 2006/1028 Sch 1 para 2 (29 April 2006).
2   Functions of Board of Trade and of President of Board of Trade now exercisable concurrently by Secretary of State: SI 1970/1537 art 2(1).

Register of designs, etc

[17   Register of designs etc

(1) The registrar shall maintain the register of designs, in which shall be entered—

(a)   the names and addresses of proprietors of registered designs;
(b)   notices of assignments and of transmissions of registered designs; and
(c)   such other matters as may be prescribed or as the registrar may think fit.

(2) No notice of any trust, whether express, implied or constructive, shall be entered in the registrar of designs, and the registrar shall not be affected by any such notice.

(3) The register need not be kept in documentary form.

(4) Subject to the provisions of this Act and to rules made by the Secretary of State under it, the public shall have a right to inspect the register at the Patent Office at all convenient times.

(5) Any person who applies for a certified copy of an entry in the register or a certified extract from the register shall be entitled to obtain such a copy or extract on payment of a fee prescribed in relation to certified copies and extracts; and rules made by the Secretary of State under this Act may provide that any person who applies for an uncertified copy or extract shall be entitled to such a copy or extract on payment of a fee prescribed in relation to uncertified copies and extracts.

(6) Applications under subsection (5) above or rules made by virtue of that subsection shall be made in such manner as may be prescribed.

(7) In relation to any portion of the register kept otherwise than in documentary form—

(a)   the right of inspection conferred by subsection (4) above is a right to inspect the material on the register; and
(b)   the right to a copy or extract conferred by subsection (5) above or rules is a right to a copy or extract in a form in which it can be taken away and in which it is visible and legible.

(8) [The] register shall be prima facie evidence of anything required or authorised by this Act to be entered in it and in Scotland shall be sufficient evidence of any such thing.

(9) A certificate purporting to be signed by the registrar and certifying that any entry which he is authorised by or under this Act to make has or has not been made, or that any other thing which he is so authorised to do has or has not been done, shall be prima facie evidence, and in Scotland shall be sufficient evidence, of the matters so certified.

(10) Each of the following—

(a)   a copy of an entry in the register or an extract from the register which is supplied under subsection (5) above;

(b)   a copy of any representation, specimen or document kept in the Patent Office or an extract from any such document,

which purports to be a certified copy or certified extract shall, […] be admitted in evidence without further proof and without production of any original; and in Scotland such evidence shall be sufficient evidence.

[…]

(12) In this section "certified copy" and "certified extract" mean a copy and extract certified by the registrar and sealed with the seal of the Patent Office.]

NOTES

1   Section 17 substituted by Patents, Designs and Marks Act 1986 s 1 Sch 1 para 3.
2   Words repealed by Criminal Justice Act 2003 c 44 Sch 37(6) para 1 (4 April 2005).
3   Repealed by Youth Justice and Criminal Evidence Act 1999 c. 23 Sch 6 para 1 (14 April 2000 as SI 2000/1034).

18   Certificate of registration

(1) The registrar shall grant a certificate of registration in the prescribed form to the registered proprietor of a design when the design is registered.

(2) The registrar may, in a case where he is satisfied that the certificate of registration has been lost or destroyed, or in any other case in which he thinks it expedient, furnish one or more copies of the certificate.

NOTES

1   Functions of Board of Trade and of President of Board of Trade now exercisable concurrently by Secretary of State: SI 1970/1537 art 2(1).

19   Registration of assignments, etc

(1) Where any person becomes entitled by assignment, transmission or operation of law to a registered design or to a share in a registered design, or becomes entitled as mortgagee, licensee or otherwise to any other interest in a registered design, he shall apply to the registrar in the prescribed manner for the registration of his title as proprietor or co-proprietor or, as the case may be, of notice of his interest, in the register of designs.

(2) Without prejudice to the provisions of the foregoing subsection, an application for the registration of the title of any person becoming entitled by assignment to a registered design or a share in a registered design, or becoming entitled by virtue of a mortgage, licence or other instrument to any other interest in a registered design, may be made in the prescribed manner by the assign or, mortgagor, licensor or other party to that instrument, as the case may be.

(3) Where application is made under this section for the registration of the title of any person, the registrar shall, upon proof of title to his satisfaction—

(a) where that person is entitled to a registered design or a share in a registered design, register him in the register of designs as proprietor or co-proprietor of the design, and enter in that register particulars of the instrument or event by which he derives title; or

(b) where that person is entitled to any other interest in the registered design, enter in that register notice of his interest, with particulars of the instrument (if any) creating it.

[(3A) Where [national unregistered design right][2] subsists in a registered design, the registrar shall not register an interest under subsection (3) unless he is satisfied that the person entitled to that interest is also entitled to a corresponding interest in the [national unregistered design right][2] .

(3B) Where [national unregistered design right][3] subsists in a registered design and the proprietor of the registered design is also the design right owner, an assignment of the [national unregistered design right][3] shall be taken to be also an assignment of the right in the registered design, unless a contrary intention appears.][1]

(4) [...][4]

(5) Except for the purposes of an application to rectify the register under the following provisions of this Act, a document in respect of which no entry has been made in the register of designs under subsection (3) of this section shall not be admitted in any court as evidence of the title of any person to a registered design or share of or interest in a registered design unless the court otherwise directs.

NOTES

1 Section 19(3A)(3B) inserted by Copyright, Designs and Patents Act 1988 s 272 Sch 3 para 10.

2 Words substituted by Registered Designs Regulations 2001/3949 Sch 1 para 6(2) (9 December 2001).

3 Words substituted by Registered Designs Regulations 2001/3949 Sch 1 para 6(3) (9 December 2001).

4 Repealed by Intellectual Property (Enforcement, etc) Regulations 2006/1028 Sch 4 para 1 (29 April 2006).

20 Rectification of register

(1) The court may, on the application of [the relevant person] , order the register of designs to be rectified by the making of any entry therein or the variation or deletion of any entry therein.

[(1A) In subsection (1) above

"the relevant person" means—

(a) in the case of an application invoking any ground referred to in [section 11ZA(1)(c)] of this Act, any person concerned by the use in question;

(b) in the case of an application invoking the ground mentioned in [section 11ZA(1A)] of this Act, the appropriate person;

(c) in the case of an application invoking any ground mentioned in section 11ZA(2), (3) or (4) of this Act, the person able to make the objection;

(d) in any other case, any person aggrieved.

(1B) In subsection (1A) above "the appropriate person" means , in relation to an earlier design protected by virtue of registration under this Act [or the Community Design Regulation] or an application for such registration, the registered proprietor of the design [, the holder of the registered Community design] or (as the case may be) the applicant .]

(2) In proceedings under this section the court may determine any question which it may be necessary or expedient to decide in connection with the rectification of the register.

(3) Notice of any application to the court under this section shall be given in the prescribed manner to the registrar, who shall be entitled to appear and be heard on the application, and shall appear if so directed by the court.

(4) Any order made by the court under this section shall direct that notice of the order shall be served on the registrar in the prescribed manner; and the registrar shall, on receipt of the notice, rectify the register accordingly.

[(5) A rectification of the register under this section has effect as follows—

(a) an entry made has effect from the date on which it should have been made,

(b) an entry varied has effect as if it had originally been made in its varied form, and (c) an entry deleted shall be deemed never to have had effect,

unless, in any case, the court directs otherwise.]

[(6) Orders which may be made by the court under this section include, in particular, declarations of partial invalidity.]

NOTES
1 Words substituted by Registered Designs Regulations 2001/3949 reg 8(2) (9 December 2001).
2 Added by Registered Designs Regulations 2001/3949 reg 8 (3) (9 December 2001).
3 Words substituted subject to transitional provisions specified in SI 2006/1974 art 18 by Regulatory Reform (Registered Designs) Order 2006/1974 art 10(2) (1 October 2006: substitution has effect subject to transitional provisions specified in SI 2006/1974 art 18).
4 Words substituted subject to transitional provisions specified in SI 2006/1974

art 18 by Regulatory Reform (Registered Designs) Order 2006/1974 art 10(3) (1 October 2006: substitution has effect subject to transitional provisions specified in SI 2006/1974 art 18).

5   Words inserted by Registered Designs Regulations 2003/550 reg 2(4)(b) (1 April 2003: insertion has effect subject to transitional provisions specified in SI 2003/550 regs 3–5).

6   Words inserted by Registered Designs Regulations 2003/550 reg 2(4)(a) (1 April 2003: insertion has effect subject to transitional provisions specified in SI 2003/550 regs 3–5).

7   Section 20(5) inserted by Copyright, Designs and Patents Act 1988 s 272 Sch 3 para 11.

8   Added by Registered Designs Regulations 2001/3949 reg 8(4) (9 December 2001).

21   Power to correct clerical errors

(1) The registrar may, in accordance with the provisions of this section, correct any error in an application for the registration or in the representation of a design, or any error in the register of designs.

(2) A correction may be made in pursuance of this section either upon a request in writing made by any person interested and accompanied by the prescribed fee, or without such a request.

(3) Where the registrar proposes to make any such correction as aforesaid otherwise than in pursuance of a request made under this section, he shall give notice of the proposal to the registered proprietor or the applicant for registration of the design, as the case may be, and to any other person who appears to him to be concerned, and shall give them an opportunity to be heard before making the correction.

NOTES
1   Functions of Board of Trade and of President of Board of Trade now exercisable concurrently by Secretary of State: SI 1970/1537 art 2(1).

22   Inspection of registered designs

[(1) Where a design has been registered under this Act, there shall be open to inspection at the Patent Office on and after the day on which the certificate of registration is [granted] —

   (a)   the representation or specimen of the design [.]
   (b)   [...]

This subsection has effect subject to [subsection (4)] and to any rules made under section 5(2) of this Act.]

[...]

[(4) Where registration of a design has been refused pursuant to an application under this Act, or an application under this Act has been abandoned in relation to any design—

   (a)   the application, so far as relating to that design, and
   (b)   any representation, specimen or other document which has been filed and relates to that design,

shall not at any time be open to inspection at the Patent Office or be published by the registrar.]

NOTES
1   Section 22(1) substituted by Copyright, Designs and Patents Act 1988 s 272 Sch 3 para 12(2).
2   Word substituted by Regulatory Reform (Registered Designs) Order 2006/1974 art 16(2)(a) (1 October 2006).
3   And the word "and" immediately preceding it is repealed by Registered Designs Regulations 2001/3949 Sch 2 para 1 (9 December 2001).
4   Words substituted subject to transitional provisions specified in SI 2006/1974 art 18 by Regulatory Reform (Registered Designs) Order 2006/1974 art 16(2)(b) (1 October 2006: substitution has effect subject to transitional provisions specified in SI 2006/1974 art 18).
5   Repeal has effect subject to transitional provisions specified in SI 2006/1974 art 18 by Regulatory Reform (Registered Designs) Order 2006/1974 art 16(3) (1 October 2006: repealed subject to transitional provisions specified in SI 2006/1974 art 18).
6   Substituted by Regulatory Reform (Registered Designs) Order 2006/1974 art 15 (1 October 2006).

[23   Information as to existence of right in registered design

On the request of a person furnishing such information as may enable the registrar to identify the design, and on payment of the prescribed fee, the registrar shall inform him—

(a)   whether the design is registered […] , and
(b)   whether any extension of the period of the right in the registered design has been granted,

and shall state the date of registration and the name and address of the registered proprietor.]

NOTES
1   Section 23 substituted by Copyright, Designs and Patents Act 1988 s 272 Sch 3 para 13.
2   Words repealed by Registered Designs Regulations 2001/3949 Sch 2 para 1 (9 December 2001).

Repealed

[…]

NOTES
1   Repealed by Patents, Designs and Marks Act 1986 s 3(1) Sch 3 Pt. I.
2   Functions of Board of Trade and of President of Board of Trade now exercisable concurrently by Secretary of State: SI 1970/1537 art 2(1).

Legal proceedings and Appeals

[24A   Action for infringement

(1) An infringement of the right in a registered design is actionable by the registered proprietor.

(2) In an action for infringement all such relief by way of damages, injunctions, accounts or otherwise is available to him as is available in respect of the infringement of any other property right.

(3) This section has effect subject to section 24B of this Act (exemption of innocent infringer from liability).]

NOTES
1   Added by Intellectual Property (Enforcement, etc) Regulations 2006/1028 Sch 1 para 3 (29 April 2006).
2   Functions of Board of Trade and of President of Board of Trade now exercisable concurrently by Secretary of State: SI 1970/1537 art 2(1).

[24B   Exemption of innocent infringer from liability

(1) In proceedings for the infringement of the right in a registered design damages shall not be awarded, and no order shall be made for an account of profits, against a defendant who proves that at the date of the infringement he was not aware, and had no reasonable ground for supposing, that the design was registered.

(2) For the purposes of subsection (1), a person shall not be deemed to have been aware or to have had reasonable grounds for supposing that the design was registered by reason only of the marking of a product with—

(a)   the word "registered" or any abbreviation thereof, or
(b)   any word or words expressing or implying that the design applied to, or incorporated in, the product has been registered,

unless the number of the design accompanied the word or words or the abbreviation in question.

(3) Nothing in this section shall affect the power of the court to grant an injunction in any proceedings for infringement of the right in a registered design.]

NOTES
1   Added by Intellectual Property (Enforcement, etc.) Regulations 2006/1028 Sch 1 para 3 (29 April 2006).
2   Functions of Board of Trade and of President of Board of Trade now exercisable concurrently by Secretary of State: SI 1970/1537 art 2(1).

[24C   Order for delivery up

(1) Where a person—

(a)   has in his possession, custody or control for commercial purposes an infringing article, or
(b)   has in his possession, custody or control anything specifically designed or adapted for making articles to a particular design which is a registered design, knowing or having reason to believe that it has been or is to be used to make an infringing article,

the registered proprietor in question may apply to the court for an order that the infringing article or other thing be delivered up to him or to such other person as the court may direct.

(2) An application shall not be made after the end of the period specified in the following provisions of this section; and no order shall be made unless the court also makes, or it appears to the court that there are grounds for making, an order under section 24D of this Act (order as to disposal of infringing article, &c.).

(3) An application for an order under this section may not be made after the end of the period of six years from the date on which the article or thing in question was made, subject to subsection (4).

(4) If during the whole or any part of that period the registered proprietor—

    (a)   is under a disability, or
    (b)   is prevented by fraud or concealment from discovering the facts entitling him to apply for an order,

an application may be made at any time before the end of the period of six years from the date on which he ceased to be under a disability or, as the case may be, could with reasonable diligence have discovered those facts.

(5) In subsection (4) "disability"—

    (a)   in England and Wales, has the same meaning as in the Limitation Act 1980;
    (b)   in Scotland, means legal disability within the meaning of the Prescription and Limitation (Scotland) Act 1973;
    (c)   in Northern Ireland, has the same meaning as in the Statute of Limitations (Northern Ireland) 1958.

(6) A person to whom an infringing article or other thing is delivered up in pursuance of an order under this section shall, if an order under section 24D of this Act is not made, retain it pending the making of an order, or the decision not to make an order, under that section.

(7) The reference in subsection (1) to an act being done in relation to an article for "commercial purposes" are to its being done with a view to the article in question being sold or hired in the course of a business.

(8) Nothing in this section affects any other power of the court.]

NOTES
    1   Added by Intellectual Property (Enforcement, etc.) Regulations 2006/1028 Sch 1 para 3 (29 April 2006).
    2   Functions of Board of Trade and of President of Board of Trade now exercisable concurrently by Secretary of State: SI 1970/1537 art 2(1).

[24D   Order as to disposal of infringing articles, &c

(1) An application may be made to the court for an order that an infringing article or other thing delivered up in pursuance of an order under section 24C of this Act shall be—

(a) forfeited to the registered proprietor, or

(b) destroyed or otherwise dealt with as the court may think fit,

or for a decision that no such order should be made.

(2) In considering what order (if any) should be made, the court shall consider whether other remedies available in an action for infringement of the right in a registered design would be adequate to compensate the registered proprietor and to protect his interests.

(3) Where there is more than one person interested in an article or other thing, the court shall make such order as it thinks just and may (in particular) direct that the thing be sold, or otherwise dealt with, and the proceeds divided.

(4) If the court decides that no order should be made under this section, the person in whose possession, custody or control the article or other thing was before being delivered up is entitled to its return.

(5) References in this section to a person having an interest in an article or other thing include any person in whose favour an order could be made in respect of it—

(a) under this section;

(b) under section 19 of Trade Marks Act 1994 (including that section as applied by regulation 4 of the Community Trade Mark Regulations 2006 (SI 2006/1027));

(c) under section 114, 204 or 231 of the Copyright, Designs and Patents Act 1988; or

(d) under regulation 1C of the Community Design Regulations 2005 (SI 2005/2339).]

NOTES

1   Added by Intellectual Property (Enforcement, etc) Regulations 2006/1028 Sch 1 para 3 (29 April 2006).

2   Functions of Board of Trade and of President of Board of Trade now exercisable concurrently by Secretary of State: SI 1970/1537 art 2(1).

[24E   Jurisdiction of county court and sheriff court

(1) In Northern Ireland a county court may entertain proceedings under the following provisions of this Act—

(a) section 24C (order for delivery up of infringing article, &c.),

(b) section 24D (order as to disposal of infringing article, &c.), or

(c) section 24F(8) (application by exclusive licensee having concurrent rights),

where the value of the infringing articles and other things in question does not exceed the county court limit for actions in tort.

(2) In Scotland proceedings for an order under any of those provisions may be brought in the sheriff court.

(3) Nothing in this section shall be construed as affecting the jurisdiction of the Court of Session or the High Court in Northern Ireland.]

NOTES

1   Added by Intellectual Property (Enforcement, etc.) Regulations 2006/1028 Sch 1 para 3 (29 April 2006).

2   Functions of Board of Trade and of President of Board of Trade now exercisable concurrently by Secretary of State: SI 1970/1537 art 2(1).

[24F   Rights and remedies of exclusive licensee

(1) In relation to a registered design, an exclusive licensee has, except against the registered proprietor, the same rights and remedies in respect of matters occurring after the grant of the licence as if the licence had been an assignment.

(2) His rights and remedies are concurrent with those of the registered proprietor; and references to the registered proprietor in the provisions of this Act relating to infringement shall be construed accordingly.

(3) In an action brought by an exclusive licensee by virtue of this section a defendant may avail himself of any defence which would have been available to him if the action had been brought by the registered proprietor.

(4) Where an action for infringement of the right in a registered design brought by the registered proprietor or an exclusive licensee relates (wholly or partly) to an infringement in respect of which they have concurrent rights of action, the proprietor or, as the case may be, the exclusive licensee may not, without the leave of the court, proceed with the action unless the other is either joined as a claimant or added as a defendant.

(5) A registered proprietor or exclusive licensee who is added as a defendant in pursuance of subsection (4) is not liable for any costs in the action unless he takes part in the proceedings.

(6) Subsections (4) and (5) do not affect the granting of interlocutory relief on the application of the registered proprietor or an exclusive licensee.

(7) Where an action for infringement of the right in a registered design is brought which relates (wholly or partly) to an infringement in respect of which the registered proprietor and an exclusive licensee have concurrent rights of action—

(a)   the court shall, in assessing damages, take into account—

   (i)   the terms of the licence, and
   (ii) any pecuniary remedy already awarded or available to either of them in respect of the infringement;

(b)   no account of profits shall be directed if an award of damages has been made, or an account of profits has been directed, in favour of the other of them in respect of the infringement; and

(c)   the court shall if an account of profits is directed apportion the profits between them as the court considers just, subject to any agreement between them; and these provisions apply whether or not the proprietor and the exclusive licensee are both parties to the action.

(8) The registered proprietor shall notify any exclusive licensee having concurrent rights before applying for an order under section 24C of this Act (order for

delivery up of infringing article, &c); and the court may on the application of the licensee make such order under that section as it thinks fit having regard to the terms of the licence.]

[24G   Meaning of "infringing article"

(1) In this Act "infringing article", in relation to a design, shall be construed in accordance with this section.

(2) An article is an infringing article if its making to that design was an infringement of the right in a registered design.

(3) An article is also an infringing article if—

(a)   it has been or is proposed to be imported into the United Kingdom, and

(b)   its making to that design in the United Kingdom would have been an infringement of the right in a registered design or a breach of an exclusive licensing agreement relating to that registered design.

(4) Where it is shown that an article is made to a design which is or has been a registered design, it shall be presumed until the contrary is proved that the article was made at a time when the right in the registered design subsisted.

(5) Nothing in subsection (3) shall be construed as applying to an article which may be lawfully imported into the United Kingdom by virtue of an enforceable Community right within the meaning of section 2(1) of the European Communities Act 1972.]

25   Certificate of contested validity of registration

(1) If in any proceedings before the court the validity of the registration of a design is contested, and it is found by the court that the design is [, to any extent,] validly registered, the court may certify that the validity of the registration of the design was contested in those proceedings.

(2) Where any such certificate has been granted, then if in any subsequent proceedings before the court for infringement of [the right in the registered design] or for [invalidation] of the registration of the design, a final order or judgment is made or given in favour of the registered proprietor, he shall, unless the court otherwise directs, be entitled to his costs as between solicitor and client:

Provided that this subsection shall not apply to the costs of any appeal in any such proceedings as aforesaid.

NOTES
1 Words inserted by Registered Designs Regulations 2001/3949 Sch 1 para 8(2) (9 December 2001).
2 Words substituted by Copyright, Designs and Patents Act 1988 s 272 Sch 3 para 14.
3 Word substituted by Registered Designs Regulations 2001/3949 Sch 1 para 8(3) (9 December 2001).

26 Remedy for groundless threats of infringement proceedings

(1) Where any person (whether entitled to or interested in a registered design or an application for registration of a design or not) by circulars, advertisements or otherwise threatens any other person with proceedings for infringement of [the right in a registered design], any person aggrieved thereby may bring an action against him for any such relief as is mentioned in the next following subsection.

(2) Unless in any action brought by virtue of this section the defendant proves that the acts in respect of which proceedings were threatened constitute or, if done, would constitute, an infringement of [the right in a registered design] the registration of which is not shown by the [claimant] to be invalid, the [claimant] shall be entitled to the following relief, that is to say:—

(a) a declaration to the effect that the threats are unjustifiable;
(b) an injunction against the continuance of the threats; and
(c) such damages, if any, as he has sustained thereby.

[(2A) Proceedings may not be brought under this section in respect of a threat to bring proceedings for an infringement alleged to consist of the making or importing of anything.]

(3) For the avoidance of doubt it is hereby declared that a mere notification that a design is registered does not constitute a threat of proceedings within the meaning of this section.

NOTES
1 Words substituted by Copyright, Designs and Patents Act 1988 s 272 Sch 3 para 15(2).
2 Word substituted by Intellectual Property (Enforcement, etc.) Regulations 2006/1028 Sch 1 para 4 (29 April 2006).
3 Section 26(2A) inserted by Copyright, Designs and Patents Act 1988 s 272 Sch 3 para 15(3).

[27 The court

(1) In this Act "the court" means —

(a) in England and Wales the High Court or any patents county court having jurisdiction by virtue of an order under section 287 of the Copyright, Designs and Patents Act 1988,

(b)   in Scotland, the Court of Session, and

(c)   in Northern Ireland, the High Court.

(2) Provision may be made by rules of court with respect to proceedings in the High Court in England and Wales for references and applications under this Act to be dealt with by such judge of that court as the [Lord Chief Justice of England and Wales may, after consulting the Lord Chancellor, select] for the purpose.

[(3) The Lord Chief Justice may nominate a judicial office holder (as defined in section 109(4) of the Constitutional Reform Act 2005) to exercise his functions under subsection (2).]]

NOTES

1   Section 27 substituted by Copyright, Designs and Patents Act 1988 s 272 Sch 3 para 16.

2   Words substituted by Constitutional Reform Act 2005 Sch 4(1) para 36(2) (3 April 2006).

3   Added by Constitutional Reform Act 2005 Sch 4(1) para 36(3) (3 April 2006).

28   The Appeal Tribunal.

(1) Any appeal from the registrar under this Act shall lie to the Appeal Tribunal.

[(2) The Appeal Tribunal shall consist of—

(a)   one or more judges of the High Court nominated [by the Lord Chief Justice of England and Wales after consulting the Lord Chancellor] , and

(b)   one judge of the Court of Session nominated by the Lord President of that Court.]

[(2A) At any time when it consists of two or more judges, the jurisdiction of the Appeal Tribunal—

(a)   where in the case of any particular appeal the senior of those judges so directs, shall be exercised in relation to that appeal by both of the judges, or (if there are more than two) by two of them, sitting together, and

(b)   in relation to any appeal in respect of which no such direction is given, may be exercised by any one of the judges;

and, in the exercise of that jurisdiction, different appeals may be heard at the same time by different judges.]

(3) The expenses of the Appeal Tribunal shall be defrayed and the fees to be taken therein may be fixed as if the Tribunal were a court of the High Court.

(4) The Appeal Tribunal may examine witnesses on oath and administer oaths for that purpose.

(5) Upon any appeal under this Act the Appeal Tribunal may by order award to any party such costs [...] as the Tribunal may consider reasonable and direct how and by what parties the costs [...] are to be paid[and any such order may be enforced—]

[(a)   in England and Wales or Northern Ireland, in the same way as an order of the High Court;

(b)   in Scotland, in the same way as a decree for expenses granted by the Court of Session.]

[…]

(7) Upon any appeal under this Act the Appeal Tribunal may exercise any power which could have been exercised by the registrar in the proceeding from which the appeal is brought.

(8) Subject to the foregoing provisions of this section the Appeal Tribunal may make rules for regulating all matters relating to proceedings before it under this Act. [including right of audience]

[(8A) At any time when the Appeal Tribunal consists of two or more judges, the power to make rules under sub-section (8) of this section shall be exercisable by the senior of those judges:

Provided that another of those judges may exercise of that power if it appears to him that it is necessary for rules to be made and that the judge (or, if more than one, each of the judges) senior to him is for the time being prevented by illness, absence or otherwise from making them.]

(9) An appeal to the Appeal Tribunal under this Act shall not be deemed to be a proceeding in the High Court.

[(10) In this section "the High Court" means the High Court in England and Wales; and for the purposes of this section the seniority of judges shall be reckoned by reference to the dates on which they were appointed judges of that court or the Court of Session.]

[(11) The Lord Chief Justice may nominate a judicial office holder (as defined in section 109(4) of the Constitutional Reform Act 2005) to exercise his functions under subsection (2)(a).]

NOTES
1   Section 28(2) substituted by Copyright, Designs and Patents Act 1988 s 272 Sch 3 para 17(2).
2   Words substituted by Constitutional Reform Act 2005 Sch 4(1) para 37(2) (3 April 2006).
3   Section 28(2)(2A) substituted for s 28(2) by Administration of Justice Act 1969 s 24(1)(2).
4   Words repealed by Intellectual Property (Enforcement, etc.) Regulations 2006/1028 Sch 4 para 1 (29 April 2006).
5   Words substituted by Copyright, Designs and Patents Act 1988 s 272 Sch 3 para 17(3).
6   Repealed by Administration of Justice Act 1970 Sch 11.
7   Words inserted by Administration of Justice Act 1970 s 10(5).
8   Section 28(8A) inserted by Administration of Justice Act 1969 s 24(1)(3).
9   Section 28(10) substituted by Copyright, Designs and Patents Act 1988 s 272 Sch 3 para 17(4).
10   Added by Constitutional Reform Act 2005 c. 4 Sch 4(1) para 37(3) (3 April 2006).

Powers and Duties of Registrar

29 Exercise of discretionary powers of registrar

Without prejudice to any provisions of this Act requiring the registrar to hear any party to proceedings thereunder, or to give to any such party an opportunity to be heard, [rules made by the Secretary of State under this Act shall require the registrar to give] to any applicant for registration of a design an opportunity to be heard before exercising adversely to the applicant any discretion vested in the registrar by or under this Act.

NOTES

1 Words substituted by Copyright, Designs and Patents Act 1988 s 272 Sch 3 para 18.
2 Functions of Board of Trade and of President of Board of Trade now exercisable concurrently by Secretary of State: SI 1970/1537 art 2(1).

[30 Costs and security for costs

(1) Rules made by the Secretary of State under this Act may make provision empowering the registrar, in any proceedings before him under this Act—

(a)   to award any party such costs as he may consider reasonable, and
(b)   to direct how and by what parties they are to be paid.

(2) Any such order of the registrar may be enforced—

(a)   in England and Wales or Northern Ireland, in the same way as an order of the High Court;
(b)   in Scotland, in the same way as a decree for expenses granted by the Court of Session.

(3) Rules made by the Secretary of State under this Act may make provision empowering the registrar to require a person, in such cases as may be prescribed, to give security for the costs of—

(a)   an application for [invalidation] of the registration of a design,
(b)   [...]
(c)   an appeal from any decision of the registrar under this Act,

and enabling the application or appeal to be treated as abandoned in default of such security being given.]

NOTES

1 Section 30 substituted by Copyright, Designs and Patents Act 1988 s 272 Sch 3 para 19.
2 Word substituted by Registered Designs Regulations 2001/3949 Sch 1 para 9 (9 December 2001).
3 Repealed by Registered Designs Regulations 2001/3949 Sch 2 para 1 (9 December 2001).

[31 Evidence before registrar

Rules made by the Secretary of State under this Act may make provision—

(a)   as to the giving of evidence in proceedings before the registrar under this Act by affidavit or statutory declaration;

(b)   conferring on the registrar the powers of an official referee of the [Senior Courts] [or of the Court of Judicature] as regards the examination of witnesses on oath and the discovery and production of documents; and

(c)   applying in relation to the attendance of witness in proceedings before the registrar the rules applicable to the attendance of witnesses in proceedings before such a referee.]

NOTES

1   Section 31 substituted by Copyright, Designs and Patents Act 1988 s 272 Sch 3 para 20.

2   Words substituted by Constitutional Reform Act 2005 Sch 11(2) para 4(1) (1 October 2009).

3   Words inserted by Constitutional Reform Act 2005 Sch 11(4) para 18 (1 October 2009).

Repealed

[…]

NOTES

1   Repealed by Copyright, Designs and Patents Act 1988 ss 272, 303(2) Sch 3 para 21 Sch 8.

2   Functions of Board of Trade and of President of Board of Trade now exercisable concurrently by Secretary of State: SI 1970/1537 art 2(1).

Offences

33   Offences under s 5

(1) If any person fails to comply with any direction given under section five of this Act or makes or causes to be made an application for the registration of a design in contravention of that section, he shall be guilty of an offence and liable—

[(a)   on conviction on indictment to imprisonment for a term not exceeding two years or a fine, or both;

(b)   on summary conviction to imprisonment for a term not exceeding six months or a fine not exceeding the statutory maximum, or both.]

[…]

NOTES

1   Section 33(1)(a)(b) substituted by Copyright, Designs and Patents Act 1988 s 272 Sch 3 para 22(2)(4).

2   Repealed by Copyright, Designs and Patents Act 1988 ss 272, 303(2) Sch 3 para 22(3)(4) Sch 8.

3   Functions of Board of Trade and of President of Board of Trade now exercisable concurrently by Secretary of State: SI 1970/1537 art 2(1).

Offences

34 Falsification of register, etc

If any person makes or causes to be made a false entry in the register of designs, or a writing falsely purporting to be a copy of an entry in that register, or produces or tenders or causes to be produced or tendered in evidence any such writing, knowing the entry or writing to be false, he [

shall be guilty of an offence and liable—

(a) on conviction on indictment to imprisonment for a term not exceeding two years or a fine, or both;

(b) on summary conviction to imprisonment for a term not exceeding six months or a fine not exceeding the statutory maximum, or both.].

NOTES
1 Words substituted by Copyright, Designs and Patents Act 1988 s 272 Sch 3 para 23(1)(2).
2 Functions of Board of Trade and of President of Board of Trade now exercisable concurrently by Secretary of State: SI 1970/1537 art 2(1).

35 Fine for falsely representing a design as registered

(1) If any person falsely represents that a design applied to [, or incorporated in, any product]1 sold by him is registered […] , he shall be liable on summary conviction to [a fine not exceeding level 3 on the standard scale]; and for the purposes of this provision a person who sells [a product] having stamped, engraved or impressed thereon or otherwise applied thereto the word "registered", or any other word expressing or implying that the design applied to [, or incorporated in, the product] is registered, shall be deemed to represent that the design applied to [, or incorporated in, the product] is registered […] .

(2) If any person, after [the right in a registered design] has expired, marks [any product] to which the design has been applied [or in which it has been incorporated] with the word "registered", or any word or words implying that there is a [subsisting right in the design under this Act] , or causes any [such product] to be so marked, he shall be liable on summary conviction to [a fine not exceeding level 1 on the standard scale]

[(3) For the purposes of this section, the use in the United Kingdom in relation to a design—

(a) of the word ""registered"", or

(b) of any other word or symbol importing a reference (express or implied) to registration,

shall be deemed to be a representation as to registration under this Act unless it is shown that the reference is to registration elsewhere than in the United Kingdom and that the design is in fact so registered.]

NOTES
1 Words substituted by Registered Designs Regulations 2001/3949 Sch 1 para 10(2)(a) (9 December 2001).

2 Words repealed by Registered Designs Regulations 2001/3949 Sch 2 para 1 (9 December 2001).
3 Words substituted by Copyright, Designs and Patents Act 1988 s 272 Sch 3 para 24(2)(4).
4 Words substituted by Registered Designs Regulations 2001/3949 Sch 1 para 10(2)(c) (9 December 2001).
5 Words substituted by Registered Designs Regulations 2001/3949 Sch 1 para 10(2)(d) (9 December 2001).
6 Words substituted by Copyright, Designs and Patents Act 1988 s 272 Sch 3 para 24(3)(a).
7 Words substituted by Registered Designs Regulations 2001/3949 Sch 1 para 10(3)(a) (9 December 2001).
8 Words inserted by Registered Designs Regulations 2001/3949 Sch 1 para 10(3)(b) (9 December 2001).
9 Words substituted by Copyright, Designs and Patents Act 1988 s 272 Sch 3 para 24(3)(b).
10 Words substituted by Registered Designs Regulations 2001/3949 Sch 1 para 10(3)(c) (9 December 2001).
11 Words substituted by Copyright, Designs and Patents Act 1988 s 272 Sch 3 para 24(3)(c).
12 Added by Community Design Regulations 2005/2339 reg 6 (1 October 2005).

[35 Offence by body corporate: liability of officers

(1) Where an offence under this Act committed by a body corporate is proved to have been committed with the consent or connivance of a director, manager, secretary or other similar officer of the body, or a person purporting to act in any such capacity, he as well as the body corporate is guilty of the offence and liable to be proceeded against and punished accordingly.

(2) In relation to a body corporate whose affairs are managed by its members "director" means a member of the body corporate.]

NOTES
1 Section 35A inserted by Copyright, Designs and Patents Act 1988 s 272 Sch 3 para 25(1)(2).
2 Functions of Board of Trade and of President of Board of Trade now exercisable concurrently by Secretary of State: SI 1970/1537 art 2(1).

Rules, etc

36 General power of Board of Trade to make rules, etc

(1) Subject to the provisions of this Act, [the Secretary of State] may make such rules [as he thinks expedient] for regulating the business of the Patent Office in relation to designs and for regulating all matters by this Act placed under the direction or control of the registrar or [the Secretary of State],

[(1A) Rules may, in particular, make provision—

(a) prescribing the form of applications for registration of designs and of any representations or specimens of designs or other documents which may be filed at the Patent Office, and requiring copies to be furnished of any such representations, specimens or documents;

[(ab) requiring applications for registration of designs to specify—

     (i) the products to which the designs are intended to be applied or in which they are intended to be incorporated;

    (ii) the classification of the designs by reference to such test as may be prescribed;]

(b) regulating the procedure to be followed in connection with any application or request to the registrar or in connection with any proceeding before him, and authorising the rectification of irregularities of procedure;

(c) providing for the appointment of advisers to assist the registrar in proceedings before him;

(d) regulating the keeping of the register of designs;

(e) authorising the publication and sale of copies of representations of designs and other documents in the Patent Office;

(f) prescribing anything authorised or required by this Act to be prescribed by rules.

(1B) The remuneration of an adviser appointed to assist the registrar shall be determined by the Secretary of State with the consent of the Treasury and shall be defrayed out of money provided by Parliament.]

(2) Rules made under this section may provide for the establishment of branch offices for designs and may authorise any document or thing required by or under this Act to be filed or done at the Patent Office to be filed or done at the branch office at Manchester or any other branch office established in pursuance of the rules.

NOTES

1 Words substituted by Copyright, Designs and Patents Act 1988 s 272 Sch 3 para 26(2).

2 Words substituted by Copyright, Designs and Patents Act 1988 s 272 Sch 3 para 26(3).

3 Added by Registered Designs Regulations 2001/3949 Sch 1 para 11 (9 December 2001).

37 Provisions as to rules and Orders

(1) […]

(2) Any rules made by [the Secretary of State] in pursuance of [section 15 of this Act] , and any order made, direction given, or other action taken under the rules by the registrar, may be made, given or taken so as to have effect as respects things done or omitted to be done on or after such date, whether before or after the coming into operation of the rules or of this Act, as may be specified in the rules.

(3) Any power to make rules conferred by this Act on [the Secretary of State] or on the Appeal Tribunal shall be exercisable by statutory instrument; and the Statutory Instruments Act 1946, shall apply to a statutory instrument containing rules made by the Appeal Tribunal in like manner as if the rules had been made by a Minister of the Crown.

(4) Any statutory instrument containing rules made by [the Secretary of State] under this Act shall be subject to annulment in pursuance of a resolution of either House of Parliament.

(5) Any Order in Council made under this Act may be revoked or varied by a subsequent Order in Council.

NOTES
1   Repealed by Copyright, Designs and Patents Act 1988 ss 272, 303(2) Sch 3 para 27(2) Sch 8.
2   Words substituted by Copyright, Designs and Patents Act 1988 s 272 Sch 3 para 27(3).
3   Words substituted by Registered Designs Regulations 2001/3949 Sch 1 para 12 (9 December 2001).

[37A   Use of electronic communications

(1) The registrar may give directions as to the form and manner in which documents to be delivered to the registrar—

(a)   in electronic form; or
(b)   using electronic communications,

are to be delivered to him.

(2) A direction under subsection (1) may provide that in order for a document to be delivered in compliance with the direction it shall be accompanied by one or more additional documents specified in the direction.

(3) Subject to subsections (11) and (12), if a document to which a direction under subsection (1) or (2) applies is delivered to the registrar in a form or manner which does not comply with the direction the registrar may treat the document as not having been delivered.

(4) Subsection (5) applies in relation to a case where—

(a)   a document is delivered using electronic communications, and
(b)   there is a requirement for a fee to accompany the document.

(5) The registrar may give directions specifying—

(a)   how the fee shall be paid; and
(b)   when the fee shall be deemed to have been paid.

(6) The registrar may give directions specifying that a person who delivers a document to the registrar in electronic form or using electronic communications cannot treat the document as having been delivered unless its delivery has been acknowledged.

(7) The registrar may give directions specifying how a time of delivery is to be accorded to a document delivered to him in electronic form or using electronic communications.

(8) A direction under this section may be given—

(a)   generally;

(b)   in relation to a description of cases specified in the direction; (c) in relation to a particular person or persons.

(9) A direction under this section may be varied or revoked by a subsequent direction under this section.

(10) The delivery using electronic communications to any person by the registrar of any document is deemed to be effected, unless the registrar has otherwise specified, by transmitting an electronic communication containing the document to an address provided or made available to the registrar by that person as an address of his for the receipt of electronic communications; and unless the contrary is proved such delivery is deemed to be effected immediately upon the transmission of the communication.

(11) A requirement of this Act that something must be done in the prescribed manner is satisfied in the case of something that is done—

(a)   using a document in electronic form, or
(b)   using electronic communications,

only if the directions under this section that apply to the manner in which it is done are complied with.

(12) In the case of an application made as mentioned in subsection (11)(a) or (b) above, a reference in this Act to the application not having been made in accordance with rules under this Act includes a reference to its not having been made in accordance with any applicable directions under this section.

(13) This section applies—

(a)   to delivery at the Patent Office as it applies to delivery to the registrar; and
(b)   to delivery by the Patent Office as it applies to delivery by the registrar.]

NOTES
1   Added by Registered Designs Act 1949 and Patents Act 1977 (Electronic Communications) Order 2006/1229 art 2 (1 October 2006).
2   Functions of Board of Trade and of President of Board of Trade now exercisable concurrently by Secretary of State: SI 1970/1537 art 2(1).

38   Proceedings of Board of Trade

[…]

[…]

[…]

NOTES
1   Repealed by Copyright, Designs and Patents Act 1988 ss 272, 303(2) Sch 3 para 28 Sch 8.
2   Functions of Board of Trade and of President of Board of Trade now exercisable concurrently by Secretary of State: SI 1970/1537 art 2(1).

Supplemental

39 Hours of business and excluded days

(1) Rules made by [the Secretary of State] under this Act may specify the hour at which the Patent Office shall be deemed to be closed on any day for purposes of the transaction by the public of business under this Act or of any class of such business, and may specify days as excluded days for any such purposes.

(2) Any business done under this Act on any day after the hour specified as aforesaid in relation to business of that class, or an a day which is an excluded day in relation to business of that class, shall be deemed to have been done on the next following day not being an excluded day; and where the time for doing anything under this Act expires on an excluded day, that time shall be extended to the next following day not being an excluded day.

NOTES
1 Words substituted by Copyright, Designs and Patents Act 1988 s 272 Sch 3 para 29.
2 Functions of Board of Trade and of President of Boa.d of Trade now exercisable concurrently by Secretary of State :SI 1970/1537 art 2(1)

40 Fees

There shall be paid in respect of the registration of designs and applications therefor, and in respect of other matters relating to designs arising under this Act, such fees as may be prescribed by rules made by [the Secretary of State] with the consent of the Treasury.

NOTES
1 Words substituted by Copyright, Designs and Patents Act 1988 s 272 Sch 3 para 30.
2 Functions of Board of Trade and of President of Board of Trade now exercisable concurrently by Secretary of State: SI 1970/1537 art 2(1).

41 Service of notices, etc, by post

Any notice required or authorised to be given by or under this Act, and any application or other document so authorised or required to be made or filed, may be given, made or filed by post.

NOTES
1 Functions of Board of Trade and of President of Board of Trade now exercisable concurrently by Secretary of State: SI 1970/1537 art 2(1).

42 Annual report of registrar

The Comptroller-General of Patents, Designs and Trade Marks shall, in his annual report with respect to the execution of [the Patents Act 1977], include a report with respect to the execution of this Act as if it formed a part of or was included in that Act.

NOTES
  1   Words substituted by Patents Act 1977 Sch 5 para 3.
  2   Functions of Board of Trade and of President of Board of Trade now exercisable
      concurrently by Secretary of State: SI 1970/1537 art 2(1).

43   Savings

[…]

(2) Nothing in this Act shall affect the right of the Crown or of any person deriving title directly or indirectly from the Crown to sell or use [products] forfeited under the laws relating to customs or excise.

NOTES
  1   Repealed by Registered Designs Regulations 2001/3949 Sch 2 para 1
      (9 December 2001).
  2   Word substituted by Registered Designs Regulations 2001/3949 Sch 1 para 13
      (9 December 2001).

44   Interpretation

(1) In this Act, except where the context otherwise requires, the following expressions have the meanings hereby respectively assigned by them, that is to say—

  ["Appeal Tribunal" means the Appeal Tribunal constituted and acting in accordance with section 28 of this Act as amended by the Administration of Justice Act 1969;]

[…]

  "assignee" includes the personal representative of a deceased assignee, and references to the assignee of any person include references to the assignee of the personal representative or assignee of that person;
  ["author" in relation to a design, has the meaning given by section 2(3) and (4);]

[…]

  ["Community Design Regulation" means Council Regulation (EC) 6/2002 of 12th December 2001 on Community Designs;]
  ["complex product" has the meaning assigned to it by section 1(3) of this Act;]

[…]

  ["the court" shall be construed in accordance with section 27 of this Act;]
  "design" has the meaning assigned to it by [[section 1(2)] of this Act];
  ["electronic communication" has the same meaning as in the Electronic Communications Act 2000;]
  ["employee", "employment" and "employer" refer to employment under a contract of service or of apprenticeship,] […]
  ["national unregistered design right" means design right within the meaning of Part III of the Copyright, Designs and Patents Act 1988;]

"prescribed" means prescribed by rules made by [the Secretary of State] under this Act;

["product" has the meaning assigned to it by section 1(3) of this Act;]

"proprietor" has the meaning assigned to it by section two of this Act;

["registered Community design" means a design that complies with the conditions contained in, and is registered in the manner provided for in, the Community Design Regulation;]

"registered proprietor" means the person or persons for the time being entered in the register of designs as proprietor of the design;

"registrar" means the Comptroller-General of Patents Designs and Trade Marks;

[…]

[…]

(4) For the purposes of [subsection (1) of section 14] of this Act, the expression "personal representative", in relation to a deceased person, includes the legal representative of the deceased appointed in any country outside the United Kingdom.

NOTES

1   Definition substituted by Administration of Justice Act 1969 Sch 1.

2   Definitions repealed by Registered Designs Regulations 2001/3949 Sch 2 para 1 (9 December 2001).

3   Words inserted by Copyright, Designs and Patents Act 1988 s 272 Sch 3 para 31(3).

4   Definition repealed by Copyright, Designs and Patents Act 1988 ss 272, 303(2) Sch 3 para 31(4) Sch 8.

5   Definition inserted by Registered Designs Regulations 2003/550 reg 2 (5) (1 April 2003: insertion has effect subject to transitional provisions specified in SI 2003/550 regs 3–5).

6   Definition inserted by Registered Designs Regulations 2001/3949 Sch 1 para 14(3) (9 December 2001).

7   Definition repealed by Registered Designs Regulations 2001/3949 Sch 2 para 1 (9 December 2001).

8   Definition substituted by Copyright, Designs and Patents Act 1988 s 272 Sch 3 para 31(6).

9   Words substituted by Copyright, Designs and Patents Act 1988 s 272 Sch 3 para 31(7).

10 Words substituted by Registered Designs Regulations 2001/3949 Sch 1 para 14(2) (9 December 2001).

11 Definition inserted by Registered Designs Act 1949 and Patents Act 1977 (Electronic Communications) Order 2006/1229 art 3 (1 October 2006).

12 Definitions inserted by Copyright, Designs and Patents Act 1988 s 272 Sch 3 para 31(8).

13 Definition repealed by Copyright, Designs and Patents Act 1988 ss 272, 303(2) Sch 3 para 31(9) Sch 8.

14 Words substituted by Copyright, Designs and Patents Act 1988 s 272 Sch 3 para 31(10).

15 Repealed by Registered Designs Regulations 2001/3949 Sch 2 para 1 (9 December 2001).

16 Words substituted by Registered Designs Regulations 2001/3949 Sch 1 para 14(4) (9 December 2001).

[45 Application to Scotland

(1) In the application of this Act to Scotland—

"account of profits" means accounting and payment of profits;
"accounts" means count, reckoning and payment;
"arbitrator" means arbiter;
"assignment" means assignation;
"claimant" means pursuer;
"costs" means expenses;
"defendant" means defender;
"delivery up" means delivery;
"injunction" means interdict;
"interlocutory relief" means interim remedy.

(2) References to the Crown shall be construed as including references to the Crown in right of the Scottish Administration.]

NOTES
  1 Substituted by Intellectual Property (Enforcement, etc.) Regulations 2006/1028 Sch 1 para 5 (29 April 2006).

46 Application to Northern Ireland

In the application of this Act to Northern Ireland—

  (1) [...]

  (2) [...]

[(3) References to enactments include enactments comprised in Northern Ireland legislation:]

[(3A) References to the Crown include the Crown in right of Her Majesty's Government in Northern Ireland:]

(4) References to a Government department shall be construed as including references to [a Northern Ireland department] [and in relation to a Northern Ireland department references to the Treasury shall be construed as references to the Department of Finance and Personnel]:

[(4A) Any reference to a claimant includes a reference to a plaintiff.]

  (5) [...]

NOTES
  1 Repealed by Copyright, Designs and Patents Act 1988 ss 272, 303(2) Sch 3 para 33(2) Sch 8.
  2 Section 46(3) substituted by Copyright, Designs and Patents Act 1988 s 272 Sch 3 para 33(3).
  3 Section 46(3A) inserted by Copyright, Designs and Patents Act 1988 s 272 Sch 3 para 33(4).
  4 Words substituted by Copyright, Designs and Patents Act 1988 ss 272, 305(3) Sch 3 para 33(5).
  5 Words inserted by Copyright, Designs and Patents Act 1988 s 272 Sch 3 para 33(5).

6   Added by Intellectual Property (Enforcement, etc.) Regulations 2006/1028 Sch 1
     para 6 (29 April 2006).
7   Repealed by Northern Ireland Act 1962 (c. 30) Sch 4 Pt IV.

[47   Application to Isle of Man

This Act extends to the Isle of Man, subject to any modifications contained in
an Order made by Her Majesty in Council, and accordingly, subject to any such
Order, references in this Act to the United Kingdom shall be construed as
including the Isle of Man.]

NOTES
    1   Section 47 substituted by Copyright, Designs and Patents Act 1988 s 272 Sch 3
         para 34.
    2   Functions of Board of Trade and of President of Board of Trade now exercisable
         concurrently by Secretary of State: SI 1970/1537 art 2(1).

[47A   Territorial waters and the Continental shelf

(1) For the purposes of this Act the territorial waters of the United Kingdom
shall be treated as part of the United Kingdom.

(2) This Act applies to things done in the United Kingdom sector of the
continental shelf on a structure or vessel which is present there for purposes
directly connected with the exploration of the sea bed or subsoil or the
exploitation of their natural resources as it applies to things done in the United
Kingdom.

(3) The United Kingdom sector of the continental shelf means the areas
designated by order under section 1(7) of the Continental Shelf Act 1964.]

NOTES
    1   Section 47A inserted by Copyright, Designs and Patents Act 1988 s 272 Sch 3
         para 35.
    2   Functions of Board of Trade and of President of Board of Trade now exercisable
         concurrently by Secretary of State: SI 1970/1537 art 2(1).

48   Repeals, savings, and transitional provisions

(1) [...]

(2) Subject to the provisions of this section, any Order in Council, rule, order,
requirement, certificate, notice, decision, direction, authorisation, consent,
application, request or thing made, issued, given or done under any enactment
repealed by this Act shall, if in force at the commencement of this Act, and so
far as it could have been made, issued, given or done under this Act, continue in
force and have effect as if made, issued, given or done under the corresponding
enactment of this Act.

(3) Any register kept under the Patents and Designs Act 1907, shall be deemed
to form part of the corresponding register under this Act.

(4) Any design registered before the commencement of this Act shall be deemed to be registered under this Act in respect of articles of the class in which it is registered.

(5) [...]

(6) Any document referring to any enactment repealed by this Act shall be construed as referring to the corresponding enactment of this Act.

(7) Nothing in the foregoing provisions of this section shall be taken as prejudicing the operation of [section 16(1) and section 17(2)(a) of the Interpretation Act 1978], (which [relate] to the effect of repeals).

NOTES
 1 Repealed by Copyright, Designs and Patents Act 1988 ss 272, 303(2) Sch 3 para 36 Sch 8.
 2 Repealed by Registered Designs Regulations 2001/3949 Sch 2 para 1 (9 December 2001).
 3 Words substituted by virtue of Interpretation Act 1978 s 25(2).

49   Short title and commencement

(1) This Act may be cited as the Registered Designs Act 1949.

(2) This Act shall come into operation on the first day of January, nineteen hundred and fifty, immediately after the coming into operation of the Patents and Designs Act 1949.

NOTES
 1 Functions of Board of Trade and of President of Board of Trade now exercisable concurrently by Secretary of State: SI 1970/1537 art 2(1).

Schedule A1
GROUNDS FOR REFUSAL OF REGISTRATION IN RELATION TO EMBLEMS ETC.

[1   Grounds for refusal in relation to certain emblems etc

(1) A design shall be refused registration under this Act if it involves the use of—

(a)   the Royal arms, or any of the principal armorial bearings of the Royal arms, or any insignia or device so nearly resembling the Royal arms or any such armorial bearing as to be likely to be mistaken for them or it;

(b)   a representation of the Royal crown or any of the Royal flags;

(c)   a representation of Her Majesty or any member of the Royal family, or any colourable imitation thereof; or

(d)   words, letters or devices likely to lead persons to think that the applicant either has or recently has had Royal patronage or authorisation;

unless it appears to the registrar that consent for such use has been given by or on behalf of Her Majesty or (as the case may be) the relevant member of the Royal family.

(2) A design shall be refused registration under this Act if it involves the use of—

    (a)   the national flag of the United Kingdom (commonly known as the Union Jack); or

    (b)   the flag of England, Wales, Scotland, Northern Ireland or the Isle of Man,

and it appears to the registrar that the use would be misleading or grossly offensive.

(3) A design shall be refused registration under this Act if it involves the use of—

    (a)   arms to which a person is entitled by virtue of a grant of arms by the Crown; or

    (b)   insignia so nearly resembling such arms as to be likely to be mistaken for them;

unless it appears to the registrar that consent for such use has been given by or on behalf of the person concerned and the use is not in any way contrary to the law of arms.

(4) A design shall be refused registration under this Act if it involves the use of a controlled representation within the meaning of the Olympic Symbol etc. (Protection) Act 1995 unless it appears to the registrar that—

    (a)   the application is made by the person for the time being appointed under section 1(2) of the Olympic Symbol etc. (Protection) Act 1995 (power of Secretary of State to appoint a person as the proprietor of the Olympics association right); or

    (b)   consent for such use has been given by or on behalf of the person mentioned in paragraph (a) above.]

NOTES

1   Added by Registered Designs Regulations 2001/3949 reg 3 (9 December 2001).
2   Functions of Board of Trade and of President of Board of Trade now exercisable concurrently by Secretary of State: SI 1970/1537 art 2(1).

[2 Grounds for refusal in relation to emblems etc. of Paris Convention countries

(1) A design shall be refused registration under this Act if it involves the use of the flag of a Paris Convention country unless—

    (a)   the authorisation of the competent authorities of that country has been given for the registration; or

    (b)   it appears to the registrar that the use of the flag in the manner proposed is permitted without such authorisation.

(2) A design shall be refused registration under this Act if it involves the use of the armorial bearings or any other state emblem of a Paris Convention country

which is protected under the Paris Convention unless the authorisation of the competent authorities of that country has been given for the registration.

(3) A design shall be refused registration under this Act if—

    (a)   the design involves the use of an official sign or hallmark adopted by a Paris Convention country and indicating control and warranty;

    (b)   the sign or hallmark is protected under the Paris Convention; and

    (c)   the design could be applied to or incorporated in goods of the same, or a similar, kind as those in relation to which the sign or hallmark indicates control and warranty;

unless the authorisation of the competent authorities of that country has been given for the registration.

(4) The provisions of this paragraph as to national flags and other state emblems, and official signs or hallmarks, apply equally to anything which from a heraldic point of view imitates any such flag or other emblem, or sign or hallmark.

(5) Nothing in this paragraph prevents the registration of a design on the application of a national of a country who is authorised to make use of a state emblem, or official sign or hallmark, of that country, notwithstanding that it is similar to that of another country.]

NOTES

1   Added by Registered Designs Regulations 2001/3949 reg 3 (9 December 2001).

2   Functions of Board of Trade and of President of Board of Trade now exercisable concurrently by Secretary of State: SI 1970/1537 art 2(1).

[3   Grounds for refusal in relation to emblems etc. of certain international organisations

(1) This paragraph applies to—

    (a)   the armorial bearings, flags or other emblems; and

    (b)   the abbreviations and names,

of international intergovernmental organisations of which one or more Paris Convention countries are members.

(2) A design shall be refused registration under this Act if it involves the use of any such emblem, abbreviation or name which is protected under the Paris Convention unless—

    (a)   the authorisation of the international organisation concerned has been given for the registration; or

    (b)   it appears to the registrar that the use of the emblem, abbreviation or name in the manner proposed—

        (i)   is not such as to suggest to the public that a connection exists between the organisation and the design; or

        (ii)   is not likely to mislead the public as to the existence of a connection between the user and the organisation.

(3) The provisions of this paragraph as to emblems of an international organisation apply equally to anything which from a heraldic point of view imitates any such emblem.

(4) Nothing in this paragraph affects the rights of a person whose *bona fide* use of the design in question began before 4th January 1962 (when the relevant provisions of the Paris Convention entered into force in relation to the United Kingdom).]

NOTES
1   Added by Registered Designs Regulations 2001/3949 reg 3 (9 December 2001).
2   Functions of Board of Trade and of President of Board of Trade now exercisable concurrently by Secretary of State: SI 1970/1537 art 2(1).

[4   Paragraphs 2 and 3: supplementary

(1) For the purposes of paragraph 2 above state emblems of a Paris Convention country (other than the national flag), and official signs or hallmarks, shall be regarded as protected under the Paris Convention only if, or to the extent that—

(a)   the country in question has notified the United Kingdom in accordance with Article 6*ter*(3) of the Convention that it desires to protect that emblem, sign or hallmark;
(b)   the notification remains in force; and
(c)   the United Kingdom has not objected to it in accordance with Article 6*ter*(4) or any such objection has been withdrawn.

(2) For the purposes of paragraph 3 above the emblems, abbreviations and names of an international organisation shall be regarded as protected under the Paris Convention only if, or to the extent that—

(a)   the organisation in question has notified the United Kingdom in accordance with Article 6*ter*(3) of the Convention that it desires to protect that emblem, abbreviation or name;
(b)   the notification remains in force; and
(c)   the United Kingdom has not objected to it in accordance with Article 6*ter*(4) or any such objection has been withdrawn.

(3) Notification under Article 6*ter*(3) of the Paris Convention shall have effect only in relation to applications for the registration of designs made more than two months after the receipt of the notification.]

NOTES
1   Added by Registered Designs Regulations 2001/3949 reg 3 (9 December 2001).
2   Functions of Board of Trade and of President of Board of Trade now exercisable concurrently by Secretary of State: SI 1970/1537 art 2(1).

[5   Interpretation

In this Schedule—

"a Paris Convention country" means a country, other than the United Kingdom, which is a party to the Paris Convention; and "the Paris Convention" means the Paris Convention for the Protection of Industrial Property of 20th March 1883.]

NOTES
1   Added by Registered Designs Regulations 2001/3949 reg3 (9 December 2001)
2   Functions of Board of Trade and of President of Board of Trade now exercisable concurrently by Secretary of State: SI 1970/1537 art 2(1)

Schedule 1
PROVISIONS AS TO THE USE OF REGISTERED DESIGNS FOR THE SERVICES OF THE CROWN AND AS TO THE RIGHTS OF THIRD PARTIES IN RESPECT OF SUCH USE

1   Use of registered designs for services of the Crown.

(1) Notwithstanding anything in this Act, any Government department, and any person authorised in writing by a Government department, may use any registered design for the services of the Crown in accordance with the following provisions of this paragraph.

(2) If and so far as the design has before the date of registration thereof been duly recorded by or applied by or on behalf of a Government department otherwise than in consequence of the communication of the design directly or indirectly by the registered proprietor or any person from whom he derives title, any use of the design by virtue of this paragraph may be made free of any royalty or other payment to the registered proprietor.

(3) If and so far as the design has not been so recorded or applied as aforesaid, any use of the design made by virtue of this paragraph at any time after the date of registration thereof, or in consequence of any such communication as aforesaid, shall be made upon such terms as may be agreed upon, either before or after the use, between the Government department and the registered proprietor with the approval of the Treasury, or as may in default of agreement be determined by the court on a reference under paragraph 3 of this Schedule.

(4) The authority of a Government department in respect of a design may be given under this paragraph either before or after the design is registered and either before or after the acts in respect of which the authority is given are done, and may be given to any person whether or not he is authorised directly or indirectly by the registered proprietor to use the design.

(5) Where any use of a design is made by or with the authority of a Government department under this paragraph, then, unless it appears to the department that it would be contrary to the public interest so to do, the department shall notify the registered proprietor as soon as practicable after the use is begun, and furnish him with such information as to the extent of the use as he may from time to time require.

[(6) For the purposes of this and the next following paragraph "the services of the Crown" shall be deemed to include—

(a)   the supply to the government of any country outside the United Kingdom, in pursuance of an agreement or arrangement between Her Majesty's Government in the United Kingdom and the government of that country, of [products] required—

  (i)   for the defence of that country; or
  (ii) for the defence of any other country whose government is party to any agreement or arrangement with Her Majesty's said Government in respect of defence matters;

(b)   the supply to the United Nations, or to the government of any country belonging to that organisation, in pursuance of an agreement or arrangement between Her Majesty's Government and that organisation or government, of [products] required for any armed forced operating in pursuance of a resolution of that organisation or any organ of that organisation;

and the power of a Government department or a person authorised by a Government department under this paragraph to use a design shall include power to sell to any such government or to the said organisation any [products] the supply of which is authorised by this sub-paragraph, and to sell to any person any [products] made in the exercise of the powers conferred by this paragraph which are no longer required for the purpose for which they were made.]

(7) The purchaser of any [products] sold in the exercise of powers conferred by this paragraph, and any person claiming through him, shall have power to deal with them in the same manner as if the rights in the registered design were held on behalf of His Majesty.

NOTES
  1   Para. 1(6) substituted by Defence Contracts Act 1958 s 1(1)(4).
  2   Words substituted by Registered Designs Regulations 2001/3949 Sch 1 para 15(2) (9 December 2001).

2   Rights of third parties in respect of Crown use

(1) In relation to any use of a registered design, or a design in respect of which an application for registration is pending, made for the services of the Crown—

(a)   by a Government department or a person authorised by a Government department under the last foregoing paragraph; or
(b)   by the registered proprietor or applicant for registration to the order of a Government department,

the provisions of any licence, assignment or agreement made, whether before or after the commencement of this Act, between the registered proprietor or applicant for registration or any person who derives title from him or from whom he derives title and any person other than a Government department shall be of no effect so far as those provisions restrict or regulate the use of the design, or any model, document or information relating thereto, or provide for the making of payments in respect of any such use, or calculated by reference thereto; and the reproduction or publication of any model or document in connection with the said use shall not be deemed to be an infringement of any copyright [or [national unregistered design right]] subsisting in the model or document [or of any topography right]3.

(2) Where an exclusive licence granted otherwise than for royalties or other benefits determined by reference to the use of the design is in force under the registered design then—

(a) in relation to any use of the design which, but for the provisions of this and the last foregoing paragraph, would constitute an infringement of the rights of the licensee, sub-paragraph (3) of the last foregoing paragraph shall have effect as if for the reference to the registered proprietor there were substituted a reference to the licensee; and

(b) in relation to any use of the design by the licensee by virtue of an authority given under the last foregoing paragraph, that paragraph shall have effect as if the said sub-paragraph (3) were omitted.

(3) Subject to the provisions of the last foregoing sub-paragraph, where the registered design or the right to apply for or obtain registration of the design has been assigned to the registered proprietor in consideration of royalties or other benefits determined by reference to the use of the design, then—

(a) in relation to any use of the design by virtue of paragraph 1 of this Schedule, sub-paragraph (3) of that paragraph shall have effect as if the reference to the registered proprietor included a reference to the assignor, and any sum payable by virtue of that sub-paragraph shall be divided between the registered proprietor and the assignor in such proportion as may be agreed upon between them or as may in default of agreement be determined by the court on a reference under the next following paragraph; and

(b) in relation to any use of the design made for the services of the Crown by the registered proprietor to the order of a Government department, sub-paragraph (3) of paragraph 1 of this Schedule shall have effect as if that use were made by virtue of an authority given under that paragraph.

(4) Where, under sub-paragraph (3) of paragraph 1 of this Schedule, payments are required to be made by a Government department to a registered proprietor in respect of any use of a design, any person being the holder of an exclusive licence under the registered design (not being such a licence as is mentioned in sub-paragraph (2) of this paragraph) authorising him to make that use of the design shall be entitled to recover from the registered proprietor such part (if any) of those payments as may be agreed upon between that person and the registered proprietor, or as may in default of agreement be determined by the court under the next following paragraph to be just having regard to any expenditure incurred by that person—

(a) in developing the said design; or

(b) in making payments to the registered proprietor, other than royalties or other payments determined by reference to the use of the design, in consideration of the licence;

and if, at any time before the amount of any such payment has been agreed upon between the Government department and the registered proprietor, that person gives notice in writing of his interest to the department, any agreement as to the amount of that payment shall be of no effect unless it is made with his consent.

(5) In this paragraph "exclusive licence" means a licence from a registered proprietor which confers on the licensee, or on the licensee and persons authorised by him, to the exclusion of all other persons (including the registered proprietor), any right in respect of the registered design.

NOTES
1   Words inserted by Copyright, Designs and Patents Act 1988 s 272 Sch 3 para 37(2).
2   Words substituted by Registered Designs Regulations 2001/3949 Sch 1 para 15(3) (9 December 2001).
3   Words inserted by SI 1987/1497, reg 9(2) para 2 Table B it is provided that Sch 1 para 2(1) shall apply as if there were inserted at the end thereof the words, "or of any topography right".

[2A   Compensation for loss of profit

(1) Where Crown use is made of a registered design, the government department concerned shall pay—

    (a)   to the registered proprietor, or
    (b)   if there is an exclusive licence in force in respect of the design, to the exclusive licensee,

compensation for any loss resulting from his not being awarded a contract to supply the [products] to which the design is applied [or in which it is incorporated] .

(2) Compensation is payable only to the extent that such a contract could have been fulfilled from his existing manufacturing capacity; but is payable notwithstanding the existence of circumstances rendering him ineligible for the award of such a contract.

(3) In determining the loss, regard shall be had to the profit which would have been made on such a contract and to the extent to which any manufacturing capacity was under used.

(4) No compensation is payable in respect of any failure to secure contracts for the supply of [products] to which the design is applied [or in which it is incorporated] otherwise than for the services of the Crown.

(5) The amount payable under this paragraph shall, if not agreed between the registered proprietor or licensee and the government department concerned with the approval of the Treasury, be determined by the court on a reference under paragraph 3, and it is in addition to any amount payable under paragraph 1 or 2 of this Schedule.

(6) In this paragraph—

"Crown use", in relation to a design, means the doing of anything by virtue of paragraph 1 which would otherwise be an infringement of the right in the design; and

"the government department concerned", in relation to such use, means the government department by whom or on whose authority the act was done.]

NOTES

1   Sch 1 Para. 2A inserted by Copyright, Designs and Patents Act 1988 s 271(1).
2   Words substituted by Registered Designs Regulations 2001/3949 Sch 1 para 15(4)(a) (9 December 2001).
3   Words inserted by Registered Designs Regulations 2001/3949 Sch 1 para 15(4)(b) (9 December 2001).
4   Word substituted by Registered Designs Regulations 2001/3949 Sch 1 para 15(4)(a) (9 December 2001).

3   Reference of disputes as to Crown use

[(1) Any dispute as to—

(a)   the exercise by a Government department, or a person authorised by a Government department, of the powers conferred by paragraph 1 of this Schedule,

(b)   terms for the use of a design for the services of the Crown under that paragraph,

(c)   the right of any person to receive any part of a payment made under paragraph 1(3), or

(d)   the right of any person to receive a payment under paragraph 2A,

may be referred to the court by either party to the dispute.]

(2) In any proceedings under this paragraph to which a Government department are a party, the department may—

(a)   if the registered proprietor is a party to the proceedings [and the department are a relevant person within the meaning of section 20 of this Act] , apply for [invalidation] of the registration of the design upon any ground upon which the registration of a design may be [declared invalid] on an application to the court under section twenty of this Act;

(b)   in any case [and provided that the department would be the relevant person within the meaning of section 20 of this Act if they had made an application on the grounds for invalidity being raised] , put in issue the validity of the registration of the design without applying for its [invalidation] .

(3) If in such proceedings as aforesaid any question arises whether a design has been recorded or applied as mentioned in paragraph 1 of this Schedule, and the disclosure of any document recording the design, or of any evidence of the application thereof, would in the opinion of the department be prejudicial to the public interest, the disclosure may be made confidentially to counsel for the other party or to an independent expert mutually agreed upon.

(4) In determining under this paragraph any dispute between a Government department and any person as to terms for the use of a design for the services of the Crown, the court shall have regard to any benefit or compensation which that person or any person from whom he derives title may have received, or may be entitled to receive, directly or indirectly from any Government department in respect of the design in question. (5) In any proceedings under this paragraph the court may at any time order the whole proceedings or any question or issue of fact arising therein to be referred to a special or official referee or an arbitrator on such terms as the court may direct; and references to the court in the foregoing provisions of this paragraph shall be construed accordingly.

NOTES

1   Sch. 1 para 3(1) substituted by Copyright, Designs and Patents Act 1988 s 271(2).
2   Words inserted by Registered Designs Regulations 2001/3949 Sch 1 para 15(5)(a) (9 December 2001).
3   Word substituted by Registered Designs Regulations 2001/3949 Sch 1 para 15(5)(b) (9 December 2001).
4   Words substituted by Registered Designs Regulations 2001/3949 Sch 1 para 15(5)(c) (9 December 2001).
5   Words inserted by Registered Designs Regulations 2001/3949 Sch 1 para 15(6)(a) (9 December 2001).
6   Word substituted by Registered Designs Regulations 2001/3949 Sch 1 para 15(6)(b) (9 December 2001).

4   Special provisions as to Crown use during emergency.

(1) During any period of emergency within the meaning of this paragraph, the powers exercisable in relation to a design by a Government department, or a person authorised by a Government department under paragraph 1 of this Schedule shall include power to use the design for any purpose which appears to the department necessary or expedient—

(a)   for the efficient prosecution of any war in which His Majesty may be engaged;

(b)   for the maintenance of supplies and services essential to the life of the community;

(c)   for securing a sufficiency of supplies and services essential to the well-being of the community;

(d)   for promoting the productivity of industry, commerce and agriculture;

(e)   for fostering and directing exports and reducing imports, or imports of any classes, from all or any countries and for redressing the balance of trade;

(f)   generally for ensuring that the whole resources of the community are available for use, and are used, in a manner best calculated to serve the interests of the community; or

(g)   for assisting the relief of suffering and the restoration and distribution of essential supplies and services in any part of His Majesty's dominions or any foreign countries that are in grave distress as the result of war;

and any reference in this Schedule to the services of the Crown shall be construed as including a reference to the purposes aforesaid.

(2) In this paragraph the expression "period of emergency" means [a period] beginning on such date as may be declared by Order in Council to be the commencement, and ending on such date as may be so declared to be the termination, of a period of emergency for the purposes of this paragraph.

[(3) No Order in Council under this paragraph shall be submitted to Her Majesty unless a draft of it has been laid before and approved by a resolution of each House of Parliament.]

NOTES
1 Words substituted by Copyright, Designs and Patents Act 1988 s 272 Sch 3 para 37(4).
2 Sch. 1 para 4(3) substituted by Copyright, Designs and Patents Act 1988 s 272 Sch 3 para 37(5).
3 Functions of Board of Trade and of President of Board of Trade now exercisable concurrently by Secretary of State: SI 1970/1537 art 2(1).

Copyright (Industrial Process and Excluded Articles) (No. 2) Order

1989/1070

The Secretary of State, in exercise of the powers conferred upon him by section 52(4) of the Copyright, Designs and Patents Act 1988 ("the Act"), hereby makes the following Order:

Made   26 June 1989

1 This Order may be cited as the Copyright (Industrial Process and Excluded Articles) (No. 2) Order 1989 and shall come into force on 1st August 1989.

2 An article is to be regarded for the purposes of section 52 of the Act (limitation of copyright protection for design derived from artistic work) as made by an industrial process if—

(a) it is one of more than fifty articles which—

   (i) all fall to be treated for the purposes of Part I of the Act as copies of a particular artistic work, but
   (ii) do not all together constitute a single set of articles as defined in section 44(1) of the Registered Designs Act 1949; or

(b) it consists of goods manufactured in lengths or pieces, not being hand-made goods.

3 (1) There are excluded from the operation of section 52 of the Act—

(a) works of sculpture, other than casts or models used or intended to be used as models or patterns to be multiplied by any industrial process;
(b) wall plaques, medals and medallions; and

(c) printed matter primarily of a literary or artistic character, including book jackets, calendars, certificates, coupons, dress-making patterns, greetings cards, labels, leaflets, maps, plans, playing cards, postcards, stamps, trade advertisements, trade forms and cards, transfers and similar articles.

(2) Nothing in article 2 of this Order shall be taken to limit the meaning of "industrial process" in paragraph (1)(a) of this article.

4 The Copyright (Industrial Designs) Rules 1957 and the Copyright (Industrial Process and Excluded Articles) Order 1989 are hereby revoked.

NOTES
1 The Order was made on 13 June 1989, but was not laid before Parliament.

Copyright, Designs and Patents Act 1988 (Commencement No. 1) Order 1989

1989/816

The Secretary of State, in exercise of the powers conferred upon him by section 305(3) of the Copyright, Designs and Patents Act 1988, hereby makes the following Order:

1. This Order may be cited as the Copyright, Designs and Patents Act 1988 (Commencement No. 1) Order 1989.

2. The following provisions of the Copyright, Designs and Patents Act 1988 shall come into force on 1st August 1989:

Part I (copyright);
Part II (rights in performances);
Part III (design right);
Part IV (registered designs), except–
section 272 in so far as it relates to paragraph 21 of Schedule 3, and section 273;
Part VI (patents), except–
sections 293 and 294, and section 295 in so far as it relates to paragraphs 1 to 11 and 17 to 30 of Schedule 5;
Part VII (miscellaneous and general), except—
section 301, section 303(1) in so far as it relates to paragraphs 15, 18(2) and 21 of Schedule 7, and section 303(2) in so far as it relates to the references in Schedule 8 to section 32 of the Registered Designs Act 1949 and to the provisions of the Patents Act 1977, other than section 49(3) of, and paragraphs 1 and 3 of Schedule 5 to, that Act
[, section 304(4) and (6)];
Schedule 1 (copyright: transitional provisions and savings);
Schedule 2 (rights in performances: permitted acts);
Schedule 3 (minor and consequential amendments to the Registered Designs Act 1949), other than paragraph 21;

Schedule 5 (patents: miscellaneous amendments), other than paragraphs 1 to 11 and 17 to 30;

Schedule 7 (consequential amendments), other than paragraphs 15, 18(2) and 21;

Schedule 8 (repeals), except in so far as it relates to–

section 32 of the Registered Designs Act 1949, and the provisions of the Patents Act 1977, other than section 49(3) of, and paragraphs 1 and 3 of Schedule 5 to, that Act.

NOTES
1. Reference added in the list of provisions of Part VII of the 1988 Act by Copyright, Designs and Patents Act 1988 (Commencement No. 4) Order 1989/1303 art 3 (July 27, 1989)

Design Right (Semiconductor Topographies) Regulations

1989/1100

Whereas a draft of the following Regulations has been approved by resolution of each House of Parliament:

Now, therefore, the Secretary of State, being designated[1] for the purposes of section 2(2) of the European Communities Act 1972 in relation to the conferment and protection of exclusive rights in the topographies of semiconductor products, in exercise of the powers conferred on him by the said section 2(2) hereby makes the following Regulations:

NOTES
1 SI 1987/448.

1 Citation and commencement

These Regulations may be cited as the Design Right (Semiconductor Topographies) Regulations 1989 and shall come into force on 1st August 1989.

2—Interpretation

(1) In these Regulations—

"the Act" means the Copyright, Designs and Patents Act 1988;

"semiconductor product" means an article the purpose, or one of the purposes, of which is the performance of an electronic function and which consists of two or more layers, at least one of which is composed of semiconducting material and in or upon one or more of which is fixed a pattern appertaining to that or another function; and

"semiconductor topography" means a design within the meaning of section 213(2) of the Act which is a design of either of the following:

(a) the pattern fixed, or intended to be fixed, in or upon—

      (i)   a layer of a semiconductor product, or

     (ii)   a layer of material in the course of and for the purpose of the manufacture of a semiconductor product, or

  (b)   the arrangement of the patterns fixed, or intended to be fixed, in or upon the layers of a semiconductor product in relation to one another.

(2) Except where the context otherwise requires, these Regulations shall be construed as one with Part III of the Act (design right).

3   Application of Copyright, Designs and Patents Act 1988, Part III

In its application to a design which is a semiconductor topography, Part III of the Act shall have effect subject to regulations 4 to 9 below.

4—Qualification

(1) Section 213(5) of the Act has effect subject to paragraphs (2) to (4) below.

[(2) Part III of the Act has effect as if for section 217(3) there was substituted the following—

"(3) In this section 'qualifying country' means—

  (a)   the United Kingdom,

  (b)   another member State,

  (c)   the Isle of Man, Gibraltar, the Channel Islands or any colony,

  (d)   a country listed in the Schedule to the Design Right (Semiconductor Topographies) Regulations 1989."][1].

(3) Where a semiconductor topography is created in pursuance of a commission or in the course of employment and the designer of the topography is, by virtue of section 215 of the Act (as substituted by regulation 5 below), the first owner of design right in that topography, section 219 of the Act does not apply and section 218(2) to (4) of the Act shall apply to the topography as if it had not been created in pursuance of a commission or in the course of employment.

(4) Section 220 of the Act has effect subject to regulation 7 below and as if for subsection (1) there was substituted the following:

"220—

(1) A design which does not qualify for design right protection under section 218 or 219 (as modified by regulation 4(3) of the Design Right (Semiconductor Topographies) Regulations 1989) or under the said regulation 4(3) qualifies for design right protection if the first marketing of articles made to the design—

  (a)   is by a qualifying person who is exclusively authorised to put such articles on the market in every member State of the European Economic Community, and

  (b)   takes place within the territory of any member State.";

and subsection (4) of section 220 accordingly has effect as if the words "in the United Kingdom" were omitted.

NOTES
1 Substituted by Design Right (Semiconductor Topographies) (Amendment) Regulations 2006/1833 reg 3 (August 1, 2006)

5 Ownership of design right

Part III of the Act has effect as if for section 215 of the Act there was substituted the following:

"215—

(1) The designer is the first owner of any design right in a design which is not created in pursuance of a commission or in the course of employment.

(2) Where a design is created in pursuance of a commission, the person commissioning the design in the first owner of any design right in it subject to any agreement in writing to the contrary.

(3) Where, in a case not falling within subsection (2) a design is created by an employee in the course of his employment, his employer is the first owner of any design right in the design subject to any agreement in writing to the contrary.

(4) If a design qualifies for design right protection by virtue of section 220 (as modified by regulation 4(4) of the Design Right (Semiconductor Topographies) Regulations 1989), the above rules do not apply and, subject to regulation 7 of the said Regulations, the person by whom the articles in question are marketed is the first owner of the design right."

6—Duration of design right

(1) Part III of the Act has effect as if for section 216 of the Act there was substituted the following:

"216

The design right in a semiconductor topography expires—

(a) ten years from the end of the calendar year in which the topography or articles made to the topography were first made available for sale or hire anywhere in the world by or with the licence of the design right owner, or

(b) if neither the topography nor articles made to the topography are so made available within a period of fifteen years commencing with the earlier of the time when the topography was first recorded in a design document or the time when an article was first made to the topography, at the end of that period."

(2) Subsection (2) of section 263 of the Act has effect as if the words "or a semiconductor topography" were inserted after the words "in relation to an article".

(3) The substitute provision set out in paragraph (1) above has effect subject to regulation 7 below.

7 Confidential information

In determining, for the purposes of section 215(4), 216 or 220 of the Act (as modified by these Regulations), whether there has been any marketing, or anything has been made available for sale or hire, no account shall be taken of any sale or hire, or any offer or exposure for sale or hire, which is subject to an obligation of confidence in respect of information about the semiconductor topography in question unless either—

(a) the article or semiconductor topography sold or hired or offered or exposed for sale or hire has been sold or hired on a previous occasion (whether or not subject to an obligation of confidence), or

(b) the obligation is imposed at the behest of the Crown, or of the government of any country outside the United Kingdom, for the protection of security in connection with the production of arms, munitions or war material.

8—Infringement

(1) Section 226 of the Act has effect as if for subsection (1) there was substituted the following:

"226—

(1) Subject to subsection (1A), the owner of design right in a design has the exclusive right to reproduce the design—

(a) by making articles to that design, or

(b) by making a design document recording the design for the purpose of enabling such articles to be made.

(1A) Subsection (1) does not apply to—

(a) the reproduction of a design privately for non-commercial aims; or

(b) the reproduction of a design for the purpose of analysing or evaluating the design or analysing, evaluating or teaching the concepts, processes, systems or techniques embodied in it."

(2) Section 227 of the Act does not apply if the article in question has previously been sold or hired within—

(a) the United Kingdom by or with the licence of the owner of design right in the semiconductor topography in question, or

(b) the territory of any other member State of the European Economic Community or the territory of Gibraltar by or with the consent of the person for the time being entitled to import it into or sell or hire it within that territory.

(3) Section 228(6) of the Act does not apply.

(4) It is not an infringement of design right in a semiconductor topography to—

(a)   create another original semiconductor topography as a result of an analysis or evaluation of the first topography or of the concepts, processes, systems or techniques embodied in it, or

(b)   reproduce that other topography.

(5) Anything which would be an infringement of the design right in a semiconductor topography if done in relation to the topography as a whole is an infringement of the design right in the topography if done in relation to a substantial part of the topography.

9   Licences of right

Section 237 of the Act does not apply.

10—Revocation and transitional provisions

(1) The Semiconductor Products (Protection of Topography) Regulations 1987 are hereby revoked.

(2) Sub-paragraph (1) of paragraph 19 of Schedule 1 to the Act shall not apply in respect of a semiconductor topography created between 7th November 1987 and 31st July 1989.

(3) In its application to copyright in a semiconductor topography created before 7th November 1987, sub-paragraph (2) of the said paragraph 19 shall have effect as if the reference to sections 237 to 239 were a reference to sections 238 and 239; and subparagraph (3) of that paragraph accordingly shall not apply to such copyright.

Schedule 1
QUALIFYING COUNTRIES

Part 1
DESCRIPTIONS OF ADDITIONAL CLASSES

[1

[Existing Sch 1 is not repealed but has been substituted for a new Sch.1 consisting of para 1]²]¹.

NOTES
   1   Schedule (Parts I to III) substituted by Schedule (Parts I and II) by Design Right (Semiconductor Topographies) (Amendment) Regulations 1993/2497 Sch 1 para 1 (10 November 1993).
   2   Existing Sch 1 consisting of Parts I and II substituted for a new Sch 1 consisting of para 1 by Design Right (Semiconductor Topographies) (Amendment) Regulations 2006/1833 Sch 1 para 1 (1 August 2006).

[2

[Existing Sch.1 is not repealed but has been substituted for a new Sch.1 consisting of para 1]²]¹.

NOTES
1   Schedule (Parts I to III) substituted by Schedule (Parts I and II) by Design Right
    (Semiconductor Topographies) (Amendment) Regulations 1993/2497 Sch 1
    para 1 (10 November 1993).
2   Existing Sch 1 consisting of Parts I and II substituted for a new Sch 1 consisting
    of para 1 by Design Right (Semiconductor Topographies) (Amendment)
    Regulations 2006/1833 Sch 1 para 1 (1 August 2006).

[3

[Existing Sch 1 is not repealed but has been substituted for a new Sch.1
consisting of para.1]^2]^1.

NOTES
1   Schedule (Parts I to III) substituted by Schedule (Parts I and II) by Design Right
    (Semiconductor Topographies) (Amendment) Regulations 1993/2497 Sch 1
    para 1 (November 10, 1993).
2   Existing Sch 1 consisting of Parts I and II substituted for a new Sch 1 consisting
    of para 1 by Design Right (Semiconductor Topographies) (Amendment)
    Regulations 2006/1833 Sch 1 para 1 (1 August 2006).

[4

[Existing Sch 1 is not repealed but has been substituted for a new Sch.1
consisting of para 1]^2]^1.

NOTE
1   Schedule (Parts I to III) substituted by Schedule (Parts I and II) by Design Right
    (Semiconductor Topographies) (Amendment) Regulations 1993/2497 Sch 1
    para 1 (10 November 1993).
2   Existing Sch 1 consisting of Parts I and II substituted for a new Sch 1 consisting
    of para 1 by Design Right (Semiconductor Topographies) (Amendment)
    Regulations 2006/1833 Sch 1 para 1 (1 August 2006).

Part II
SPECIFIED COUNTRIES: CITIZENS, SUBJECTS, HABITUAL RESIDENTS, BODIES CORPORATE AND OTHER BODIES HAVING LEGAL PERSONALITY

[[Existing Sch 1 is not repealed but has been substituted for a new Sch.1
consisting of para 1]^2]^1.

NOTES
1   Schedule (Parts I to III) substituted by Schedule (Parts I and II) by Design Right
    (Semiconductor Topographies) (Amendment) Regulations 1993/2497 Sch.1
    para.1 (November 10, 1993).
2   Existing Sch.1 consisting of Parts I and II substituted for a new Sch.1 consisting
    of para.1 by Design Right (Semiconductor Topographies) (Amendment)
    Regulations 2006/1833 Sch 1 para 1 (August 1, 2006).

Schedule 1
QUALIFYING COUNTRIES

[Albania
Angola
Antigua and Barbuda
Argentina
Armenia
Australia
Bahrain, Kingdom of
Bangladesh
Barbados
Belize
Benin
Bolivia
Botswana
Brazil
Brunei Darussalam
Bulgaria
Burkina Faso
Burundi
Cambodia
Cameroon
Canada
Central African Republic
Chad
Chile
China
Colombia
Congo
Costa Rica
Côte d'Ivoire Croatia
Cuba
Democratic Republic of the Congo
Djibouti
Dominica
Dominican Republic
Ecuador
Egypt
El Salvador
Fiji
Former Yugoslav Republic of Macedonia
French overseas territories
Gabon
The Gambia
Georgia
Ghana
Grenada
Guatemala

Guinea
Guinea Bissau
Guyana
Haiti
Honduras
Hong Kong
Iceland
India
Indonesia
Israel
Jamaica
Japan
Jordan
Kenya
Korea, Republic of
Kuwait
Kyrgyz Republic
Lesotho Liechtenstein
Macao, China
Madagascar
Malawi
Malaysia
Maldives
Mali
Mauritania
Mauritius
Mexico
Moldova
Mongolia
Morocco
Mozambique
Myanmar
Namibia
Nepal
Netherlands Antilles
New Zealand
Nicaragua
Niger
Nigeria
Norway
Oman
Pakistan
Panama
Papua New Guinea
Paraguay
Peru
Philippines
Qatar
Romania

Rwanda
Saint Kitts and Nevis
Saint Lucia
Saint Vincent & the Grenadines Saudi Arabia
Senegal
Sierra Leone
Singapore
Solomon Islands
South Africa
Sri Lanka
Suriname
Swaziland
Switzerland
Chinese Taipei
Tanzania
Thailand
Togo
[Tonga][2]
Trinidad and Tobago
Tunisia
Turkey
Uganda
[Ukraine][2]
United Arab Emirates
United States of America
Uruguay
Venezuela
[Vietnam][2]
Zambia
Zimbabwe][1]

NOTES
1 Existing Sch 1 consisting of Parts I and II substituted for a new Sch 1 consisting of para 1 by Design Right (Semiconductor Topographies) (Amendment) Regulations 2006/1833 Sch 1 para 1 (1 August 2006).
2 Entries inserted by Design Right (Semiconductor Topographies) (Amendment) (No.2) Regulations 2008/1434 reg 3 (1 July 2008).

Design Right (Proceedings before Comptroller) Rules

1989/1130

The Secretary of State, in exercise of the powers conferred upon him by section 250 of the Copyright, Designs and Patents Act 1988[1], with the consent of the Treasury pursuant to subsection (3) of that section as to the fees prescribed under these Rules, and after consultation with the Council on

Tribunals in accordance with section 10(1) of the Tribunal and Inquiries Act 1971, hereby makes the following Rules:–

NOTES

1   under sub-paragraph (6) of paragraph 19 of Schedule 1 to the Copyright, Designs and Patents Act 1988 the provisions of section 250 apply in relation to proceedings brought under or by virtue of that paragraph as to proceedings under Part III of the Act.

1

These Rules may be cited as the Design Right (Proceedings before Comptroller) Rules 1989 and shall come into force on 1st August 1989.

2—

(1) In these Rules, unless the context otherwise requires—

"the Act" means the Copyright, Designs and Patents Act 1988;

"applicant" means a person who has referred a dispute or made an application to the Comptroller;

"application" means an application to the Comptroller to settle or vary the terms of a licence of right or to adjust the terms of a licence;

"dispute" means a dispute as to any of the matters referred to in rule 3(1); and

"proceedings" means proceedings before the Comptroller in respect of a dispute or application.

(2) A rule or schedule referred to by number means the rule or schedule so numbered in these Rules; and a requirement under these Rules to use a form set out in Schedule 1 is satisfied by the use either of a replica of that form or of a form which contains the information required by the form set out in the said Schedule and which is acceptable to the Comptroller.

3—Commencement of proceedings

(1) Proceedings under section 246 of the Act in respect of a dispute as to–

(a)   the subsistence of design right,

(b)   the term of design right, or

(c)   the identity of the person in whom design right first vested,

shall be commenced by the service by the applicant on the Comptroller of a notice in Form 1 in Schedule 1. There shall be served with that notice a statement in duplicate setting out the name and address of the other party to the dispute (hereinafter in this rule referred to as the respondent), the issues in dispute, the applicant's case and the documents relevant to his case.

(2) Within 14 days of the receipt of the notice the Comptroller shall send a copy of the notice, together with a copy of the applicant's statement, to the respondent.

(3) Within 28 days of the receipt by him of the documents referred to in paragraph (2) above, the respondent shall serve on the Comptroller a counter-statement and shall at the same time serve a copy of it on the applicant. Such counter-statement shall set out full particulars of the grounds on which he contests the applicant's case, any issues on which he and the applicant are in agreement and the documents relevant to his case.

(4) Within 21 days of the service on him of the counter-statement, the applicant may serve a further statement on the Comptroller setting out the grounds on which the contests the respondent's case, and shall at the same time serve a copy of it on the respondent.

(5) No amended statement or further statement shall be served by either party except by leave or direction of the Comptroller.

4—Comptroller's directions

(1) The Comptroller shall give such directions as to the further conduct of proceedings as he considers appropriate [including directing the party or parties to attend a case management conference or a pre-hearing review or both][1].

(2) If a party fails to comply with any direction given under this rule, the Comptroller may in awarding costs take account of such default.

NOTES
1 Words added by Design Right (Proceedings before Comptroller) (Amendment) Rules 1999/3195 rule 3. (December 22, 1999: 1999–12-22; save that rules 3, 4 and 6 shall not apply to any proceedings already begun before the Comptroller at the time of entry into force of these Rules but that they should apply to such proceedings from 2000–04-26).

5—Procedure and evidence at hearing

(1) Unless the Comptroller otherwise directs, all evidence in the proceedings shall be by statutory declaration [, witness statement][1] or affidavit.

(2) Where the Comptroller thinks fit in any particular case to take oral evidence in lieu of or in addition to evidence by statutory declaration [, witness statement][1] or affidavit he may so direct and, unless he directs otherwise, shall allow any witness to be cross-examined on his evidence.

(3) A party to the proceedings who desires to make oral representations shall so notify the Comptroller and the Comptroller shall, unless he and the parties agree to a shorter period, give at least 14 days' notice of the time and place of the hearing to the parties.

(4) If a party intends to refer at a hearing to any document not already referred to in the proceedings, he shall, unless the Comptroller and the other party agree to a shorter period, give 14 days' notice of his intention, together with particulars of every document to which he intends to refer, to the Comptroller and the other party.

(5) At any stage of the proceedings the Comptroller may direct that such documents, information or evidence as he may require shall be filed within such time as he may specify.

(6) The hearing of any proceedings, or part of proceedings, under this rule shall be in public, unless the Comptroller, after consultation with the parties, otherwise directs.

[(7) The Comptroller may give a direction as he thinks fit in any particular case that evidence shall be given by affidavit or statutory declaration instead of or in addition to a witness statement.

(8) Where in proceedings before the Comptroller, a party adduces evidence of a statement made by a person otherwise than while giving oral evidence in the proceedings and does not call that person as a witness, the Comptroller may, if he thinks fit, permit any other party to the proceedings to call that person as a witness and cross-examine him on the statement as if he had been called by the first-mentioned party and as if the statement were his evidence in chief.][2]

NOTES

1   Words added by Design Right (Proceedings before Comptroller) (Amendment) Rules 1999/3195 rule 4(a) (22 December 1999; save that rules 3, 4 and 6 shall not apply to any proceedings already begun before the Comptroller at the time of entry into force of these Rules but that they should apply to such proceedings from 2000–04-26).

2   Added by Design Right (Proceedings before Comptroller) (Amendment) Rules 1999/3195 rule 4(b) (22 December 1999; save that rules 3, 4 and 6 shall not apply to any proceedings already begun before the Comptroller at the time of entry into force of these Rules but that they should apply to such proceedings from 26 April 2000).

6—Representation and rights of audience

(1) Any party to the proceedings may appear in person or be represented by counsel or a solicitor (of any part of the United Kingdom) or, subject to paragraph (4) below, a patient agent or any other person whom he desires to represent him.

(2) Anything required or authorised by these Rules to be done by or in relation to any person may be done by or in relation to his agent.

(3) Where after a person has become a party to the proceedings he appoints an agent for the first time or appoints an agent in substitution for another, the newly appointed agent shall give written notice of his appointment to the Comptroller and to every other party to the proceedings.

(4) The Comptroller may refuse to recognise as such an agent in respect of any proceedings before him–

   (a)   a person who has been convicted of an offences under section 88 of the Patents Act 1949 or section 114 of the Patents Act 1977 [or section 276 of the Act][1];

   (b)   any individual whose name has been erased from and not restored to, or who is suspended from, the register of patent agents (kept in pursuance of rules made under [section 275 of the Act][2]) on the ground of misconduct;

   (c)   a person who is found by the Secretary of State to have been guilty of such conduct as would, in the case of an individual registered in the register of patent agents, render him liable to have his name erased from the register on the ground of misconduct;

(d)   a partnership or body corporate of which one of the partners or directors is a person whom the Comptroller could refuse to recognise under sub-paragraphs (a), (b), or (c) above.[³]⁴

NOTES
1   Words added by Design Right (Proceedings before Comptroller) (Amendment) Rules 1990/1453 rule 2(a) (13 August 1990).
2   Words substituted by Design Right (Proceedings before Comptroller) (Amendment) Rules 1990/1453 rule 2(b) (13 August 1990).
3   Modified by Legal Services Act 2007 (Consequential Amendments) Order 2009/3348 art.8 (1 January 2010 being the day on which 2007 c 29 s 13 comes into force).
4.   In relation to England and Wales:
6.— Representation and rights of audience
(1) Any party to the proceedings may appear in person or be represented by counsel or a solicitor (of any part of the United Kingdom) or, subject to paragraph (4) below, a patient attorney or any other person whom he desires to represent him.
(2) Anything required or authorised by these Rules to be done by or in relation to any person may be done by or in relation to his agent. (3) Where after a person has become a party to the proceedings he appoints an agent for the first time or appoints an agent in substitution for another, the newly appointed agent shall give written notice of his appointment to the Comptroller and to every other party to the proceedings.
(4) The Comptroller may refuse to recognise as such an agent in respect of any proceedings before him–
(a)   a person who has been convicted of an offences under section 88 of the Patents Act 1949 or section 114 of the Patents Act 1977or section 276 of the Act;
(b)   a person whose name has been erased from and not restored to, or who is suspended from, the register of patent attorneys (kept in accordance with section 275 of the Act) on the ground of misconduct;
(c)   a person who is found by the Secretary of State to have been guilty of such conduct as would, in the case of a person registered in the register of patent attorneys, render the person liable to have the person's name erased from the register on the ground of misconduct;
(d)   a partnership or body corporate of which one of the partners or directors is a person whom the Comptroller could refuse to recognise under sub-paragraphs (a), (b), or (c) above.

7—Application to be made a party to proceedings

(1) A person who claims to have a substantial interest in a dispute in respect of which proceedings have been commenced may apply to the Comptroller to be made a party to the dispute in Form 2 in Schedule 1, supported by a statement of his interest. He shall serve a copy of his application, together with his statement, on every party to the proceedings.

(2) The Comptroller shall, upon being satisfied of the substantial interest of that person in the dispute, grant the application and shall give such directions or

further directions under rule 4(1) as may be necessary to enable that person to participate in the proceedings as a party to the dispute.

8 Withdrawal of reference

A party (including a person made a party to the proceedings under rule 7) may at any time before the Comptroller's decision withdraw from the proceedings by serving a notice to that effect on the Comptroller and every other party to the proceedings, but such withdrawal shall be without prejudice to the Comptroller's power to make an order as to the payment of costs incurred up to the time of service of the notice.

9 Decision of the Comptroller

After hearing the party or parties desiring to be heard, or if none of the parties so desires, then without a hearing, the Comptroller shall decide the dispute and notify his decision to the parties, giving written reasons for his decision if so required by any party.

10—Commencement of proceedings

(1) Proceedings in respect of an application to the Comptroller–

(a) under section 247 of the Act, to settle the terms of a licence available as of right by virtue of section 237 or under an order under section 238 of the Act, or

(b) under paragraph 19(2) of Schedule 1 to the Act, to settle the terms of a licence available as of right in respect of a design recorded or embodied in a design document or model before 1st August 1989, or

(c) brought by virtue of paragraph 19(5) of Schedule 1 to the Act, to adjust the terms of a licence granted before 1st August 1989 in respect of a design referred to in sub-paragraph (b) above,

shall be commenced by the service by the applicant on the Comptroller of a notice in Form 3 in Schedule 1.

(2) There shall be served with the notice a statement in duplicate setting out–

(a) in the case of an application referred to in paragraph (1)(a) or (b) above, the terms of the licence which the applicant requires the Comptroller to settle and, unless the application is one to which rule 13 relates, the name and address of the owner of the design right or, as the case may be, the copyright owner of the design;

(b) in the case of an application referred to in paragraph (1)(c) above, the date and terms of the licence and the grounds on which the applicant requires the Comptroller to adjust those terms and the name and address of the grantor of the licence.

(3) Within 14 days of the receipt of the notice the Comptroller shall send a copy of it, together with a copy of the applicant's statement, to the person (hereinafter in this rule referred to as the respondent) shown in the application as the design right owner, copyright owner or grantor of the licence, as appropriate.

Design Right (Proceedings before Comptroller) Rules 1989

(4) Within 6 weeks of the receipt by him of the notice sent under paragraph (3) above the respondent shall, if he does not agreed to the terms of the licence required by the applicant to be settled or, as the case may be, adjusted, serve a notice of objection on the Comptroller with a statement setting out the grounds of his objection and at the same time shall serve a copy of the same on the applicant.

(5) Within 4 weeks of the receipt of the notice of objection the applicant may serve on the Comptroller a counter-statement and at the same time serve a copy of it on the respondent.

(6) No amended statement or further statement shall be served by either party except by leave or direction of the Comptroller.

11 Directions, procedure and evidence

Rules 4, 5, 6 and 8 shall apply in respect of proceedings under rule 10 as they apply in respect of proceedings under rule 3.

12 Decision of the Comptroller

After hearing the party or parties desiring to be heard, or if none of the parties so desires, then without a hearing, the Comptroller shall decide the application and notify his decision to the parties, giving written reasons for his decision if so required by any party.

13—Commencement of proceedings

(1) Where a person making an application under rule 10(1)(a) or (b) is unable (after making such inquiries as he considers reasonable) to discover the identity of the design right owner or, as the case may be, the copyright owner, he shall serve with his notice under that rule a statement to that effect, setting out particulars of the inquiries made by him as to the identity of the owner of the right and the result of those inquiries.

(2) The Comptroller may require the applicant to make such further inquiries into the identity of the owner of the right as he thinks fit and, may for that purpose, require him to publish in such a manner as the Comptroller considers appropriate particulars of the application.

(3) The Comptroller shall, upon being satisfied from the applicant's statement or the further inquiries made under paragraph (2) above that the identity of the owner of the right cannot be discovered, consider the application and settle the terms of the licence.

14—Commencement of proceedings

(1) Where the Comptroller has, in settling the terms of the licence under rule 13, ordered that the licence shall be free of any obligation as to royalties or other payments, the design right owner or copyright owner (as the case may be) may serve on the Comptroller a notice in Form 4 in Schedule 1 applying for the terms of the licence to be varied from the date of his application. There shall be

served with the notice a statement in duplicate setting out the particulars of the grounds for variation and the terms required to be varied.

(2) Within 14 days of the receipt of the notice the Comptroller shall send a copy of the notice, together with the design right or copyright owner's statement, to the applicant under rule 10 (hereinafter in this rule referred to as the licensee).

(3) The licensee shall, if he does not agree to the terms as required to be varied by the design right or copyright owner, within 6 weeks of the receipt of the notice serve notice of objection on the Comptroller with a statement setting out the grounds of his objection and at the same time shall serve a copy of the same on the design right or copyright owner, as the case may be.

(4) Within 4 weeks of the receipt of the notice of objection the design right or copyright owner may serve on the Comptroller a counter-statement, and at the same time shall serve a copy of it on the licensee.

(5) No amended statement or further statement shall be served by either party except by leave or direction of the Comptroller.

15   Directions, procedure and evidence

Rules 4, 5, 6 and 8 shall apply in respect of proceedings under rule 14 as they apply in respect of proceedings under rule 3.

16   Decision of the Comptroller

After hearing the party or parties desiring to be heard, or if none of the parties so desires, then without a hearing, the Comptroller shall decide the application and notify his decision to the parties, giving written reasons for his decision if so required by any party.

17   Rectification of irregularities

Any document filed in any proceedings may, if the Comptroller thinks fit, be amended, and any irregularity in procedure may be rectified by the Comptroller on such terms as he may direct.

18—Evidence

(1) Any statutory declaration or affidavit filed in any proceedings shall be made and subscribed as follows—

- (a)   in the United Kingdom, before any justice of the peace or any commissioner or other officer authorised by law in any part of the United Kingdom to administer an oath for the purpose of any legal proceedings;
- (b)   in any other part of Her Majesty's dominions or in the Republic of Ireland, before any court, judge, justice of the peace or any officer authorised by law to administer an oath there for the purpose of any legal proceedings; and

(c) elsewhere, before a British Minister, or person exercising the functions of a British Minister, or a Consul, Vice-Consul or other person exercising the functions of a British Consul or before a notary public, judge or magistrate.

(2) Any document purporting to have fixed, impressed or subscribed thereto or thereon the seal or signature of any person authorised by paragraph (1) above to take a declaration may be admitted by the Comptroller without proof of the genuineness of the seal or signature or of the official character of the person or his authority to take the declaration.

(3) In England and Wales, the Comptroller shall, in relation to the giving of evidence (including evidence on oath), the attendance of witnesses and the discovery and production of documents, have all the powers of a judge of the High Court, other than the power to punish summarily for contempt of court.

(4) In Scotland, the Comptroller shall, in relation to the giving of evidence (including evidence on oath), have all the powers which a Lord Ordinary of the Court of Session has in an action before him, other than the power to punish summarily for contempt of court, and, in relation to the attendance of witnesses and the recovery and production of documents, have all the powers of the Court of Session.

[18(A)

Any witness statement filed under these Rules shall–

(a) be a written statement signed and dated by a person which contains the evidence which the person signing it would be allowed to give orally; and

(b) include a statement by the intended witness that he believes the facts in it are true.]¹.

NOTES
1   Added by Design Right (Proceedings before Comptroller) (Amendment) Rules 1999/3195 rule 5. (22 December 1999; save that rules 3, 4 and 6 shall not apply to any proceedings already begun before the Comptroller at the time of entry into force of these Rules but that they should apply to such proceedings from 26 April 2000).

19   Appointment of advisers

The Comptroller may appoint an adviser to assist him in any proceedings and shall settle the question or instructions to be submitted or given to such an adviser.

20—Time

[(1) The times or periods prescribed by these Rules for doing any act or taking any proceedings thereunder may be extended or shortened by the Comptroller if he thinks fit, upon such notice and upon such terms as he may direct, and an extension may be granted although the time for doing such act or taking such proceedings has already expired.]¹.

Appendix 3 Legislation

(2) Where the last day for the doing of any act falls on a day on which the Patent Office is closed and by reason thereof the act cannot be done on that day, it may be done on the next day on which the Office is open.

NOTES
1 Substituted by Design Right (Proceedings before Comptroller) (Amendment) Rules 1999/3195 rule 6. (22 December 1999; save that rules 3, 4 and 6 shall not apply to any proceedings already begun before the Comptroller at the time of entry into force of these Rules but that they should apply to such proceedings from 26 April 2000).

21 Hours of business

For the purposes of these Rules the Patent Office shall be open Monday to Friday–

(a) between [9.00 a.m.][1] and midnight, for the filing of applications, forms and other documents, and
(b) between [9.00 a.m.][1] and [5.00 p.m.][2] for all other purposes,

excluding Good Friday, Christmas Day [, Tuesday 4th January 2000] and any day specified or proclaimed to be a bank holiday under section 1 of the Banking and Financial Dealings Act 1971.

NOTES
1 Words substituted by Design Right (Proceedings before Comptroller) (Amendment) Rules 1999/3195 rule 7(a) (22 December 1999; save that rules 3, 4 and 6 shall not apply to any proceedings already begun before the Comptroller at the time of entry into force of these Rules but that they should apply to such proceedings from 26 April 2000).
2 Words substituted by Design Right (Proceedings before Comptroller) (Amendment) Rules 1999/3195 rule 7(b) (22 December 1999; save that rules 3, 4 and 6 shall not apply to any proceedings already begun before the Comptroller at the time of entry into force of these Rules but that they should apply to such proceedings from 26 April 2000).
3 Words added by Design Right (Proceedings before Comptroller) (Amendment) Rules 1999/3195 rule 7(c) (22 December 1999; save that rules 3,4 and 6 shall not apply to any proceedings already begun before the Comptroller at the time of entry into force of these Rules but that they should apply to such proceedings from 26 April 2000).

22—Costs

(1) The Comptroller may, in respect of any proceedings, by order award such costs or, in Scotland, such expenses as he considers reasonable and direct how, to what party and from what parties they are to be paid.

(2) Where any applicant or a person making an application under rule 7 neither resides nor carries on business in the United Kingdom or another member State of the European Economic Community the Comptroller may require him to give security for the costs or expenses of the proceedings and in default of such security being given may treat the reference or application as abandoned.

23—Service and translation of documents

(1) Every person concerned in any proceedings to which these Rules relate shall furnish to the Comptroller an address for service […]¹, and that address may be treated for all purposes connected with such proceedings as the address of the person concerned.

[(1A) The address for service shall be an address in the United Kingdom, another EEA state or the Channel Islands.]².

(2) Where any document or part of a document which is in a language other than English is served on the Comptroller or any party to proceedings or filed with the Comptroller in pursuance of these Rules, it shall be accompanied by a translation into English of the document or part, verified to the satisfaction of the Comptroller as corresponding to the original text.

NOTES
  1   Words repealed by Patents, Trade Marks and Designs (Address For Service and Time Limits, etc) Rules 2006/760 rule 3(2) (6 April 2006).
  2   Substituted by Patents, Trade Marks and Designs (Address for Service) Rules 2009/546 rule 3 (6 April 2009).

24   Fees

The fees specified in Schedule 2 shall be payable in respect of the matters there mentioned.

Appendix 3 Legislation

Schedule I
FORMS

Design Right
Form I

Reference of dispute to Comptroller

<table>
<tr><td></td><td>For Official Use</td></tr>
</table>

Design Right Form 1
Notice of counter-statement

Reference of dispute to Comptroller

Copyright, Designs
& Patents Act 1988

Notes
Please type or write in dark ink using
BLOCK LETTERS. For details of
prescribed fees please contact the
Intellectual Property Office.

Rule 3 of the Design Right
(proceedings before Comptroller)
Rules 1989 is the main rule governing
the completion and filing of this form.

This form must be filed together with
a statement in duplicate setting out
the matters referred to in Rule 3(1).

4. Identification may be made by
providing drawings, photographs
or other identifying material.

 Please tick
correct box
where appropriate

1. Your reference
2. Please give full name and address of person making the reference.
Name
Address
Postcode
ADP number (if known)
3. Please give an address for service in the United Kingdom to which all correspondence will be sent.
Name
Address
Postcode
ADP number (if known)
4. Please identify the design which is the subject of the proceedings.
5. The dispute to be settled is in respect of:
the subsistence of the design right ☐
the term of the design right ☐
the identity of the person in whom design right first vested ☐
6. Please give the name and address of the other party to the dispute.
Name
Address
Postcode
ADP number (if known)

Signature	Date

Reminder
Have you attached: the statement case in duplicate? ☐
the prescribed fee? ☐

Issued 2007

Design Right (Proceedings before Comptroller) Rules 1989

Design Right
Form 2

Application to be made a party to proceedings

<table>
<tr><td></td><td>For Official Use</td></tr>
</table>

Design Right Form 2
Application to be made a party to proceedings

Reference of dispute to Comptroller

Copyright, Designs
& Patents Act 1988

Notes
Please type or write in dark ink using
BLOCK LETTERS. For details of
prescribed fees please contact the
UK Intellectual Property Office.

Rule 7 of the Design Right
(Proceedings before Comptroller)
Rules 1989 is the main rule governing
the completion and filing of this form.

A statement to show your substantial
interest in the dispute in respect of
which proceedings have been
commenced must accompany this
form. You must also serve a copy of
the form and statement on every
party to the proceedings.

1. Your reference

2. Please give full name and address of person applying to be made a party to dispute.

Name

Address

Postcode

ADP number (if known)

3. Please give an address for service in the United Kingdom to which all correspondence will be sent.

Name

Address

Postcode

ADP number (if known)

4. Please identify the proceedings relating to the dispute in which you claim to have a substantial interest.

Signature	Date

Reminder
Have you attached: a statement of your interest? ☐
                       the prescribed fee? ☐

☑ Please tick
correct box
where appropriate

Issued 2007

223

Appendix 3 Legislation

Design Right
Form 3

Application to settle terms of Licence of Right or to adjust terms of Licence granted before 1st August 1989

Design Right Form 3

Application to settle terms of Licence of Right
or to adjust terms of Licence granted before
1st August 1989

For Official Use

Copyright, Designs
& Patents Act 1988

Notes
Please type or write in dark ink using
BLOCK LETTERS. For details of
prescribed fees please contact the
Intellectual Property Office.

Rule 10 and 13 of the Design Right
(Proceedings before Comptroller)
Rules 1989 are the main rules
governing the completion and filing of
this form.

This form must be filed, by the person
requiring the settlement or adjustment
of the licence, together with a
statement in duplicate setting out the
terms required. Where the
applicant has been unable to discover
the identity of the design right or
copyright owner a statement must also
be filed setting out the particulars of
and result of the inquiries made to try
to identify the owner.

4. Identification may be made by
providing drawings, photographs
or other identifying material.

5. Give the name and address of the
design right or copyright owner (if
known).

☑ Please tick
   correct box
   where appropriate

---

1. Your reference

2. Please give full name and address of applicant.

Name

Address
                                               Postcode
ADP number (if known)

3. Please give an address for service in the United Kingdom to which all
correspondence will be sent.

Name

Address
                                               Postcode
ADP number (if known)

4. Please identify the design which is the subject of the proceedings.

5. Please give the name and address of the respondent

Name

Address
                                               Postcode
ADP number (if known)

6. Application is made to the Comptroller to settle the terms of a licence for the
design which is available as of right by virtue of:
                                         Section 237 ☐

                              an order under Section 238 ☐

Signature	Date

Reminder
Have you attached: the statement in duplicate of the terms required? ☐
                                               the prescribed fee? ☐
                         a statement of inquiries made to identify the
                  design right or copyright owner (if inquiries unsuccessful)? ☐

Issued 2007

Design Right (Proceedings before Comptroller) Rules 1989

Design Right
Form 4

Application by Design Right or Copyright owner to vary terms of licence of right

For Official Use

Design Right Form 4

Application by Design Right or
Copyright owner to vary terms of licence of right

Copyright, Designs
& Patents Act 1988

Notes
Please type or write in dark ink using
BLOCK LETTERS. For details of
prescribed fees please contact the
Intellectual Property Office.

Rule 14 of the Design Right
(Proceedings before Comptroller)
Rules 1989 is the main rule governing
the completion and filing of this form.

This form must be filed together with
a statement in duplicate setting out
the particular of the grounds for
variation and the terms required to be
varied.

1. Your reference
2. Please give full name and address of applicant.   Name   Address   Postcode   ADP number (if known)
3. Please give an address for service in the United Kingdom to which all correspondence will be sent.   Name   Address   Postcode   ADP number (if known)
4. Please identify the licence which is the subject of the application.
5. Please give the name and address of the licence holder.   Name   Address   Postcode   ADP number (if known)

Signature	Date

Reminder
Have you attached: a statement in duplicate of the grounds for variation and the terms required? ☐
the prescribed fee? ☐

 Please tick
correct box
where appropriate

Issued 2007

225

Schedule 2
FEES

[1.	On reference of dispute (Form 1) under rule 3(1)	£65
2.	On application (Form 2) under rule 7(1)	£40
3.	On application (Form 3) under rule 10(1)	£65
4.	On application (Form 4) under rule 14(1)	£65

]¹.

[…]².

[…]³.

NOTES

1 Substituted by Design Right (Proceedings before Comptroller) (Amendment) Rules 1992/615 rule 2 (11 May 1992).

2 Substituted by Design Right (Proceedings before Comptroller) (Amendment) Rules 1991/1626 rule 2 (12 August 1991).

3 Substituted by Design Right (Proceedings before Comptroller) (Amendment) (No. 2) Rules 1990/1699 rule 2 (10 September 1990).

Registered Designs Regulations 2001

2001/3949

Whereas a draft of the following Regulations has been approved by resolution of each House of Parliament:

Now, therefore, the Secretary of State, being designated for the purposes of section 2(2) of the European Communities Act 1972 in relation to measures relating to the legal protection of designs, in exercise of the powers conferred on her by the said section 2(2) hereby makes the following Regulations:

NOTES

1. SI 2000/1813.

1 Citation, commencement and extent

(1) These Regulations may be cited as the Registered Designs Regulations 2001 and shall come into force on the day after the day on which they are made.

(2) Subject to paragraph (3), these Regulations extend to England and Wales, Scotland and Northern Ireland.

(3) The amendments made by these Regulations to the Chartered Associations (Protection of Names and Uniforms) Act 1926 do not extend to Northern Ireland.

2. Designs registrable under the 1949 Act

For section 1 of the Registered Designs Act 1949 (designs registrable under Act) there shall be substituted—

1 Registration of designs

(1) A design may, subject to the following provisions of this Act, be registered under this Act on the making of an application for registration.

(2) In this Act "design" means the appearance of the whole or a part of a product resulting from the features of, in particular, the lines, contours, colours, shape, texture or materials of the product or its ornamentation.

(3) In this Act—

"complex product" means a product which is composed of at least two replaceable component parts permitting disassembly and reassembly of the product; and

"product" means any industrial or handicraft item other than a computer program; and, in particular, includes packaging, get-up, graphic symbols, typographic type-faces and parts intended to be assembled into a complex product.

1A Substantive grounds for refusal of registration.

(1) The following shall be refused registration under this Act—

(a) anything which does not fulfil the requirements of section 1(2) of this Act;

(b) designs which do not fulfil the requirements of sections 1B to 1D of this Act;

(c) designs to which a ground of refusal mentioned in Schedule A1 to this Act applies.

(2) A design ("the later design") shall be refused registration under this Act if it is not new or does not have individual character when compared with a design which—

(a) has been made available to the public on or after the relevant date; but

(b) is protected as from a date prior to the relevant date by virtue of registration under this Act or an application for such registration.

(3) In subsection (2) above "the relevant date" means the date on which the application for the registration of the later design was made or is treated by virtue of section 3B(2), (3) or (5) or 14(2) of this Act as having been made.

1B Requirement of novelty and individual character

(1) A design shall be protected by a right in a registered design to the extent that the design is new and has individual character.

(2) For the purposes of subsection (1) above, a design is new if no identical design or no design whose features differ only in immaterial details has been made available to the public before the relevant date.

(3) For the purposes of subsection (1) above, a design has individual character if the overall impression it produces on the informed user differs from the overall impression produced on such a user by any design which has been made available to the public before the relevant date.

(4) In determining the extent to which a design has individual character, the degree of freedom of the author in creating the design shall be taken into consideration.

(5) For the purposes of this section, a design has been made available to the public before the relevant date if—

    (a)   it has been published (whether following registration or otherwise), exhibited, used in trade or otherwise disclosed before that date; and

    (b)   the disclosure does not fall within subsection (6) below.

(6) A disclosure falls within this subsection if—

    (a)   it could not reasonably have become known before the relevant date in the normal course of business to persons carrying on business in the European Economic Area and specialising in the sector concerned;

    (b)   it was made to a person other than the designer, or any successor in title of his, under conditions of confidentiality (whether express or implied);

    (c)   it was made by the designer, or any successor in title of his, during the period of 12 months immediately preceding the relevant date;

    (d)   it was made by a person other than the designer, or any successor in title of his, during the period of 12 months immediately preceding the relevant date in consequence of information provided or other action taken by the designer or any successor in title of his; or

    (e)   it was made during the period of 12 months immediately preceding the relevant date as a consequence of an abuse in relation to the designer or any successor in title of his.

(7) In subsections (2), (3), (5) and (6) above "the relevant date" means the date on which the application for the registration of the design was made or is treated by virtue of section 3B(2), (3) or (5) or 14(2) of this Act as having been made.

(8) For the purposes of this section, a design applied to or incorporated in a product which constitutes a component part of a complex product shall only be considered to be new and to have individual character—

    (a)   if the component part, once it has been incorporated into the complex product, remains visible during normal use of the complex product; and

    (b)   to the extent that those visible features of the component part are in themselves new and have individual character.

(9) In subsection (8) above "normal use" means use by the end user; but does not include any maintenance, servicing or repair work in relation to the product.

IC   Designs dictated by their technical function

(1) A right in a registered design shall not subsist in features of appearance of a product which are solely dictated by the product's technical function.

(2) A right in a registered design shall not subsist in features of appearance of a product which must necessarily be reproduced in their exact form and dimensions so as to permit the product in which the design is incorporated or to which it is applied to be mechanically connected to, or placed in, around or against, another product so that either product may perform its function.

(3) Subsection (2) above does not prevent a right in a registered design subsisting in a design serving the purpose of allowing multiple assembly or connection of mutually interchangeable products within a modular system.

ID   Designs contrary to public policy or morality

A right in a registered design shall not subsist in a design which is contrary to public policy or to accepted principles of morality."

NOTES
1. Section 1 as originally enacted was substituted by section 265 of the Copyright, Designs and Patents Act 1988 ("the 1988 Act") but not in relation to applications for registration made before 1st August 1989. Subsection (6) was added by section 13(1) of the Olympic Symbol etc. (Protection) Act 1995 (c. 32) in relation to applications for registration made on or after 20 September 1995.

3   Designs registrable under the 1949 Act: emblems etc.

Before Schedule 1 to the Registered Designs Act 1949 there shall be inserted—

SCHEDULE A1
GROUNDS FOR REFUSAL OF REGISTRATION IN RELATION TO EMBLEMS ETC.

1.   — Grounds for refusal in relation to certain emblems etc.

(1) A design shall be refused registration under this Act if it involves the use of—

(a)   the Royal arms, or any of the principal armorial bearings of the Royal arms, or any insignia or device so nearly resembling the Royal arms or any such armorial bearing as to be likely to be mistaken for them or it;

(b)   a representation of the Royal crown or any of the Royal flags;

(c)   a representation of Her Majesty or any member of the Royal family, or any colourable imitation thereof; or

(d)   words, letters or devices likely to lead persons to think that the applicant either has or recently has had Royal patronage or authorisation;

unless it appears to the registrar that consent for such use has been given by or on behalf of Her Majesty or (as the case may be) the relevant member of the Royal family.

(2) A design shall be refused registration under this Act if it involves the use of—

(a)   the national flag of the United Kingdom (commonly known as the Union Jack); or

(b)   the flag of England, Wales, Scotland, Northern Ireland or the Isle of Man,

and it appears to the registrar that the use would be misleading or grossly offensive.

(3) A design shall be refused registration under this Act if it involves the use of—

(a)   arms to which a person is entitled by virtue of a grant of arms by the Crown; or

(b)   insignia so nearly resembling such arms as to be likely to be mistaken for them;

unless it appears to the registrar that consent for such use has been given by or on behalf of the person concerned and the use is not in any way contrary to the law of arms.

(4) A design shall be refused registration under this Act if it involves the use of a controlled representation within the meaning of the Olympic Symbol etc. (Protection) Act 1995 unless it appears to the registrar that—

(a)   the application is made by the person for the time being appointed under section 1(2) of the Olympic Symbol etc. (Protection) Act 1995 (power of Secretary of State to appoint a person as the proprietor of the Olympics association right); or

(b)   consent for such use has been given by or on behalf of the person mentioned in paragraph (a) above.

2.   — Grounds for refusal in relation to emblems etc. of Paris Convention countries

(1) A design shall be refused registration under this Act if it involves the use of the flag of a Paris Convention country unless—

(a)   the authorisation of the competent authorities of that country has been given for the registration; or

(b)   it appears to the registrar that the use of the flag in the manner proposed is permitted without such authorisation.

(2) A design shall be refused registration under this Act if it involves the use of the armorial bearings or any other state emblem of a Paris Convention country which is protected under the Paris Convention unless the authorisation of the competent authorities of that country has been given for the registration.

(3) A design shall be refused registration under this Act if—

(a)   the design involves the use of an official sign or hallmark adopted by a Paris Convention country and indicating control and warranty;

(b)   the sign or hallmark is protected under the Paris Convention; and

(c)   the design could be applied to or incorporated in goods of the same, or a similar, kind as those in relation to which the sign or hallmark indicates control and warranty;

unless the authorisation of the competent authorities of that country has been given for the registration.

(4) The provisions of this paragraph as to national flags and other state emblems, and official signs or hallmarks, apply equally to anything which from a heraldic point of view imitates any such flag or other emblem, or sign or hallmark.

(5) Nothing in this paragraph prevents the registration of a design on the application of a national of a country who is authorised to make use of a state emblem, or official sign or hallmark, of that country, notwithstanding that it is similar to that of another country.

3. — Grounds for refusal in relation to emblems etc. of certain international organisations

(1) This paragraph applies to—

(a)   the armorial bearings, flags or other emblems; and

(b)   the abbreviations and names,

of international intergovernmental organisations of which one or more Paris Convention countries are members.

(2) A design shall be refused registration under this Act if it involves the use of any such emblem, abbreviation or name which is protected under the Paris Convention unless—

(a)   the authorisation of the international organisation concerned has been given for the registration; or

(b)   it appears to the registrar that the use of the emblem, abbreviation or name in the manner proposed—

(i)   is not such as to suggest to the public that a connection exists between the organisation and the design; or

(ii)   is not likely to mislead the public as to the existence of a connection between the user and the organisation.

(3) The provisions of this paragraph as to emblems of an international organisation apply equally to anything which from a heraldic point of view imitates any such emblem.

(4) Nothing in this paragraph affects the rights of a person whose *bona fide* use of the design in question began before 4th January 1962 (when the relevant provisions of the Paris Convention entered into force in relation to the United Kingdom).

4. — Paragraphs 2 and 3: supplementary

(1) For the purposes of paragraph 2 above state emblems of a Paris Convention country (other than the national flag), and official signs or hallmarks, shall be regarded as protected under the Paris Convention only if, or to the extent that—

> (a) the country in question has notified the United Kingdom in accordance with Article 6*ter*(3) of the Convention that it desires to protect that emblem, sign or hallmark;
>
> (b) the notification remains in force; and
>
> (c) the United Kingdom has not objected to it in accordance with Article 6*ter*(4) or any such objection has been withdrawn.

(2) For the purposes of paragraph 3 above the emblems, abbreviations and names of an international organisation shall be regarded as protected under the Paris Convention only if, or to the extent that—

> (a) the organisation in question has notified the United Kingdom in accordance with Article 6*ter*(3) of the Convention that it desires to protect that emblem, abbreviation or name;
>
> (b) the notification remains in force; and
>
> (c) the United Kingdom has not objected to it in accordance with Article 6*ter*(4) or any such objection has been withdrawn.

(3) Notification under Article 6*ter*(3) of the Paris Convention shall have effect only in relation to applications for the registration of designs made more than two months after the receipt of the notification.

5. Interpretation

In this Schedule—

> "a Paris Convention country" means a country, other than the United Kingdom, which is a party to the Paris Convention; and
>
> "the Paris Convention" means the Paris Convention for the Protection of Industrial Property of 20th March 1883.

4. Registration of designs: general

For section 3 of the Registered Designs Act 1949 (proceedings for registration) there shall be substituted—

"3. — Applications for registration.

(1) An application for the registration of a design shall be made in the prescribed form and shall be filed at the Patent Office in the prescribed manner.

(2) An application for the registration of a design shall be made by the person claiming to be the proprietor of the design.

(3) An application for the registration of a design in which national unregistered design right subsists shall be made by the person claiming to be the design right owner.

(4) For the purpose of deciding whether, and to what extent, a design is new or has individual character, the registrar may make such searches (if any) as he thinks fit.

(5) An application for the registration of a design which, owing to any default or neglect on the part of the applicant, has not been completed so as to enable registration to be effected within such time as may be prescribed shall be deemed to be abandoned.

3A. — Determination of applications for registration.

(1) Subject as follows, the registrar shall not refuse an application for the registration of a design.

(2) If it appears to the registrar that an application for the registration of a design has not been made in accordance with any rules made under this Act, he may refuse the application.

(3) If it appears to the registrar that an application for the registration of a design has not been made in accordance with sections 3(2) and (3) and 14(1) of this Act, he shall refuse the application.

(4) If it appears to the registrar that any ground for refusal of registration mentioned in section 1A of this Act applies in relation to an application for the registration of a design, he shall refuse the application.

3B. — Modification of applications for registration.

(1) The registrar may, at any time before an application for the registration of a design is determined, permit the applicant to make such modifications of the application as the registrar thinks fit.

(2) Where an application for the registration of a design has been modified before it has been determined in such a way that the design has been altered significantly, the registrar may, for the purposes of deciding whether and to what extent the design is new or has individual character, direct that the application shall be treated as having been made on the date on which it was so modified.

(3) Where—

    (a) an application for the registration of a design has disclosed more than one design and has been modified before it has been determined to exclude one or more designs from the application; and

    (b) a subsequent application for the registration of a design so excluded has, within such period (if any) as has been prescribed for such applications, been made by the person who made the earlier application or his successor in title,

the registrar may, for the purpose of deciding whether and to what extent the design is new or has individual character, direct that the subsequent application shall be treated as having been made on the date on which the earlier application was, or is treated as having been, made.

(4) Where an application for the registration of a design has been refused on any ground mentioned in section 1A(1)(b) or (c) of this Act, the application may be modified by the applicant if it appears to the registrar that—

(a)   the identity of the design is retained; and
(b)   the modifications have been made in accordance with any rules made under this Act.

(5) An application modified under subsection (4) above shall be treated as the original application and, in particular, as made on the date on which the original application was made or is treated as having been made.

(6) Any modification under this section may, in particular, be effected by making a partial disclaimer in relation to the application.

3C.   — Date of registration of designs.

(1) Subject as follows, a design, when registered, shall be registered as of the date on which the application was made or is treated as having been made.

(2) Subsection (1) above shall not apply to an application which is treated as having been made on a particular date by section 14(2) of this Act or by virtue of the operation of section 3B(3) or (5) of this Act by reference to section 14(2) of this Act.

(3) A design, when registered, shall be registered as of—

(a)   in the case of an application which is treated as having been made on a particular date by section 14(2) of this Act, the date on which the application was made;
(b)   in the case of an application which is treated as having been made on a particular date by virtue of the operation of section 3B(3) of this Act by reference to section 14(2) of this Act, the date on which the earlier application was made;

(c) in the case of an application which is treated as having been made on a particular date by virtue of the operation of section 3B(5) of this Act by reference to section 14(2) of this Act, the date on which the original application was made.

3D.   Appeals in relation to applications for registration.

An appeal lies from any decision of the registrar under section 3A or 3B of this Act."

NOTES
1. Section 3(2) to (7) was substituted by section 272 of, and paragraph 1 of Schedule 3 to, the 1988 Act.

5.   Right given by registration under the 1949 Act

For section 7 of the Registered Designs Act 1949 (right given by registration) there shall be substituted—

"7. — Right given by registration.

(1) The registration of a design under this Act gives the registered proprietor the exclusive right to use the design and any design which does not produce on the informed user a different overall impression.

(2) For the purposes of subsection (1) above and section 7A of this Act any reference to the use of a design includes a reference to—

    (a) the making, offering, putting on the market, importing, exporting or using of a product in which the design is incorporated or to which it is applied; or

    (b) stocking such a product for those purposes.

(3) In determining for the purposes of subsection (1) above whether a design produces a different overall impression on the informed user, the degree of freedom of the author in creating his design shall be taken into consideration.

(4) The right conferred by subsection (1) above is subject to any limitation attaching to the registration in question (including, in particular, any partial disclaimer or any declaration by the registrar or a court of partial invalidity).

7A. — Infringements of rights in registered designs.

(1) Subject as follows, the right in a registered design is infringed by a person who, without the consent of the registered proprietor, does anything which by virtue of section 7 of this Act is the exclusive right of the registered proprietor.

(2) The right in a registered design is not infringed by—

    (a) an act which is done privately and for purposes which are not commercial;

    (b) an act which is done for experimental purposes;

    (c) an act of reproduction for teaching purposes or for the purposes of making citations provided that the conditions mentioned in subsection (3) below are satisfied;

    (d) the use of equipment on ships or aircraft which are registered in another country but which are temporarily in the United Kingdom;

    (e) the importation into the United Kingdom of spare parts or accessories for the purposes of repairing such ships or aircraft; or (f) the carrying out of repairs on such ships or aircraft.

(3) The conditions mentioned in this subsection are—

    (a) the act of reproduction is compatible with fair trade practice and does not unduly prejudice the normal exploitation of the design; and

    (b) mention is made of the source.

(4) The right in a registered design is not infringed by an act which relates to a product in which any design protected by the registration is incorporated or to which it is applied if the product has been put on the market in the European Economic Area by the registered proprietor or with his consent.

(5) The right in a registered design of a component part which may be used for the purpose of the repair of a complex product so as to restore its original appearance is not infringed by the use for that purpose of any design protected by the registration.

(6) No proceedings shall be taken in respect of an infringement of the right in a registered design committed before the date on which the certificate of registration of the design under this Act is granted."

NOTES
1. Section 7 as originally enacted was substituted by section 268 of the 1988 Act but not in relation to a design registered in pursuance of an application made before 1st August 1989.

6. — Removal of compulsory licence regimes

(1) Section 10 of the Registered Designs Act 1949 (compulsory licence in respect of registered design) shall be omitted.

(2) In section 11A of that Act (powers exercisable for protection of the public interest), in subsection (3) (power to ensure licences available as of right)—

(a) paragraph (b) and the word ""or"" immediately preceding it shall be omitted; and
(b) the words from ""or may, instead"" to the end of the subsection shall be omitted.

NOTES
1. Section 11A was inserted by section 270 of the 1988 Act.

7. Cancellation and invalidation of registration

For section 11 of the Registered Designs Act 1949[1] (cancellation of registration) there shall be substituted—

"11. Cancellation of registration.

The registrar may, upon a request made in the prescribed manner by the registered proprietor, cancel the registration of a design.

11ZA. — Grounds for invalidity of registration.

(1) The registration of a design may be declared invalid on any of the grounds mentioned in section 1A of this Act.

(2) The registration of a design may be declared invalid on the ground of the registered proprietor not being the proprietor of the design and the proprietor of the design objecting.

(3) The registration of a design involving the use of an earlier distinctive sign may be declared invalid on the ground of an objection by the holder of rights to the sign which include the right to prohibit in the United Kingdom such use of the sign.

(4) The registration of a design constituting an unauthorised use of a work protected by the law of copyright in the United Kingdom may be declared invalid on the ground of an objection by the owner of the copyright.

(5) In this section and sections 11ZB, 11ZC and 11ZE of this Act (other than section 11ZE(1)) references to the registration of a design include references to the former registration of a design; and these sections shall apply, with necessary modifications, in relation to such former registrations.

11ZB. — Applications for declaration of invalidity.

(1) Any person interested may make an application to the registrar for a declaration of invalidity on the ground mentioned in section 1A(1)(a) or (b) of this Act.

(2) Any person concerned by the use in question may make an application to the registrar for a declaration of invalidity on the ground mentioned in section 1A(1)(c) of this Act.

(3) The relevant person may make an application to the registrar for a declaration of invalidity on the ground mentioned in section 1A(2) of this Act.

(4) In subsection (3) above "the relevant person" means, in relation to an earlier design protected by virtue of registration under this Act or an application for such registration, the registered proprietor of the design or (as the case may be) the applicant.

(5) The person able to make an objection under subsection (2), (3) or (4) of section 11ZA of this Act may make an application to the registrar for a declaration of invalidity on the ground mentioned in that subsection.

(6) An application may be made under this section in relation to a design at any time after the design has been registered.

11ZC. — Determination of applications for declaration of invalidity.

(1) This section applies where an application has been made to the registrar for a declaration of invalidity in relation to a registration.

(2) If it appears to the registrar that the application has not been made in accordance with any rules made under this Act, he may refuse the application.

(3) If it appears to the registrar that the application has not been made in accordance with section 11ZB of this Act, he shall refuse the application.

(4) Subject to subsections (2) and (3) above, the registrar shall make a declaration of invalidity if it appears to him that the ground of invalidity specified in the application has been established in relation to the registration.

(5) Otherwise the registrar shall refuse the application.

(6) A declaration of invalidity may be a declaration of partial invalidity.

11ZD. — Modification of registration.

(1) Subsections (2) and (3) below apply where the registrar intends to declare the registration of a design invalid on any ground mentioned in section 1A(1)(b) or (c) or 11ZA(3) or (4) of this Act.

(2) The registrar shall inform the registered proprietor of that fact.

(3) The registered proprietor may make an application to the registrar for the registrar to make such modifications to the registration of the design as the registered proprietor specifies in his application.

(4) Such modifications may, in particular, include the inclusion on the register of a partial disclaimer by the registered proprietor.

(5) If it appears to the registrar that the application has not been made in accordance with any rules made under this Act, the registrar may refuse the application.

(6) If it appears to the registrar that the identity of the design is not retained or the modified registration would be invalid by virtue of section 11ZA of this Act, the registrar shall refuse the application.

(7) Otherwise the registrar shall make the specified modifications.

(8) A modification of a registration made under this section shall have effect, and be treated always to have had effect, from the grant of registration.

11ZE. — Effect of cancellation or invalidation of registration.

(1) A cancellation of registration under section 11 of this Act takes effect from the date of the registrar's decision or from such other date as the registrar may direct.

(2) Where the registrar declares the registration of a design invalid to any extent, the registration shall to that extent be treated as having been invalid from the date of registration or from such other date as the registrar may direct.

11ZF. Appeals in relation to cancellation or invalidation.

An appeal lies from any decision of the registrar under section 11 to 11ZE of this Act."

NOTES

1. Words in subsection (2) of section 11 were repealed by section 303(2) of, and Schedule 8 to, the 1988 Act. Subsections (3) to (5) of section 11 were substituted for subsection (2A) of that section (as inserted by section 44(3) of the Copyright Act 1956 (c. 74)) by section 272 of, and paragraph 6 of Schedule 3 to, the 1988 Act.

8. — Rectification of register

(1) Section 20 of the Registered Designs Act 1949 (rectification of register) shall be amended as follows.

(2) In subsection (1) (applications for rectification) for the words ""any person aggrieved" "there shall be substituted ""the relevant person"".

(3) After subsection (1) there shall be inserted—

"(1A) In subsection (1) above

"the relevant person" means—

(a) in the case of an application invoking any ground referred to in section 1A(1)(c) of this Act, any person concerned by the use in question;

(b) in the case of an application invoking the ground mentioned in section 1A(2) of this Act, the appropriate person;

(c) in the case of an application invoking any ground mentioned in section 11ZA(2), (3) or (4) of this Act, the person able to make the objection;

(d) in any other case, any person aggrieved.

(1B) In subsection (1A) above "the appropriate person" means, in relation to an earlier design protected by virtue of registration under this Act or an application for such registration, the registered proprietor of the design or (as the case may be) the applicant."

(4) After subsection (5) there shall be added—

"(6) Orders which may be made by the court under this section include, in particular, declarations of partial invalidity."

NOTES
1. Section 20(5) was added by section 272 of, and paragraph 11 of Schedule 3 to, the 1988 Act.

9. — Other modifications of enactments

(1) The amendments specified in Schedule 1 (consequential amendments) shall have effect.

(2) The repeals specified in Schedule 2 shall have effect.

10. — Transitional provisions: pending applications

(1) This Regulation applies to applications for registration under the Registered Designs Act 1949 which have been made but not finally determined before the coming into force of these Regulations ("pending applications").

(2) The Act of 1949 as it has effect immediately before the coming into force of these Regulations shall continue to apply in relation to pending applications so far as it relates to the determination of such applications.

(3) Accordingly the amendments and repeals made by these Regulations shall not apply in relation to the determination of such applications.

11. — Transitional provisions: transitional registrations

(1) This Regulation applies to any registration under the Registered Designs Act 1949 which results from the determination of a pending application (within the meaning of Regulation 10).

(2) The Act of 1949 as it has effect immediately before the coming into force of these Regulations shall continue to apply in relation to registrations to which this Regulation applies ("transitional registrations") so far as the Act relates to the cancellation or invalidation of such registrations (other than cancellation by virtue of section 11(3) of that Act).

(3) Accordingly the amendments and repeals made by these Regulations shall, so far as they relate to the cancellation or invalidation of registrations, not apply in relation to transitional registrations.

(4) The amendments and repeals made by these Regulations shall otherwise (and subject to paragraphs (5) to (9) and Regulation 14) apply in relation to transitional registrations.

(5) In the application by virtue of paragraph (4) of the amendments made by Regulation 5, the fact that transitional registrations are in respect of any articles, or sets of articles, shall be disregarded.

(6) The amendments made by Regulation 4 shall not operate so as to determine the dates of registration of designs to which transitional registrations apply; and these dates shall be determined by reference to the Act of 1949 as it has effect immediately before the coming into force of these Regulations.

(7) Where—

    (a)   any such date of registration for the purposes of calculating the period for which the right in a registered design subsists, or any extension of that period, under section 8 of the Act of 1949 is determined by virtue of section 14(2) of that Act; and

    (b)   that date is earlier than the date which would otherwise have been the date of registration for those purposes;

the difference between the two dates shall be added to the first period of five years for which the right in the registered design is to subsist.

(8) Any reference in section 8 of the Act of 1949 to a period of five years shall, in the case of any such period which is extended by virtue of paragraph (7), be treated as a reference to the extended period.

(9) The repeal by these Regulations of the proviso in section 4(1) of the Act of 1949 and of the reference to it in section 8 of that Act shall not apply to the right in a design to which a transitional registration applies.

12. — Transitional provisions: post-1989 registrations

(1) This Regulation applies to—

    (a)   any registration under the Registered Designs Act 1949 which—

        (i)   has resulted from an application made on or after 1st August 1989 and before the coming into force of these Regulations; and

        (ii)   has given rise to a right in a registered design which is in force at the coming into force of these Regulations;

    (b)   any registration under the Act of 1949 which—

    (i)   has resulted from an application made on or after 1st August 1989 and before the coming into force of these Regulations; and

    (ii)   has given rise to a right in a registered design which is not in force at the coming into force of these Regulations but which is capable of being treated as never having ceased to be in force by virtue of section 8(4) of the Act of 1949 or of being restored by virtue of sections 8A and 8B of that Act; and

(c)   any registration which subsequently ceases to fall within sub-paragraph (b) because the right in the registered design has been treated or restored as mentioned in paragraph (ii) of that sub-paragraph.

(2) The Act of 1949 as it has effect immediately before the coming into force of these Regulations shall continue to apply in relation to registrations to which this Regulation applies ("post-1989 registrations") so far as the Act relates to the cancellation or invalidation of such registrations (other than cancellation by virtue of section 11(3) of that Act and by reference to an expiry of copyright occurring on or after the coming into force of these Regulations).

(3) Accordingly the amendments and repeals made by these Regulations shall, so far as they relate to the cancellation or invalidation of registrations, not apply in relation to post-1989 registrations.

(4) The amendments and repeals made by these Regulations shall otherwise apply (subject to paragraphs (5) to (9) and Regulation 14) in relation to post-1989 registrations.

(5) In the application by virtue of paragraph (4) of the amendments made by Regulation 5, the fact that post-1989 registrations are in respect of any articles, or sets of articles, shall be disregarded.

(6) The amendments made by Regulation 4 shall not operate so as to alter the dates of registration of designs to which post-1989 registrations apply. (7) Where—

(a)   any such date of registration for the purposes of calculating the period for which the right in a registered design subsists, or any extension of that period, under section 8 of the Act of 1949 was determined by virtue of section 14(2) of that Act; and

(b)   that date is earlier than the date which would otherwise have been the date of registration for those purposes;

the difference between the two dates shall be added to any period of five years which is current on the coming into force of these Regulations or, if no such period is current but a subsequent extension or restoration is effected under section 8, or sections 8A and 8B, of the Act of 1949, to the period resulting from that extension or restoration.

(8) Any reference in section 8 of the Act of 1949 to a period of five years shall, in the case of any such period which is extended by virtue of paragraph (7), be treated as a reference to the extended period.

(9) The repeal by these Regulations of the proviso in section 4(1) of the Act of 1949 and the reference to it in section 8 of that Act shall not apply to the right in a design to which a post-1989 registration applies.

13.— Transitional provisions: pre-1989 registrations

(1) This Regulation applies to—

(a) any registration under the Registered Designs Act 1949 which—

(i) has resulted from an application made before 1st August 1989; and

(ii) has given rise to a copyright in a registered design which is in force at the coming into force of these Regulations;

(b) any registration under the Act of 1949 which—
has resulted from an application made before 1st August 1989; and has given rise to a copyright in a registered design which is not in force at the coming into force of these Regulations but which would be capable of coming back into force by virtue of an extension of the period of copyright under section 8(2) of the Act of 1949 if that provision were amended as set out in paragraph (8); and

(c) any registration which subsequently ceases to fall within sub-paragraph (b) because the copyright in the registered design has come back into force by virtue of an extension of the period of copyright under section 8(2) of the Act of 1949 as amended by paragraph (8).

(2) Subject as follows, the amendments and repeals made by these Regulations shall not apply to any provision of the Act of 1949 which only has effect in relation to applications for registration made before 1st August 1989 or any registrations resulting from such applications.

(3) Any such provision and any other provision of the Act of 1949 as it has effect immediately before the coming into force of these Regulations in relation to registrations which fall within paragraph (1) ("pre-1989 registrations") shall continue to apply so far as it relates to the cancellation or invalidation of pre-1989 registrations (other than cancellation by virtue of section 11(3) of that Act and by reference to an expiry of copyright occurring on or after the coming into force of these Regulations).

(4) Accordingly the amendments and repeals made by these Regulations shall, so far as they relate to the cancellation or invalidation of registrations, not apply in relation to pre-1989 registrations.

(5) The amendments and repeals made by these Regulations shall otherwise apply (subject to paragraphs (2) and (9) to (12) and Regulation 14) in relation to pre-1989 registrations.

(6) Amendments and repeals corresponding to the amendments and repeals made by these Regulations (other than those relating to the cancellation or invalidation of registrations) shall be treated as having effect, with necessary modifications and subject to Regulation 14, in relation to any provision of the

Act of 1949 which only has effect in relation to applications for registration made before 1st August 1989 or any registrations resulting from such applications.

(7) In the application by virtue of paragraph (6) of amendments corresponding to those made by Regulation 5, the fact that pre-1989 registrations are in respect of any articles, or sets of articles, shall be disregarded.

(8) In section 8(2) of the Act of 1949 as it has effect in relation to pre-1989 registrations (period of copyright)—

(a) after the words "second period", where they appear for the second time, there shall be inserted "and for a fourth period of five years from the expiration of the third period and for a fifth period of five years from the expiration of the fourth period";

(b) after the words "second or third" there shall be inserted "or fourth or fifth"; and

(c) after the words "second period", where they appear for the third time, there shall be inserted "or the third period or the fourth period".

(9) The amendments made by Regulation 4 shall not operate so as to alter the dates of registration of designs to which pre-1989 registrations apply.

(10) Where—

(a) the date of registration for the purposes of calculating the period of copyright, or any extension of that period, under section 8(2) of the Act of 1949 as it has effect in relation to pre-1989 registrations was determined by virtue of section 14(2) of that Act; and

(b) that date is earlier than the date which would otherwise have been the date of registration for those purposes;

the difference between the two dates shall be added to any period of five years which is current on the coming into force of these Regulations or, if no such period is current but a subsequent extension is effected under section 8 of the Act of 1949 as amended by paragraph (8), to the period resulting from that extension.

(11) Any reference in section 8(2) of the Act of 1949 as amended by paragraph (8) to a period of five years shall, in the case of any such period which is extended by virtue of paragraph (10), be treated as a reference to the extended period.

(12) The repeal by these Regulations of the proviso in section 4(1) of the Act of 1949 shall not apply to the right in a design to which a pre-1989 registration applies.

14.— Other transitional provisions

(1) Any licence which—

(a) permits anything which would otherwise be an infringement under the Registered Designs Act 1949 of the right in a registered design or the copyright in a registered design; and

(b) was granted by the registered proprietor of the design, or under section 10 or 11A of the Act of 1949, before the coming into force of these Regulations,

shall continue in force, with necessary modifications, on or after the making of these Regulations.

(2) In determining the effect of any such licence on or after the coming into force of these Regulations, regard shall be had to the purpose for which the licence was granted; and, in particular, a licence granted for the full term or extent of the right in a registered design or the copyright in a registered design shall be treated as applying, subject to its other terms and conditions, to the full term or extent of that right as extended by virtue of these Regulations.

(3) The right in a registered design conferred by virtue of these Regulations in relation to registrations to which Regulation 11, 12 or 13 applies shall not enable the registered proprietor to prevent any person from continuing to carry out acts begun by him before the coming into force of these Regulations and which, at that time, the registered proprietor or, in the case of registrations to which Regulation 11 applies, a registered proprietor would have been unable to prevent.

(4) The right in a registered design conferred by virtue of these Regulations in relation to registrations to which Regulation 12 or 13 applies shall, in particular, not apply in relation to infringements committed in relation to those registrations before the coming into force of these Regulations.

(5) The repeals by these Regulations in section 5 of the Registered Designs Act 1949 shall not apply in relation to any evidence filed in support of an application made before the coming into force of these Regulations.

(6) The amendments and repeals made by these Regulations in section 22 of the Act of 1949 (other than the amendment to the proviso insubsection (2) of that section) shall not apply in relation to any registration which has resulted from an application made before the coming into force of these Regulations.

(7) The amendment to the proviso in section 22(2) of the Act of 1949 shall not apply where—

(a) the registration of the first-mentioned design resulted from an application made before the coming into force of these Regulations; and
(b) the application for the registration of the other design was also made before the coming into force of these Regulations. (8) The amendments and repeals made by these Regulations in section 35 of the Act of 1949 shall not apply in relation to any offences committed before the coming into force of these Regulations.

(9) The repeal by these Regulations of provisions in section 44 of the Act of 1949 which relate to the meaning of a set of articles shall not apply so far as those provisions are required for the purposes of paragraph 6(2)(a) of Schedule 1 to the Copyright, Designs and Patents Act 1988.

(10) Any amendment or repeal by these Regulations of a provision in section 44 of the Act of 1949 or in any enactment other than the Act of 1949 shall not

apply so far as that provision is required for the purposes of any other transitional provision made by these Regulations.

(11) The Act of 1949 as it has effect immediately before the coming into force of these Regulations shall continue to apply in relation to former registrations, whose registration resulted from an application made before the coming into force of these Regulations, so far as the Act relates to the cancellation or invalidation of such registrations.

(12) Paragraph (13) applies in relation to any registration to which Regulation 11, 12 or 13 applies which is in respect of any features of shape, configuration, pattern or ornament which do not fall within the new definition of ""'design"" inserted into section 1 of the Act of 1949 by Regulation 2 of these Regulations.

(13) The Act of 1949 shall, so far as it applies in relation to any such registration, apply as if the features concerned were included within the new definition of "design" in that Act.

Chartered Associations (Protection of Names and Uniforms) Act 1926

1. In section 3 of the Chartered Associations (Protection of Names and Uniforms) Act 1926 (savings)—

(a) for the word "article", in the first place where it appears, there shall be substituted "product";
(b) for the words from "in respect of" to "1907", there shall be substituted "where a design is applied to, or incorporated in, the product and the design is protected by virtue of registration under the Registered Designs Act 1949";
(c) for the words "such registered design", in both places where they appear, there shall be substituted "the design"; and
(d) for the words "such article" there shall be substituted "the product".

Registered Designs Act 1949

2. In section 8B(6) of the Registered Designs Act 1949 (effect of order for restoration of right)—

(a) for the words "an article" there shall be substituted "a product"; and
(b) for the words "the article" there shall be substituted "the product".

NOTES
1. Section 8B was inserted by section 269 of the 1988 Act.

3. In section 9(1) of that Act (exemption of innocent infringer from liability for damages)—

(a) for the words "an article" there shall be substituted "a product"; and
(b) for the words "the article" there shall be substituted ", or incorporated in, the product".

NOTES
1. Section 9 was amended by section 272 of, and paragraph 5 of Schedule 3 to, the 1988 Act.

4.— (1) Section 14 of that Act (registration of design where application for protection in convention country has been made) shall be amended as follows.

(2) In subsection (2)—

(a) after the word "whether" there shall be inserted "(and to what extent)"; and

(b) after the word "new" there shall be inserted "or has individual character".

(3) In subsection (3) for the words "section 3(4)" there shall be substituted "section 3B(2) or (3)".

NOTES

1. Section 14(2) and (3) were substituted by section 272 of, and paragraph 7 of Schedule 3 to, the 1988 Act.

5. In section 15(2) of that Act (extension of time for applications under section 14 in certain cases)—

(a) in paragraph (a), for the word "articles" there shall be substituted "products"; and

(b) in paragraph (e)—

(i) for the word "articles" there shall be substituted "products"; and

(ii) after the word "applied" there shall be inserted "or in which it is incorporated".

6.— (1) Section 19 (registration of assignments etc.) of that Act shall be amended as follows.

(2) In subsection (3A) for the words "design right", in both places where they appear, there shall be substituted "national unregistered design right".

(3) In subsection (3B) for the words "design right", in the first and third places where they appear, there shall be substituted "national unregistered design right".

NOTES

1. Section 19(3A) and (3B) were inserted by section 272 of, and paragraph 10 of Schedule 3 to, the 1988 Act.

7.— (1) Section 22 of that Act (inspection of registered designs) shall be amended as follows.

(2) In subsection (2) for the words from the beginning to "no" there shall be substituted—

"Where—

(a) a design has been registered;

(b) a product to which the design was intended to be applied or in which it was intended to be incorporated was specified, in accordance with rules made under section 36 of this Act, in the application for the registration of the design; and

    (c)   the product so specified falls within any class prescribed for the purposes of this subsection, no".

(3) Also in subsection (2)—

    (a)   for the word "articles" there shall be substituted "products"; and

    (b)   for the words from "it is the same" to "trade" there shall be substituted ", by reference to the first-mentioned design, it is not new or does not have individual character".

(4) In subsection (3) for the words from "design" to "class" there shall be substituted "registered design and a specified product which falls within any class" .

NOTES
    1.   Section 22(2) and (3) were amended by section 272 of, and paragraph 12 of Schedule 3 to, the 1988 Act.

8.— (1) Section 25 of that Act (certificate of contested validity of registration) shall be amended as follows.

(2) In subsection (1) after the words "the design is" there shall be inserted ", to any extent,".

(3) In subsection (2) for the word "cancellation" there shall be substituted "invalidation".

NOTES
    1.   Section 25(2) was amended by section 272 of, and paragraph 14 of Schedule 3 to, the 1988 Act.

9. In section 30(3)(a) of that Act (costs and security for costs) for the word "cancellation" there shall be substituted "invalidation".

NOTES
    1.   Section 30 was substituted by section 272 of, and paragraph 19 of Schedule 3 to, the 1988 Act.

10.— (1) Section 35 of that Act (fine for falsely representing a design as registered) shall be amended as follows.

(2) In subsection (1)—

    (a)   for the words "any article" there shall be substituted ", or incorporated in, any product";

    (b)   the words "in respect of that article" shall be omitted;

    (c)   for the words "an article" there shall be substituted "a product";

    (d)   for the words "the article", in the first and second places where they appear, there shall be substituted ", or incorporated in, the product"; and

    (e)   the words "in respect of the article" shall be omitted.

(3) In subsection (2)—

(a)   for the words "any article" there shall be substituted "any product";

(b)   after the word "applied" there shall be inserted "or in which it has been incorporated"; and

(c)   for the words "such article" there shall be substituted "such product".

NOTES
  1. Section 35 was amended by section 272 of, and paragraph 24 of Schedule 3 to, the 1988 Act but not, in the case of the amendment to section 35(1), in relation to offences committed before 1st August 1989.

11. In section 36(1A) of that Act (general power of Secretary of State to make rules etc.), after paragraph (a), there shall be inserted—

"(ab) requiring applications for registration of designs to specify—

(i)   the products to which the designs are intended to be applied or in which they are intended to be incorporated;

(ii) the classification of the designs by reference to such test as may be prescribed;".

NOTES
  1. Section 36 was amended by section 272 of, and paragraph 26 of Schedule 3 to, the 1988 Act.

12. In section 37(2) of that Act for the words from "section", where it first appears, to "Act", where it first appears, there shall be substituted "section 15 of this Act".

13. In section 43(2) of that Act (savings) for the word "articles" there shall be substituted "products".

14.— (1) Section 44 of that Act (interpretation) shall be amended as follows.

(2) In subsection (1), in the definition of "design" for the words "section 1(1)" there shall be substituted "section 1(2)".

(3) In subsection (1), at the appropriate places, there shall be inserted—

"complex product" has the meaning assigned to it by section 1(3) of this Act;";

"national unregistered design right" means design right within the meaning of Part III of the Copyright, Designs and Patents Act 1988;";

"product" has the meaning assigned to it by section 1(3) of this Act;".

(4) In subsection (4) for the words from "section", where it first appears, to "Act" there shall be substituted "section 14 of this Act".

NOTES
  1. The definition of "design" was amended by section 272 of, and paragraph 31(7) of Schedule 3 to, the 1988 Act.

15.— (1) Schedule 1 to that Act (use of registered designs for the services of the Crown) shall be amended as follows.

(2) In paragraph 1(6) and (7), for the word "articles", in each place where it appears, there shall be substituted "products".

(3) In paragraph 2(1) for the words "design right" there shall be substituted "national unregistered design right".

(4) In paragraph 2A(1) and (4)—

(a)   for the word "articles" there shall be substituted "products"; and
(b)   after the word "applied" there shall be inserted "or in which it is incorporated".

(5) In paragraph 3(2)(a)—

(a)   after the word "proceedings" there shall be inserted "and the department are a relevant person within the meaning of section 20 of this Act";
(b)   for the word "cancellation" there shall be substituted "invalidation"; and
(c)   for the word "cancelled" there shall be substituted "declared invalid".

(6) In paragraph 3(2)(b)—

(a)   after the word "case" there shall be inserted "and provided that the department would be the relevant person within the meaning of section 20 of this Act if they had made an application on the grounds for invalidity being raised"; and
(b)   for the word "cancellation" there shall be substituted "invalidation".

NOTES
1. Paragraph 1(6) was substituted by section 1(1) and (4) of the Defence Contracts Act 1958 (c. 38).
2. The words "design right" were inserted into paragraph 2(1) by section 272 of, and paragraph 37(2) of Schedule 3 to, the 1988 Act.
3. Paragraph 2A was inserted by section 271 of the 1988 Act in relation to any Crown use of a registered design after 1st August 1989 even if the terms for such use were settled before that date.

Copyright, Designs and Patents Act 1988

16. In section 53(1)(b) of the Copyright, Designs and Patents Act 1988 (things done in reliance on registration of design) after the word "cancellation" there shall be inserted "or invalidation".

Schedule 2 REPEALS

Chapter	Short title	Extent of repeal
1949 c. 88.	The Registered Designs Act 1949.	In section 2(2), the words from ", or the" to "any article," and the words from "or as", where they appear for a second time, to the end of the subsection.
		Section 4.

Chapter	Short title	Extent of repeal
		In section 5, in subsection (2), paragraph (b) and the word "and" immediately preceding it and, in subsection (3)(b), the words from ", or any" to "above,".
		Section 6.
		Section 8(5) and (6).
		Section 10.
		In section 11A(3), paragraph (b) and the word "or" immediately preceding it, and the words from "or may, instead" to the end of the subsection.
		Section 11A(4) and (5).
		Section 11B.
		Section 16.
		In section 22(1), paragraph (b) and the word "and" immediately preceding it.
		In section 23(a), the words "and, if so, in respect of what articles"".
		In section 30(3), paragraph (b).
		In section 35(1), the words "in respect of that article" and the words "in respect of the article".
		Section 43(1).
		In section 44, in subsection (1), the definitions of "article", "artistic work", "corresponding design" and "set of articles" and subsections (2) and (3).
		Section 48(5).
1988 c. 48.	The Copyright, Designs and Patents Act 1988.	Section 265.
		Section 268.
		In Schedule 3, paragraphs 1, 2, 3(4), 4, 6, 9 and 31(2) and (5).

Chapter	Short title	Extent of repeal
1995 c. 21.	The Merchant Shipping Act 1995.	In Schedule 13, paragraph 26.
1995 c. 32.	The Olympic Symbol etc. (Protection) Act 1995.	Section 13(1).

Registered Designs Regulations 2003

SI 2003/550

The Secretary of State, being designated for the purposes of section 2(2) of the European Communities Act 1972 in relation to measures relating to the legal protection of designs, in exercise of powers conferred on her by the said section 2(2) hereby makes the following Regulations:

NOTES
1   SI 2000/1813.

I   Citation, commencement and extent

(1) These Regulations may be cited as the Registered Designs Regulations 2003 and shall come into force on 1st April 2003.

(2) These Regulations extend to England and Wales, Scotland and Northern Ireland.

2   Amendment to the Registered Designs Act 1949

(1) The Registered Designs Act 1949 ("the Act") shall be amended as follows.

(2) In section 1A(2)(b) of the Act, after "this Act""there shall be inserted "or the Community Design Regulation".

(3) In section 11ZB(4) of the Act—

    (a)   after "this Act" there shall be inserted "or the Community Design Regulation"; and

    (b)   after "the design" there shall be inserted ", the holder of the registered Community design".

(4) In section 20(1B) of the Act—

    (a)   after "this Act" there shall be inserted "or the Community Design Regulation"; and

    (b)   after "the design" there shall be inserted ", the holder of the registered Community design".

(5) In section 44(1) of the Act, at the appropriate places, there shall be inserted—

> "Community Design Regulation" means Council Regulation (EC) 6/2002 of 12th December 2001 on Community Designs;";
>
> "registered Community design" means a design that complies with the conditions contained in, and is registered in the manner provided for in, the Community Design Regulation;".

NOTES

    1 Sections 1A, 11ZB and 20(1B) were added by the Registered Designs Regulations 2001 (SI 2001/3949).

3 Transitional provisions: pending applications

(1) This Regulation applies to applications for registration under the Act that have been made after the coming into force of the Registered Designs Regulations 2001 ("2001 Regulations") and before the coming into force of these Regulations but that have not been finally determined before the coming into force of these Regulations ("pending applications").

(2) The Act as it has effect immediately before the coming into force of these Regulations shall continue to apply in relation to pending applications.

(3) Accordingly the amendments made by these Regulations shall not apply in relation to such applications.

NOTES

    1. The Registered Designs Regulations came into force on 9th December 2001.

4 Transitional provisions: transitional registrations

(1) This Regulation applies to any registration under the Act that results from the determination of a pending application (within the meaning of Regulation 3).

(2) The Act as it has effect immediately before the coming into force of these Regulations shall continue to apply in relation to registrations to which this Regulation applies ("transitional registrations").

(3) Accordingly the amendments made by these Regulations shall not apply in relation to transitional registrations.

5 Transitional provisions: resulting registrations

(1) This Regulation applies to any registration made under the Act before the coming into force of these Regulations that results from the determination of an application made under the Act after the coming into force of the 2001 Regulations.

(2) The Act as it has effect immediately before the coming into force of these Regulations shall continue to apply in relation to registrations to which this Regulation applies ("resulting registrations").

(3) Accordingly the amendments made by these Regulations shall not apply in relation to resulting registrations.

Regulatory Reform (Registered Designs) Order 2006

SI 2006/1974

The Secretary of State for Trade and Industry ("the Secretary of State") has—

(a)   consulted, in accordance with section 5(1) of the Regulatory Reform Act 2001,

    (i)   such organisations as appear to him to be representative of interests substantially affected by his proposals for this Order,

    (ii)   the Comptroller-General of Patents, Designs and Trade Marks,

    (iii)   the Law Commission,

    (iv)   the National Assembly for Wales,

    (v)   such other persons as he considers appropriate;

(b)   following that consultation, considered it appropriate to proceed with the making of this Order;

(c)   laid a document containing his proposals before Parliament as required by section 6 of the Regulatory Reform Act 2001 and the period for Parliamentary consideration under section 8 of that Act has expired;

(d)   had regard to the representations made during this period, in particular the Seventeenth Report of Session 2005– 6 of the Delegated Powers and Regulatory Reform Committee of the House of Lords and the Fifth Report of Session 2005– 6 of the Regulatory Reform Committee of the House of Commons ;

(e)   laid a draft of this Order before Parliament with a statement giving details of those representations and the changes he has made to his proposals in light of them;

(f)   reached the opinion that this Order does not remove any necessary protection or prevent any person from continuing to exercise any right or freedom which he might reasonably expect to continue to exercise.

The draft of this Order has been approved by a resolution of each House of Parliament pursuant to section 4(2) of the Regulatory Reform Act 2001.

Accordingly, the Secretary of State makes the following Order in exercise of the powers conferred by section 1 of the Regulatory Reform Act 2001:

NOTES

1   A consultation document on the modernisation of design practice entitled "Consultation on the Modernisation of the UK System of Registration of Designs" was published by the Patent Office on 7 July 2005. Copies may be obtained from the Trade Marks and Designs Directorate, The Patent Office, Concept House, Cardiff Road, Newport, NP10 8QQ.

2   Seventeenth Report published on 3 April 2006, HL 160.

3   Fifth Report published on 26 May 2006, HC 1142.

Appendix 3 Legislation

Introductory

1 (1) This Order may be cited as the Regulatory Reform (Registered Designs) Order 2006 and it shall come into force on 1st October 2006.

(2) This Order extends to England and Wales, Scotland and Northern Ireland.

2 The Registered Designs Act 1949 shall be amended as follows.

NOTES

    1   Section 8 was inserted by section 269 of the Copyright, Designs and Patents Act 1988 (c. 48), sections 14 and 20 were amended by section 272 of, and paragraphs 7 and 11 of Schedule 3 to, that Act; sections 1A, 3 to 3B, 11ZA to 11ZD were inserted by the Registered Designs Regulations 2001 (SI 2001/3939), sections 14 and 20 were also amended by those Regulations; further amendments to sections 1A, 11ZB and 20 were made by the Registered Designs Regulations 2003 (SI 2003/550); there are other amendments but none is relevant.

Substantive examination for novelty

3 Section 1A (substantive grounds for refusal of registration) shall be omitted.

4 In section 3 (applications for registration), subsection (4) shall be omitted.

5 In section 3A (determination of applications for registration), for subsection (4) there shall be substituted—

> "(4) If it appears to the registrar that the application for registration includes—
> (a) something which does not fulfil the requirements of section 1(2) of this Act;
> (b) a design that does not fulfil the requirements of section 1C or 1D of this Act; or
> (c) a design to which a ground of refusal mentioned in Schedule A1 to this Act applies,
> he shall refuse to register that thing or that design.".

6 In section 3B (modification of applications for registration), in subsection (4), for "section 1A(1)(b) or (c)" there shall be substituted "section 3A(4)(b) or (c)".

7 (1) Section 11ZA (grounds for invalidity of registration) shall be amended as follows.

(2) In subsection (1), for "on any of the grounds mentioned in section 1A of this Act." there shall be substituted—

> "(a) on the ground that it does not fulfil the requirements of section 1(2) of this Act;
> (b) on the ground that it does not fulfil the requirements of sections 1B to 1D of this Act; or
> (c) where any ground of refusal mentioned in Schedule A1 to this Act applies.".

(3) After subsection (1), there shall be inserted—

"(1A) The registration of a design ("the later design") may be declared invalid if it is not new or does not have individual character when compared to a design which—

(a) has been made available to the public on or after the relevant date; but

(b) is protected as from a date prior to the relevant date by virtue of registration under this Act or the Community Design Regulation or an application for such registration.

(1B) In subsection (1A) "the relevant date" means the date on which the application for the registration of the later design was made or is treated by virtue of section 3B(2), (3) or (5) or 14(2) of this Act as having been made.".

8 (1) Section 11ZB (applications for declaration of invalidity) shall be amended as follows.

(2) In subsection (1), for "on the ground mentioned in section 1A(1)(a) or (b)" there shall be substituted "under section 11ZA(1)(a) or (b)".

(3) In subsection (2), for "on the ground mentioned in section 1A(1)(c)" there shall be substituted "under section 11ZA(1)(c)".

(4) In subsection (3), for "on the ground mentioned in section 1A(2)" there shall be substituted "under section 11ZA(1A)".

(5) In subsection (5), for "on the ground mentioned in" there shall be substituted "under".

9 In section 11ZD (modification of registration), for the words in subsection (1) from "on any ground" to "or (4)" there shall be substituted "under section 11ZA(1)(b) or (c), (1A), (3) or (4)".

10 (1) Section 20 (rectification of register) shall be amended as follows.

(2) In subsection (1A)(a), for "section 1A(1)(c)" there shall be substituted "section 11ZA(1)(c)".

(3) In subsection (1A)(b), for "section 1A(2)" there shall be substituted "section 11ZA(1A)".

Multiple applications

11 (1) Section 3 (applications for registration) shall be amended as follows.

(2) In subsection (1), after "a design"there shall be inserted "or designs".

(3) In subsection (2), after "design", in both places it occurs, there shall be inserted "or designs".

(4) In subsection (3), after "a design"there shall be inserted "or designs".

12 (1) Section 3A (determination of applications for registration) shall be amended as follows.

(2) In subsection (1), for "an application for the registration of a design" there shall be substituted "to register a design included in an application under this Act".

(3) In subsection (2)—

(a)   for "a design" there shall be inserted "or designs"; and
(b)   for "the application" there shall be substituted "to register any design included in it".

(4) In subsection (3), for the words from "an application" to the end of the subsection there shall be substituted "the applicant is not under section 3(2) or (3) or 14 entitled to apply for the registration of a design included in the application, he shall refuse to register that design.".

13 (1) Section 3B (modification of applications for registration) shall be amended as follows.

(2) In subsection (1), after "a design" there shall be inserted "or designs".

(3) In subsection (2)—

(a)   after "a design" there shall be inserted "or designs";
(b)   for "the design", where it first occurs, there shall be substituted "any design included in the application"; and
(c)   after "direct that the application" there shall be inserted "so far as relating to that design".

(4) In subsection (3), for "a design has disclosed more than one design and" there shall be substituted "more than one design".

(5) In subsection (4)—

(a)   "an application for" shall be omitted; and
(b)   after "the application" there shall be inserted "for the design".

14 (1) Section 14 (registration of design where application for protection in convention country has been made) is amended as follows.

(2) In subsection (1), after "a design" there shall be inserted "or designs".

(3) In subsection (2), after "a design" there shall be inserted "or designs".

15 In section 22 (inspection of registered designs), for subsection (4) there shall be substituted—

"(4) Where registration of a design has been refused pursuant to an application under this Act, or an application under this Act has been abandoned in relation to any design—

(a)   the application, so far as relating to that design, and
(b)   any representation, specimen or other document which has been filed and relates to that design,

shall not at any time be open to inspection at the Patent Office or be published by the registrar.".

Inspection

16 (1) Section 22 (inspection of registered designs) shall be amended as follows.

(2) In subsection (1)—

   (a)   for "issued" there shall be substituted "granted"; and

   (b)   for "the following provisions of this section" there shall be substituted "subsection (4)".

(3) Subsections (2) and (3) shall be omitted.

Lowering the standard of care for restoration of lapsed right in design

17 In section 8A (restoration of lapsed right in design), in subsection (4)—

   (a)   for "proprietor took reasonable care" there shall be substituted "failure of the proprietor"; and

   (b)   after "section 8(2) or (4)" there shall be inserted "was unintentional".

Transitional provisions

18 (1) The amendments made to the Registered Designs Act 1949 by articles 7 to 10 shall not apply to post-1989 registrations or pre-1989 registrations.

(2) In paragraph (1)—

"post-1989 registrations" means registrations to which regulation 12 of the Registered Designs Regulations 2001 applies;

"pre-1989 registrations" means registrations which fall within regulation 13(1) of those Regulations.

19 The amendments made to section 22 of the Registered Designs Act 1949 by article 16(2)(b) and (3) shall not apply to any registration under the Act which has resulted from an application made before the coming into force of this Order.

Registered Designs Rules 2006

SI 2006/1975

The Secretary of State makes the following Rules in exercise of the powers conferred upon him by sections 29 to 31 and 36 of the Registered Designs Act 1949.

In accordance with section 8(1) of the Tribunals and Inquiries Act 1992 the Secretary of State has consulted the Council on Tribunals.

NOTES
1. Sections 29 to 31 and 36 were amended by section 272 of, and paragraphs 18 to 20 and 26 of Schedule 3 to, the Copyright, Designs and Patents Act 1988 and sections 30 and 36 were amended by regulation 9 of, and paragraphs 9 and 11 of Schedule 1 and Schedule 2 to, SI 2001/3949.

Part 1

INTRODUCTORY

1   Citation and commencement

These Rules may be cited as the Registered Designs Rules 2006 and shall come into force on 1st October 2006.

2   Interpretation

(1) In these Rules—

"the Act" means the Registered Designs Act 1949;
"the journal" means the journal published under rule 44(1); and
"section" means a section of the Act.

(2) Where a time or period has been altered under rules 19(1) or 39 to 41, any reference in these Rules to the time or period shall be construed as a reference to the time or period as altered.

3   Forms

(1) The forms of which the use is required by these Rules are those set out in Schedule 1.

(2) Such a requirement to use a form is satisfied by the use of a form which is acceptable to the registrar and contains the information required by the form as so set out.

Part 2

APPLICATIONS FOR REGISTRATION

Applications for registration and formal requirements

4   Applications

(1) An application for the registration of a design or designs shall be made on Form DF2A and—

(a)   shall include the identity of the person making the application; and
(b)   in relation to each design, shall either—

(i)   include a representation of the design; or
(ii)   be accompanied by a specimen of the design,

and it shall be accompanied by the prescribed fee.

(2) But an application for the registration of a design or designs, which is a subsequent application for the purposes of section 3B(3), shall be made on Form DF2B and be accompanied by the prescribed fee.

(3) Where an application includes a representation of the design, the applicant may give his consent for its publication on Form DF2A or Form DF2B.

(4) Where a person purports to file something under section 3(1) and—

(a)   it is not in the form prescribed by either paragraph (1) or (2); or

(b)   it is not accompanied by the prescribed fee,

the registrar shall notify that person accordingly.

(5) A representation or specimen filed under paragraph (1)(b) may be accompanied by a brief description of the design.

(6) A specimen may not be filed under paragraph (1)(b) if it is hazardous or perishable; and where such a specimen is so filed it shall be disregarded.

(7) An application for the registration of a design which is a repeating surface pattern shall only be treated as such if—

(a)   the representation or specimen filed under paragraph (1)(b) includes the complete pattern and a sufficient portion of the repeat in length and width to show how the pattern repeats; and (b) the application contains a statement that it relates to a repeating surface pattern.

5   Formal requirements

(1) An application for the registration of a design shall comply with the first and second requirement.

(2) The first requirement is that the applicant has specified the product to which the design is intended to be applied or in which it is intended to be incorporated.

(3) The second requirement is that the dimensions of any specimen of the design filed under rule 4(1)(b)(ii) shall not exceed 29.7cm × 21cm × 1cm.

(4) Where the applicant files a representation of the design after being notified under rule 8(1) that the application does not comply with the second requirement—

(a)   that representation shall be deemed to have been filed under rule 4(1)(b)(i); and

(b)   any specimen filed under rule 4(1)(b)(ii) shall be treated as not having been filed.

(5) Nothing done to comply with the first requirement shall be taken to affect the scope of the protection conferred by the registration of a design.

Disclaimers

6   Partial disclaimers

An application for the registration of a design may be accompanied by a disclaimer which—

    (a)   limits the scope or extent of protection being applied for in relation to the design; or

    (b)   indicates that the application for registration relates to a design that forms only a part of the appearance of a product.

Convention applications

7 Convention applications

(1) Where an application for the registration of a design or designs is made by virtue of section 14 the applicant shall comply with the following provisions.

(2) The application shall contain a declaration specifying—

    (a)   the date of making of each convention application; and

    (b)   the country it was made in or in respect of.

(3) The applicant shall, before the end of the period of 3 months beginning with the date on which the application was filed, file at the Patent Office a copy of the representation of the design that was the subject of each convention application.

(4) A copy of the representation filed under paragraph (3) shall be—

    (a)   duly certified by the authority with which it was filed; or

    (b)   verified to the satisfaction of the registrar.

(5) Paragraph (3) shall not apply where a copy of the convention application is kept at the Patent Office.

(6) Where any document relating to the convention application is in a language other than English or Welsh, the registrar may direct the applicant to provide a translation of the whole or any part of that document.

(7) The translation shall be filed before the end of the period of 3 months beginning with the date of the direction.

(8) Where the applicant—

    (a)   fails to file a copy of the representation of the design which has been certified or verified in accordance with paragraph (4); or

    (b)   fails to comply with a direction given under paragraph (6),

the convention application shall be disregarded for the purposes of section 14(2).

(9) In this rule "convention application" means an application for the protection of a design which has been made in a convention country.

Examination of application, representations for publication and time limits

8 Substantive and formal examination of application

(1) Where it appears to the registrar that he should refuse to register a design included in an application—

(a) by reason of the application for the registration of that design not being made in accordance with any of these Rules, other than rule 9(2) (see section 3A(2)); or

(b) by reason of section 3A(3) or (4),

he shall notify the applicant accordingly.

(2) The notification shall include a statement of why it appears to the registrar that he should refuse to register the design (for the purposes of this rule the "statement of objections").

(3) The applicant may, before the end of the period of 2 months beginning with the date of the notification, send his written observations on the statement of objections to the registrar.

(4) The registrar shall give the applicant an opportunity to be heard.

(5) Where the registrar refuses to register a design included in an application, he shall send to the applicant the written reasons for his decision.

(6) The date on which the written reasons were sent to the applicant shall be deemed to be the date of the decision for the purposes of any appeal.

9 Representation of design for publication

(1) Where the registrar decides that he should not refuse to register the design for the reasons mentioned in rule 8(1)(a) or (b) and—

(a) no representation of the design has been filed; or

(b) a representation has been filed but it is not suitable for publication,

the registrar shall direct the applicant to provide a suitable representation.

(2) Where a direction is given, the applicant shall, before the end of the period of 3 months beginning with the date of the direction, file a suitable representation (otherwise the registrar may refuse to register the design: see section 3A(2)).

(3) Where a suitable representation has been filed, the applicant shall file his consent for its publication on Form DF2C.

(4) But paragraph (3) shall not apply where the applicant consented to publication in accordance with rule 4(3).

(5) In this rule "suitable representation" means a representation of the design which is suitable for publication.

10 Time limits under section 3(5) and section 3B

(1) The time prescribed for the purposes of section 3(5) shall be 12 months beginning with the date on which the application for registration of the design was made or treated as made (disregarding section 14).

(2) The period prescribed for the purposes of section 3B(3) shall be the period of 2 months beginning with the date on which the earlier application was modified under section 3B(3).

Part 3

DESIGNS AFTER REGISTRATION

Publication

11 Publication

(1) When a design has been registered, the registrar shall publish a representation of that design in the journal as soon as possible after the certificate of registration is granted.

(2) When the registrar publishes the representation, he may also publish any other information he thinks is relevant to that design.

(3) The representation published under paragraph (1) shall be the representation filed under rule 4(1)(b)(i) or 9(2) or as mentioned in rule 5(4).

Duration of rights and surrender

12 Extension of duration of right in registered design

(1) An application for an extension under section 8(2) or 8(4) shall be made on Form DF9A.

(2) An application under section 8(2) may only be made during the period of 6 months ending with the date on which the relevant period of 5 years expires.

(3) On receipt of the prescribed renewal fee the registrar shall notify the registered proprietor of the extension of the right in the registered design.

(4) Where the right in a registered design has ceased to have effect by reason of section 8(3), the registrar shall, before the end of the period of 6 weeks beginning with the date on which the right ceased, send written notice to the registered proprietor of that fact.

(5) But paragraph (4) shall not apply where the renewal fee and the prescribed additional fee is paid before a notice is sent.

13 Restoration of a lapsed right in a design under section 8A

(1) An application for the restoration of the right in a design under section 8A shall—

(a)   be made on Form DF29; and
(b)   be supported by evidence of the statements made in the application.

(2) The period prescribed for the purposes of section 8A(1) shall be the period of 12 months beginning with the date on which the registered design ceased to have effect.

(3) The notice of the application shall be published in the journal.

(4) Where, upon consideration of that evidence, the registrar is not satisfied that a case for an order under section 8A has been made out, he shall notify the applicant accordingly.

(5) The applicant may, before the end of the period of 1 month beginning with the date of that notification, request to be heard by the registrar.

(6) Where the applicant requests a hearing, the registrar shall give him an opportunity to be heard; after which the registrar shall determine whether the application under section 8A shall be granted or refused.

(7) Where the registrar decides not to make the order he shall give the applicant written reasons for his refusal.

14 Cancellation of registration

A request under section 11 to cancel the registration of a design shall be made on Form DF19C.

Part 4

PROCEEDINGS HEARD BEFORE THE REGISTRAR

Conduct of proceedings

15 Procedure for applying for a declaration of invalidity

(1) An application for a declaration of invalidity under section 11ZB shall—

    (a)   be made on Form DF19A; and

    (b)   include a statement of the grounds on which the application is made.

(2) The statement of grounds shall include a concise statement of the facts and grounds on which the applicant relies and shall be verified by a statement of truth.

(3) The registrar shall send a copy of Form DF19A and the statement of case to the registered proprietor.

(4) The registrar shall specify a period within which the registered proprietor shall file a counter-statement.

(5) The registered proprietor, within that period, shall—

    (a)   file his counter-statement on Form DF19B; and

    (b)   send a copy of it to the applicant,

otherwise the registrar may treat him as not opposing the application.

(6) In his counter-statement the registered proprietor shall—

    (a)   include a concise statement of the facts on which he relies;

(b)　state which of the allegations in the statement of grounds he denies;

(c)　state which of the allegations he is unable to admit or deny, but which he requires the applicant to prove;

(d)　state which allegations he admits,

and it shall be verified by a statement of truth.

(7) In this Part—

(a)　"statement of case" means the statement of grounds filed by the applicant or the counter-statement filed by the registered proprietor; and (b) references to the statement of case include part of the statement of case.

16　Evidence rounds

(1) When the period specified under rule 15(4) has expired, the registrar shall specify the periods within which evidence may be filed by the parties.

(2) Where the applicant for a declaration of invalidity files no evidence (other than his statement of grounds) in support of his application, the registrar may treat him as having withdrawn his application.

(3) The registrar may, at any time if he thinks fit, give leave to either party to file evidence upon such terms as he thinks fit.

(4) Under this rule, evidence shall only be considered to be filed when—

(a)　it has been received by the registrar; and

(b)　it has been sent to all other parties to the proceedings.

(5) The registrar shall give the parties an opportunity to be heard.

(6) Where any party requests to be heard, the registrar shall send to the parties notice of a date for the hearing.

17　Decision of registrar on invalidity

(1) When the registrar has made a decision on the application for a declaration of invalidity, he shall send to the parties written notice of it, stating the reasons for his decision.

(2) The date on which the decision was sent to the applicant shall be deemed to be the date of the decision for the purposes of any appeal.

18　Exercise of discretionary powers of registrar

The registrar shall give to any applicant for registration of a design an opportunity to be heard before exercising adversely to the applicant any discretion vested in the registrar by or under the Act.

Conduct of proceedings

19　General powers of registrar in relation to proceedings before him

(1) The registrar may extend or shorten (or further extend or shorten) any period which has been specified under any provision of this Part.

(2) At any stage of proceedings before him, the registrar may direct that the parties to the proceedings attend a case management conference or pre-hearing review.

(3) Except where the Act or these Rules otherwise provide, the registrar may give such directions as to the management of the proceedings as he thinks fit, and in particular he may—

(a)   require a document, information or evidence to be filed;
(b)   require a translation of any document;
(c)   require a party or a party's legal representative to attend a hearing;
(d)   hold a hearing and receive evidence by telephone or by using any other method of direct oral communication;
(e)   allow a statement of case to be amended;
(f)   stay the whole, or any part, of the proceedings either generally or until a specified date or event;
(g)   consolidate proceedings;
(h)   direct that part of any proceedings be dealt with as separate proceedings.

(4) The registrar may control the evidence by giving directions as to—

(a)   the issues on which he requires evidence;
(b)   the nature of the evidence which he requires to decide those issues; and
(c)   the way in which the evidence is to be placed before him,

and the registrar may use his power under this paragraph to exclude evidence which would otherwise be admissible.

(5) When the registrar gives directions under any provision of this Part, he may—

(a)   make them subject to conditions; and
(b)   specify the consequences of failure to comply with the directions or a condition.

20   Hearings in public

(1) Subject to paragraphs (3) and (4), any hearing before the registrar of proceedings between two or more parties relating to an application for a registered design or a registered design, shall be held in public.

(2) Any party to the proceedings may apply to the registrar for the hearing to be held in private.

(3) The registrar shall only grant an application under paragraph (2) where—

(a)   it is in the interests of justice for the hearing to be in held in private; and
(b)   all the parties to the proceedings have had an opportunity to be heard on the matter,

and where the application is granted the hearing shall be in private.

(4) Any hearing of an application under paragraph (2) shall be held in private.

(5) In this rule a reference to a hearing includes any part of a hearing.

[…]

NOTES
   1   Revoked by Tribunals, Courts and Enforcement Act 2007 (Transitional and Consequential Provisions) Order 2008/2683 Sch.1 para 318 (3 November 2008)

21   Evidence in proceedings before the registrar

(1) Subject as follows, evidence filed under this Part may be given—

    (a)   by witness statement, statement of case, affidavit, statutory declaration; or

    (b)   in any other form which would be admissible as evidence in proceedings before the court.

(2) A witness statement or a statement of case may only be given in evidence if it includes a statement of truth.

(3) The general rule is that evidence at hearings is to be by witness statement unless the registrar or any enactment requires otherwise.

(4) For the purposes of this Part, a statement of truth—

    (a)   means a statement that the person making the statement believes that the facts stated in a particular document are true; and

    (b)   shall be dated and signed by—

        (i)   in the case of a witness statement, the maker of the statement,

        (ii)   in any other case, the party or his legal representative.

(5) In this Part, a witness statement is a written statement signed by a person that contains the evidence which that person would be allowed to give orally.

Miscellaneous

22   Costs of proceedings

The registrar may, in any proceedings before him under the Act, award to any party by order such costs as he considers reasonable, and direct how and by what parties they are to be paid.

23   Security for costs

(1) The registrar may require a person to give security for the costs of any application or appeal mentioned in section 30(3) if—

    (a)   he is satisfied, having regard to all the circumstances of the case, that it is just to require such security; and

    (b)   one or more of the conditions in paragraph (2) applies.

(2) The conditions are—

(a)   the person is resident outside the United Kingdom but—

    (i)   not resident in a Brussels Contracting State,

    (ii)   a Lugano Contracting State, or

    (iii)   a Regulation State,

as defined in section 1(3) of the Civil Jurisdiction and Judgments Act 1982;

(b)   the person is a company or other body (whether incorporated inside or outside the United Kingdom) and there is reason to believe that it will be unable to pay the other person's costs if ordered to do so;

(c)   the person has changed his address since filing an address for service with a view to evading the consequences of the proceedings;

(d)   the person has furnished an incorrect address for service;

(e)   the person has taken steps in relation to his assets that would make it difficult to enforce an order for costs against him;

(f)   the person has failed to pay a costs order in relation to previous proceedings before the registrar or a court (whether or not the proceedings were between the same parties).

(3) In default of such security being given the registrar may treat the application or appeal as abandoned.

24 Registrar shall have the powers of official referee

The registrar shall have the powers of an official referee of the Supreme Court as regards—

(a) the attendance of witnesses and their examination on oath; and

(b) the discovery and production of documents,

but he shall have no power to punish summarily for contempt.

25 Minimum notice of hearing

The registrar shall not give a person less than 14 days notice of any hearing under the Act.

Part 5

THE REGISTER AND OTHER INFORMATION

Certificate of registration and registrable interests

26 Certificate of registration

(1) The certificate of registration of a design shall include—

(a)   the name of the registered proprietor;

(b)   the date of registration; and

(c)   the registration number of the design.

(2) Any request by the registered proprietor for a copy of the certificate of registration shall—

(a)   be in writing; and
(b)   be accompanied by the prescribed fee.

(3) Before considering the request, the registrar may require the person making the request to provide such information or evidence as the registrar thinks fit.

27   Registration of interests

(1) The following matters are prescribed for the purposes of section 17(1)(c)—

(a)   the registered proprietor's address for service;
(b)   the grant or cancellation of a licence under a registered design;
(c)   the granting or cancelling of a security interest (whether fixed or floating) over a registered design or any right in or under it;
(d)   an order of a court or other competent authority transferring a registered design or any right in or under it.

(2) An application to the registrar to enter in the register a matter not mentioned in section 17(1)(a) or (b) or paragraph (1) shall be made in writing.

(3) An application under section 19(1) or (2) shall be made on Form DF12A.

(4) Where the registrar has doubts about whether he should enter a matter in the register—

(a)   he shall inform the person making the application of the reasons for his doubts; and
(b)   he may require that person to furnish evidence in support of the application.

Inspection and information about registered designs

28   Inspection of register, representations and specimens

(1) The register and any representation or specimen of a registered design shall be open for inspection at the Patent Office during the hours the Patent Office is open for all classes of public business (see rule 45(2)).

(2) Whilst a direction under section 5(1) in respect of a design remains in force, no representation or specimen of the design shall be open to inspection.

29   Inspection of documents

(1) Where a design has been registered under the Act, there shall be open to inspection at the Patent Office on and after the date on which the certificate of registration is granted every document kept at the Patent Office in connection with that design.

(2) But no document may be inspected—

(a)   before the end of the period of 14 days beginning with the day—

    (i)   it was filed at the Patent Office; or

    (ii)   received by the registrar or the Patent Office;

(b)   where that document was prepared by the registrar or the Patent Office for internal use only;

(c)   where the document includes matter—

    (i)   which in the registrar's opinion disparages any person in a way likely to damage him; or

    (ii)   the inspection of which would in his opinion be generally expected to encourage offensive, immoral or anti-social behaviour.

(3) Unless, in a particular case, the registrar otherwise directs, no document may be inspected—

(a)   where—

    (i)   the document was prepared by the registrar or the Patent Office other than for internal use; and

    (ii)   it contains information which the registrar considers should remain confidential;

(b)   where it is treated as a confidential document (under rule 30).

(4) In this rule and rule 30 references to a document include part of a document.

30   Confidential information

(1) Where a person files a document at the Patent Office or sends it to the registrar or the Patent Office, any person may request that the document be treated as a confidential document.

(2) A request to treat a document as confidential shall—

(a)   be made before the end of the period of 14 days beginning with the date on which the document was filed at the Patent Office or received by the registrar or at the Patent Office;

(b)   include reasons for the request.

(3) Where a request has been made under paragraph (1), the document shall be treated as confidential until the registrar refuses that request or makes a direction under paragraph (4).

(4) Where it appears that there is good reason for the document to remain confidential, the registrar may direct that the document shall be treated as a confidential document; otherwise he shall refuse the request made under paragraph (1).

(5) But, where the registrar believes there is no longer a good reason for the direction under paragraph (4) to remain in force, he shall revoke it.

31 Information about rights in registered designs

(1) A request for information under section 23 shall be made on Form DF21 and be accompanied by the prescribed fee.

(2) The request shall—

    (a)   where the registration number is known by the person making the request, include that number; or

    (b)   in any other case, be accompanied by a representation or specimen of the product—

        (i)   in which the design has been incorporated; or

        (ii)   to which the design has been applied.

Copies of documents

32 Copies of entries in, or extracts from, the register

An application under section 17(5) for a certified copy of an entry in the register or a certified extract from the register shall be made on Form DF23 and be accompanied by the prescribed fee.

33 Copies of representations and specimens

(1) A person may apply to the registrar for a certified copy of any representation or specimen of a design; and that person shall be entitled to such a copy.

(2) An application under paragraph (1) shall be made in writing and be accompanied by the prescribed fee.

Alterations and rectification

34 Alteration of name or address

(1) Any person may request that an alteration to his name or address—

    (a)   be entered in the register; or

    (b)   be made to any application or other document filed at the Patent Office.

(2) A request under paragraph (1) shall in relation to an alteration to—

    (a)   his name, be made on Form DF16A; and

    (b)   his address, be made on Form DF16A or in writing.

(3) Where the registrar has doubts about whether he should make the alteration to a name or address—

    (a)   he shall inform the person making the request of the reason for his doubts; and

    (b)   he may require that person to furnish evidence in support of the request.

(4) Where the registrar has no doubts (or no longer has doubts) about whether he should make the alteration, it shall be entered in the register or made to the application or document.

35 Notice of rectification of the register

(1) The prescribed manner of giving notice to the registrar for the purposes of section 20(3) is by giving written notice.

(2) The prescribed manner of service on the registrar for the purposes of section 20(4) is by filing a copy of the order at the Patent Office.

Part 6

MISCELLANEOUS

Agents and advisers

36 Agents

(1) Any act required or authorised by the Act to be done by or to any person in connection with the registration of a design, or any procedure relating to a registered design, may be done by or to an agent authorised by that person orally or in writing.

(2) But an agent shall only be treated as authorised under paragraph (1) where—

    (a)   he was nominated by the applicant at the time of—

        (i)   making his application for registration;

        (ii)   making his application for a declaration of invalidity under section 11ZB; or

        (iii) making his application under section 19(1) or (2); or

    (b)   he has filed Form DF1A.

(3) Where an agent has been authorised under paragraph (1), the registrar may, if he thinks fit in any particular case, require the signature or presence of his principal.

37 Appointing advisers

(1) The registrar may appoint an adviser to assist him in any proceedings before him.

(2) The registrar shall settle any question or instructions to be submitted or given to the adviser.

Correction of irregularities and extensions of time

38 Correction of irregularities

Where the registrar thinks fit, he may rectify any irregularity of procedure—

(a) after giving the parties such notice, and

(b) subject to such conditions,

as he may direct.

39 Extension of times or periods prescribed by Rules

(1) The registrar may, if he thinks fit, extend (or further extend) any time or period prescribed by these Rules, except the periods prescribed by—

(a) rule 10(1) (period prescribed for the purposes of section 3(5)); and

(b) rule 13(2) (period for making an application for restoration),

(but those periods may be extended under rules 38, 40 and 41).

(2) Any extension under paragraph (1) shall be made—

(a) after giving the parties such notice, and

(b) subject to such conditions,

as the registrar may direct.

(3) An extension may be granted under paragraph (1) notwithstanding that the time or period prescribed by the relevant rule has expired.

40 Interrupted days

(1) The registrar may certify any day as an interrupted day where—

(a) there is an event or circumstance causing an interruption in the normal operation of the Patent Office; or

(b) there is a general interruption or subsequent dislocation in the postal services of the United Kingdom.

(2) Any certificate of the registrar made under paragraph (1) shall be posted in the Patent Office and advertised in the journal.

(3) The registrar shall, where the time for doing anything under these Rules expires on an interrupted day, extend that time to the next following day not being an interrupted day (or an excluded day).

(4) In this rule—

"interrupted day" means a day which has been certified as such under paragraph (1); and

"excluded day" means a day specified as such by rule 46.

41 Delays in communication services

(1) The registrar shall extend any time or period in these Rules where he is satisfied that the failure to do something under these Rules was wholly or mainly attributed to a delay in, or failure of, a communication service.

(2) Any extension under paragraph (1) shall be—

    (a)   made after giving the parties such notice; and

    (b)   subject to such conditions,

as the registrar may direct.

(3) In this rule "communication service" means a service by which documents may be sent and delivered and includes post, electronic communications and courier.

Address for service

42   Address for service

(1) For the purposes of any proceedings under the Act, an address for service shall be furnished by—

    (a)   an applicant for the registration of a design;

    (b)   a person who makes an application under section 11ZB for a declaration of invalidity of a registered design;

    (c)   the registered proprietor of the design who opposes such an application.

(2) The proprietor of a registered design, or any person who has registered any interest in a registered design, may furnish an address for service on Form DF1A.

(3) Where a person has furnished an address for service under paragraph (1) or (2), he may substitute a new address for service by notifying the registrar on Form DF1A.

[(4) An address for service furnished under this Rule shall be an address in the United Kingdom, another EEA state or the Channel Islands.]

(6) In this rule "EEA State" means a member State, Iceland, Liechtenstein or Norway.

NOTES

    1   Rule 42(4) substituted for rule 42(4)–(5) by Patents, Trade Marks and Designs (Address for Service) Rules 2009/546 rule 6 (6 April 2009)

43   Failure to furnish an address for service

(1) Where—

    (a)   a person has failed to furnish an address for service under rule 42(1); and

    (b)   the registrar has sufficient information enabling him to contact that person,

the registrar shall direct that person to furnish an address for service.

Appendix 3 Legislation

(2) Where a direction has been given under paragraph (1), the person directed shall, before the end of the period of 2 months beginning with the date of the direction, furnish an address for service.

(3) Paragraph (4) applies where—

(a) a direction was given under paragraph (1) and the period prescribed by paragraph (2) has expired; or

(b) the registrar had insufficient information to give a direction under paragraph (1),

and the person has failed to furnish an address for service.

(4) Where this paragraph applies—

(a) in the case of an applicant for the registration of a design, the application shall be treated as withdrawn;

(b) in the case of a person applying under section 11ZB for a declaration of invalidity, his application shall be treated as withdrawn; and

(c) in the case of the proprietor who is opposing an application under section 11ZB, he shall be deemed to have withdrawn from the proceedings.

(5) In this rule an "address for service" means an address which complies with the requirements of [rule 42(4)].

NOTES
1 Words repealed by Patents, Trade Marks and Designs (Address for Service) Rules 2009/546 rule 7 (6 April 2009).

Miscellaneous

44   The journal

(1) The registrar shall publish a journal which shall contain—

(a) everything which is required by the Act or these Rules to be published; and

(b) any other information that the registrar may consider to be generally useful or important.

(2) In these Rules "the journal" means the journal published under paragraph (1).

45   Hours of business

(1) For the transaction of relevant business by the public the Patent Office shall be open—

(a) on Monday to Friday between 9.00am and midnight; and

(b) on Saturday between 9.00am and 1.00pm.

(2) For the transaction of all other business by the public under the Act the Patent Office shall be open between 9.00am and 5.00pm.

(3) In this Part "relevant business" means the filing of any application or other document except—

(a)   an application for an extension under section 8; or

(b)   an application for the registration of a design or designs made by virtue of section 14.

46   Excluded days

(1) The following shall be excluded days for the transaction by the public of business under the Act—

(a)   a Sunday;

(b)   Good Friday;

(c)   Christmas day; or

(d)   a day which is specified or proclaimed to be a bank holiday by or under section 1 of the Banking and Financial Dealings Act 1971.

(2) A Saturday shall be an excluded day for the transaction by the public of business under the Act, except relevant business (see rule 45(1)).

47   Transitional provisions and revocation

(1) Schedule 2 (transitional provisions) shall have effect.

(2) The instruments set out in Schedule 3 (revocations) are revoked to the extent specified.

Form number	Title	Rule
DF1A	Appointment or change of agent or contact address	36 and 42
DF2A	Application to register one or more designs	4
DF2B	Application to register one or more designs divided from an earlier application	4
DF2C	Application to publish one or more designs	9
DF9A	Renewal of design registration	12
DF12A	Application to record a change of ownership or to record or cancel a licence or security	27
DF16A	Change of proprietor's name or address	34
DF19A	Request to invalidate a design registration	15
DF19B	Notice of counter-statement	15
DF19C	Notice by proprietor to cancel a registration	14
DF21	Request for a search of the UK designs register	31
DF23	Request for a Certified Copy	32
DF29	Request to restore a registration	13

Schedule 2
TRANSITIONAL PROVISIONS

Part I

PROVISIONS RELATING TO PENDING APPLICATIONS

1. Interpretation

In this Part—

> "the old Rules" means the Registered Designs Rules 1995 as they had effect immediately before the coming into force of these Rules; and
> "the RRO" means the Regulatory Reform (Registered Designs) Order 2006.

NOTES
> 1. Amended by SI 1999/3196, 2001/3950, 2006/760 and 2006/1029.

2. Statement of objections

Where—

(a) the registrar sent the applicant a statement of objections under rule 29 of the old Rules; and

(b) the applicant has not sent to the registrar his observations in writing on the objections,

the objections shall be treated as the "statement of objections" under rule 8 of these Rules and the date on which the objections were sent shall be treated as the date on which the applicant was notified under rule 8(1).

3. Period prescribed for the purposes of section 3B(3)

Where—

(a) the period prescribed by rule 10 of these Rules has expired before the date on which these Rules come into force; and

(b) the period prescribed for the purposes of section 3B by rule 36A of the old Rules has not expired before the date on which these Rules come into force,

the period prescribed for the purposes of section 3B(3) shall be that mentioned in rule 36A of the old Rules.

4. Publication

Rules 9 and 11 shall not apply where the application for registration of a design under the Act was made before these Rules come into force.

5. Restoration

An application made in accordance with rule 41(2) of the old Rules shall be treated as made in accordance with rule 13(1) of these Rules.

66
666

666666666666666666666666666666666666666666666666666666666666666666666666666666666666666666666666666666666666666666666666666666666666666666666

6. Inspection of register

Where the amendments made to section 22, by article 16(2)(b) and (3) of the RRO, do not apply to a registration under the Act (by reason of article 19 of the RRO), rule 69 of the old Rules shall continue to have effect in relation to that registration.

7. Inspection of documents

Rules 29 and 30 shall not apply to any document filed at the Patent Office before these Rules come into force.

8. Requests for certified copies

A request under rule 72 of the old Rules for a certified copy of any representation, specimen or document kept at the Patent Office shall be treated as an application under rule 33(1) of these Rules.

9. Invalidity proceedings

(1) The time the registrar allowed under rule 53 of the old Rules for the filing of the counter-statement shall be treated as the period specified under rule 15(4) of these Rules.

(2) Where—

    (a)   an application for a declaration of invalidity which was made before these Rules came into force; and

    (b)   a counter-statement has been filed by the registered proprietor,

the registrar shall, within 28 days of these Rules coming into force, specify the periods within which any evidence may be filed, in accordance with rule 16(1).

Part 2

PROVISIONS RELATING TO APPLICATIONS UNDER THE OLD ACT

10. Interpretation

In this Part, "the old Act" means the Registered Designs Act 1949 as it had effect on 27th October 2001.

11. Application of this Part

This Part applies to—

    (a)   transitional registrations, within the meaning of regulation 11 of the Registered Designs Regulations 2001;

    (b)   post-1989 registrations, within the meaning of regulation 12 of those Regulations; and

    (c)   pre-1989 registrations, within the meaning of regulation 13 of those Regulations.

12. Meaning of applied industrially

For the purposes of section 6 of the old Act, the circumstances in which a design shall be regarded as "applied industrially" are—

    (a)   where the design is applied to more than fifty articles, which do not all together constitute a single set of articles (within the meaning of section 44(1) of the old Act); or

    (b)   where the design is applied to goods manufactured in lengths or pieces, not being hand-made goods.

13. Applications under section 11(2) of old Act

(1) Part 4 of these Rules applies to an application under section 11(2) of the old Act for the cancellation of registration as it applies to an application for a declaration of invalidity under section 11ZB of the Act.

(2) Where an application is made under section 11(2) of the old Act, any reference in rule 15(1) to an application for a declaration of invalidity under section 11ZB of the Act shall be construed as a reference to an application under the relevant provision of the old Act.

(3) For the purposes of rule 23(1), an application under section 11(2) of the old Act shall be treated as if it were mentioned in section 30(3) of the Act.

Schedule 3

REVOCATIONS

Title and number	Extent of revocation
Registered Designs Rules 1995 (SI 1995/2912)	The whole rules.
Registered Designs (Amendment) Rules 1999 (SI 1999/3196)	The whole rules.
Registered Designs (Amendment) Rules 2001 (SI 2001/3950)	The whole rules.
Patents, Trade Marks and Designs (Address For Service, etc) Rules 2006 (SI 2006/760)	Rules 10 to 14.
Trade Marks and Designs (Address For Service) (Amendment) Rules 2006 (2006/1029)	Rule 2.

Commission Regulation (EC) No 2245/2002 of 21 October 2002 implementing Council Regulation (EC) No 6/2002 on Community designs

THE COMMISSION OF THE EUROPEAN COMMUNITIES,

Having regard to the Treaty establishing the European Community,

Having regard to Council Regulation (EC) No 6/2002 of 12 December 2001 on Community designs(1), and in particular Article 107(3) thereof,

Whereas:

(1) Regulation (EC) No 6/2002 creates a system enabling a design having effect throughout the Community to be obtained on the basis of an application to the Office for Harmonisation in the Internal Market (trade marks and designs) (hereinafter 'the Office').

(2) For this purpose, Regulation (EC) No 6/2002 contains the necessary provisions for a procedure leading to the registration of a Community design, as well as for the administration of registered Community designs, for appeals against decisions of the Office and for proceedings for the invalidation of a Community design.

(3) The present Regulation lays down the necessary measures for implementing the provisions of Regulation (EC) No 6/2002.

(4) This Regulation should ensure the smooth and efficient operation of design proceedings before the Office.

(5) The measures provided for in this Regulation are in accordance with the opinion of the Committee established under Article 109 of Regulation (EC) No 6/2002,

HAS ADOPTED THIS REGULATION:

CHAPTER I

APPLICATION PROCEDURE

Article 1 — Content of the application

1. The application for a registered Community design shall contain:

(a) a request for registration of the design as a registered Community design;

(b) the name, address and nationality of the applicant and the State in which the applicant is domiciled or in which it has its seat or establishment. Names of natural persons shall take the form of the family name and the given name(s). Names of legal entities shall be indicated by their official designation, which may be abbreviated in a customary manner; furthermore, the State whose law governs such entities shall be indicated.

The telephone numbers as well as fax numbers and details of other data-communications links, such as electronic mail, may be given. Only one address shall, in principle, be indicated for each applicant; where several addresses are indicated, only the address mentioned first shall be taken into account, except where the applicant designates one of the addresses as an address for service. If the Office has given the applicant an identification number, it shall be sufficient to mention that number together with the name of the applicant;

(c)   a representation of the design in accordance with Article 4 of this Regulation or, if the application concerns a two-dimensional design and contains a request for deferment of publication in accordance with Article 50 of Regulation (EC) No 6/2002, a specimen in accordance with Article 5 of this Regulation;

(d)   an indication, in accordance with Article 3(3), of the products in which the design is intended to be incorporated or to which it is intended to be applied;

(e)   if the applicant has appointed a representative, the name of that representative and the address of his/her place of business in accordance with point (b); if the representative has more than one business address or if there are two or more representatives with different business addresses, the application shall indicate which address shall be used as an address for service; where no such indication is made, only the first-mentioned address shall be taken into account as an address for service. If there is more than one applicant, the application may indicate the appointment of one applicant or representative as common representative. If an appointed representative has been given an identification number by the Office, it shall be sufficient to mention that number together with the name of the representative;

(f)   if applicable, a declaration that priority of a previous application is claimed pursuant to Article 42 of Regulation (EC) No 6/2002, stating the date on which the previous application was filed and the country in which or for which it was filed;

(g)   if applicable, a declaration that exhibition priority is claimed pursuant to Article 44 of Regulation (EC) No 6/2002, stating the name of the exhibition and the date of the first disclosure of the products in which the design is incorporated or to which it is applied;

(h)   a specification of the language in which the application is filed, and of the second language pursuant to Article 98(2) of Regulation (EC) No 6/2002;

(i)   he signature of the applicant or his/her representative in accordance with Article 65.

2. The application may contain:

(a)   a single description per design not exceeding 100 words explaining the representation of the design or the specimen; the description must relate only to those features which appear in the reproductions of the design or the specimen; it shall not contain statements as to the purported novelty or individual character of the design or its technical value;

(b) a request for deferment of publication of registration in accordance with Article 50(1) of Regulation (EC) No 6/2002;

(c) an indication of the 'Locarno classification' of the products contained in the application, that is to say, of the class or classes and the subclass or subclasses to which they belong in accordance with the Annex to the Agreement establishing an international classification for industrial designs, signed at Locarno on 8 October 1968 (hereinafter 'the Locarno Agreement'), referred to in Article 3 and subject to Article 2(2);

(d) the citation of the designer or of the team of designers or a statement signed by the applicant to the effect that the designer or team of designers has waived the right to be cited under Article 36(3)(e) of Regulation (EC) No 6/2002.

Article 2 — Multiple application

1. An application may be a multiple application requesting the registration of several designs.

2. When several designs other than ornamentation are combined in a multiple application, the application shall be divided if the products in which the designs are intended to be incorporated or to which they are intended to be applied belong to more than one class of the Locarno Classification.

3. For each design contained in the multiple application the applicant shall provide a representation of the design in accordance with Article 4 and the indication of the product in which the design is intended to be incorporated or to be applied.

4. The applicant shall number the designs contained in the multiple application consecutively, using arabic numerals.

Article 3 — Classification and indication of products

1. Products shall be classified in accordance with Article 1 of the Locarno Agreement, as amended and in force at the date of filing of the design.

2. The classification of products shall serve exclusively administrative purposes.

3. The indication of products shall be worded in such a way as to indicate clearly the nature of the products and to enable each product to be classified in only one class of the Locarno classification, preferably using the terms appearing in the list of products set out therein.

4. The products shall be grouped according to the classes of the Locarno classification, each group being preceded by the number of the class to which that group of products belongs and presented in the order of the classes and subclasses under that classification.

Article 4 — Representation of the design

1. The representation of the design shall consist in a graphic or photographic reproduction of the design, either in black and white or in colour. It shall meet the following requirements:

(a) save where the application is filed by electronic means pursuant to Article 67, the representation must be filed on separate sheets of paper or reproduced on the page provided for that purpose in the form made available by the Office pursuant to Article 68;

(b) in the case of separate sheets of paper, the design shall be reproduced on opaque white paper and either pasted or printed directly on it. Only one copy shall be filed and the sheets of paper shall not be folded or stapled;

(c) the size of the separate sheet shall be DIN A4 size (29,7 cm x 21 cm) and the space used for the reproduction shall be no larger than 26,2 cm x 17 cm. A margin of at least 2,5 cm shall be left on the left-hand side; at the top of each sheet of paper the number of views shall be indicated pursuant to paragraph 2 and, in the case of a multiple application, the consecutive number of the design; no explanatory text, wording or symbols, other than the indication 'top' or the name or address of the applicant, may be displayed thereon;

(d) where the application is filed by electronic means, the graphic or photographic reproduction of the designs shall be in a data format determined by the President of the Office; the manner of identifying the different designs contained in a multiple application, or the different views, shall be determined by the President of the Office;

(e) the design shall be reproduced on a neutral background and shall not be retouched with ink or correcting fluid. It shall be of a quality permitting all the details of the matter for which protection is sought to be clearly distinguished and permitting it to be reduced or enlarged to a size no greater than 8 cm by 16 cm per view for entry in the Register of Community Designs provided for in Article 72 of Regulation (EC) No 6/2002, hereinafter 'the Register', and for direct publishing in the Community Designs Bulletin referred to in Article 73 of that Regulation.

2. The representation may contain no more than seven different views of the design. Any one graphic or photographic reproduction may contain only one view. The applicant shall number each view using arabic numerals. The number shall consist of separate numerals separated by a point, the numeral to the left of the point indicating the number of the design, that to the right indicating the number of the view.

In cases where more than seven views are provided, the Office may disregard for registration and publication any of the extra views. The Office shall take the views in the consecutive order in which the views are numbered by the applicant.

3. Where an application concerns a design that consists in a repeating surface pattern, the representation of the design shall show the complete pattern and a sufficient portion of the repeating surface.

The size limits set out in paragraph 1(c) shall apply.

4. Where an application concerns a design consisting in a typographic typeface, the representation of the design shall consist in a string of all the letters of the alphabet, in both upper and lower case, and of all the arabic numerals, together with a text of five lines produced using that typeface, both letters and numerals being in the size pitch 16.

Article 5 — Specimens

1. Where the application concerns a two-dimensional design and contains a request for a deferment of publication, in accordance with Article 50(1) of Regulation (EC) No 6/2002, the representation of the design may be replaced by a specimen pasted on a sheet of paper.

Applications for which a specimen is submitted must be sent by a single mail or directly delivered to the office of filing.

Both the application and the specimen shall be submitted at the same time.

2. The specimens shall not exceed 26,2 cm x 17 cm in size, 50 grams in weight or 3 mm in thickness. The specimen shall be capable of being stored, unfolded, alongside documents of the size prescribed in Article 4(1)(c).

3. Specimens that are perishable or dangerous to store shall not be filed.

The specimen shall be filed in five copies; in the case of a multiple application, five copies of the specimen shall be filed for each design.

4. Where the design concerns a repeating surface pattern, the specimen shall show the complete pattern and a sufficient portion of the repeating surface in length and width. The limits set out in paragraph 2 shall apply.

Article 6 — Fees for the application

1. The following fees shall be paid at the time when the application is submitted to the Office:

    (a)   the registration fee;
    (b)   the publication fee or a deferment fee if deferment of publication has been requested;
    (c)   an additional registration fee in respect of each additional design included in a multiple application;
    (d)   an additional publication fee in respect of each additional design included in a multiple application, or an additional deferment fee in respect of each additional design included in a multiple application if deferment of publication has been requested.

2. Where the application includes a request for deferment of publication of registration, the publication fee and any additional publication fee in respect of each additional design included in a multiple application shall be paid within the time limits specified in Article 15(4).

Article 7 — Filing of the application

1. The Office shall mark the documents making up the application with the date of its receipt and the file number of the application.

Each design contained in a multiple application shall be numbered by the Office in accordance with a system determined by the President.

The Office shall issue to the applicant without delay a receipt which shall specify the file number, the representation, description or other identification of the design, the nature and the number of the documents and the date of their receipt.

In the case of a multiple application, the receipt issued by the Office shall specify the first design and the number of designs filed.

2. If the application is filed with the central industrial property office of a Member State or at the Benelux Design Office in accordance with Article 35 of Regulation (EC) No 6/2002, the office of filing shall number each page of the application, using arabic numerals. The office of filing shall mark the documents making up the application with the date of receipt and the number of pages before forwarding the application to the Office.

The office of filing shall issue to the applicant without delay a receipt specifying the nature and the number of the documents and the date of their receipt.

3. If the Office receives an application forwarded by the central industrial property office of a Member State or the Benelux Design Office, it shall mark the application with the date of receipt and the file number and shall issue to the applicant without delay a receipt in accordance with the third and fourth subparagraphs of paragraph 1, indicating the date of receipt at the Office.

Article 8 — Claiming priority

1. Where the priority of one or more previous applications is claimed in the application pursuant to Article 42 of Regulation (EC) No 6/2002, the applicant shall indicate the file number of the previous application and file a copy of it within three months of the filing date referred to in Article 38 of that Regulation. The President of the Office shall determine the evidence to be provided by the applicant.

2. Where, subsequent to the filing of the application, the applicant wishes to claim the priority of one or more previous applications pursuant to Article 42 of Regulation (EC) No 6/2002, he/she shall submit, within one month of the filing date, the declaration of priority, stating the date on which and the country in or for which the previous application was made.

The applicant shall submit to the Office the indications and evidence referred to in paragraph 1 within three months of receipt of the declaration of priority.

Article 9 — Exhibition priority

1. Where exhibition priority has been claimed in the application pursuant to Article 44 of Regulation (EC) No 6/2002, the applicant shall, together with the

application or at the latest within three months of the filing date, file a certificate issued at the exhibition by the authority responsible for the protection of industrial property at the exhibition.

That certificate shall declare that the design was incorporated in or applied to the product and disclosed at the exhibition, and shall state the opening date of the exhibition and, where the first disclosure of the product did not coincide with the opening date of the exhibition, the date of such first disclosure. The certificate shall be accompanied by an identification of the actual disclosure of the product, duly certified by that authority.

2. Where the applicant wishes to claim an exhibition priority subsequent to the filing of the application, the declaration of priority, indicating the name of the exhibition and the date of the first disclosure of the product in which the design was incorporated or to which it was applied, shall be submitted within one month of the filing date. The indications and evidence referred to in paragraph 1 shall be submitted to the Office within three months of receipt of the declaration of priority.

Article 10 — Examination of requirements for a filing date and of formal requirements

1. The Office shall notify the applicant that a date of filing cannot be granted if the application does not contain:

(a) a request for registration of the design as a registered Community design;

(b) information identifying the applicant;

(c) a representation of the design pursuant to Article 4(1)(d) and (e) or, where applicable, a specimen.

2. If the deficiencies indicated in paragraph 1 are remedied within two months of receipt of the notification, the date on which all the deficiencies are remedied shall determine the date of filing.

If the deficiencies are not remedied before the time limit expires, the application shall not be dealt with as a Community design application. Any fees paid shall be refunded.

3. The Office shall call upon the applicant to remedy the deficiencies noted within a time limit specified by it where, although a date of filing has been granted, the examination reveals that:

(a) the requirements set out in Articles 1, 2, 4 and 5 or the other formal requirements for applications laid down in the Regulation (EC) No 6/2002 or in this Regulation have not been complied with;

(b) the full amount of the fees payable pursuant to Article 6(1), read in conjunction with Commission Regulation (EC) No 2246/2002(2), has not been received by the Office;

(c) where priority has been claimed pursuant to Articles 8 and 9, either in the application itself or within one month after the date of filing, the other requirements set out in those Articles have not been complied with;

(d) in the case of a multiple application, the products in which the designs are intended to be incorporated or to which they are intended to be applied belong to more than one class of the Locarno classification.

In particular, the Office shall call upon the applicant to pay the required fees within two months of the date of notification, together with the late payment fees provided for in Article 107(2)(a) to (d) of Regulation (EC) No 6/2002 and as set out in Regulation (EC) No 2246/2002.

In the case of the deficiency referred to in point (d) of the first subparagraph, the Office shall call upon the applicant to divide the multiple application in order to ensure compliance with the requirements under Article 2(2). It shall also call upon the applicant to pay the total amount of the fees for all the applications resulting from the separation of the multiple application, within such a time limit as it may specify.

After the applicant has complied with the request to divide the application within the time limit set, the date of filing of the resulting application or applications shall be the date of filing granted to the multiple application initially filed.

4. If the deficiencies referred to in paragraph 3(a) and (d) are not remedied before the time limit expires, the Office shall reject the application.

5. If the fees payable pursuant to Article 6(1)(a) and (b) are not paid before the time limit expires, the Office shall reject the application.

6. If any additional fees payable pursuant to Article 6(1)(c) or (d) in respect of multiple applications are not paid or not paid in full before the time limit expires, the Office shall reject the application in respect of all the additional designs which are not covered by the amount paid.

In the absence of any criteria for determining which designs are intended to be covered, the Office shall take the designs in the numerical order in which they are represented in accordance with Article 2(4). The Office shall reject the application in so far as it concerns designs for which additional fees have not been paid or have not been paid in full.

7. If the deficiencies referred to in paragraph 3(c) are not remedied before the time limit expires, the right of priority for the application shall be lost.

8. If any of the deficiencies referred to in paragraph 3 is not remedied before the time limit expires and such deficiency concerns only some of the designs contained in a multiple application, the Office shall reject the application, or the right of priority shall be lost, only in so far as those designs are concerned.

Article 11 — Examination of grounds for non-registrability

1. Where, pursuant to Article 47 of Regulation (EC) No 6/2002, the Office finds, in the course of carrying out the examination under Article 10 of this Regulation, that the design for which protection is sought does not correspond to the definition of design provided in Article 3(a) of Regulation (EC) No 6/2002 or that the design is contrary to public policy or to accepted

principles of morality, it shall inform the applicant that the design is non-registrable, specifying the ground for non-registrability.

2. The Office shall specify a time limit within which the applicant may submit his/her observations, withdraw the application or amend it by submitting an amended representation of the design, provided that the identity of the design is retained.

3. Where the applicant fails to overcome the grounds for non-registrability within the time limit, the Office shall refuse the application. If those grounds concern only some of the designs contained in a multiple application, the Office shall refuse the application only in so far as those designs are concerned.

Article 12 — Withdrawal or correction of the application

1. The applicant may at any time withdraw a Community design application or, in the case of a multiple application, withdraw some of the designs contained in the application.

2. Only the name and address of the applicant, errors of wording or of copying, or obvious mistakes may be corrected, at the request of the applicant and provided that such correction does not change the representation of the design.

3. An application for the correction of the application pursuant to paragraph 2 shall contain:

(a) the file number of the application;
(b) the name and the address of the applicant in accordance with Article 1(1)(b);
(c) where the applicant has appointed a representative, the name and the business address of the representative in accordance with Article 1(1)(e);
(d) the indication of the element of the application to be corrected and that element in its corrected version.

4. If the requirements for the correction of the application are not fulfilled, the Office shall communicate the deficiency to the applicant. If the deficiency is not remedied within the time limits specified by the Office, the Office shall reject the application for correction.

5. A single application may be made for the correction of the same element in two or more applications submitted by the same applicant.

6. Paragraphs 2 to 5 shall apply mutatis mutandis to applications to correct the name or the business address of a representative appointed by the applicant.

CHAPTER II

REGISTRATION PROCEDURE

Article 13 — Registration of the design

1. If the application satisfies the requirements referred to in Article 48 of Regulation (EC) No 6/2002, the design contained in that application and the particulars set out in Article 69(2) of this Regulation shall be recorded in the Register.

2. If the application contains a request for deferment of publication pursuant to Article 50 of Regulation (EC) No 6/2002, that fact and the date of expiry of the period of deferment shall be recorded.

3. The fees payable pursuant to Article 6(1) shall not be refunded even if the design applied for is not registered.

Article 14 — Publication of the registration

1. The registration of the design shall be published in the Community Designs Bulletin.

2. Subject to paragraph 3, the publication of the registration shall contain:

(a) the name and address of the holder of the Community design (hereinafter 'the holder');

(b) where applicable, the name and business address of the representative appointed by the holder other than a representative falling within the first subparagraph of Article 77(3) of Regulation (EC) No 6/2002; if more than one representative has the same business address, only the name and business address of the first-named representative shall be published, the name being followed by the words 'et al'; if there are two or more representatives with different business addresses, only the address for service determined pursuant to Article 1(1)(e) of this Regulation shall be published; where an association of representatives is appointed pursuant to Article 62(9) only the name and business address of the association shall be published;

(c) the representation of the design pursuant to Article 4; where the representation of the design is in colour, the publication shall be in colour;

(d) where applicable, an indication that a description has been filed pursuant to Article 1(2)(a);

(e) an indication of the products in which the design is intended to be incorporated or to which it is intended to be applied, preceded by the number of the relevant classes and subclasses of the Locarno classification, and grouped accordingly;

(f) where applicable, the name of the designer or the team of designers;

(g) the date of filing and the file number and, in the case of a multiple application, the file number of each design;

(h) where applicable, particulars of the claim of priority pursuant to Article 42 of Regulation (EC) No 6/2002;

(i)   where applicable, particulars of the claim of exhibition priority pursuant to Article 44 of Regulation (EC) No 6/2002;

(j)   the date and the registration number and the date of the publication of the registration;

(k)   the language in which the application was filed and the second language indicated by the applicant pursuant to Article 98(2) of Regulation (EC) No 6/2002.

3. If the application contains a request for deferment of publication pursuant to Article 50 of Regulation (EC) No 6/2002, a mention of the deferment shall be published in the Community Designs Bulletin, together with the name of the holder, the name of the representative, if any, the date of filing and registration, and the file number of the application. Neither the representation of the design nor any particulars identifying its appearance shall be published.

Article 15 — Deferment of publication

1. Where the application contains a request for deferment of publication pursuant to Article 50 of Regulation (EC) No 6/2002, the holder shall, together with the request or at the latest three months before the 30-month deferment period expires:

(a)   pay the publication fee referred to in Article 6(1)(b);

(b)   in the case of a multiple registration, pay the additional publication fees, referred to in Article 6(1)(d);

(c)   in cases where a representation of the design has been replaced by a specimen in accordance with Article 5, file a representation of the design in accordance with Article 4. This applies to all the designs contained in a multiple application for which publication is requested;

(d)   in the case of a multiple registration, clearly indicate which of the designs contained therein is to be published or which of the designs are to be surrendered, or, if the period of deferment has not yet expired, for which designs deferment is to be continued.

Where the holder requests publication before the expiry of the 30-month deferment period, he/she shall, at the latest three months before the requested date of publication, comply with the requirements set out in points (a) to (d) of the first paragraph.

2. If the holder fails to comply with the requirements set out in paragraph 1(c) or (d), the Office shall call upon him/her to remedy the deficiencies within a specified time limit which shall in no case expire after the 30-month deferment period.

3. If the holder fails to remedy the deficiencies referred to in paragraph 2 within the applicable time limit:

(a)   the registered Community design shall be deemed from the outset not to have had the effects specified in Regulation (EC) No 6/2002;

(b)   where the holder has requested earlier publication as provided for under the second subparagraph of paragraph 1, the request shall be deemed not to have been filed.

4. If the holder fails to pay the fees referred to in paragraph 1(a) or (b), the Office shall call upon him/her to pay those fees together with the fees for late payment provided for in Article 107(2)(b) or (d) of Regulation (EC) No 6/2002 and as set out in Regulation (EC) No 2246/2002, within a specified time limit which shall in no case expire after the 30-month deferment period.

If no payment has been made within that time limit, the Office shall notify the holder that the registered Community design has from the outset not had the effects specified in Regulation (EC) No 6/2002.

If, in respect of a multiple registration, a payment is made within that time limit but is insufficient to cover all the fees payable pursuant to paragraph 1(a) and (b), as well as the applicable fee for late payment, all the designs in respect of which the fees have not been paid shall be deemed from the outset not to have had the effects specified in Regulation (EC) No 6/2002.

Unless it is clear which designs the amount paid is intended to cover, and in the absence of other criteria for determining which designs are intended to be covered, the Office shall take the designs in the numerical order in which they are represented in accordance with Article 2(4).

All designs for which the additional publication fee has not been paid or has not been paid in full, together with the applicable fee for late payment, shall be deemed from the outset not to have had the effects specified in Regulation (EC) No 6/2002.

Article 16 — Publication after the period for deferment

1. Where the holder has complied with the requirements laid down in Article 15, the Office shall, at the expiry of the period for deferment or in the case of a request for earlier publication, as soon as is technically possible:

(a) publish the registered Community design in the Community Designs Bulletin, with the indications set out in Article 14(2), together with an indication of the fact that the application contained a request for deferment of publication pursuant to Article 50 of Regulation (EC) No 6/2002 and, where applicable, that a specimen was filed in accordance with Article 5 of this Regulation;

(b) make available for public inspection any file relating to the design;

(c) open to public inspection all the entries in the Register, including any entries withheld from inspection pursuant to Article 73.

2. Where Article 15(4) applies, the actions referred to in paragraph 1 of this Article shall not take place in respect of those designs contained in the multiple registration which are deemed from the outset not to have had the effects specified in Regulation (EC) No 6/2002.

Article 17 — Certificate of registration

1. After publication, the Office shall issue to the holder a certificate of registration which shall contain the entries in the Register provided for in Article 69(2) and a statement to the effect that those entries have been recorded in the Register.

2. The holder may request that certified or uncertified copies of the certificate of registration be supplied to him/her upon payment of a fee.

Article 18 — Maintenance of the design in an amended form

1. Where, pursuant to Article 25(6) of Regulation (EC) No 6/2002, the registered Community design is maintained in an amended form, the Community design in its amended form shall be entered in the Register and published in the Community Designs Bulletin.

2. Maintenance of a design in an amended form may include a partial disclaimer, not exceeding 100 words, by the holder or an entry in the Register of Community Designs of a court decision or a decision by the Office declaring the partial invalidity of the design right.

Article 19 — Change of the name or address of the holder or of his/her registered representative

1. A change of the name or address of the holder which is not the consequence of a transfer of the registered design shall, at the request of the holder, be recorded in the Register.

2. An application for a change of the name or address of the holder shall contain:

(a)   the registration number of the design;

(b)   the name and the address of the holder as recorded in the Register. If the holder has been given an identification number by the Office, it shall be sufficient to indicate that number together with the name of the holder;

(c)   the indication of the name and address of the holder, as changed, in accordance with Article 1(1)(b);

(d)   where the holder has appointed a representative, the name and business address of the representative, in accordance with Article 1(1)(e).

3. The application referred to in paragraph 2 shall not be subject to payment of a fee.

4. A single application may be made for a change of the name or address in respect of two or more registrations of the same holder.

5. If the requirements set out in paragraphs 1 and 2 are not fulfilled, the Office shall communicate the deficiency to the applicant.

If the deficiency is not remedied within the time limits specified by the Office, the Office shall reject the application.

6. Paragraphs 1 to 5 shall apply mutatis mutandis to a change of the name or address of the registered representative.

7. Paragraphs 1 to 6 shall apply mutatis mutandis to applications for Community designs. The change shall be recorded in the files kept by the Office concerning the Community design application.

Article 20 — Correction of mistakes and errors in the Register and in the publication of the registration

Where the registration of a design or the publication of the registration contains a mistake or error attributable to the Office, the Office shall correct the error or mistake of its own motion or at the request of the holder.

Where such a request is made by the holder, Article 19 shall apply mutatis mutandis. The request shall not be subject to payment of a fee.

The Office shall publish the corrections made pursuant to this Article.

CHAPTER III

RENEWAL OF REGISTRATION

Article 21 — Notification of expiry of registration

At least six months before expiry of the registration, the Office shall inform the holder, and any person having a right entered in the Register, including a licence, in respect of the Community design, that the registration is approaching expiry. Failure to give notification shall not affect the expiry of the registration.

Article 22 — Renewal of registration

1. An application for renewal of registration shall contain:

(a) where the application is filed by the holder, his/her name and address in accordance with Article 1(1)(b);

(b) where the application is filed by a person expressly authorised to do so by the holder, the name and address of that person and evidence that he/she is authorised to file the application;

(c) where the applicant has appointed a representative, the name and business address of the representative in accordance with Article 1(1)(e);

(d) the registration number;

(e) where applicable, an indication that renewal is requested for all the designs covered by a multiple registration or, if the renewal is not requested for all such designs, an indication of those designs for which renewal is requested.

2. The fees payable pursuant to Article 13 of Regulation (EC) No 6/2002 for the renewal of a registration shall consist of:

(a) a renewal fee, which, in cases where several designs are covered by a multiple registration, shall be proportionate to the number of designs covered by the renewal;

(b) where applicable, the additional fee for late payment of the renewal fee or late submission of the request for renewal, pursuant to Article 13 of Regulation (EC) No 6/2002, as specified in Regulation (EC) No 2246/2002.

3. Where the application for renewal is filed within the time limits provided for in Article 13(3) of Regulation (EC) No 6/2002, but the other conditions for

renewal provided for in Article 13 thereof and in this Regulation are not satisfied, the Office shall inform the applicant of the deficiencies.

If the application is filed by a person whom the holder has expressly authorised to do so, the holder of the design shall receive a copy of the notification.

4. Where an application for renewal is not submitted or is submitted after expiry of the time limit provided for in the second sentence of Article 13(3) of Regulation (EC) No 6/2002, or if the fees are not paid or are paid only after expiry of the relevant time limit, or if the deficiencies are not remedied within the time limit specified by the Office, the Office shall determine that the registration has expired and shall notify accordingly the holder and, where appropriate, the applicant for renewal and the person recorded in the Register as having rights in the design.

In the case of a multiple registration, where the fees paid are insufficient to cover all the designs for which renewal is requested, such a determination shall be made only after the Office has established which designs the amount paid is intended to cover.

In the absence of other criteria for determining which designs are intended to be covered, the Office shall take the designs in the numerical order in which they are represented in accordance with Article 2(4).

The Office shall determine that the registration has expired with regard to all designs for which the renewal fees have not been paid or have not been paid in full.

5. Where the determination made pursuant to paragraph 4 has become final, the Office shall cancel the design from the Register with effect from the day following the day on which the existing registration expired.

6. Where the renewal fees provided for in paragraph 2 have been paid but the registration is not renewed, those fees shall be refunded.

CHAPTER IV

TRANSFER, LICENCES AND OTHER RIGHTS, CHANGES

Article 23 — Transfer

1. An application for registration of a transfer pursuant to Article 28 of Regulation (EC) No 6/2002 shall contain:

    (a)   the registration number of the Community design;
    (b)   particulars of the new holder in accordance with Article 1(1)(b);
    (c)   where not all of the designs covered by a multiple registration are included in the transfer, particulars of the registered designs to which the transfer relates;
    (d)   documents duly establishing the transfer.

2. The application may contain, where applicable, the name and business address of the representative of the new holder, to be set out in accordance with Article 1(1)(e).

3. The application shall not be deemed to have been filed until the required fee has been paid. If the fee is not paid or is not paid in full, the Office shall notify the applicant accordingly.

4. The following shall constitute sufficient proof of transfer under paragraph 1(d):

(a) the application for registration of the transfer is signed by the registered holder or his/her representative and by the successor in title or his/her representative; or

(b) the application, if submitted by the successor in title, is accompanied by a declaration, signed by the registered holder or his/her representative, that he/she agrees to the registration of the successor in title; or

(c) the application is accompanied by a completed transfer form or document, signed by the registered holder or his/her representative and by the successor in title or his/her representative.

5. Where the conditions applicable to the registration of a transfer are not fulfilled, the Office shall notify the applicant of the deficiencies.

If the deficiencies are not remedied within the time limit specified by the Office, it shall reject the application for registration of the transfer.

6. A single application for registration of a transfer may be submitted for two or more registered Community designs, provided that the registered holder and the successor in title are the same in each case.

7. Paragraphs 1 to 6 shall apply mutatis mutandis to the transfer of applications for registered Community designs. The transfer shall be recorded in the files kept by the Office concerning the Community design application.

Article 24 — Registration of licences and other rights

1. Article 23(1)(a), (b) and (c) and Article 23(2), (3), (5) and (6) shall apply mutatis mutandis to the registration of the grant or transfer of a licence, to registration of the creation or transfer of a right in rem in respect of a registered Community design, and to registration of enforcement measures. However, where a registered Community design is involved in insolvency proceedings, the request of the competent national authority for an entry in the Register to this effect shall not be subject to payment of a fee.

In the case of a multiple registration, each registered Community design may, separately from the others, be licensed, the subject of a right in rem, levy of execution or insolvency proceedings.

2. Where the registered Community design is licensed for only a part of the Community, or for a limited period of time, the application for registration of the licence shall indicate the part of the Community or the period of time for which the licence is granted.

3. Where the conditions applicable to registration of licences and other rights, set out in Articles 29, 30 or 32 of Regulation (EC) No 6/2002, in paragraph 1 of this Article, and in the other applicable Articles of this Regulation are not fulfilled, the Office shall notify the applicant of the deficiencies.

If the deficiencies are not remedied within a time limit specified by the Office, it shall reject the application for registration.

4. Paragraphs 1, 2 and 3 shall apply mutatis mutandis to licences and other rights concerning applications for registered Community designs. Licences, rights in rem and enforcement measures shall be recorded in the files kept by the Office concerning the Community design application.

5. The request for a non-exclusive licence pursuant to Article 16(2) of Regulation (EC) No 6/2002 shall be made within three months of the date of the entry in the Register of the newly entitled holder.

Article 25 — Special provisions for the registration of a licence

1. A licence in respect of a registered Community design shall be recorded in the Register as an exclusive licence if the holder of the design or the licensee so requests.

2. A licence in respect of a registered Community design shall be recorded in the Register as a sub-licence where it is granted by a licensee whose licence is recorded in the Register.

3. A licence in respect of a registered Community design shall be recorded in the Register as a territorially limited licence if it is granted for a part of the Community.

4. A licence in respect of a registered Community design shall be recorded in the Register as a temporary licence if it is granted for a limited period of time.

Article 26 — Cancellation or modification of the registration of licences and other rights

1. A registration effected under Article 24 shall be cancelled upon application by one of the persons concerned.

2. The application shall contain:

(a) the registration number of the registered Community design, or in the case of a multiple registration, the number of each design; and
(b) particulars of the right whose registration is to be cancelled.

3. Application for cancellation of the registration of a licence or other right shall not be deemed to have been filed until the required fee has been paid.

If the fee is not paid or is not paid in full, the Office shall notify the applicant accordingly. A request from a competent national authority for cancellation of an entry where a registered Community design is involved in insolvency proceedings shall not be subject to payment of a fee.

4. The application shall be accompanied by documents showing that the registered right no longer exists or by a statement by the licensee or the holder of another right to the effect that he/she consents to cancellation of the registration.

5. Where the requirements for cancellation of the registration are not satisfied, the Office shall notify the applicant of the deficiencies. If the deficiencies are

not remedied within the time limit specified by the Office, it shall reject the application for cancellation of the registration.

6. Paragraphs 1, 2, 4 and 5 shall apply mutatis mutandis to a request for modification of a registration effected pursuant to Article 24.

7. Paragraphs 1 to 6 shall apply mutatis mutandis to entries made in the files pursuant to Article 24(4).

CHAPTER V

SURRENDER AND INVALIDITY

Article 27 — Surrender

1. A declaration of surrender pursuant to Article 51 of Regulation (EC) No 6/2002 shall contain:

(a) the registration number of the registered Community design;
(b) the name and address of the holder in accordance with Article 1(1)(b);
(c) where a representative has been appointed, the name and business address of the representative in accordance with Article 1(1)(e);
(d) where surrender is declared only for some of the designs contained in a multiple registration, an indication of the designs for which the surrender is declared or the designs which are to remain registered;
(e) where, pursuant to Article 51(3) of Regulation (EC) No 6/2002, the registered Community design is partially surrendered, a representation of the amended design in accordance with Article 4 of this Regulation.

2. Where a right of a third party relating to the registered Community design is entered in the Register, it shall be sufficient proof of his/her agreement to the surrender that a declaration of consent to the surrender is signed by the holder of that right or his/her representative.

Where a licence has been registered, surrender of the design shall be registered three months after the date on which the holder satisfies the Office that he/she has informed the licensee of his/her intention to surrender it. If the holder proves to the Office before the expiry of that period that the licensee has given his/her consent, the surrender shall be registered forthwith.

3. Where a claim relating to the entitlement to a registered Community design has been brought before a court pursuant to Article 15 of Regulation (EC) No 6/2002, a declaration of consent to the surrender, signed by the claimant or his/her representative, shall be sufficient proof of his/her agreement to the surrender.

4. If the requirements governing surrender are not fulfilled, the Office shall communicate the deficiencies to the declarant. If the deficiencies are not remedied within the time limit specified by the Office, the Office shall reject the entry of the surrender in the Register.

Article 28 — Application for a declaration of invalidity

1. An application to the Office for a declaration of invalidity pursuant to Article 52 of Regulation (EC) No 6/2002 shall contain:

(a) as concerns the registered Community design for which the declaration of invalidity is sought:

    (i) its registration number;

    (ii) the name and address of its holder;

(b) as regards the grounds on which the application is based:

    (i) a statement of the grounds on which the application for a declaration of invalidity is based;

    (ii) additionally, in the case of an application pursuant to Article 25(1)(d) of Regulation (EC) No 6/2002, the representation and particulars identifying the prior design on which the application for a declaration of invalidity is based and showing that the applicant is entitled to invoke the earlier design as a ground for invalidity pursuant to Article 25(3) of that Regulation;

    (iii) additionally, in the case of an application pursuant to Article 25(1)(e) or (f) of Regulation (EC) No 6/2002, the representation and particulars identifying the distinctive sign or the work protected by copyright on which the application for a declaration of invalidity is based and particulars showing that the applicant is the holder of the earlier right pursuant to Article 25(3) of that Regulation;

    (iv) additionally, in the case of an application pursuant to Article 25(1)(g) of the Regulation (EC) No 6/2002, the representation and particulars of the relevant item as referred to in that Article and particulars showing that the application is filed by the person or entity concerned by the improper use pursuant to Article 25(4) of that Regulation;

    (v) where the ground for invalidity is that the registered Community design does not fulfil the requirements set out in Article 5 or 6 of Regulation (EC) No 6/2002, the indication and the reproduction of the prior designs that could form an obstacle to the novelty or individual character of the registered Community design, as well as documents proving the existence of those earlier designs;

    (vi) an indication of the facts, evidence and arguments submitted in support of those grounds;

(c) as concerns the applicant:

    (i) his/her name and address in accordance with Article 1(1)(b);

    (ii) if the applicant has appointed a representative, the name and the business address of the representative, in accordance with Article 1(1)(e);

(iii) additionally, in the case of an application pursuant to Article 25(1)(c) of Regulation (EC) No 6/2002, particulars showing that the application is made by a person or by persons duly entitled pursuant to Article 25(2) of that Regulation.

2. The application shall be subject to the fee referred to in Article 52(2) of Regulation (EC) No 6/2002.

3. The Office shall inform the holder that an application for declaration of invalidity has been filed.

Article 29 — Languages used in invalidity proceedings

1. The application for a declaration of invalidity shall be filed in the language of proceedings pursuant to Article 98(4) of Regulation (EC) No 6/2002.

2. Where the language of proceedings is not the language used for filing the application and the holder has filed his/her observations in the language of filing, the Office shall arrange to have those observations translated into the language of proceedings.

3. Three years after the date fixed in accordance with Article 111(2) of Regulation (EC) No 6/2002, the Commission will submit to the Committee mentioned in Article 109 of Regulation (EC) No 6/2002 a report on the application of paragraph 2 of this Article and, if appropriate, proposals for fixing a limit for the expenses borne by the Office in this respect as provided for in the fourth subparagraph of Article 98(4) of Regulation (EC) No 6/2002.

4. The Commission may decide to submit the report and possible proposals referred to in paragraph 3 at an earlier date, and the Committee shall discuss them as a matter of priority if the facilities in paragraph 2 lead to disproportionate expenditure.

5. Where the evidence in support of the application is not filed in the language of the invalidity proceedings, the applicant shall file a translation of that evidence into that language within two months of the filing of such evidence.

6. Where the applicant for a declaration of invalidity or the holder informs the Office, within two months of receipt by the holder of the communication referred to in Article 31(1) of this Regulation, that they have agreed on a different language of proceedings pursuant to Article 98(5) of Regulation (EC) No 6/2002, the applicant shall, where the application was not filed in that language, file a translation of the application in that language within one month of the said date.

Article 30 — Rejection of the application for declaration of invalidity as inadmissible

1. If the Office finds that the application for declaration of invalidity does not comply with Article 52 of Regulation (EC) No 6/2002, Article 28(1) of this Regulation or any other provision of Regulation (EC) No 6/2002 or this Regulation, it shall inform the applicant accordingly and shall call upon him/her to remedy the deficiencies within such time limit as it may specify.

If the deficiencies are not remedied within the specified time limit, the Office shall reject the application as inadmissible.

2. Where the Office finds that the required fees have not been paid, it shall inform the applicant accordingly and shall inform him/her that the application will be deemed not to have been filed if the required fees are not paid within a specified time limit.

If the required fees are paid after the expiry of the time limit specified, they shall be refunded to the applicant.

3. Any decision to reject an application for a declaration of invalidity pursuant to paragraph 1 shall be communicated to the applicant.

Where, pursuant to paragraph 2, an application is deemed not to have been filed, the applicant shall be informed accordingly.

Article 31 — Examination of the application for a declaration of invalidity

1. If the Office does not reject the application for declaration of invalidity in accordance with Article 30, it shall communicate such application to the holder and shall request him/her to file his/her observations within such time limits as it may specify.

2. If the holder files no observations, the Office may base its decision concerning invalidity on the evidence before it.

3. Any observations filed by the holder shall be communicated to the applicant, who may be called upon by the Office to reply within specified time limits.

4. All communications pursuant to Article 53(2) of Regulation (EC) No 6/2002 and all observations filed in that respect shall be sent to the parties concerned.

5. The Office may call upon the parties to make a friendly settlement.

Article 32 — Multiple applications for a declaration of invalidity

1. Where a number of applications for a declaration of invalidity have been filed relating to the same registered Community design, the Office may deal with them in one set of proceedings.

The Office may subsequently decide no longer to deal with them in that way.

2. If a preliminary examination of one or more applications reveals that the registered Community design may be invalid, the Office may suspend the other invalidity proceedings.

The Office shall inform the remaining applicants of any relevant decisions taken during such proceedings as are continued.

3. Once a decision declaring the invalidity of the design has become final, the applications in respect of which the proceedings have been suspended in accordance with paragraph 2 shall be deemed to have been disposed of and the applicants concerned shall be informed accordingly. Such disposition shall be considered to constitute a case which has not proceeded to judgment for the purposes of Article 70(4) of Regulation (EC) No 6/2002.

4. The Office shall refund 50 % of the invalidity fee referred to in Article 52(2) of Regulation (EC) No 6/2002 paid by each applicant whose application is deemed to have been disposed of in accordance with paragraphs 1, 2 and 3 of this Article.

Article 33 — Participation of an alleged infringer

Where, pursuant to Article 54 of Regulation (EC) No 6/2002, an alleged infringer seeks to join the proceedings, he/she shall be subject to the relevant provisions of Articles 28, 29 and 30 of this Regulation, and shall in particular file a reasoned statement and pay the fee referred to in Article 52(2) of Regulation (EC) No 6/2002.

CHAPTER VI

APPEALS

Article 34 — Content of the notice of appeal

1. The notice of appeal shall contain:

- (a) the name and address of the appellant in accordance with Article 1(1)(b);
- (b) where the appellant has appointed a representative, the name and the business address of the representative in accordance with Article 1(1)(e);
- (c) a statement identifying the decision which is contested and the extent to which amendment or cancellation of the decision is requested.

2. The notice of appeal shall be filed in the language of the proceedings in which the decision subject to the appeal was taken.

Article 35 — Rejection of the appeal as inadmissible

1. If the appeal does not comply with Articles 55, 56 and 57 of Regulation (EC) No 6/2002 and Article 34(1)(c) and (2) of this Regulation, the Board of Appeal shall reject it as inadmissible, unless each deficiency has been remedied before the relevant time limit laid down in Article 57 of Regulation (EC) No 6/2002 has expired.

2. If the Board of Appeal finds that the appeal does not comply with other provisions of Regulation (EC) No 6/2002 or other provisions of this Regulation, in particular with Article 34(1)(a) and (b), it shall inform the appellant accordingly and shall request him/her to remedy the deficiencies noted within such time limit as it may specify. If the deficiencies are not remedied in good time, the Board of Appeal shall reject the appeal as inadmissible.

3. If the fee for appeal has been paid after expiry of the time limits for the filing of an appeal pursuant to Article 57 of Regulation (EC) No 6/2002, the appeal shall be deemed not to have been filed and the appeal fee shall be refunded to the appellant.

Article 36 — Examination of appeals

1. Save as otherwise provided, the provisions relating to proceedings before the department which has made the decision against which the appeal is brought shall be applicable to appeal proceedings mutatis mutandis.

2. The Board of Appeal's decision shall contain:

(a) a statement that it is delivered by the Board;
(b) the date when the decision was taken;
(c) the names of the Chairman and the other members of the Board of Appeal taking part;
(d) the name of the competent employee of the registry;
(e) the names of the parties and of their representatives;
(f) a statement of the issues to be decided;
(g) a summary of the facts;
(h) the reasons;
(i) the order of the Board of Appeal, including, where necessary, a decision on costs.

3. The decision shall be signed by the Chairman and the other members of the Board of Appeal and by the employee of the registry of the Board of Appeal.

Article 37 — Reimbursement of appeal fees

The reimbursement of appeal fees shall be ordered in the event of interlocutory revision or where the Board of Appeal deems an appeal to be allowable, if such reimbursement is equitable by reason of a substantial procedural violation. In the event of interlocutory revision, reimbursement shall be ordered by the department whose decision has been impugned, and in other cases by the Board of Appeal.

CHAPTER VII

DECISIONS AND COMMUNICATIONS OF THE OFFICE

Article 38 — Form of decisions

1. Decisions of the Office shall be in writing and shall state the reasons on which they are based.

Where oral proceedings are held before the Office, the decision may be given orally. Subsequently, the decision in writing shall be notified to the parties.

2. Decisions of the Office which are open to appeal shall be accompanied by a written communication indicating that notice of appeal must be filed in writing at the Office within two months of the date of notification of the decision from which appeal is to be made. The communications shall also draw the attention of the parties to the provisions laid down in Articles 55, 56 and 57 of Regulation (EC) No 6/2002.

The parties may not plead any failure to communicate the availability of such appeal proceedings.

Article 39 — Correction of errors in decisions

In decisions of the Office, only linguistic errors, errors of transcription and obvious mistakes may be corrected. They shall be corrected by the department which took the decision, acting of its own motion or at the request of an interested party.

Article 40 — Noting of loss of rights

1. If the Office finds that the loss of any rights results from Regulation (EC) No 6/2002 or this Regulation without any decision having been taken, it shall communicate this to the person concerned in accordance with Article 66 of Regulation (EC) No 6/2002, and shall draw his/her attention to the legal remedies set out in paragraph 2 of this Article.

2. If the person concerned considers that the finding of the Office is inaccurate, he/she may, within two months of notification of the communication referred to in paragraph 1, apply for a decision on the matter by the Office.

Such decision shall be given only if the Office disagrees with the person requesting it; otherwise the Office shall amend its finding and inform the person requesting the decision.

Article 41 — Signature, name, seal

1. Any decision, communication or notice from the Office shall indicate the department or division of the Office as well as the name or the names of the official or officials responsible. They shall be signed by the official or officials, or, instead of a signature, carry a printed or stamped seal of the Office.

2. The President of the Office may determine that other means of identifying the department or division of the Office and the name of the official or officials responsible or an identification other than a seal may be used where decisions, communications or notices are transmitted by fax or any other technical means of communication.

CHAPTER VIII

ORAL PROCEEDINGS AND TAKING OF EVIDENCE

Article 42 — Summons to oral proceedings

1. The parties shall be summoned to oral proceedings provided for in Article 64 of Regulation (EC) No 6/2002 and their attention shall be drawn to paragraph 3 of this Article. At least one month's notice of the summons shall be given unless the parties agree to a shorter time limit.

2. When issuing the summons, the Office shall draw attention to the points which in its opinion need to be discussed in order for the decision to be taken.

3. If a party who has been duly summoned to oral proceedings before the Office does not appear as summoned, the proceedings may continue without him/her.

Article 43 — Taking of evidence by the Office

1. Where the Office considers it necessary to hear the oral evidence of parties, of witnesses or of experts or to carry out an inspection, it shall take a decision to that end, stating the means by which it intends to obtain evidence, the relevant facts to be proved and the date, time and place of the hearing or inspection.

If oral evidence from witnesses and experts is requested by a party, the decision of the Office shall determine the period of time within which the party filing the request must make known to the Office the names and addresses of the witnesses and experts whom the party wishes to be heard.

2. The period of notice given in the summons of a party, witness or expert to give evidence shall be at least one month, unless they agree to a shorter time limit.

The summons shall contain:

    (a)   an extract from the decision mentioned in the first subparagraph of paragraph 1, indicating in particular the date, time and place of the hearing ordered and stating the facts regarding which the parties, witnesses and experts are to be heard;

    (b)   the names of the parties to proceedings and particulars of the rights which the witnesses or experts may invoke pursuant to Article 45(2) to (5).

Article 44 — Commissioning of experts

1. The Office shall decide in what form the report made by an expert whom it appoints shall be submitted.

2. The terms of reference of the expert shall include:

    (a)   a precise description of his/her task;

    (b)   the time limit laid down for the submission of the expert's report;

    (c)   the names of the parties to the proceedings;

    (d)   particulars of the claims which the expert may invoke pursuant to Article 45(2), (3) and (4).

3. A copy of any written report shall be submitted to the parties.

4. The parties may object to an expert on grounds of incompetence or on the same grounds as those on which objection may be made to an examiner or to a member of a Division or Board of Appeal pursuant to Article 132(1) and (3) of Council Regulation (EC) No 40/94(3). The department of the Office concerned shall rule on the objection.

Article 45 — Costs of taking of evidence

1. The taking of evidence by the Office may be made conditional upon deposit with it, by the party who has requested the evidence to be taken, of a sum which shall be fixed by reference to an estimate of the costs.

2. Witnesses and experts who are summoned by and appear before the Office shall be entitled to reimbursement of reasonable expenses for travel and

subsistence. An advance for those expenses may be granted to them by the Office. The first sentence shall apply also to witnesses and experts who appear before the Office without being summoned by it and who are heard as witnesses or experts.

3. Witnesses entitled to reimbursement under paragraph 2 shall also be entitled to appropriate compensation for loss of earnings, and experts shall be entitled to fees for their services. Those payments shall be made to the witnesses and experts after they have fulfilled their duties or tasks, where such witnesses and experts have been summoned by the Office on its own initiative.

4. The amounts and the advances for expenses to be paid pursuant to paragraphs 1, 2 and 3 shall be determined by the President of the Office and shall be published in the Official Journal of the Office.

The amounts shall be calculated on the same basis as the compensation and salaries received by officials in grades A 4 to A 8 as laid down in the Staff Regulations of officials of the European Communities and in Annex VII thereto.

5. Final liability for the amounts due or paid pursuant to paragraphs 1 to 4 shall lie with:

- (a) the Office where the Office, on its own initiative, considered it necessary to hear the oral evidence of witnesses or experts; or
- (b) the party concerned where that party requested the giving of oral evidence by witnesses or experts, subject to the decision on apportionment and fixing of costs pursuant to Articles 70 and 71 of Regulation (EC) No 6/2002 and Article 79 of this Regulation.

The party referred to in point (b) of the first subparagraph shall reimburse the Office for any advances duly paid.

Article 46 — Minutes of oral proceedings and of evidence

1. Minutes of oral proceedings or the taking of evidence shall be drawn up, containing the essentials of the oral proceedings or of the taking of evidence, the relevant statements made by the parties, the testimony of the parties, witnesses or experts and the result of any inspection.

2. The minutes of the testimony of a witness, expert or party shall be read out or submitted to him/her so that he/she may examine them. It shall be noted in the minutes that this formality has been carried out and that the person who gave the testimony approved the minutes. Where his/her approval is not given, his/her objections shall be noted.

3. The minutes shall be signed by the employee who drew them up and by the employee who conducted the oral proceedings or taking of evidence.

4. The parties shall be provided with a copy of the minutes.

5. Upon request, the Office shall make available to the parties transcripts of recordings of the oral proceedings, in typescript or in any other machine-readable form.

The release of transcripts of those recordings shall be subject to the payment of the costs incurred by the Office in making such transcript. The amount to be charged shall be determined by the President of the Office.

CHAPTER IX

NOTIFICATIONS

Article 47 — General provisions on notifications

1. In proceedings before the Office, any notifications to be made by the Office shall take the form of the original document, of a copy thereof certified by, or bearing the seal of, the Office or of a computer print-out bearing such seal. Copies of documents emanating from the parties themselves shall not require such certification.

2. Notifications shall be made:

    (a)   by post in accordance with Article 48;

    (b)   by hand delivery in accordance with Article 49;

    (c)   by deposit in a post box at the Office in accordance with Article 50;

    (d)   by fax and other technical means in accordance with Article 51;

    (e)   by public notification in accordance with Article 52.

Article 48 — Notification by post

1. Decisions subject to a time limit for appeal, summonses and other documents as determined by the President of the Office shall be notified by registered letter with acknowledgement of delivery.

Decisions and communications subject to another time limit shall be notified by registered letter, unless the President of the Office determines otherwise.

All other communications shall be ordinary mail.

2. Notifications to addressees having neither their domicile nor their principal place of business nor an establishment in the Community and who have not appointed a representative in accordance with Article 77(2) of Regulation (EC) No 6/2002 shall be effected by posting the document requiring notification by ordinary mail to the last address of the addressee known to the Office.

Notification shall be deemed to have been effected when the posting has taken place.

3. Where notification is effected by registered letter, whether or not with acknowledgement of delivery, it shall be deemed to be delivered to the addressee on the 10th day following that of its posting, unless the letter has failed to reach the addressee or has reached him/her at a later date.

In the event of any dispute, it shall be for the Office to establish that the letter has reached its destination or to establish the date on which it was delivered to the addressee, as the case may be.

4. Notification by registered letter, with or without acknowledgement of delivery, shall be deemed to have been effected even if the addressee refuses to accept the letter.

5. To the extent that notification by post is not covered by paragraphs 1 to 4, the law of the State on the territory of which notification is made shall apply.

Article 49 — Notification by hand delivery

Notification may be effected on the premises of the Office by hand delivery of the document to the addressee, who shall on delivery acknowledge its receipt.

Article 50 — Notification by deposit in a post box at the Office

Notification may also be effected to addressees who have been provided with a post box at the Office, by depositing the document therein. A written notification of deposit shall be inserted in the files. The date of deposit shall be recorded on the document. Notification shall be deemed to have taken place on the fifth day following deposit of the document in the post box at the Office.

Article 51 — Notification by fax and other technical means

1. Notification by fax shall be effected by transmitting either the original or a copy, as provided for in Article 47(1), of the document to be notified. The details of such transmission shall be determined by the President of the Office.

2. Details of notification by other technical means of communication shall be determined by the President of the Office.

Article 52 — Public notification

1. If the address of the addressee cannot be established, or if notification in accordance with Article 48(1) has proved to be impossible even after a second attempt by the Office, notification shall be effected by public notice.

Such notice shall be published at least in the Community Designs Bulletin.

2. The President of the Office shall determine how the public notice is to be given and shall fix the beginning of the time limit of one month on the expiry of which the document shall be deemed to have been notified.

Article 53 — Notification to representatives

1. If a representative has been appointed or where the applicant first named in a common application is considered to be the common representative pursuant to Article 61(1), notifications shall be addressed to that appointed or common representative.

2. If several representatives have been appointed for a single interested party, notification to any one of them shall be sufficient, unless a specific address for service has been indicated in accordance with Article 1(1)(e).

3. If several interested parties have appointed a common representative, notification of a single document to the common representative shall be sufficient.

Article 54 — Irregularities in notification

Where a document has reached the addressee, if the Office is unable to prove that it has been duly notified or if provisions relating to its notification have not been observed, the document shall be deemed to have been notified on the date established by the Office as the date of receipt.

Article 55 — Notification of documents in the case of several parties

Documents emanating from parties which contain substantive proposals, or a declaration of withdrawal of a substantive proposal, shall be notified to the other parties as a matter of course. Notification may be dispensed with where the document contains no new pleadings and the matter is ready for decision.

CHAPTER X

TIME LIMITS

Article 56 — Calculation of time limits

1. Time limits shall be laid down in terms of full years, months, weeks or days.

2. The beginning of any time limit shall be calculated starting on the day following the day on which the relevant event occurred, the event being either a procedural step or the expiry of another time limit. Where that procedural step is a notification, the event considered shall be the receipt of the document notified, unless otherwise provided.

3. Where a time limit is expressed as one year or a certain number of years, it shall expire in the relevant subsequent year in the month having the same name and on the day having the same number as the month and the day on which the relevant event occurred. Where the relevant month has no day with the same number the time limit shall expire on the last day of that month.

4. Where a time limit is expressed as one month or a certain number of months, it shall expire in the relevant subsequent month on the day which has the same number as the day on which the relevant event occurred. Where the day on which the relevant event occurred was the last day of a month or where the relevant subsequent month has no day with the same number the time limit shall expire on the last day of that month.

5. Where a time limit is expressed as one week or a certain number of weeks, it shall expire in the relevant subsequent week on the day having the same name as the day on which the relevant event occurred.

Article 57 — Duration of time limits

1. Where Regulation (EC) No 6/2002 or this Regulation provide for a time limit to be specified by the Office, such time limit shall, when the party concerned has its domicile or its principal place of business or an establishment within the Community, be not less than one month, or, when those conditions are not fulfilled, not less than two months, and no more than six months.

The Office may, when this is appropriate under the circumstances, grant an extension of a time limit specified if such extension is requested by the party concerned and the request is submitted before the original time limit expires.

2. Where there are two or more parties, the Office may make the extension of a time limit subject to the agreement of the other parties.

Article 58 — Expiry of time limits in special cases

1. If a time limit expires on a day on which the Office is not open for receipt of documents or on which, for reasons other than those referred to in paragraph 2, ordinary mail is not delivered in the locality in which the Office is located, the time limit shall extend until the first day thereafter on which the Office is open for receipt of documents and on which ordinary mail is delivered.

The days on which the Office is not open for receipt of documents shall be determined by the President of the Office before the commencement of each calendar year.

2. If a time limit expires on a day on which there is a general interruption or subsequent dislocation in the delivery of mail in a Member State or between a Member State and the Office, the time limit shall extend until the first day following the end of the period of interruption or dislocation, for parties having their residence or registered office in the State concerned or who have appointed representatives with a place of business in that State.

In the event of the Member State concerned being the State in which the Office is located, the first subparagraph shall apply to all parties.

The period referred to in the first subparagraph shall be as determined by the President of the Office.

3. Paragraphs 1 and 2 shall apply mutatis mutandis to the time limits provided for in Regulation (EC) No 6/2002 or this Regulation in the case of transactions to be carried out with the competent authority within the meaning of Article 35(1)(b) and (c) of Regulation (EC) No 6/2002.

4. If an exceptional occurrence such as natural disaster or strike interrupts or dislocates the proper functioning of the Office so that any communication from the Office to parties concerning the expiry of a time limit is delayed, acts to be completed within such a time limit may still be validly completed within one month of the notification of the delayed communication.

The date of commencement and the end of any such interruption or dislocation shall be as determined by the President of the Office.

CHAPTER XI

INTERRUPTION OF PROCEEDINGS AND WAIVING OF ENFORCED RECOVERY PROCEDURES

Article 59 — Interruption of proceedings

1. Proceedings before the Office shall be interrupted:

(a) in the event of the death or legal incapacity of the applicant for or holder of a registered Community design or of the person authorised by national law to act on his/her behalf;

(b) in the event that the applicant for or holder of a registered Community design is, as a result of some action taken against his/her property, prevented for legal reasons from continuing the proceedings before the Office;

(c)   in the event of the death or legal incapacity of the representative of an applicant for or holder of a registered Community design or of his/her being prevented for legal reasons resulting from action taken against his/her property from continuing the proceedings before the Office.

To the extent that the events referred to in point (a) of the first subparagraph do not affect the authorisation of a representative appointed under Article 78 of Regulation (EC) No 6/2002, proceedings shall be interrupted only on application by such representative.

2. When, in the cases referred to in points (a) and (b) of the first subparagraph of paragraph 1, the Office has been informed of the identity of the person authorised to continue the proceedings before the Office, the Office shall communicate to such person and to any interested third parties that the proceedings shall be resumed as from a date to be fixed by the Office.

3. In the case referred to in paragraph 1(c), the proceedings shall be resumed when the Office has been informed of the appointment of a new representative of the applicant or when the Office has notified to the other parties the communication of the appointment of a new representative of the holder of the design.

If, three months after the beginning of the interruption of the proceedings, the Office has not been informed of the appointment of a new representative, it shall communicate that fact to the applicant for or holder of the registered Community design:

(a)   where Article 77(2) of Regulation (EC) No 6/2002 is applicable, that the Community design application will be deemed to be withdrawn if the information is not submitted within two months after that communication is notified; or

(b)   where Article 77(2) of Regulation (EC) No 6/2002 is not applicable, that the proceedings will be resumed with the applicant for or holder as from the date on which that communication is notified.

4. The time limits, other than the time limit for paying the renewal fees, in force as regards the applicant for or holder of the Community design at the date of interruption of the proceedings, shall begin again as from the day on which the proceedings are resumed.

Article 60 — Waiving of enforced recovery procedures

The President of the Office may waive action for the enforced recovery of any sum due where the sum to be recovered is minimal or where such recovery is too uncertain.

CHAPTER XII

REPRESENTATION

Article 61 — Appointment of a common representative

1. If there is more than one applicant and the application for a registered Community design does not name a common representative, the applicant first named in the application shall be considered to be the common representative.

However, if one of the applicants is obliged to appoint a professional representative, such representative shall be considered to be the common representative unless the applicant named first in the application has also appointed a professional representative.

The first and second subparagraphs shall apply mutatis mutandis to third parties acting in common in applying for a declaration of invalidity, and to joint holders of a registered Community design.

2. If, during the course of proceedings, transfer is made to more than one person, and such persons have not appointed a common representative, paragraph 1 shall apply.

If such application is not possible, the Office shall require such persons to appoint a common representative within two months. If this request is not complied with, the Office shall appoint the common representative.

Article 62 — Authorisations

1. Legal practitioners and professional representatives entered on the lists maintained by the Office pursuant to Article 78(1)(b) or (c) of Regulation (EC) No 6/2002 may file with the Office a signed authorisation for inclusion in the files.

Such authorisation shall be filed if the Office expressly requires it or, where there are several parties to the proceedings in which the representative acts before the Office, one of the parties expressly request it.

2. Employees acting on behalf of natural or legal persons pursuant to Article 77(3) of Regulation (EC) No 6/2002 shall file with the Office a signed authorisation for insertion in the files.

3. The authorisation may be filed in any of the official languages of the Community. It may cover one or more applications or registered Community designs or may be in the form of a general authorisation allowing the representative to act in respect of all proceedings before the Office to which the person who has issued it is a party.

4. Where, pursuant to paragraphs 1 or 2, an authorisation has to be filed, the Office shall specify a time limit within which such authorisation shall be filed. If the authorisation is not filed in due time, proceedings shall be continued with the represented person. Any procedural steps other than the filing of the application taken by the representative shall be deemed not to have been taken if the represented person does not approve them. The application of Article 77(2) of Regulation (EC) No 6/2002 shall remain unaffected.

5. Paragraphs 1, 2 and 3 shall apply mutatis mutandis to a document withdrawing an authorisation.

6. Any representative who has ceased to be authorised shall continue to be regarded as the representative until the termination of his/her authorisation has been communicated to the Office.

7. Subject to any provisions to the contrary contained therein, an authorisation shall not terminate vis-à-vis the Office upon the death of the person who gave it.

8. Where several representatives are appointed by the same party, they may, notwithstanding any provisions to the contrary in their authorisations, act either collectively or individually.

9. The authorisation of an association of representatives shall be deemed to be an authorisation of any representative who can establish that he/she practises within that association.

Article 63 — Representation

Any notification or other communication addressed by the Office to the duly authorised representative shall have the same effect as if it had been addressed to the represented person.

Any communication addressed to the Office by the duly authorised representative shall have the same effect as if it originated from the represented person.

Article 64 — Amendment of the special list of professional representatives for design matters

1. The entry of a professional representative in the special list of professional representatives for design matters, as referred to in Article 78(4) of Regulation (EC) No 6/2002, shall be deleted at his/her request.

2. The entry of a professional representative shall be deleted automatically:

(a) in the event of the death or legal incapacity of the professional representative;

(b) where the professional representative is no longer a national of a Member State, unless the President of the Office has granted an exemption pursuant to Article 78(6)(a) of Regulation (EC) No 6/2002;

(c) where the professional representative no longer has his/her place of business or employment in the Community;

(d) where the professional representative no longer possesses the entitlement referred to in the first sentence of Article 78(4)(c) of Regulation (EC) No 6/2002.

3. The entry of a professional representative shall be suspended of the Office's own motion where his/her entitlement to represent natural or legal persons before the Benelux Design Office or the central industrial property office of the Member State as referred to in the first sentence of Article 78(4)(c) of Regulation (EC) No 6/2002 has been suspended.

4. A person whose entry has been deleted shall, upon request pursuant to Article 78(5) of Regulation (EC) No 6/2002, be reinstated in the list of professional representatives if the conditions for deletion no longer exist.

5. The Benelux Design Office and the central industrial property offices of the Member States concerned shall, where they are aware thereof, promptly inform the Office of any relevant events referred to in paragraphs 2 and 3.

6. The amendments of the special list of professional representatives for design matters shall be published in the Official Journal of the Office.

CHAPTER XIII

WRITTEN COMMUNICATIONS AND FORMS

Article 65 — Communication in writing or by other means

1. Subject to paragraph 2, applications for the registration of a Community design as well as any other application or declaration provided for in Regulation (EC) No 6/2002 and all other communications addressed to the Office shall be submitted as follows:

    (a)   by submitting a signed original of the document in question to the Office, by post, personal delivery, or by any other means; annexes to documents submitted need not be signed;

    (b)   by transmitting a signed original by fax in accordance with Article 66; or

    (c)   by transmitting the contents of the communication by electronic means in accordance with Article 67.

2. Where the applicant avails himself of the possibility provided for in Article 36(1)(c) of Regulation (EC) No 6/2002 of filing a specimen of the design, the application and the specimen shall be submitted to the Office by a single mail in the form prescribed in paragraph 1(a) of this Article. If the application and the specimen, or specimens in the case of a multiple application, are not submitted by a single mail the Office shall not give a filing date until the last item has been received pursuant to Article 10(1) of this Regulation.

Article 66 — Communication by fax

1. Where an application for registration of a Community design is submitted by fax and the application contains a reproduction of the design pursuant to Article 4(1) which does not satisfy the requirements of that Article, the required reproduction suitable for registration and publication shall be submitted to the Office in accordance with Article 65(1)(a).

Where the reproduction is received by the Office within a time limit of one month from the date of the receipt of the fax, the application shall be deemed to have been received by the Office on the date on which the fax was received.

Where the reproduction is received by the Office after the expiry of that time limit, the application shall be deemed to have been received by the Office on the date on which the reproduction was received.

2. Where a communication received by fax is incomplete or illegible, or where the Office has reasonable doubts as to the accuracy of the transmission, the Office shall inform the sender accordingly and shall call upon him/her, within a time limit to be specified by the Office, to retransmit the original by fax or to submit the original in accordance with Article 65(1)(a).

Where that request is complied with within the time limit specified, the date of the receipt of the retransmission or of the original shall be deemed to be the date of the receipt of the original communication, provided that where the deficiency concerns the granting of a filing date for an application to register a Community design, the provisions on the filing date shall apply.

Where the request is not complied with within the time limit specified, the communication shall be deemed not to have been received.

3. Any communication submitted to the Office by fax shall be considered to be duly signed if the reproduction of the signature appears on the printout produced by the fax.

4. The President of the Office may determine additional requirements for communication by fax, such as the equipment to be used, technical details of communication, and methods of identifying the sender.

Article 67 — Communication by electronic means

1. Applications for registration of a Community design may be submitted by electronic means, including the representation of the design, and notwithstanding Article 65(2) in the case of filing a specimen.

The conditions shall be laid down by the President of the Office.

2. The President of the Office shall determine the requirements for communication by electronic means, such as the equipment to be used, technical details of communication, and methods of identifying the sender.

3. Where a communication is sent by electronic means, Article 66(2) shall apply mutatis mutandis.

4. Where a communication is sent to the Office by electronic means, the indication of the name of the sender shall be deemed to be equivalent to the signature.

Article 68 — Forms

1. The Office shall make available free of charge forms for the purpose of:

  (a) filing an application for a registered Community design;
  (b) applying for the correction of an application or a registration;
  (c) applying for the registration of a transfer and the transfer form and transfer document referred to in Article 23(4);
  (d) applying for the registration of a licence;
  (e) applying for renewal of registration of a registered Community design;
  (f) applying for a declaration of invalidity of a registered Community design;

(g)   applying for restitutio in integrum;

(h)   taking an appeal;

(i)   authorising a representative, in the form of an individual authorisation and in the form of a general authorisation.

2. The Office may make other forms available free of charge.

3. The Office shall make available the forms referred to in paragraphs 1 and 2 in all the official languages of the Community.

4. The Office shall place the forms at the disposal of the Benelux Design Office and of the Member States' central industrial property offices free of charge.

5. The Office may also make available the forms in machine-readable form.

6. Parties to proceedings before the Office should use the forms provided by the Office, or copies of those forms, or forms with the same content and format as those forms, such as forms generated by means of electronic data processing.

7. Forms shall be completed in such a manner as to permit an automated input of the content into a computer, such as by character recognition or scanning.

CHAPTER XIV

INFORMATION TO THE PUBLIC

Article 69 — Register of Community Designs

1. The Register may be maintained in the form of an electronic database.

2. The Register shall contain the following entries:

(a)   the date of filing the application;

(b)   the file number of the application and the file number of each individual design included in a multiple application;

(c)   the date of the publication of the registration;

(d)   the name, the address and the nationality of the applicant and the State in which he/she is domiciled or has his/her seat or establishment;

(e)   the name and business address of the representative, other than an employee acting as representative in accordance with the first sub-paragraph of Article 77(3) of Regulation (EC) No 6/2002; where there is more than one representative, only the name and business address of the first named representative, the name being followed by the words 'et al', shall be recorded; where an association of representatives is appointed, only the name and address of the association shall be recorded;

(f)   the representation of the design;

(g)   an indication of the products by their names, preceded by the numbers of the classes and subclasses of the Locarno classification, and grouped accordingly;

(h)   particulars of claims of priority pursuant to Article 42 of Regulation (EC) No 6/2002;

(i)   particulars of claims of exhibition priority pursuant to Article 44 of
       Regulation (EC) No 6/2002;
(j)   where applicable, the citation of the designer or of the team of
       designers pursuant to Article 18 of Regulation (EC) No 6/2002, or a
       statement that the designer or the team of designers has waived the
       right to be cited;
(k)   the language in which the application was filed and the second
       language which the applicant has indicated in his/her application,
       pursuant to Article 98(2) of Regulation (EC) No 6/2002;
(l)   the date of registration of the design in the Register and the registra-
       tion number;
(m)   a mention of any request for deferment of publication pursuant to
       Article 50(3) of Regulation (EC) No 6/2002, specifying the date of
       expiry of the period of deferment;
(n)   a mention that a specimen was filed pursuant to Article 5;
(o)   a mention that a description was filed pursuant to Article 1(2)(a).

3. In addition to the entries set out in paragraph 2 the Register shall contain the
following entries, each accompanied by the date of recording such entry:

(a)   changes in the name, the address or the nationality of the holder or in
       the State in which he/she is domiciled or has his/her seat or establish-
       ment;
(b)   changes in the name or business address of the representative, other
       than a representative falling within the first subparagraph of Arti-
       cle 77(3) of Regulation (EC) No 6/2002;
(c)   when a new representative is appointed, the name and business
       address of that representative;
(d)   a mention that a multiple application or registration has been divided
       into separate applications or registrations pursuant to Article 37(4) of
       Regulation (EC) No 6/2002;
(e)   the notice of an amendment to the design pursuant to Article 25(6) of
       Regulation (EC) No 6/2002, including, if applicable, a reference to
       the disclaimer made or the court decision or the decision by the
       Office declaring the partial invalidity of the design right, as well as
       corrections of mistakes and errors pursuant to Article 20 of this
       Regulation;
(f)   a mention that entitlement proceedings have been instituted under
       Article 15(1) of Regulation (EC) No 6/2002 in respect of a registered
       Community design;
(g)   the final decision or other termination of proceedings pursuant to
       Article 15(4)(b) of Regulation (EC) No 6/2002 concerning entitle-
       ment proceedings;
(h)   a change of ownership pursuant to Article 15(4)(c) of Regulation
       (EC) No 6/2002;
(i)   transfers pursuant to Article 28 of Regulation (EC) No 6/2002;
(j)   the creation or transfer of a right in rem pursuant to Article 29 of
       Regulation (EC) No 6/2002 and the nature of the right in rem;

(k) levy of execution pursuant to Article 30 of Regulation (EC) No 6/2002 and insolvency proceedings pursuant to Article 31 of that Regulation;

(l) the grant or transfer of a licence pursuant to Article 16(2) or Article 32 of Regulation (EC) No 6/2002 and, where applicable, the type of licence pursuant to Article 25 of this Regulation;

(m) renewal of the registration pursuant to Article 13 of Regulation (EC) No 6/2002 and the date from which it takes effect;

(n) a record of the determination of the expiry of the registration;

(o) a declaration of total or partial surrender by the holder pursuant to Article 51(1) and (3) of Regulation (EC) No 6/2002;

(p) the date of submission of an application or of the filing of a counterclaim for a declaration of invalidity pursuant, respectively, to Article 52 or Article 86(2) of Regulation (EC) No 6/2002;

(q) the date and content of the decision on the application or counter-claim for declaration of invalidity or any other termination of proceedings pursuant, respectively, to Article 53 or Article 86(4) of Regulation (EC) No 6/2002;

(r) a mention pursuant to Article 50(4) of Regulation (EC) No 6/2002 that the registered Community design is deemed from the outset not to have had the effects specified in that Regulation;

(s) the cancellation of the representative recorded pursuant to paragraph 2(e);

(t) the modification or cancellation from the Register of the items referred to in points (j), (k) and (l).

4. The President of the Office may determine that items other than those referred to in paragraphs 2 and 3 shall be entered in the Register.

5. The holder shall be notified of any change in the Register.

6. Subject to Article 73, the Office shall provide certified or uncertified extracts from the Register on request, on payment of a fee.

CHAPTER XV

COMMUNITY DESIGNS BULLETIN AND DATA BASE

Article 70 — Community Designs Bulletin

1. The Office shall determine the frequency of the publication of the Community Designs Bulletin and the manner in which such publication shall take place.

2. Without prejudice to the provisions of Article 50(2) of Regulation (EC) No 6/2002 and subject to Articles 14 and 16 of this Regulation relating to deferment of publication, the Community Designs Bulletin shall contain publications of registration and of entries made in the Register as well as other particulars relating to registrations of designs whose publication is prescribed by Regulation (EC) No 6/2002 or by this Regulation.

3. Where particulars whose publication is prescribed in Regulation (EC) No 6/2002 or in this Regulation are published in the Community Designs Bulletin, the date of issue shown on the Bulletin shall be taken as the date of publication of the particulars.

4. The information the publication of which is prescribed in Articles 14 and 16 shall, where appropriate, be published in all the official languages of the Community.

Article 71 — Database

1. The Office shall maintain an electronic database with the particulars of applications for registration of Community designs and entries in the Register. The Office may, subject to the restrictions prescribed by Article 50(2) and (3) of Regulation (EC) No 6/2002, make available the contents of that database for direct access or on CD-ROM or in any other machine-readable form.

2. The President of the Office shall determine the conditions of access to the database and the manner in which the contents of this database may be made available in machine-readable form, including the charges for those acts.

CHAPTER XVI

INSPECTION OF FILES AND KEEPING OF FILES

Article 72 — Parts of the file excluded from inspection

The parts of the file which shall be excluded from inspection pursuant to Article 74(4) of Regulation (EC) No 6/2002 shall be:

(a) documents relating to exclusion or objection pursuant to Article 132 of Regulation (EC) No 40/94, the provisions of that Article being considered for this purpose as applying mutatis mutandis to regis-tered Community designs and to applications for these;

(b) draft decisions and opinions, and all other internal documents used for the preparation of decisions and opinions;

(c) parts of the file which the party concerned showed a special interest in keeping confidential before the application for inspection of the files was made, unless inspection of such part of the file is justified by overriding legitimate interests of the party seeking inspection.

Article 73 — Inspection of the Register of Community Designs

Where the registration is subject to a deferment of publication pursuant to Article 50(1) of Regulation (EC) No 6/2002:

(a) access to the Register to persons other than the holder shall be limited to the name of the holder, the name of any representative, the date of filing and registration, the file number of the application and the mention that publication is deferred;

(b) the certified or uncertified extracts from the Register shall contain only the name of the holder, the name of any representative, the date of filing and registration, the file number of the application and the mention that publication is deferred, except where the request has been made by the holder or his/her representative.

Article 74 — Procedures for the inspection of files

1. Inspection of the files of registered Community designs shall either be of the original document, or of copies thereof, or of technical means of storage if the files are so stored.

The request for inspection of the files shall not be deemed to have been made until the required fee has been paid.

The means of inspection shall be determined by the President of the Office.

2. Where inspection of the files relates to an application for a registered Community design or to a registered Community design which is subject to deferment of publication, which, being subject to such deferment, has been surrendered before or on the expiry of that period or which, pursuant to Article 50(4) of Regulation (EC) No 6/2002, is deemed from the outset not to have had the effects specified in that Regulation, the request shall contain an indication and evidence to the effect that:

(a) the applicant for or holder of the Community design has consented to the inspection; or

(b) the person requesting the inspection has established a legitimate interest in the inspection of the file, in particular where the applicant for or holder of the Community design has stated that after the design has been registered he/she will invoke the rights under it against the person requesting the inspection.

3. Inspection of the files shall take place on the premises of the Office.

4. On request, inspection of the files shall be effected by means of issuing copies of file documents. Such copies shall incur fees.

5. The Office shall issue on request certified or uncertified copies of the application for a registered Community design or of those file documents of which copies may be issued pursuant to paragraph 4 upon payment of a fee.

Article 75 — Communication of information contained in the files

Subject to the restrictions provided for in Article 74 of Regulation (EC) No 6/2002 and Articles 72 and 73 of this Regulation, the Office may, upon request, communicate information from any file of a Community design applied for or of a registered Community design, subject to payment of a fee.

However, the Office may require the applicant to inspect the file in situ, should it deem that to be appropriate in view of the quantity of information to be supplied.

Article 76 — Keeping of files

1. The Office shall keep the files relating to Community design applications and to registered Community designs for at least five years from the end of the year in which:

(a)   the application is rejected or withdrawn;
(b)   the registration of the registered Community design expires defini-tively;
(c)   the complete surrender of the registered Community design is regis-tered pursuant to Article 51 of Regulation (EC) No 6/2002;
(d)   the registered Community design is definitively removed from the Register;
(e)   the registered Community design is deemed not to have had the effects specified in Regulation (EC) No 6/2002 pursuant to Arti-cle 50(4) thereof.

2. The President of the Office shall determine the form in which the files shall be kept.

CHAPTER XVII

ADMINISTRATIVE COOPERATION

Article 77 — Exchange of information and communications between the Office and the authorities of the Member States

1. The Office and the central industrial property offices of the Member States and the Benelux Design Office shall, upon request, communicate to each other relevant information about the filing of applications for registered Community designs, Benelux designs or national registered designs and about proceedings relating to such applications and the designs registered as a result thereof. Such communications shall not be subject to the restrictions provided for in Arti-cle 74 of Regulation (EC) No 6/2002.

2. Communications between the Office and the courts or authorities of the Member States which arise out of the application of Regulation (EC) No 6/2002 or this Regulation shall be effected directly between those authorities.

Such communication may also be effected through the central industrial property offices of the Member States or the Benelux Design Office.

3. Expenditure in respect of communications pursuant to paragraphs 1 and 2 shall be chargeable to the authority making the communications, which shall be exempt from fees.

Article 78 — Inspection of files by or via courts or authorities of the Member States

1. Inspection of files relating to Community designs applied for or registered Community designs by courts or authorities of the Member States shall if so requested be of the original documents or of copies thereof. Article 74 shall not apply.

2. Courts or public prosecutors' offices of the Member States may, in the course of proceedings before them, open files or copies thereof transmitted by the Office to inspection by third parties. Such inspection shall be subject to Article 74 of Regulation (EC) No 6/2002.

3. The Office shall not charge any fee for inspections pursuant to paragraphs 1 and 2.

4. The Office shall, at the time of transmission of the files or copies thereof to the courts or public prosecutors' offices of the Member States, indicate the restrictions to which the inspection of files relating to Community designs applied for or registered Community designs is subject pursuant to Article 74 of Regulation (EC) No 6/2002 and Article 72 of this Regulation.

CHAPTER XVIII

COSTS

Article 79 — Apportionment and fixing of costs

1. Apportionment of costs pursuant to Article 70(1) and (2) of Regulation (EC) No 6/2002 shall be dealt with in the decision on the application for a declaration of invalidity of a registered Community design, or in the decision on the appeal.

2. Apportionment of costs pursuant to Article 70(3) and (4) of Regulation (EC) No 6/2002 shall be dealt with in a decision on costs by the Invalidity Division or the Board of Appeal.

3. A bill of costs, with supporting evidence, shall be attached to the request for the fixing of costs provided for in the first sentence of Article 70(6) of Regulation (EC) No 6/2002.

The request shall be admissible only if the decision in respect of which the fixing of costs is required has become final. Costs may be fixed once their credibility is established.

4. The request provided for in the second sentence of Article 70(6) of Regulation (EC) No 6/2002 for a review of the decision of the registry on the fixing of costs, stating the reasons on which it is based, must be filed at the Office within one month of the date of notification of the awarding of costs.

It shall not be deemed to be filed until the fee for reviewing the amount of the costs has been paid.

5. The Invalidity Division or the Board of Appeal, as the case may be, shall take a decision on the request referred to in paragraph 4 without oral proceedings.

6. The fees to be borne by the losing party pursuant to Article 70(1) of Regulation (EC) No 6/2002 shall be limited to the fees incurred by the other party for the application for a declaration of invalidity and/or for the appeal.

7. Costs essential to the proceedings and actually incurred by the successful party shall be borne by the losing party in accordance with Article 70(1) of Regulation (EC) No 6/2002 on the basis of the following maximum rates:

    (a)   travel expenses of one party for the outward and return journey between the place of residence or the place of business and the place where oral proceedings are held or where evidence is taken, as follows:

    (i)   the cost of the first-class rail fare including usual transport supplements where the total distance by rail does not exceed 800 km;

    (ii)   the cost of the tourist-class air fare where the total distance by rail exceeds 800 km or the route includes a sea crossing;

(b)   subsistence expenses of one party equal to the daily subsistence allowance for officials in grades A 4 to A 8 as laid down in Article 13 of Annex VII to the Staff Regulations of officials of the European Communities;

(c)   travel expenses of representatives within the meaning of Article 78(1) of Regulation (EC) No 6/2002 and of witnesses and of experts, at the rates provided for in point (a);

(d)   subsistence expenses of representatives within the meaning of Article 78(1) of Regulation (EC) No 6/2002 and of witnesses and experts, at the rates referred to in point (b);

(e)   costs entailed in the taking of evidence in the form of examination of witnesses, opinions by experts or inspection, up to EUR 300 per proceedings;

(f)   costs of representation, within the meaning of Article 78(1) of Regulation (EC) No 6/2002:

    (i)   of the applicant in proceedings relating to invalidity of a registered Community design up to EUR 400;

    (ii)   of the holder in proceedings relating to invalidity of a registered Community design up to EUR 400;

    (iii)   of the appellant in appeal proceedings up to EUR 500;

    (iv)   of the defendant in appeal proceedings up to EUR 500;

(g)   where the successful party is represented by more than one representative within the meaning of Article 78(1) of the Regulation (EC) No 6/2002, the losing party shall bear the costs referred to in points (c), (d) and (f) for one such person only;

(h)   the losing party shall not be obliged to reimburse the successful party for any costs, expenses and fees other than those referred to in points (a) to (g).

Where the taking of evidence in any of the proceedings referred to in point (f) of the first subparagraph involves the examination of witnesses, opinions by experts or inspection, an additional amount shall be granted for representation costs of up to EUR 600 per proceedings.

CHAPTER XIX

LANGUAGES

Article 80 — Applications and declarations

Without prejudice to Article 98(4) of Regulation (EC) No 6/2002:

(a)   any application or declaration relating to an application for a regis-
      tered Community design may be filed in the language used for filing
      the application or in the second language indicated by the applicant in
      his/her application;
(b)   any application or declaration other than an application for declara-
      tion of invalidity pursuant to Article 52 of Regulation (EC)
      No 6/2002, or declaration of surrender pursuant to Article 51 of that
      Regulation relating to a registered Community design may be filed in
      one of the languages of the Office;
(c)   when any of the forms provided by the Office pursuant to Article 68
      is used, such forms may be used in any of the official languages of the
      Community, provided that the form is completed in one of the
      languages of the Office, as far as textual elements are concerned.

Article 81 — Written proceedings

1. Without prejudice to Article 98(3) and (5) of Regulation (EC) No 6/2002 and
save as otherwise provided in this Regulation, in written proceedings before the
Office a party may use any language of the Office.

If the language chosen is not the language of the proceedings, the party shall
supply a translation into that language within one month of the date of the
submission of the original document.

Where the applicant for a registered Community design is the sole party to
proceedings before the Office and the language used for the filing of the
application for the registered Community design is not one of the languages of
the Office, the translation may also be filed in the second language indicated by
the applicant in his/her application.

2. Save as otherwise provided in this Regulation, documents to be used in
proceedings before the Office may be filed in any official language of the
Community.

Where the language of such documents is not the language of the proceedings
the Office may require that a translation be supplied, within a time limit
specified by it, in that language or, at the choice of the party to the proceeding,
in any language of the Office.

Article 82 — Oral proceedings

1. Any party to oral proceedings before the Office may, in place of the language
of proceedings, use one of the other official languages of the Community, on
condition that he/she makes provision for interpretation into the language of
proceedings.

Where the oral proceedings are held in a proceeding concerning the application
for registration of a design the applicant may use either the language of the
application or the second language indicated by him/her.

2. In oral proceedings concerning the application for registration of a design,
the staff of the Office may use either the language of the application or the
second language indicated by the applicant.

In all other oral proceedings, the staff of the Office may use, in place of the language of the proceedings, one of the other languages of the Office, on condition that the party or parties to the proceedings agree(s) to such use.

3. With regard to the taking of evidence, any party to be heard, witness or expert who is unable to express himself/herself adequately in the language of proceedings, may use any of the official languages of the Community.

Where the taking of evidence is decided upon following a request by a party to the proceedings, parties to be heard, witnesses or experts who express themselves in languages other than the language of proceedings may be heard only if the party who made the request makes provision for interpretation into that language.

In proceedings concerning the application for registration of a design, in place of the language of the application, the second language indicated by the applicant may be used.

In any proceedings with only one party, the Office may at the request of the party concerned permit derogation from the provisions in this paragraph.

4. If the parties and the Office so agree, any official language of the Community may be used in oral proceedings.

5. The Office shall, if necessary, make provision at its own expense for interpretation into the language of proceedings, or, where appropriate, into its other languages, unless this interpretation is the responsibility of one of the parties to the proceedings.

6. Statements by staff of the Office, by parties to the proceedings and by witnesses and experts, made in one of the languages of the Office during oral proceedings shall be entered in the minutes in the language employed. Statements made in any other language shall be entered in the language of proceedings.

Corrections to the application for or the registration of a Community design shall be entered in the minutes in the language of proceedings.

Article 83 — Certification of translations

1. When a translation of any document is to be filed, the Office may require the filing, within a time limit to be specified by it, of a certificate that the translation corresponds to the original text.

Where the certificate relates to the translation of a previous application pursuant to Article 42 of Regulation (EC) No 6/2002, such time limit shall not be less than three months after the date of filing of the application.

Where the certificate is not filed within that time limit, the document shall be deemed not to have been received.

2. The President of the Office may determine the manner in which translations are certified.

Article 84 — Legal authenticity of translations

In the absence of evidence to the contrary, the Office may assume that a translation corresponds to the relevant original text.

CHAPTER XX

RECIPROCITY, TRANSITION PERIOD AND ENTRY INTO FORCE

Article 85 — Publication of reciprocity

1. If necessary, the President of the Office shall request the Commission to enquire whether a State which is not party to the Paris Convention for the Protection of Industrial Property or to the Agreement establishing the World Trade Organisation grants reciprocal treatment within the meaning of Article 41(5) Regulation (EC) No 6/2002.

2. If the Commission determines that reciprocal treatment in accordance with paragraph 1 is granted, it shall publish a communication to that effect in the Official Journal of the European Communities.

3. Article 41(5) of Regulation (EC) No 6/2002 shall apply from the date of publication in the Official Journal of the European Communities of the communication referred to in paragraph 2, unless the communication states an earlier date from which it is applicable.

Article 41(5) of Regulation (EC) No 6/2002 shall cease to be applicable from the date of publication in the Official Journal of the European Communities of a communication of the Commission stating that reciprocal treatment is no longer granted, unless the communication states an earlier date from which it is applicable.

4. Communications referred to in paragraphs 2 and 3 shall also be published in the Official Journal of the Office.

Article 86 — Transition period

1. Any application for registration of a Community design filed no more than three months before the date fixed pursuant to Article 111(2) of Regulation (EC) No 6/2002 shall be marked by the Office with the filing date determined pursuant to that provision and with the actual date of receipt of the application.

2. With regard to the application, the priority period of six months provided for in Articles 41 and 44 of Regulation (EC) No 6/2002 shall be calculated from the date fixed pursuant to Article 111(2) of that Regulation.

3. The Office may issue a receipt to the applicant prior to the date fixed pursuant to Article 111(2) of Regulation (EC) No 6/2002.

4. The Office may examine the applications prior to the date fixed pursuant to Article 111(2) of Regulation (EC) No 6/2002 and communicate with the applicant with a view to remedying any deficiencies prior to that date.

Any decisions with regard to such applications may be taken only after that date.

5. Where the date of receipt of an application for the registration of a Community design by the Office, by the central industrial property office of a Member State or by the Benelux Design Office is before the commencement of the three-month period specified in Article 111(3) of Regulation (EC) No 6/2002 the application shall be deemed not to have been filed.

The applicant shall be informed accordingly and the application shall be sent back to him/her.

Article 87 — Entry into force

This Regulation shall enter into force on the seventh day following its publication in the Official Journal of the European Communities.

This Regulation shall be binding in its entirety and directly applicable in all Member States.

Done at Brussels, 21 October 2002.

For the Commission

Frederik Bolkestein

Member of the Commission

Council Regulation (EC) No 6/2002 of 12 December 2001 on Community designs

THE COUNCIL OF THE EUROPEAN UNION,

Having regard to the Treaty establishing the European Community, and in particular Article 308 thereof,

Having regard to the proposal from the Commission(1),

Having regard to the opinion of the European Parliament(2),

Having regard to the opinion of the Economic and Social Committee(3),

Whereas:

(1) A unified system for obtaining a Community design to which uniform protection is given with uniform effect throughout the entire territory of the Community would further the objectives of the Community as laid down in the Treaty.

(2) Only the Benelux countries have introduced a uniform design protection law. In all the other Member States the protection of designs is a matter for the relevant national law and is confined to the territory of the Member State concerned. Identical designs may be therefore protected differently in different Member States and for the benefit of different owners. This inevitably leads to conflicts in the course of trade between Member States.

(3) The substantial differences between Member States' design laws prevent and distort Community-wide competition. In comparison with domestic trade in, and competition between, products incorporating a design, trade and

competition within the Community are prevented and distorted by the large number of applications, offices, procedures, laws, nationally circumscribed exclusive rights and the combined administrative expense with correspondingly high costs and fees for the applicant. Directive 98/71/EC of the European Parliament and of the Council of 13 October 1998 on the legal protection of designs(4) contributes to remedying this situation.

(4) The effect of design protection being limited to the territory of the individual Member States whether or not their laws are approximated, leads to a possible division of the internal market with respect to products incorporating a design which is the subject of national rights held by different individuals, and hence constitutes an obstacle to the free movement of goods.

(5) This calls for the creation of a Community design which is directly applicable in each Member State, because only in this way will it be possible to obtain, through one application made to the Office for Harmonisation in the Internal Market (Trade Marks and Design) in accordance with a single procedure under one law, one design right for one area encompassing all Member States.

(6) Since the objectives of the proposed action, namely, the protection of one design right for one area encompassing all the Member States, cannot be sufficiently achieved by the Member States by reason of the scale and the effects of the creation of a Community design and a Community design authority and can therefore, and can therefore be better achieved at Community level, the Community may adopt measures, in accordance with the principle of subsidiarity as set out in Article 5 of the Treaty. In accordance with the principle of proportionality, as set out in that Article, this Regulation does not go beyond what is necessary in order to achieve those objectives.

(7) Enhanced protection for industrial design not only promotes the contribution of individual designers to the sum of Community excellence in the field, but also encourages innovation and development of new products and investment in their production.

(8) Consequently a more accessible design-protection system adapted to the needs of the internal market is essential for Community industries.

(9) The substantive provisions of this Regulation on design law should be aligned with the respective provisions in Directive 98/71/EC.

(10) Technological innovation should not be hampered by granting design protection to features dictated solely by a technical function. It is understood that this does not entail that a design must have an aesthetic quality. Likewise, the interoperability of products of different makes should not be hindered by extending protection to the design of mechanical fittings. Consequently, those features of a design which are excluded from protection for those reasons should not be taken into consideration for the purpose of assessing whether other features of the design fulfil the requirements for protection.

(11) The mechanical fittings of modular products may nevertheless constitute an important element of the innovative characteristics of modular products and present a major marketing asset, and therefore should be eligible for protection.

(12) Protection should not be extended to those component parts which are not visible during normal use of a product, nor to those features of such part which are not visible when the part is mounted, or which would not, in themselves, fulfil the requirements as to novelty and individual character. Therefore, those features of design which are excluded from protection for these reasons should not be taken into consideration for the purpose of assessing whether other features of the design fulfil the requirements for protection.

(13) Full-scale approximation of the laws of the Member States on the use of protected designs for the purpose of permitting the repair of a complex product so as to restore its original appearance, where the design is applied to or incorporated in a product which constitutes a component part of a complex product upon whose appearance the protected design is dependent, could not be achieved through Directive 98/71/EC. Within the framework of the conciliation procedure on the said Directive, the Commission undertook to review the consequences of the provisions of that Directive three years after the deadline for transposition of the Directive in particular for the industrial sectors which are most affected. Under these circumstances, it is appropriate not to confer any protection as a Community design for a design which is applied to or incorporated in a product which constitutes a component part of a complex product upon whose appearance the design is dependent and which is used for the purpose of the repair of a complex product so as to restore its original appearance, until the Council has decided its policy on this issue on the basis of a Commission proposal.

(14) The assessment as to whether a design has individual character should be based on whether the overall impression produced on an informed user viewing the design clearly differs from that produced on him by the existing design corpus, taking into consideration the nature of the product to which the design is applied or in which it is incorporated, and in particular the industrial sector to which it belongs and the degree of freedom of the designer in developing the design.

(15) A Community design should, as far as possible, serve the needs of all sectors of industry in the Community.

(16) Some of those sectors produce large numbers of designs for products frequently having a short market life where protection without the burden of registration formalities is an advantage and the duration of protection is of lesser significance. On the other hand, there are sectors of industry which value the advantages of registration for the greater legal certainty it provides and which require the possibility of a longer term of protection corresponding to the foreseeable market life of their products.

(17) This calls for two forms of protection, one being a short-term unregistered design and the other being a longer term registered design.

(18) A registered Community design requires the creation and maintenance of a register in which will be registered all those applications which comply with formal conditions and which have been accorded a date of filing. This

registration system should in principle not be based upon substantive examination as to compliance with requirements for protection prior to registration, thereby keeping to a minimum the registration and other procedural burdens on applicants.

(19) A Community design should not be upheld unless the design is new and unless it also possesses an individual character in comparison with other designs.

(20) It is also necessary to allow the designer or his successor in title to test the products embodying the design in the market place before deciding whether the protection resulting from a registered Community design is desirable. To this end it is necessary to provide that disclosures of the design by the designer or his successor in title, or abusive disclosures during a period of 12 months prior to the date of the filing of the application for a registered Community design should not be prejudicial in assessing the novelty or the individual character of the design in question.

(21) The exclusive nature of the right conferred by the registered Community design is consistent with its greater legal certainty. It is appropriate that the unregistered Community design should, however, constitute a right only to prevent copying. Protection could not therefore extend to design products which are the result of a design arrived at independently by a second designer. This right should also extend to trade in products embodying infringing designs.

(22) The enforcement of these rights is to be left to national laws. It is necessary therefore to provide for some basic uniform sanctions in all Member States. These should make it possible, irrespective of the jurisdiction under which enforcement is sought, to stop the infringing acts.

(23) Any third person who can establish that he has in good faith commenced use even for commercial purposes within the Community, or has made serious and effective preparations to that end, of a design included within the scope of protection of a registered Community design, which has not been copied from the latter, may be entitled to a limited exploitation of that design.

(24) It is a fundamental objective of this Regulation that the procedure for obtaining a registered Community design should present the minimum cost and difficulty to applicants, so as to make it readily available to small and medium-sized enterprises as well as to individual designers.

(25) Those sectors of industry producing large numbers of possibly short-lived designs over short periods of time of which only some may be eventually commercialised will find advantage in the unregistered Community design. Furthermore, there is also a need for these sectors to have easier recourse to the registered Community design. Therefore, the option of combining a number of designs in one multiple application would satisfy that need. However, the designs contained in a multiple application may be dealt with independently of each other for the purposes of enforcement of rights, licensing, rights in rem, levy of execution, insolvency proceedings, surrender, renewal, assignment, deferred publication or declaration of invalidity.

(26) The normal publication following registration of a Community design could in some cases destroy or jeopardise the success of a commercial operation involving the design. The facility of a deferment of publication for a reasonable period affords a solution in such cases.

(27) A procedure for hearing actions concerning validity of a registered Community design in a single place would bring savings in costs and time compared with procedures involving different national courts.

(28) It is therefore necessary to provide safeguards including a right of appeal to a Board of Appeal, and ultimately to the Court of Justice. Such a procedure would assist the development of uniform interpretation of the requirements governing the validity of Community designs.

(29) It is essential that the rights conferred by a Community design can be enforced in an efficient manner throughout the territory of the Community.

(30) The litigation system should avoid as far as possible 'forum shopping'. It is therefore necessary to establish clear rules of international jurisdiction.

(31) This Regulation does not preclude the application to designs protected by Community designs of the industrial property laws or other relevant laws of the Member States, such as those relating to design protection acquired by registration or those relating to unregistered designs, trade marks, patents and utility models, unfair competition or civil liability.

(32) In the absence of the complete harmonisation of copyright law, it is important to establish the principle of cumulation of protection under the Community design and under copyright law, whilst leaving Member States free to establish the extent of copyright protection and the conditions under which such protection is conferred.

(33) The measures necessary for the implementation of this Regulation should be adopted in accordance with Council Decision 1999/468/EC of 28 June 1999 laying down the procedures for the exercise of implementing powers conferred on the Commission(5),

HAS ADOPTED THIS REGULATION:

TITLE I

GENERAL PROVISIONS

Article 1 — Community design

1. A design which complies with the conditions contained in this Regulation is hereinafter referred to as a 'Community design'.

2. A design shall be protected:

   (a)   by an 'unregistered Community design', if made available to the public in the manner provided for in this Regulation;

   (b)   by a 'registered Community design', if registered in the manner provided for in this Regulation.

3. A Community design shall have a unitary character. It shall have equal effect throughout the Community. It shall not be registered, transferred or surrendered or be the subject of a decision declaring it invalid, nor shall its use be prohibited, save in respect of the whole Community. This principle and its implications shall apply unless otherwise provided in this Regulation.

Article 2 — Office

The Office for Harmonisation in the Internal Market (Trade Marks and Designs), hereinafter referred to as 'the Office', instituted by Council Regulation (EC) No 40/94 of 20 December 1993 on the Community trade mark(6), hereinafter referred to as the 'Regulation on the Community trade mark', shall carry out the tasks entrusted to it by this Regulation.

TITLE II

THE LAW RELATING TO DESIGNS

Section I
Requirements for protection

Article 3 — Definitions

For the purposes of this Regulation:

(a)   'design' means the appearance of the whole or a part of a product resulting from the features of, in particular, the lines, contours, colours, shape, texture and/or materials of the product itself and/or its ornamentation;

(b)   'product' means any industrial or handicraft item, including inter alia parts intended to be assembled into a complex product, packaging, get-up, graphic symbols and typographic typefaces, but excluding computer programs;

(c)   'complex product' means a product which is composed of multiple components which can be replaced permitting disassembly and re-assembly of the product.

Article 4 — Requirements for protection

1. A design shall be protected by a Community design to the extent that it is new and has individual character.

2. A design applied to or incorporated in a product which constitutes a component part of a complex product shall only be considered to be new and to have individual character:

(a)   if the component part, once it has been incorporated into the complex product, remains visible during normal use of the latter; and

(b)   to the extent that those visible features of the component part fulfil in themselves the requirements as to novelty and individual character.

3. 'Normal use' within the meaning of paragraph (2)(a) shall mean use by the end user, excluding maintenance, servicing or repair work.

Article 5 — Novelty

1. A design shall be considered to be new if no identical design has been made available to the public:

(a)   in the case of an unregistered Community design, before the date on which the design for which protection is claimed has first been made available to the public;

(b)   in the case of a registered Community design, before the date of filing of the application for registration of the design for which protection is claimed, or, if priority is claimed, the date of priority.

2. Designs shall be deemed to be identical if their features differ only in immaterial details.

Article 6 — Individual character

1. A design shall be considered to have individual character if the overall impression it produces on the informed user differs from the overall impression produced on such a user by any design which has been made available to the public:

(a)   in the case of an unregistered Community design, before the date on which the design for which protection is claimed has first been made available to the public;

(b)   in the case of a registered Community design, before the date of filing the application for registration or, if a priority is claimed, the date of priority.

2. In assessing individual character, the degree of freedom of the designer in developing the design shall be taken into consideration.

Article 7 — Disclosure

1. For the purpose of applying Articles 5 and 6, a design shall be deemed to have been made available to the public if it has been published following registration or otherwise, or exhibited, used in trade or otherwise disclosed, before the date referred to in Articles 5(1)(a) and 6(1)(a) or in Articles 5(1)(b) and 6(1)(b), as the case may be, except where these events could not reasonably have become known in the normal course of business to the circles specialised in the sector concerned, operating within the Community. The design shall not, however, be deemed to have been made available to the public for the sole reason that it has been disclosed to a third person under explicit or implicit conditions of confidentiality.

2. A disclosure shall not be taken into consideration for the purpose of applying Articles 5 and 6 and if a design for which protection is claimed under a registered Community design has been made available to the public:

(a)   by the designer, his successor in title, or a third person as a result of information provided or action taken by the designer or his successor in title; and

(b) during the 12-month period preceding the date of filing of the application or, if a priority is claimed, the date of priority.

3. Paragraph 2 shall also apply if the design has been made available to the public as a consequence of an abuse in relation to the designer or his successor in title.

Article 8 — Designs dictated by their technical function and designs of interconnections

1. A Community design shall not subsist in features of appearance of a product which are solely dictated by its technical function.

2. A Community design shall not subsist in features of appearance of a product which must necessarily be reproduced in their exact form and dimensions in order to permit the product in which the design is incorporated or to which it is applied to be mechanically connected to or placed in, around or against another product so that either product may perform its function.

3. Notwithstanding paragraph 2, a Community design shall under the conditions set out in Articles 5 and 6 subsist in a design serving the purpose of allowing the multiple assembly or connection of mutually interchangeable products within a modular system.

Article 9 — Designs contrary to public policy or morality

A Community design shall not subsist in a design which is contrary to public policy or to accepted principles of morality.

Section 2
Scope and term of protection

Article 10 — Scope of protection

1. The scope of the protection conferred by a Community design shall include any design which does not produce on the informed user a different overall impression.

2. In assessing the scope of protection, the degree of freedom of the designer in developing his design shall be taken into consideration.

Article 11 — Commencement and term of protection of the unregistered Community design

1. A design which meets the requirements under Section 1 shall be protected by an unregistered Community design for a period of three years as from the date on which the design was first made available to the public within the Community.

2. For the purpose of paragraph 1, a design shall be deemed to have been made available to the public within the Community if it has been published, exhibited, used in trade or otherwise disclosed in such a way that, in the normal course of business, these events could reasonably have become known to the circles specialised in the sector concerned, operating within the Community.

The design shall not, however, be deemed to have been made available to the public for the sole reason that it has been disclosed to a third person under explicit or implicit conditions of confidentiality.

Article 12 — Commencement and term of protection of the registered Community design

Upon registration by the Office, a design which meets the requirements under Section 1 shall be protected by a registered Community design for a period of five years as from the date of the filing of the application. The right holder may have the term of protection renewed for one or more periods of five years each, up to a total term of 25 years from the date of filing.

Article 13 — Renewal

1. Registration of the registered Community design shall be renewed at the request of the right holder or of any person expressly authorised by him, provided that the renewal fee has been paid.

2. The Office shall inform the right holder of the registered Community design and any person having a right entered in the register of Community designs, referred to in Article 72, hereafter referred to as the 'register' in respect of the registered Community design, of the expiry of the registration in good time before the said expiry. Failure to give such information shall not involve the responsibility of the Office.

3. The request for renewal shall be submitted and the renewal fee paid within a period of six months ending on the last day of the month in which protection ends. Failing this, the request may be submitted and the fee paid within a further period of six months from the day referred to in the first sentence, provided that an additional fee is paid within this further period.

4. Renewal shall take effect from the day following the date on which the existing registration expires. The renewal shall be entered in the register.

Section 3
Right to the Community design

Article 14 — Right to the Community design

1. The right to the Community design shall vest in the designer or his successor in title.

2. If two or more persons have jointly developed a design, the right to the Community design shall vest in them jointly.

3. However, where a design is developed by an employee in the execution of his duties or following the instructions given by his employer, the right to the Community design shall vest in the employer, unless otherwise agreed or specified under national law.

Article 15 — Claims relating to the entitlement to a Community design

1. If an unregistered Community design is disclosed or claimed by, or a registered Community design has been applied for or registered in the name of,

a person who is not entitled to it under Article 14, the person entitled to it under that provision may, without prejudice to any other remedy which may be open to him, claim to become recognised as the legitimate holder of the Community design.

2. Where a person is jointly entitled to a Community design, that person may, in accordance with paragraph 1, claim to become recognised as joint holder.

3. Legal proceedings under paragraphs 1 or 2 shall be barred three years after the date of publication of a registered Community design or the date of disclosure of an unregistered Community design. This provision shall not apply if the person who is not entitled to the Community design was acting in bad faith at the time when such design was applied for or disclosed or was assigned to him.

4. In the case of a registered Community design, the following shall be entered in the register:

    (a)   the mention that legal proceedings under paragraph 1 have been instituted;

    (b)   the final decision or any other termination of the proceedings;

    (c)   any change in the ownership of the registered Community design resulting from the final decision.

Article 16 — Effects of a judgement on entitlement to a registered Community design

1. Where there is a complete change of ownership of a registered Community design as a result of legal proceedings under Article 15(1), licences and other rights shall lapse upon the entering in the register of the person entitled.

2. If, before the institution of the legal proceedings under Article 15(1) has been registered, the holder of the registered Community design or a licensee has exploited the design within the Community or made serious and effective preparations to do so, he may continue such exploitation provided that he requests within the period prescribed by the implementing regulation a non-exclusive licence from the new holder whose name is entered in the register. The licence shall be granted for a reasonable period and upon reasonable terms.

3. Paragraph 2 shall not apply if the holder of the registered Community design or the licensee was acting in bad faith at the time when he began to exploit the design or to make preparations to do so.

Article 17 — Presumption in favour of the registered holder of the design

The person in whose name the registered Community design is registered or, prior to registration, the person in whose name the application is filed, shall be deemed to be the person entitled in any proceedings before the Office as well as in any other proceedings.

Article 18 — Right of the designer to be cited

The designer shall have the right, in the same way as the applicant for or the holder of a registered Community design, to be cited as such before the Office and in the register. If the design is the result of teamwork, the citation of the team may replace the citation of the individual designers.

Section 4
Effects of the Community design

Article 19 — Rights conferred by the Community design

1. A registered Community design shall confer on its holder the exclusive right to use it and to prevent any third party not having his consent from using it. The aforementioned use shall cover, in particular, the making, offering, putting on the market, importing, exporting or using of a product in which the design is incorporated or to which it is applied, or stocking such a product for those purposes.

2. An unregistered Community design shall, however, confer on its holder the right to prevent the acts referred to in paragraph 1 only if the contested use results from copying the protected design.

The contested use shall not be deemed to result from copying the protected design if it results from an independent work of creation by a designer who may be reasonably thought not to be familiar with the design made available to the public by the holder.

3. Paragraph 2 shall also apply to a registered Community design subject to deferment of publication as long as the relevant entries in the register and the file have not been made available to the public in accordance with Article 50(4).

Article 20 — Limitation of the rights conferred by a Community design

1. The rights conferred by a Community design shall not be exercised in respect of:

    (a)   acts done privately and for non-commercial purposes;
    (b)   acts done for experimental purposes;
    (c)   acts of reproduction for the purpose of making citations or of teaching, provided that such acts are compatible with fair trade practice and do not unduly prejudice the normal exploitation of the design, and that mention is made of the source.

2. In addition, the rights conferred by a Community design shall not be exercised in respect of:

    (a)   the equipment on ships and aircraft registered in a third country when these temporarily enter the territory of the Community;
    (b)   the importation in the Community of spare parts and accessories for the purpose of repairing such craft;
    (c)   the execution of repairs on such craft.

Article 21 — Exhaustion of rights

The rights conferred by a Community design shall not extend to acts relating to a product in which a design included within the scope of protection of the

Community design is incorporated or to which it is applied, when the product has been put on the market in the Community by the holder of the Community design or with his consent.

Article 22 — Rights of prior use in respect of a registered Community design

1. A right of prior use shall exist for any third person who can establish that before the date of filing of the application, or, if a priority is claimed, before the date of priority, he has in good faith commenced use within the Community, or has made serious and effective preparations to that end, of a design included within the scope of protection of a registered Community design, which has not been copied from the latter.

2. The right of prior use shall entitle the third person to exploit the design for the purposes for which its use had been effected, or for which serious and effective preparations had been made, before the filing or priority date of the registered Community design.

3. The right of prior use shall not extend to granting a licence to another person to exploit the design.

4. The right of prior use cannot be transferred except, where the third person is a business, along with that part of the business in the course of which the act was done or the preparations were made.

Article 23 — Government use

Any provision in the law of a Member State allowing use of national designs by or for the government may be applied to Community designs, but only to the extent that the use is necessary for essential defence or security needs.

Section 5
Invalidity

Article 24 — Declaration of invalidity

1. A registered Community design shall be declared invalid on application to the Office in accordance with the procedure in Titles VI and VII or by a Community design court on the basis of a counterclaim in infringement proceedings.

2. A Community design may be declared invalid even after the Community design has lapsed or has been surrendered.

3. An unregistered Community design shall be declared invalid by a Community design court on application to such a court or on the basis of a counterclaim in infringement proceedings.

Article 25 — Grounds for invalidity

1. A Community design may be declared invalid only in the following cases:

    (a)   if the design does not correspond to the definition under Article 3(a);

    (b)   if it does not fulfil the requirements of Articles 4 to 9;

(c)   if, by virtue of a court decision, the right holder is not entitled to the Community design under Article 14;

(d)   if the Community design is in conflict with a prior design which has been made available to the public after the date of filing of the application or, if a priority is claimed, the date of priority of the Community design, and which is protected from a date prior to the said date by a registered Community design or an application for such a design, or by a registered design right of a Member State, or by an application for such a right;

(e)   if a distinctive sign is used in a subsequent design, and Community law or the law of the Member State governing that sign confers on the right holder of the sign the right to prohibit such use;

(f)   if the design constitutes an unauthorised use of a work protected under the copyright law of a Member State;

(g)   if the design constitutes an improper use of any of the items listed in Article 6ter of the 'Paris Convention' for the Protection of Industrial Property hereafter referred to as the 'Paris Convention', or of badges, emblems and escutcheons other than those covered by the said Article 6ter and which are of particular public interest in a Member State.

2. The ground provided for in paragraph (1)(c) may be invoked solely by the person who is entitled to the Community design under Article 14.

3. The grounds provided for in paragraph (1)(d), (e) and (f) may be invoked solely by the applicant for or holder of the earlier right.

4. The ground provided for in paragraph (1)(g) may be invoked solely by the person or entity concerned by the use.

5. Paragraphs 3 and 4 shall be without prejudice to the freedom of Member States to provide that the grounds provided for in paragraphs 1(d) and (g) may also be invoked by the appropriate authority of the Member State in question on its own initiative.

6. A registered Community design which has been declared invalid pursuant to paragraph (1)(b), (e), (f) or (g) may be maintained in an amended form, if in that form it complies with the requirements for protection and the identity of the design is retained. 'Maintenance' in an amended form may include registration accompanied by a partial disclaimer by the holder of the registered Community design or entry in the register of a court decision or a decision by the Office declaring the partial invalidity of the registered Community design.

Article 26 — Consequences of invalidity

1. A Community design shall be deemed not to have had, as from the outset, the effects specified in this Regulation, to the extent that it has been declared invalid.

2. Subject to the national provisions relating either to claims for compensation for damage caused by negligence or lack of good faith on the part of the holder of the Community design, or to unjust enrichment, the retroactive effect of invalidity of the Community design shall not affect:

(a) any decision on infringement which has acquired the authority of a final decision and been enforced prior to the invalidity decision;

(b) any contract concluded prior to the invalidity decision, in so far as it has been performed before the decision; however, repayment, to an extent justified by the circumstances, of sums paid under the relevant contract may be claimed on grounds of equity.

TITLE III

COMMUNITY DESIGNS AS OBJECTS OF PROPERTY

Article 27 — Dealing with Community designs as national design rights

1. Unless Articles 28, 29, 30, 31 and 32 provide otherwise, a Community design as an object of property shall be dealt with in its entirety, and for the whole area of the Community, as a national design right of the Member State in which:

(a) the holder has his seat or his domicile on the relevant date; or

(b) where point (a) does not apply, the holder has an establishment on the relevant date.

2. In the case of a registered Community design, paragraph 1 shall apply according to the entries in the register.

3. In the case of joint holders, if two or more of them fulfil the condition under paragraph 1, the Member State referred to in that paragraph shall be determined:

(a) in the case of an unregistered Community design, by reference to the relevant joint holder designated by them by common agreement;

(b) in the case of a registered Community design, by reference to the first of the relevant joint holders in the order in which they are mentioned in the register.

4. Where paragraphs 1, 2 and 3 do not apply, the Member State referred to in paragraph 1 shall be the Member State in which the seat of the Office is situated.

Article 28 — Transfer of the registered Community design

The transfer of a registered Community design shall be subject to the following provisions:

(a) at the request of one of the parties, a transfer shall be entered in the register and published;

(b) until such time as the transfer has been entered in the register, the successor in title may not invoke the rights arising from the registration of the Community design;

(c) where there are time limits to be observed in dealings with the Office, the successor in title may make the corresponding statements to the Office once the request for registration of the transfer has been received by the Office;

(d) all documents which by virtue of Article 66 require notification to the holder of the registered Community design shall be addressed by the Office to the person registered as holder or his representative, if one has been appointed.

Article 29 — Rights in rem on a registered Community design

1. A registered Community design may be given as security or be the subject of rights in rem.

2. On request of one of the parties, the rights mentioned in paragraph 1 shall be entered in the register and published.

Article 30 — Levy of execution

1. A registered Community design may be levied in execution.

2. As regards the procedure for levy of execution in respect of a registered Community design, the courts and authorities of the Member State determined in accordance with Article 27 shall have exclusive jurisdiction.

3. On request of one of the parties, levy of execution shall be entered in the register and published.

Article 31 — Insolvency proceedings

1. The only insolvency proceedings in which a Community design may be involved shall be those opened in the Member State within the territory of which the centre of a debtor's main interests is situated.

2. In the case of joint proprietorship of a Community design, paragraph 1 shall apply to the share of the joint proprietor.

3. Where a Community design is involved in insolvency proceedings, on request of the competent national authority an entry to this effect shall be made in the register and published in the Community Designs Bulletin referred to in Article 73(1).

Article 32 — Licensing

1. A Community design may be licensed for the whole or part of the Community. A licence may be exclusive or non-exclusive.

2. Without prejudice to any legal proceedings based on the law of contract, the holder may invoke the rights conferred by the Community design against a licensee who contravenes any provision in his licensing contract with regard to its duration, the form in which the design may be used, the range of products for which the licence is granted and the quality of products manufactured by the licensee.

3. Without prejudice to the provisions of the licensing contract, the licensee may bring proceedings for infringement of a Community design only if the right holder consents thereto. However, the holder of an exclusive licence may bring such proceedings if the right holder in the Community design, having been given notice to do so, does not himself bring infringement proceedings within an appropriate period.

4. A licensee shall, for the purpose of obtaining compensation for damage suffered by him, be entitled to intervene in an infringement action brought by the right holder in a Community design.

5. In the case of a registered Community design, the grant or transfer of a licence in respect of such right shall, at the request of one of the parties, be entered in the register and published.

Article 33 — Effects vis-à-vis third parties

1. The effects vis-à-vis third parties of the legal acts referred to in Articles 28, 29, 30 and 32 shall be governed by the law of the Member State determined in accordance with Article 27.

2. However, as regards registered Community designs, legal acts referred to in Articles 28, 29 and 32 shall only have effect vis-à-vis third parties in all the Member States after entry in the register. Nevertheless, such an act, before it is so entered, shall have effect vis-à-vis third parties who have acquired rights in the registered Community design after the date of that act but who knew of the act at the date on which the rights were acquired.

3. Paragraph 2 shall not apply to a person who acquires the registered Community design or a right concerning the registered Community design by way of transfer of the whole of the undertaking or by any other universal succession.

4. Until such time as common rules for the Member States in the field of insolvency enter into force, the effects vis-à-vis third parties of insolvency proceedings shall be governed by the law of the Member State in which such proceedings are first brought under the national law or the regulations applicable in this field.

Article 34 — The application for a registered Community design as an object of property

1. An application for a registered Community design as an object of property shall be dealt with in its entirety, and for the whole area of the Community, as a national design right of the Member State determined in accordance with Article 27.

2. Articles 28, 29, 30, 31, 32 and 33 shall apply mutatis mutandis to applications for registered Community designs. Where the effect of one of these provisions is conditional upon an entry in the register, that formality shall be performed upon registration of the resulting registered Community design.

TITLE IV

APPLICATION FOR A REGISTERED COMMUNITY DESIGN

Section I
Filing of applications and the conditions which govern them

Article 35 — Filing and forwarding of applications

1. An application for a registered Community design shall be filed, at the option of the applicant:

    (a)   at the Office; or

    (b)   at the central industrial property office of a Member State; or

    (c)   in the Benelux countries, at the Benelux Design Office.

2. Where the application is filed at the central industrial property office of a Member State or at the Benelux Design Office, that office shall take all steps to forward the application to the Office within two weeks after filing. It may charge the applicant a fee which shall not exceed the administrative costs of receiving and forwarding the application.

3. As soon as the Office has received an application which has been forwarded by a central industrial property office of a Member State or by the Benelux Design Office, it shall inform the applicant accordingly, indicating the date of its receipt at the Office.

4. No less than 10 years after the entry into force of this Regulation, the Commission shall draw up a report on the operation of the system of filing applications for registered Community designs, accompanied by any proposals for revision that it may deem appropriate.

Article 36 — Conditions with which applications must comply

1. An application for a registered Community design shall contain:

    (a)   a request for registration;

    (b)   information identifying the applicant;

    (c)   a representation of the design suitable for reproduction. However, if the object of the application is a two-dimensional design and the application contains a request for deferment of publication in accordance with Article 50, the representation of the design may be replaced by a specimen.

2. The application shall further contain an indication of the products in which the design is intended to be incorporated or to which it is intended to be applied.

3. In addition, the application may contain:

    (a)   a description explaining the representation or the specimen;

    (b)   a request for deferment of publication of the registration in accordance with Article 50;

(c)   information identifying the representative if the applicant has appointed one;

(d)   the classification of the products in which the design is intended to be incorporated or to which it is intended to be applied according to class;

(e)   the citation of the designer or of the team of designers or a statement under the applicant's responsibility that the designer or the team of designers has waived the right to be cited.

4. The application shall be subject to the payment of the registration fee and the publication fee. Where a request for deferment under paragraph 3(b) is filed, the publication fee shall be replaced by the fee for deferment of publication.

5. The application shall comply with the conditions laid down in the implementing regulation.

6. The information contained in the elements mentioned in paragraph 2 and in paragraph 3(a) and (d) shall not affect the scope of protection of the design as such.

Article 37 — Multiple applications

1. Several designs may be combined in one multiple application for registered Community designs. Except in cases of ornamentation, this possibility is subject to the condition that the products in which the designs are intended to be incorporated or to which they are intended to be applied all belong to the same class of the International Classification for Industrial Designs.

2. Besides the fees referred to in Article 36(4), the multiple application shall be subject to payment of an additional registration fee and an additional publication fee. Where the multiple application contains a request for deferment of publication, the additional publication fee shall be replaced by the additional fee for deferment of publication. The additional fees shall correspond to a percentage of the basic fees for each additional design.

3. The multiple application shall comply with the conditions of presentation laid down in the implementing regulation.

4. Each of the designs contained in a multiple application or registration may be dealt with separately from the others for the purpose of applying this Regulation. It may in particular, separately from the others, be enforced, licensed, be the subject of a right in rem, a levy of execution or insolvency proceedings, be surrendered, renewed or assigned, be the subject of deferred publication or be declared invalid. A multiple application or registration may be divided into separate applications or registrations only under the conditions set out in the implementing regulation.

Article 38 — Date of filing

1. The date of filing of an application for a registered Community design shall be the date on which documents containing the information specified in Article 36(1) are filed with the Office by the applicant, or, if the application has been filed with the central industrial property office of a Member State or with the Benelux Design Office, with that office.

2. By derogation from paragraph 1, the date of filing of an application filed with the central industrial property office of a Member State or with the Benelux Design Office and reaching the Office more than two months after the date on which documents containing the information specified in Article 36(1) have been filed shall be the date of receipt of such documents by the Office.

Article 39 — Equivalence of Community filing with national filing

An application for a registered Community design which has been accorded a date of filing shall, in the Member States, be equivalent to a regular national filing, including where appropriate the priority claimed for the said application.

Article 40 — Classification

For the purpose of this Regulation, use shall be made of the Annex to the Agreement establishing an International Classification for Industrial Designs, signed at Locarno on 8 October 1968.

Section 2
Priority

Article 41 — Right of priority

1. A person who has duly filed an application for a design right or for a utility model in or for any State party to the Paris Convention for the Protection of Industrial Property, or to the Agreement establishing the World Trade Organisation, or his successors in title, shall enjoy, for the purpose of filing an application for a registered Community design in respect of the same design or utility model, a right of priority of six months from the date of filing of the first application.

2. Every filing that is equivalent to a regular national filing under the national law of the State where it was made or under bilateral or multilateral agreements shall be recognised as giving rise to a right of priority.

3. 'Regular national filing' means any filing that is sufficient to establish the date on which the application was filed, whatever may be the outcome of the application.

4. A subsequent application for a design which was the subject of a previous first application, and which is filed in or in respect of the same State, shall be considered as the first application for the purpose of determining priority, provided that, at the date of the filing of the subsequent application, the previous application has been withdrawn, abandoned or refused without being open to public inspection and without leaving any rights outstanding, and has not served as a basis for claiming priority. The previous application may not thereafter serve as a basis for claiming a right of priority.

5. If the first filing has been made in a State which is not a party to the Paris Convention, or to the Agreement establishing the World Trade Organisation, paragraphs 1 to 4 shall apply only in so far as that State, according to published

findings, grants, on the basis of a filing made at the Office and subject to conditions equivalent to those laid down in this Regulation, a right of priority having equivalent effect.

Article 42 — Claiming priority

An applicant for a registered Community design desiring to take advantage of the priority of a previous application shall file a declaration of priority and a copy of the previous application. If the language of the latter is not one of the languages of the Office, the Office may require a translation of the previous application in one of those languages.

Article 43 — Effect of priority right

The effect of the right of priority shall be that the date of priority shall count as the date of the filing of the application for a registered Community design for the purpose of Articles 5, 6, 7, 22, 25(1)(d) and 50(1).

Article 44 — Exhibition priority

1. If an applicant for a registered Community design has disclosed products in which the design is incorporated, or to which it is applied, at an official or officially recognised international exhibition falling within the terms of the Convention on International Exhibitions signed in Paris on 22 November 1928 and last revised on 30 November 1972, he may, if he files the application within a period of six months from the date of the first disclosure of such products, claim a right of priority from that date within the meaning of Article 43.

2. An applicant who wishes to claim priority pursuant to paragraph 1, under the conditions laid down in the implementing regulation, must file evidence that he has disclosed at an exhibition the products in or to which the design is incorporated or applied.

3. An exhibition priority granted in a Member State or in a third country does not extend the period of priority laid down in Article 41.

TITLE V

REGISTRATION PROCEDURE

Article 45 — Examination as to formal requirements for filing

1. The Office shall examine whether the application complies with the requirements laid down in Article 36(1) for the accordance of a date of filing.

2. The Office shall examine whether:

    (a)   the application complies with the other requirements laid down in Article 36(2), (3), (4) and (5) and, in the case of a multiple application, Article 37(1) and (2);

    (b)   the application meets the formal requirements laid down in the implementing regulation for the implementation of Articles 36 and 37;

    (c)   the requirements of Article 77(2) are satisfied;

(d)   the requirements concerning the claim to priority are satisfied, if a priority is claimed.

3. The conditions for the examination as to the formal requirements for filing shall be laid down in the implementing regulation.

Article 46 — Remediable deficiencies

1. Where, in carrying out the examination under Article 45, the Office notes that there are deficiencies which may be corrected, the Office shall request the applicant to remedy them within the prescribed period.

2. If the deficiencies concern the requirements referred to in Article 36(1) and the applicant complies with the Office's request within the prescribed period, the Office shall accord as the date of filing the date on which the deficiencies are remedied. If the deficiencies are not remedied within the prescribed period, the application shall not be dealt with as an application for a registered Community design.

3. If the deficiencies concern the requirements, including the payment of fees, as referred to in Article 45(2)(a), (b) and (c) and the applicant complies with the Office's request within the prescribed period, the Office shall accord as the date of filing the date on which the application was originally filed. If the deficiencies or the default in payment are not remedied within the prescribed period, the Office shall refuse the application.

4. If the deficiencies concern the requirements referred to in Article 45(2)(d), failure to remedy them within the prescribed period shall result in the loss of the right of priority for the application.

Article 47 — Grounds for non-registrability

1. If the Office, in carrying out the examination pursuant to Article 45, notices that the design for which protection is sought:

(a)   does not correspond to the definition under Article 3(a); or
(b)   is contrary to public policy or to accepted principles of morality, it shall refuse the application.

2. The application shall not be refused before the applicant has been allowed the opportunity of withdrawing or amending the application or of submitting his observations.

Article 48 — Registration

If the requirements that an application for a registered Community design must satisfy have been fulfilled and to the extent that the application has not been refused by virtue of Article 47, the Office shall register the application in the Community design Register as a registered Community design. The registration shall bear the date of filing of the application referred to in Article 38.

Article 49 — Publication

Upon registration, the Office shall publish the registered Community design in the Community Designs Bulletin as mentioned in Article 73(1). The contents of the publication shall be set out in the implementing regulation.

Article 50 — Deferment of publication

1. The applicant for a registered Community design may request, when filing the application, that the publication of the registered Community design be deferred for a period of 30 months from the date of filing the application or, if a priority is claimed, from the date of priority.

2. Upon such request, where the conditions set out in Article 48 are satisfied, the registered Community design shall be registered, but neither the representation of the design nor any file relating to the application shall, subject to Article 74(2), be open to public inspection.

3. The Office shall publish in the Community Designs Bulletin a mention of the deferment of the publication of the registered Community design. The mention shall be accompanied by information identifying the right holder in the registered Community design, the date of filing the application and any other particulars prescribed by the implementing regulation.

4. At the expiry of the period of deferment, or at any earlier date on request by the right holder, the Office shall open to public inspection all the entries in the register and the file relating to the application and shall publish the registered Community design in the Community Designs Bulletin, provided that, within the time limit laid down in the implementing regulation:

(a) the publication fee and, in the event of a multiple application, the additional publication fee are paid;

(b) where use has been made of the option pursuant to Article 36(1)(c), the right holder has filed with the Office a representation of the design.

If the right holder fails to comply with these requirements, the registered Community design shall be deemed from the outset not to have had the effects specified in this Regulation.

5. In the case of multiple applications, paragraph 4 need only be applied to some of the designs included therein.

6. The institution of legal proceedings on the basis of a registered Community design during the period of deferment of publication shall be subject to the condition that the information contained in the register and in the file relating to the application has been communicated to the person against whom the action is brought.

TITLE VI

SURRENDER AND INVALIDITY OF THE REGISTERED COMMUNITY DESIGN

Article 51 — Surrender

1. The surrender of a registered Community design shall be declared to the Office in writing by the right holder. It shall not have effect until it has been entered in the register.

2. If a Community design which is subject to deferment of publication is surrendered it shall be deemed from the outset not to have had the effects specified in this Regulation.

3. A registered Community design may be partially surrendered provided that its amended form complies with the requirements for protection and the identity of the design is retained.

4. Surrender shall be registered only with the agreement of the proprietor of a right entered in the register. If a licence has been registered, surrender shall be entered in the register only if the right holder in the registered Community design proves that he has informed the licensee of his intention to surrender. This entry shall be made on expiry of the period prescribed by the implementing regulation.

5. If an action pursuant to Article 14 relating to the entitlement to a registered Community design has been brought before a Community design court, the Office shall not enter the surrender in the register without the agreement of the claimant.

Article 52 — Application for a declaration of invalidity

1. Subject to Article 25(2), (3), (4) and (5), any natural or legal person, as well as a public authority empowered to do so, may submit to the Office an application for a declaration of invalidity of a registered Community design.

2. The application shall be filed in a written reasoned statement. It shall not be deemed to have been filed until the fee for an application for a declaration of invalidity has been paid.

3. An application for a declaration of invalidity shall not be admissible if an application relating to the same subject matter and cause of action, and involving the same parties, has been adjudicated on by a Community design court and has acquired the authority of a final decision.

Article 53 — Examination of the application

1. If the Office finds that the application for a declaration of invalidity is admissible, the Office shall examine whether the grounds for invalidity referred to in Article 25 prejudice the maintenance of the registered Community design.

2. In the examination of the application, which shall be conducted in accordance with the implementing regulation, the Office shall invite the parties, as often as necessary, to file observations, within a period to be fixed by the Office, on communications from the other parties or issued by itself.

3. The decision declaring the registered Community design invalid shall be entered in the register upon becoming final.

Article 54 — Participation in the proceedings of the alleged infringer

1. In the event of an application for a declaration of invalidity of a registered Community design being filed, and as long as no final decision has been taken by the Office, any third party who proves that proceedings for infringement of the same design have been instituted against him may be joined as a party in the

invalidity proceedings on request submitted within three months of the date on which the infringement proceedings were instituted.

The same shall apply in respect of any third party who proves both that the right holder of the Community design has requested that he cease an alleged infringement of the design and that he has instituted proceedings for a court ruling that he is not infringing the Community design.

2. The request to be joined as a party shall be filed in a written reasoned statement. It shall not be deemed to have been filed until the invalidity fee, referred to in Article 52(2), has been paid. Thereafter the request shall, subject to any exceptions laid down in the implementing regulation, be treated as an application for a declaration of invalidity.

TITLE VII

APPEALS

Article 55 — Decisions subject to appeal

1. An appeal shall lie from decisions of the examiners, the Administration of Trade Marks and Designs and Legal Division and Invalidity Divisions. It shall have suspensive effect.

2. A decision which does not terminate proceedings as regards one of the parties can only be appealed together with the final decision, unless the decision allows separate appeal.

Article 56 — Persons entitled to appeal and to be parties to appeal proceedings

Any party to proceedings adversely affected by a decision may appeal. Any other parties to the proceedings shall be parties to the appeal proceedings as of right.

Article 57 — Time limit and form of appeal

Notice of appeal must be filed in writing at the Office within two months after the date of notification of the decision appealed from. The notice shall be deemed to have been filed only when the fee for appeal has been paid. Within four months after the date of notification of the decision, a written statement setting out the grounds of appeal must be filed.

Article 58 — Interlocutory revision

1. If the department whose decision is contested considers the appeal to be admissible and well founded, it shall rectify its decision. This shall not apply where the appellant is opposed by another party to the proceedings.

2. If the decision is not rectified within one month after receipt of the statement of grounds, the appeal shall be remitted to the Board of Appeal without delay and without comment as to its merits.

Article 59 — Examination of appeals

1. If the appeal is admissible, the Board of Appeal shall examine whether the appeal is to be allowed.

2. In the examination of the appeal, the Board of Appeal shall invite the parties, as often as necessary, to file observations, within a period to be fixed by the Board of Appeal, on communications from the other parties or issued by itself.

Article 60 — Decisions in respect of appeals

1. Following the examination as to the merits of the appeal, the Board of Appeal shall decide on the appeal. The Board of Appeal may either exercise any power within the competence of the department which was responsible for the decision appealed against or remit the case to that department for further prosecution.

2. If the Board of Appeal remits the case for further prosecution to the department whose decision was appealed, that department shall be bound by the ratio decidendi of the Board of Appeal, in so far as the facts are the same.

3. The decisions of the Boards of Appeal shall take effect only from the date of expiry of the period referred to in Article 61(5) or, if an action has been brought before the Court of Justice within that period, from the date of rejection of such action.

Article 61 — Actions before the Court of Justice

1. Actions may be brought before the Court of Justice against decisions of the Boards of Appeal on appeals.

2. The action may be brought on grounds of lack of competence, infringement of an essential procedural requirement, infringement of the Treaty, of this Regulation or of any rule of law relating to their application or misuse of power.

3. The Court of Justice has jurisdiction to annul or to alter the contested decision.

4. The action shall be open to any party to proceedings before the Board of Appeal adversely affected by its decision.

5. The action shall be brought before the Court of Justice within two months of the date of notification of the decision of the Board of Appeal.

6. The Office shall be required to take the necessary measures to comply with the judgment of the Court of Justice.

TITLE VIII

PROCEDURE BEFORE THE OFFICE

Section I
General provisions

Article 62 — Statement of reasons on which decisions are based

Decisions of the Office shall state the reasons on which they are based. They shall be based only on reasons or evidence on which the parties concerned have had an opportunity to present their comments.

Article 63 — Examination of the facts by the Office of its own motion

1. In proceedings before it the Office shall examine the facts of its own motion. However, in proceedings relating to a declaration of invalidity, the Office shall be restricted in this examination to the facts, evidence and arguments provided by the parties and the relief sought.

2. The Office may disregard facts or evidence which are not submitted in due time by the parties concerned.

Article 64 — Oral proceedings

1. If the Office considers that oral proceedings would be expedient, they shall be held either at the instance of the Office or at the request of any party to the proceedings.

2. Oral proceedings, including delivery of the decision, shall be public, unless the department before which the proceedings are taking place decides otherwise in cases where admission of the public could have serious and unjustified disadvantages, in particular for a party to the proceedings.

Article 65 — Taking of evidence

1. In any proceedings before the Office the means of giving or obtaining evidence shall include the following:

    (a)   hearing the parties;
    (b)   requests for information;
    (c)   the production of documents and items of evidence;
    (d)   hearing witnesses;
    (e)   opinions by experts;
    (f)   statements in writing, sworn or affirmed or having a similar effect under the law of the State in which the statement is drawn up.

2. The relevant department of the Office may commission one of its members to examine the evidence adduced.

3. If the Office considers it necessary for a party, witness or expert to give evidence orally, it shall issue a summons to the person concerned to appear before it.

4. The parties shall be informed of the hearing of a witness or expert before the Office. They shall have the right to be present and to put questions to the witness or expert.

Article 66 — Notification

The Office shall, as a matter of course, notify those concerned of decisions and summonses and of any notice or other communication from which a time limit is reckoned, or of which those concerned must be notified under other provisions of this Regulation or of the implementing regulation, or of which notification has been ordered by the President of the Office.

Article 67 — Restitutio in integrum

1. The applicant for or holder of a registered Community design or any other party to proceedings before the Office who, in spite of all due care required by the circumstances having been taken, was unable to observe a time limit vis-à-vis the Office shall, upon application, have his rights re-established if the non-observance in question has the direct consequence, by virtue of the provisions of this Regulation, of causing the loss of any rights or means of redress.

2. The application must be filed in writing within two months of the removal of the cause of non-compliance with the time limit. The omitted act must be completed within this period. The application shall only be admissible within the year immediately following the expiry of the unobserved time limit. In the case of non-submission of the request for renewal of registration or of non-payment of a renewal fee, the further period of six months provided for in the second sentence of Article 13(3) shall be deducted from the period of one year.

3. The application must state the grounds on which it is based and must set out the facts on which it relies. It shall not be deemed to be filed until the fee for the re-establishment of rights has been paid.

4. The department competent to decide on the omitted act shall decide upon the application.

5. The provisions of this Article shall not be applicable to the time limits referred to in paragraph 2 and Article 41(1).

6. Where the applicant for or holder of a registered Community design has his rights re-established, he may not invoke his rights vis-à-vis a third party who, in good faith, in the course of the period between the loss of rights in the application for or registration of the registered Community design and publication of the mention of re-establishment of those rights, has put on the market products in which a design included within the scope of protection of the registered Community design is incorporated or to which it is applied.

7. A third party who may avail himself of the provisions of paragraph 6 may bring third party proceedings against the decision re-establishing the rights of the applicant for or holder of the registered Community design within a period of two months as from the date of publication of the mention of re-establishment of those rights.

8. Nothing in this Article shall limit the right of a Member State to grant restitutio in integrum in respect of time limits provided for in this Regulation and to be complied with vis-à-vis the authorities of such State.

Article 68 — Reference to general principles

In the absence of procedural provisions in this Regulation, the implementing regulation, the fees regulation or the rules of procedure of the Boards of Appeal, the Office shall take into account the principles of procedural law generally recognised in the Member States.

Article 69 — Termination of financial obligations

1. Rights of the Office to the payment of fees shall be barred four years from the end of the calendar year in which the fee fell due.

2. Rights against the Office for the refunding of fees or sums of money paid in excess of a fee shall be barred after four years from the end of the calendar year in which the right arose.

3. The periods laid down in paragraphs 1 and 2 shall be interrupted, in the case covered by paragraph 1, by a request for payment of the fee and, in the case covered by paragraph 2, by a reasoned claim in writing. On interruption it shall begin again immediately and shall end at the latest six years after the end of the year in which it originally began, unless in the meantime judicial proceedings to enforce the right have begun. In this case the period shall end at the earliest one year after the judgment has acquired the authority of a final decision.

Section 2
Costs

Article 70 — Apportionment of costs

1. The losing party in proceedings for a declaration of invalidity of a registered Community design or appeal proceedings shall bear the fees incurred by the other party as well as all costs incurred by him essential to the proceedings, including travel and subsistence and the remuneration of an agent, adviser or advocate, within the limits of scales set for each category of costs under the conditions laid down in the implementing regulation.

2. However, where each party succeeds on some and fails on other heads, or if reasons of equity so dictate, the Invalidity Division or Board of Appeal shall decide a different apportionment of costs.

3. A party who terminates the proceedings by surrendering the registered Community design or by not renewing its registration or by withdrawing the application for a declaration of invalidity or the appeal, shall bear the fees and the costs incurred by the other party as stipulated in paragraphs 1 and 2.

4. Where a case does not proceed to judgment, the costs shall be at the discretion of the Invalidity Division or Board of Appeal.

5. Where the parties conclude before the Invalidity Division or Board of Appeal a settlement of costs differing from that provided for in paragraphs 1, 2, 3 and 4, the body concerned shall take note of that agreement.

6. On request, the registry of the Invalidity Division or Board of Appeal shall fix the amount of the costs to be paid pursuant to the preceding paragraphs. The amount so determined may be reviewed by a decision of the Invalidity Division or Board of Appeal on a request filed within the period prescribed by the implementing regulation.

Article 71 — Enforcement of decisions fixing the amount of costs

1. Any final decision of the Office fixing the amount of costs shall be enforceable.

2. Enforcement shall be governed by the rules of civil procedure in force in the State in the territory of which it is carried out. The order for its enforcement shall be appended to the decision, without any other formality than verification of the authenticity of the decision, by the national authority which the government of each Member State shall designate for this purpose and shall make known to the Office and to the Court of Justice.

3. When these formalities have been completed on application by the party concerned, the latter may proceed to enforcement in accordance with the national law, by bringing the matter directly before the competent authority.

4. Enforcement may be suspended only by a decision of the Court of Justice. However, the courts of the Member State concerned shall have jurisdiction over complaints that enforcement is being carried out in an irregular manner.

Section 3
Informing the public and the official authorities of the Member States

Article 72 — Register of Community designs

The Office shall keep a register to be known as the register of Community designs, which shall contain those particulars of which the registration is provided for by this Regulation or by the implementing regulation. The register shall be open to public inspection, except to the extent that Article 50(2) provides otherwise.

Article 73 — Periodical publications

1. This Office shall periodically publish a Community Designs Bulletin containing entries open to public inspection in the register as well as other particulars the publication of which is prescribed by this Regulation or by the implementing regulation.

2. Notices and information of a general character issued by the President of the Office, as well as any other information relevant to this Regulation or its implementation, shall be published in the Official Journal of the Office.

Article 74 — Inspection of files

1. The files relating to applications for registered Community designs which have not yet been published or the files relating to registered Community designs which are subject to deferment of publication in accordance with Article 50 or which, being subject to such deferment, have been surrendered before or on the expiry of that period, shall not be made available for inspection without the consent of the applicant for or the right holder in the registered Community design.

2. Any person who can establish a legitimate interest may inspect a file without the consent of the applicant for or holder of the registered Community design prior to the publication or after the surrender of the latter in the case provided for in paragraph 1.

This shall in particular apply if the interested person proves that the applicant for or the holder of the registered Community design has taken steps with a view to invoking against him the right under the registered Community design.

3. Subsequent to the publication of the registered Community design, the file may be inspected on request.

4. However, where a file is inspected pursuant to paragraph 2 or 3, certain documents in the file may be withheld from inspection in accordance with the provisions of the implementing regulation.

Article 75 — Administrative cooperation

Unless otherwise provided in this Regulation or in national laws, the Office and the courts or authorities of the Member States shall on request give assistance to each other by communicating information or opening files for inspection.

Where the Office opens files to inspection by courts, public prosecutors' offices or central industrial property offices, the inspection shall not be subject to the restrictions laid down in Article 74.

Article 76 — Exchange of publications

1. The Office and the central industrial property offices of the Member States shall despatch to each other on request and for their own use one or more copies of their respective publications free of charge.

2. The Office may conclude agreements relating to the exchange or supply of publications.

Section 4
Representation

Article 77 — General principles of representation

1. Subject to paragraph 2, no person shall be compelled to be represented before the Office.

2. Without prejudice to the second subparagraph of paragraph 3, natural or legal persons not having either their domicile or their principal place of business or a

real and effective industrial or commercial establishment in the Community must be represented before the Office in accordance with Article 78(1) in all proceedings before the Office established by this Regulation, other than in filing an application for a registered Community design; the implementing regulation may permit other exceptions.

3. Natural or legal persons having their domicile or principal place of business or a real and effective industrial or commercial establishment in the Community may be represented before the Office by one of their employees, who must file with it a signed authorisation for inclusion in the files, the details of which are set out in the implementing regulation.

An employee of a legal person to which this paragraph applies may also represent other legal persons which have economic connections with the first legal person, even if those other legal persons have neither their domicile nor their principal place of business nor a real and effective industrial or commercial establishment within the Community.

Article 78 — Professional representation

1. Representation of natural or legal persons in proceedings before the Office under this Regulation may only be undertaken by:

(a) any legal practitioner qualified in one of the Member States and having his place of business within the Community, to the extent that he is entitled, within the said State, to act as a representative in industrial property matters; or

(b) any professional representatives whose name has been entered on the list of professional representatives referred to in Article 89(1)(b) of the Regulation on the Community trade mark; or

(c) persons whose names are entered on the special list of professional representatives for design matters referred to in paragraph 4.

2. The persons referred to in paragraph 1(c) shall only be entitled to represent third persons in proceedings on design matters before the Office.

3. The implementing regulation shall provide whether and under what conditions representatives must file with the Office a signed authorisation for insertion on the files.

4. Any natural person may be entered on the special list of professional representatives in design matters, if he fulfils the following conditions:

(a) he must be a national of one of the Member States;

(b) he must have his place of business or employment in the Community;

(c) he must be entitled to represent natural or legal persons in design matters before the central industrial property office of a Member State or before the Benelux Design Office. Where, in that State, the entitlement to represent in design matters is not conditional upon the requirement of special professional qualifications, persons applying to be entered on the list must have habitually acted in design matters before the central industrial property office of the said State for at least five years. However, persons whose professional qualification to represent natural or legal persons in design matters before the central industrial property office of one of the Member States is officially recognised in accordance with the regulations laid by such State shall not be subject to the condition of having exercised the profession.

5. Entry on the list referred to in paragraph 4 shall be effected upon request, accompanied by a certificate furnished by the central industrial property office of the Member State concerned, which must indicate that the conditions laid down in the said paragraph are fulfilled.

6. The President of the Office may grant exemption from:

(a) the requirement of paragraph 4(a) in special circumstances;
(b) the requirement of paragraph 4(c), second sentence, if the applicant furnishes proof that he has acquired the requisite qualification in another way.

7. The conditions under which a person may be removed from the list shall be laid down in the implementing regulation.

TITLE IX

JURISDICTION AND PROCEDURE IN LEGAL ACTIONS RELATING TO COMMUNITY DESIGNS

Section I
Jurisdiction and enforcement

Article 79 — Application of the Convention on Jurisdiction and Enforcement

1. Unless otherwise specified in this Regulation, the Convention on Jurisdiction and the Enforcement of Judgements in Civil and Commercial Matters, signed in Brussels on 27 September 1968(7), hereinafter referred to as the 'Convention on Jurisdiction and Enforcement', shall apply to proceedings relating to Community designs and applications for registered Community designs, as well as to proceedings relating to actions on the basis of Community designs and national designs enjoying simultaneous protection.

2. The provisions of the Convention on Jurisdiction and Enforcement which are rendered applicable by the paragraph 1 shall have effect in respect of any Member State solely in the text which is in force in respect of that State at any given time.

3. In the event of proceedings in respect of the actions and claims referred to in Article 85:

(a) Articles 2, 4, 5(1), (3), (4) and (5), 16(4) and 24 of the Convention on Jurisdiction and Enforcement shall not apply;
(b) Articles 17 and 18 of that Convention shall apply subject to the limitations in Article 82(4) of this Regulation;

(c)   the provisions of Title II of that Convention which are applicable to persons domiciled in a Member State shall also be applicable to persons who do not have a domicile in any Member State but have an establishment therein.

4. The provisions of the Convention on Jurisdiction and Enforcement shall not have effect in respect of any Member State for which that Convention has not yet entered into force. Until such entry into force, proceedings referred to in paragraph 1 shall be governed in such a Member State by any bilateral or multilateral convention governing its relationship with another Member State concerned, or, if no such convention exists, by its domestic law on jurisdiction, recognition and enforcement of decisions.

Section 2
Disputes concerning the infringement and validity of Community designs

Article 80 — Community design courts

1. The Member States shall designate in their territories as limited a number as possible of national courts and tribunals of first and second instance (Community design courts) which shall perform the functions assigned to them by this Regulation.

2. Each Member State shall communicate to the Commission not later than 6 March 2005 a list of Community design courts, indicating their names and their territorial jurisdiction.

3. Any change made after communication of the list referred to in paragraph 2 in the number, names or territorial jurisdiction of the Community design courts shall be notified without delay by the Member State concerned to the Commission.

4. The information referred to in paragraphs 2 and 3 shall be notified by the Commission to the Member States and published in the Official Journal of the European Communities.

5. As long as a Member State has not communicated the list as stipulated in paragraph 2, jurisdiction for any proceedings resulting from an action covered by Article 81 for which the courts of that State have jurisdiction pursuant to Article 82 shall lie with that court of the State in question which would have jurisdiction ratione loci and ratione materiae in the case of proceedings relating to a national design right of that State.

Article 81 — Jurisdiction over infringement and validity

The Community design courts shall have exclusive jurisdiction:

(a)   for infringement actions and – if they are permitted under national law – actions in respect of threatened infringement of Community designs;

(b)   for actions for declaration of non-infringement of Community designs, if they are permitted under national law;

(c)   for actions for a declaration of invalidity of an unregistered Community design;

(d)   for counterclaims for a declaration of invalidity of a Community design raised in connection with actions under (a).

Article 82 — International jurisdiction

1. Subject to the provisions of this Regulation and to any provisions of the Convention on Jurisdiction and Enforcement applicable by virtue of Article 79, proceedings in respect of the actions and claims referred to in Article 81 shall be brought in the courts of the Member State in which the defendant is domiciled or, if he is not domiciled in any of the Member States, in any Member State in which he has an establishment.

2. If the defendant is neither domiciled nor has an establishment in any of the Member States, such proceedings shall be brought in the courts of the Member State in which the plaintiff is domiciled or, if he is not domiciled in any of the Member States, in any Member State in which he has an establishment.

3. If neither the defendant nor the plaintiff is so domiciled or has such an establishment, such proceedings shall be brought in the courts of the Member State where the Office has its seat.

4. Notwithstanding paragraphs 1, 2 and 3:

(a)   Article 17 of the Convention on Jurisdiction and Enforcement shall apply if the parties agree that a different Community design court shall have jurisdiction;

(b)   Article 18 of that Convention shall apply if the defendant enters an appearance before a different Community design court.

5. Proceedings in respect of the actions and claims referred to in Article 81(a) and (d) may also be brought in the courts of the Member State in which the act of infringement has been committed or threatened.

Article 83 — Extent of jurisdiction on infringement

1. A Community design court whose jurisdiction is based on Article 82(1), (2) (3) or (4) shall have jurisdiction in respect of acts of infringement committed or threatened within the territory of any of the Member States.

2. A Community design court whose jurisdiction is based on Article 82(5) shall have jurisdiction only in respect of acts of infringement committed or threatened within the territory of the Member State in which that court is situated.

Article 84 — Action or counterclaim for a declaration of invalidity of a Community design

1. An action or a counterclaim for a declaration of invalidity of a Community design may only be based on the grounds for invalidity mentioned in Article 25.

2. In the cases referred to in Article 25(2), (3), (4) and (5) the action or the counterclaim may be brought solely by the person entitled under those provisions.

3. If the counterclaim is brought in a legal action to which the right holder of the Community design is not already a party, he shall be informed thereof and may be joined as a party to the action in accordance with the conditions set out in the law of the Member State where the court is situated.

4. The validity of a Community design may not be put in issue in an action for a declaration of non-infringement.

Article 85 — Presumption of validity – defence as to the merits

1. In proceedings in respect of an infringement action or an action for threatened infringement of a registered Community design, the Community design court shall treat the Community design as valid. Validity may be challenged only with a counterclaim for a declaration of invalidity. However, a plea relating to the invalidity of a Community design, submitted otherwise than by way of counterclaim, shall be admissible in so far as the defendant claims that the Community design could be declared invalid on account of an earlier national design right, within the meaning of Article 25(1)(d), belonging to him.

2. In proceedings in respect of an infringement action or an action for threatened infringement of an unregistered Community design, the Community design court shall treat the Community design as valid if the right holder produces proof that the conditions laid down in Article 11 have been met and indicates what constitutes the individual character of his Community design. However, the defendant may contest its validity by way of a plea or with a counterclaim for a declaration of invalidity.

Article 86 — Judgements of invalidity

1. Where in a proceeding before a Community design court the Community design has been put in issue by way of a counterclaim for a declaration of invalidity:

(a)   if any of the grounds mentioned in Article 25 are found to prejudice the maintenance of the Community design, the court shall declare the Community design invalid;

(b)   if none of the grounds mentioned in Article 25 is found to prejudice the maintenance of the Community design, the court shall reject the counterclaim.

2. The Community design court with which a counterclaim for a declaration of invalidity of a registered Community design has been filed shall inform the Office of the date on which the counterclaim was filed. The latter shall record this fact in the register.

3. The Community design court hearing a counterclaim for a declaration of invalidity of a registered Community design may, on application by the right holder of the registered Community design and after hearing the other parties, stay the proceedings and request the defendant to submit an application for a declaration of invalidity to the Office within a time limit which the court shall determine. If the application is not made within the time limit, the proceedings shall continue; the counterclaim shall be deemed withdrawn. Article 91(3) shall apply.

4. Where a Community design court has given a judgment which has become final on a counterclaim for a declaration of invalidity of a registered Community design, a copy of the judgment shall be sent to the Office. Any party may request information about such transmission. The Office shall mention the judgment in the register in accordance with the provisions of the implementing regulation.

5. No counterclaim for a declaration of invalidity of a registered Community design may be made if an application relating to the same subject matter and cause of action, and involving the same parties, has already been determined by the Office in a decision which has become final.

Article 87 — Effects of the judgement on invalidity

When it has become final, a judgment of a Community design court declaring a Community design invalid shall have in all the Member States the effects specified in Article 26.

Article 88 — Applicable law

1. The Community design courts shall apply the provisions of this Regulation.

2. On all matters not covered by this Regulation, a Community design court shall apply its national law, including its private international law.

3. Unless otherwise provided in this Regulation, a Community design court shall apply the rules of procedure governing the same type of action relating to a national design right in the Member State where it is situated.

Article 89 — Sanctions in actions for infringement

1. Where in an action for infringement or for threatened infringement a Community design court finds that the defendant has infringed or threatened to infringe a Community design, it shall, unless there are special reasons for not doing so, order the following measures:

   (a)   an order prohibiting the defendant from proceeding with the acts which have infringed or would infringe the Community design;
   (b)   an order to seize the infringing products;
   (c)   an order to seize materials and implements predominantly used in order to manufacture the infringing goods, if their owner knew the effect for which such use was intended or if such effect would have been obvious in the circumstances;
   (d)   any order imposing other sanctions appropriate under the circumstances which are provided by the law of the Member State in which the acts of infringement or threatened infringement are committed, including its private international law.

2. The Community design court shall take such measures in accordance with its national law as are aimed at ensuring that the orders referred to in paragraph 1 are complied with.

Article 90 — Provisional measures, including protective measures

1. Application may be made to the courts of a Member State, including Community design courts, for such provisional measures, including protective measures, in respect of a Community design as may be available under the law of that State in respect of national design rights even if, under this Regulation, a Community design court of another Member State has jurisdiction as to the substance of the matter.

2. In proceedings relating to provisional measures, including protective measures, a plea otherwise than by way of counterclaim relating to the invalidity of a Community design submitted by the defendant shall be admissible. Article 85(2) shall, however, apply mutatis mutandis.

3. A Community design court whose jurisdiction is based on Article 82(1), (2), (3) or (4) shall have jurisdiction to grant provisional measures, including protective measures, which, subject to any necessary procedure for recognition and enforcement pursuant to Title III of the Convention on Jurisdiction and Enforcement, are applicable in the territory of any Member State. No other court shall have such jurisdiction.

Article 91 — Specific rules on related actions

1. A Community design court hearing an action referred to in Article 81, other than an action for a declaration of non-infringement, shall, unless there are special grounds for continuing the hearing, of its own motion after hearing the parties, or at the request of one of the parties and after hearing the other parties, stay the proceedings where the validity of the Community design is already in issue before another Community design court on account of a counterclaim or, in the case of a registered Community design, where an application for a declaration of invalidity has already been filed at the Office.

2. The Office, when hearing an application for a declaration of invalidity of a registered Community design, shall, unless there are special grounds for continuing the hearing, of its own motion after hearing the parties, or at the request of one of the parties and after hearing the other parties, stay the proceedings where the validity of the registered Community design is already in issue on account of a counterclaim before a Community design court. However, if one of the parties to the proceedings before the Community design court so requests, the court may, after hearing the other parties to these proceedings, stay the proceedings. The Office shall in this instance continue the proceedings pending before it.

3. Where the Community design court stays the proceedings it may order provisional measures, including protective measures, for the duration of the stay.

Article 92 — Jurisdiction of Community design courts of second instance – further appeal

1. An appeal to the Community design courts of second instance shall lie from judgments of the Community design courts of first instance in respect of proceedings arising from the actions and claims referred to in Article 81.

2. The conditions under which an appeal may be lodged with a Community design court of second instance shall be determined by the national law of the Member State in which that court is located.

3. The national rules concerning further appeal shall be applicable in respect of judgments of Community design courts of second instance.

Section 3
Other disputes concerning Community designs

Article 93 — Supplementary provisions on the jurisdiction of national courts other than Community design courts

1. Within the Member State whose courts have jurisdiction under Article 79(1) or (4), those courts shall have jurisdiction for actions relating to Community designs other than those referred to in Article 81 which would have jurisdiction ratione loci and ratione materiae in the case of actions relating to a national design right in that State.

2. Actions relating to a Community design, other than those referred to in Article 81, for which no court has jurisdiction pursuant to Article 79(1) and (4) and paragraph 1 of this Article may be heard before the courts of the Member State in which the Office has its seat.

Article 94 — Obligation of the national court

A national court which is dealing with an action relating to a Community design other than the actions referred to in Article 81 shall treat the design as valid. Articles 85(2) and 90(2) shall, however, apply mutatis mutandis.

TITLE X

EFFECTS ON THE LAWS OF THE MEMBER STATES

Article 95 — Parallel actions on the basis of Community designs and national design rights

1. Where actions for infringement or for threatened infringement involving the same cause of action and between the same parties are brought before the courts of different Member States, one seized on the basis of a Community design and the other seized on the basis of a national design right providing simultaneous protection, the court other than the court first seized shall of its own motion decline jurisdiction in favour of that court. The court which would be required to decline jurisdiction may stay its proceedings if the jurisdiction of the other court is contested.

2. The Community design court hearing an action for infringement or threatened infringement on the basis of a Community design shall reject the action if a final judgment on the merits has been given on the same cause of action and between the same parties on the basis of a design right providing simultaneous protection.

3. The court hearing an action for infringement or for threatened infringement on the basis of a national design right shall reject the action if a final judgment on the merits has been given on the same cause of action and between the same parties on the basis of a Community design providing simultaneous protection.

4. Paragraphs 1, 2 and 3 shall not apply in respect of provisional measures, including protective measures.

Article 96 — Relationship to other forms of protection under national law

1. The provisions of this Regulation shall be without prejudice to any provisions of Community law or of the law of the Member States concerned relating to unregistered designs, trade marks or other distinctive signs, patents and utility models, typefaces, civil liability and unfair competition.

2. A design protected by a Community design shall also be eligible for protection under the law of copyright of Member States as from the date on which the design was created or fixed in any form. The extent to which, and the conditions under which, such a protection is conferred, including the level of originality required, shall be determined by each Member State.

TITLE XI

SUPPLEMENTARY PROVISIONS CONCERNING THE OFFICE

Section I
General provisions

Article 97 — General provision

Unless otherwise provided in this Title, Title XII of the Regulation on the Community trade mark shall apply to the Office with regard to its tasks under this Regulation.

Article 98 — Language of proceedings

1. The application for a registered Community design shall be filed in one of the official languages of the Community.

2. The applicant must indicate a second language which shall be a language of the Office the use of which he accepts as a possible language of proceedings before the Office.

If the application was filed in a language which is not one of the languages of the Office, the Office shall arrange to have the application translated into the language indicated by the applicant.

3. Where the applicant for a registered Community design is the sole party to proceedings before the Office, the language of proceedings shall be the language used for filing the application. If the application was made in a language other then the languages of the Office, the Office may send written communications to the applicant in the second language indicated by the applicant in his application.

4. In the case of invalidity proceedings, the language of proceedings shall be the language used for filing the application for a registered Community design if this is one of the languages of the Office. If the application was made in a language other than the languages of the Office, the language of proceedings shall be the second language indicated in the application.

The application for a declaration of invalidity shall be filed in the language of proceedings.

Where the language of proceedings is not the language used for filing the application for a registered Community design, the right holder of the Community design may file observations in the language of filing. The Office shall arrange to have those observations translated into the language of proceedings.

The implementing regulation may provide that the translation expenses to be borne by the Office may not, subject to a derogation granted by the Office where justified by the complexity of the case, exceed an amount to be fixed for each category of proceedings on the basis of the average size of statements of case received by the Office. Expenditure in excess of this amount may be allocated to the losing party in accordance with Article 70.

5. Parties to invalidity proceedings may agree that a different official language of the Community is to be the language of the proceedings.

Article 99 — Publication and register

1. All information the publication of which is prescribed by this Regulation or the implementing regulation shall be published in all the official languages of the Community.

2. All entries in the Register of Community designs shall be made in all the official languages of the Community.

3. In cases of doubt, the text in the language of the Office in which the application for a registered Community design was filed shall be authentic. If the application was filed in an official language of the Community other than one of the languages of the Office, the text in the second language indicated by the applicant shall be authentic.

Article 100 — Supplementary powers of the President

In addition to the functions and powers conferred on the President of the Office by Article 119 of the Regulation on the Community trade mark, the President may place before the Commission any proposal to amend this Regulation, the implementing regulation, the fees regulation and any other rule to the extent that they apply to registered Community designs, after consulting the Administrative Board and, in the case of the fees regulation, the Budget Committee.

Article 101 — Supplementary powers of the Administrative Board

In addition to the powers conferred on it by Article 121 et seq of the Regulation on the Community trade mark or by other provisions of this Regulation, the Administrative Board;

(a)   shall set the date for the first filing of applications for registered Community designs pursuant to Article 111(2);

(b)   shall be consulted before adoption of the guidelines for examination as to formal requirements, examination as to grounds for refusal of registration and invalidity proceedings in the Office and in the other cases provided for in this Regulation.

Section 2
Procedures

Article 102 — Competence

For taking decisions in connection with the procedures laid down in this Regulation the following shall be competent:

(a)   examiners;

(b)   the Administration of Trade Marks and Designs and Legal Division;

(c)   Invalidity Divisions;

(d)   Boards of Appeal.

Article 103 — Examiners

An examiner shall be responsible for taking decisions on behalf of the Office in relation to an application for a registered Community design.

Article 104 — The Administration of Trade Marks and Designs and Legal Division

1. The Administration of Trade Marks and Legal Division provided for by Article 128 of the Regulation on the Community trade mark shall become the Administration of Trade Marks and Designs and Legal Division.

2. In addition to the powers conferred upon it by the Regulation on the Community trade mark, it shall be responsible for taking those decisions required by this Regulation which do not fall within the competence of an examiner or an Invalidity Division. It shall in particular be responsible for decisions in respect of entries in the register.

Article 105 — Invalidity Divisions

1. An Invalidity Division shall be responsible for taking decisions in relation to applications for declarations of invalidity of registered Community designs.

2. An Invalidity Division shall consist of three members. At least one of the members must be legally qualified.

Article 106 — Boards of Appeal

In addition to the powers conferred upon it by Article 131 of the Regulation on the Community trade mark, the Boards of Appeal instituted by that Regulation shall be responsible for deciding on appeals from decisions of the examiners, the Invalidity Divisions and from the decisions of the Administration of Trade Marks and Designs and Legal Division as regards their decisions concerning Community designs.

TITLE XII

FINAL PROVISIONS

Article 107 — Implementing regulation

1. The rules implementing this Regulation shall be adopted in an implementing regulation.

2. In addition to the fees already provided for in this Regulation, fees shall be charged, in accordance with the detailed rules of application laid down in the implementing regulation and in a fees regulation, in the cases listed below:

   (a)   late payment of the registration fee;
   (b)   late payment of the publication fee;
   (c)   late payment of the fee for deferment of publication;
   (d)   late payment of additional fees for multiple applications;
   (e)   issue of a copy of the certificate of registration;
   (f)   registration of the transfer of a registered Community design;
   (g)   registration of a licence or another right in respect of a registered Community design;
   (h)   cancellation of the registration of a licence or another right;
   (i)   issue of an extract from the register;
   (j)   inspection of the files;
   (k)   issue of copies of file documents;
   (l)   communication of information in a file;
   (m) review of the determination of the procedural costs to be refunded;
   (n)   issue of certified copies of the application.

3. The implementing regulation and the fees regulation shall be adopted and amended in accordance with the procedure laid down in Article 109(2).

Article 108 — Rules of procedure of the Boards of Appeal

The rules of procedure of the Boards of Appeal shall apply to appeals heard by those Boards under this Regulation, without prejudice to any necessary adjustment or additional provision, adopted in accordance with the procedure laid down in Article 109(2).

Article 109 — Committee

1. The Commission shall be assisted by a Committee.

2. Where reference is made to this paragraph, Articles 5 and 7 of Decision 1999/468/EC shall apply.

The period laid down in Article 5(6) of Decision 1999/468/EC shall be set at three months.

3. The Committee shall adopt its rules of procedure

Article 110 — Transitional provision

1. Until such time as amendments to this Regulation enter into force on a proposal from the Commission on this subject, protection as a Community

design shall not exist for a design which constitutes a component part of a complex product used within the meaning of Article 19(1) for the purpose of the repair of that complex product so as to restore its original appearance.

2. The proposal from the Commission referred to in paragraph 1 shall be submitted together with, and take into consideration, any changes which the Commission shall propose on the same subject pursuant to Article 18 of Directive 98/71/EC.

Article 111 — Entry into force

1. This Regulation shall enter into force on the 60th day following its publication in the Official Journal of the European Communities.

2. Applications for registered Community designs may be filed at the Office from the date fixed by the Administrative Board on the recommendation of the President of the Office.

3. Applications for registered Community designs filed within three months before the date referred to in paragraph 2 shall be deemed to have been filed on that date.

Directive 98/7 I/EC of the European Parliament and of the Council of I3 October I998 on the legal protection of designs

THE EUROPEAN PARLIAMENT AND THE COUNCIL OF THE EURO-PEAN UNION,

Having regard to the Treaty establishing the European Community and in particular Article 100a thereof,

Having regard to the proposal by the Commission (1),

Having regard to the opinion of the Economic and Social Committee (2),

Acting in accordance with the procedure laid down in Article 189b of the Treaty (3), in the light of the joint text approved by the Conciliation Committee on 29 July 1998,

(1) Whereas the objectives of the Community, as laid down in the Treaty, include laying the foundations of an ever closer union among the peoples of Europe, fostering closer relations between Member States of the Community, and ensuring the economic and social progress of the Community countries by common action to eliminate the barriers which divide Europe; whereas to that end the Treaty provides for the establishment of an internal market character-ised by the abolition of obstacles to the free movement of goods and also for the institution of a system ensuring that competition in the internal market is not distorted; whereas an approximation of the laws of the Member States on the legal protection of designs would further those objectives;

(2) Whereas the differences in the legal protection of designs offered by the legislation of the Member States directly affect the establishment and functioning of the internal market as regards goods embodying designs; whereas such differences can distort competition within the internal market;

(3) Whereas it is therefore necessary for the smooth functioning of the internal market to approximate the design protection laws of the Member States;

(4) Whereas, in doing so, it is important to take into consideration the solutions and the advantages with which the Community design system will provide undertakings wishing to acquire design rights;

(5) Whereas it is unnecessary to undertake a full-scale approximation of the design laws of the Member States, and it will be sufficient if approximation is limited to those national provisions of law which most directly affect the functioning of the internal market; whereas provisions on sanctions, remedies and enforcement should be left to national law; whereas the objectives of this limited approximation cannot be sufficiently achieved by the Member States acting alone;

(6) Whereas Member States should accordingly remain free to fix the procedural provisions concerning registration, renewal and invalidation of design rights and provisions concerning the effects of such invalidity;

(7) Whereas this Directive does not exclude the application to designs of national or Community legislation providing for protection other than that conferred by registration or publication as design, such as legislation relating to unregistered design rights, trade marks, patents and utility models, unfair competition or civil liability;

(8) Whereas, in the absence of harmonisation of copyright law, it is important to establish the principle of cumulation of protection under specific registered design protection law and under copyright law, whilst leaving Member States free to establish the extent of copyright protection and the conditions under which such protection is conferred;

(9) Whereas the attainment of the objectives of the internal market requires that the conditions for obtaining a registered design right be identical in all the Member States; whereas to that end it is necessary to give a unitary definition of the notion of design and of the requirements as to novelty and individual character with which registered design rights must comply;

(10) Whereas it is essential, in order to facilitate the free movement of goods, to ensure in principle that registered design rights confer upon the right holder equivalent protection in all Member States;

(11) Whereas protection is conferred by way of registration upon the right holder for those design features of a product, in whole or in part, which are shown visibly in an application and made available to the public by way of publication or consultation of the relevant file;

(12) Whereas protection should not be extended to those component parts which are not visible during normal use of a product, or to those features of such part which are not visible when the part is mounted, or which would not,

in themselves, fulfil the requirements as to novelty and individual character; whereas features of design which are excluded from protection for these reasons should not be taken into consideration for the purpose of assessing whether other features of the design fulfil the requirements for protection;

(13) Whereas the assessment as to whether a design has individual character should be based on whether the overall impression produced on an informed user viewing the design clearly differs from that produced on him by the existing design corpus, taking into consideration the nature of the product to which the design is applied or in which it is incorporated, and in particular the industrial sector to which it belongs and the degree of freedom of the designer in developing the design;

(14) Whereas technological innovation should not be hampered by granting design protection to features dictated solely by a technical function; whereas it is understood that this does not entail that a design must have an aesthetic quality; whereas, likewise, the interoperability of products of different makes should not be hindered by extending protection to the design of mechanical fittings; whereas features of a design which are excluded from protection for these reasons should not be taken into consideration for the purpose of assessing whether other features of the design fulfil the requirements for protection;

(15) Whereas the mechanical fittings of modular products may nevertheless constitute an important element of the innovative characteristics of modular products and present a major marketing asset and therefore should be eligible for protection;

(16) Whereas a design right shall not subsist in a design which is contrary to public policy or to accepted principles of morality; whereas this Directive does not constitute a harmonisation of national concepts of public policy or accepted principles of morality;

(17) Whereas it is fundamental for the smooth functioning of the internal market to unify the term of protection afforded by registered design rights;

(18) Whereas the provisions of this Directive are without prejudice to the application of the competition rules under Articles 85 and 86 of the Treaty;

(19) Whereas the rapid adoption of this Directive has become a matter of urgency for a number of industrial sectors; whereas full-scale approximation of the laws of the Member States on the use of protected designs for the purpose of permitting the repair of a complex product so as to restore its original appearance, where the product incorporating the design or to which the design is applied constitutes a component part of a complex product upon whose appearance the protected design is dependent, cannot be introduced at the present stage; whereas the lack of full-scale approximation of the laws of the Member States on the use of protected designs for such repair of a complex product should not constitute an obstacle to the approximation of those other national provisions of design law which most directly affect the functioning of the internal market; whereas for this reason Member States should in the meantime maintain in force any provisions in conformity with the Treaty

relating to the use of the design of a component part used for the purpose of the repair of a complex product so as to restore its original appearance, or, if they introduce any new provisions relating to such use, the purpose of these provisions should be only to liberalise the market in such parts; whereas those Member States which, on the date of entry into force of this Directive, do not provide for protection for designs of component parts are not required to introduce registration of designs for such parts; whereas three years after the implementation date the Commission should submit an analysis of the consequences of the provisions of this Directive for Community industry, for consumers, for competition and for the functioning of the internal market; whereas, in respect of component parts of complex products, the analysis should, in particular, consider harmonisation on the basis of possible options, including a remuneration system and a limited term of exclusivity; whereas, at the latest one year after the submission of its analysis, the Commission should, after consultation with the parties most affected, propose to the European Parliament and the Council any changes to this Directive needed to complete the internal market in respect of component parts of complex products, and any other changes which it considers necessary;

(20) Whereas the transitional provision in Article 14 concerning the design of a component part used for the purpose of the repair of a complex product so as to restore its original appearance is in no case to be construed as constituting an obstacle to the free movement of a product which constitutes such a component part;

(21) Whereas the substantive grounds for refusal of registration in those Member States which provide for substantive examination of applications prior to registration, and the substantive grounds for the invalidation of registered design rights in all the Member States, must be exhaustively enumerated,

HAVE ADOPTED THIS DIRECTIVE:

Article 1 — Definitions

For the purpose of this Directive:

(a) 'design' means the appearance of the whole or a part of a product resulting from the features of, in particular, the lines, contours, colours, shape, texture and/or materials of the product itself and/or its ornamentation;

(b) 'product' means any industrial or handicraft item, including inter alia parts intended to be assembled into a complex product, packaging, get-up, graphic symbols and typographic typefaces, but excluding computer programs;

(c) 'complex product' means a product which is composed of multiple components which can be replaced permitting disassembly and reassembly of the product.

Article 2 — Scope of application

1. This Directive shall apply to:

(a)   design rights registered with the central industrial property offices of the Member States;
(b)   design rights registered at the Benelux Design Office;
(c)   design rights registered under international arrangements which have effect in a Member State;
(d)   applications for design rights referred to under (a), (b) and (c).

2. For the purpose of this Directive, design registration shall also comprise the publication following filing of the design with the industrial property office of a Member State in which such publication has the effect of bringing a design right into existence.

Article 3 — Protection requirements

1. Member States shall protect designs by registration, and shall confer exclusive rights upon their holders in accordance with the provisions of this Directive.

2. A design shall be protected by a design right to the extent that it is new and has individual character.

3. A design applied to or incorporated in a product which constitutes a component part of a complex product shall only be considered to be new and to have individual character:

(a)   if the component part, once it has been incorporated into the complex product, remains visible during normal use of the latter, and
(b)   to the extent that those visible features of the component part fulfil in themselves the requirements as to novelty and individual character.

4. 'Normal use' within the meaning of paragraph (3)(a) shall mean use by the end user, excluding maintenance, servicing or repair work.

Article 4 — Novelty

A design shall be considered new if no identical design has been made available to the public before the date of filing of the application for registration or, if priority is claimed, the date of priority. Designs shall be deemed to be identical if their features differ only in immaterial details.

Article 5 — Individual character

1. A design shall be considered to have individual character if the overall impression it produces on the informed user differs from the overall impression produced on such a user by any design which has been made available to the public before the date of filing of the application for registration or, if priority is claimed, the date of priority.

2. In assessing individual character, the degree of freedom of the designer in developing the design shall be taken into consideration.

Article 6 — Disclosure

1. For the purpose of applying Articles 4 and 5, a design shall be deemed to have been made available to the public if it has been published following registration or otherwise, or exhibited, used in trade or otherwise disclosed,

except where these events could not reasonably have become known in the normal course of business to the circles specialised in the sector concerned, operating within the Community, before the date of filing of the application for registration or, if priority is claimed, the date of priority. The design shall not, however, be deemed to have been made available to the public for the sole reason that it has been disclosed to a third person under explicit or implicit conditions of confidentiality.

2. A disclosure shall not be taken into consideration for the purpose of applying Articles 4 and 5 if a design for which protection is claimed under a registered design right of a Member State has been made available to the public:

(a)   by the designer, his successor in title, or a third person as a result of information provided or action taken by the designer, or his successor in title; and

(b)   during the 12-month period preceding the date of filing of the application or, if priority is claimed, the date of priority.

3. Paragraph 2 shall also apply if the design has been made available to the public as a consequence of an abuse in relation to the designer or his successor in title.

Article 7 — Designs dictated by their technical function and designs of interconnections

1. A design right shall not subsist in features of appearance of a product which are solely dictated by its technical function.

2. A design right shall not subsist in features of appearance of a product which must necessarily be reproduced in their exact form and dimensions in order to permit the product in which the design is incorporated or to which it is applied to be mechanically connected to or placed in, around or against another product so that either product may perform its function.

3. Notwithstanding paragraph 2, a design right shall, under the conditions set out in Articles 4 and 5, subsist in a design serving the purpose of allowing multiple assembly or connection of mutually interchangeable products within a modular system.

Article 8 — Designs contrary to public policy or morality

A design right shall not subsist in a design which is contrary to public policy or to accepted principles of morality.

Article 9 — Scope of protection

1. The scope of the protection conferred by a design right shall include any design which does not produce on the informed user a different overall impression.

2. In assessing the scope of protection, the degree of freedom of the designer in developing his design shall be taken into consideration.

Article 10 — Term of protection

Upon registration, a design which meets the requirements of Article 3(2) shall be protected by a design right for one or more periods of five years from the date of filing of the application. The right holder may have the term of protection renewed for one or more periods of five years each, up to a total term of 25 years from the date of filing.

Article 11 — Invalidity or refusal of registration

1. A design shall be refused registration, or, if the design has been registered, the design right shall be declared invalid:

(a)   if the design is not a design within the meaning of Article 1(a); or

(b)   if it does not fulfil the requirements of Articles 3 to 8; or

(c)   if the applicant for or the holder of the design right is not entitled to it under the law of the Member State concerned; or

(d)   if the design is in conflict with a prior design which has been made available to the public after the date of filing of the application or, if priority is claimed, the date of priority, and which is protected from a date prior to the said date by a registered Community design or an application for a registered Community design or by a design right of the Member State concerned, or by an application for such a right.

2. Any Member State may provide that a design shall be refused registration, or, if the design has been registered, that the design right shall be declared invalid:

(a)   if a distinctive sign is used in a subsequent design, and Community law or the law of the Member State concerned governing that sign confers on the right holder of the sign the right to prohibit such use; or

(b)   if the design constitutes an unauthorised use of a work protected under the copyright law of the Member State concerned; or

(c)   if the design constitutes an improper use of any of the items listed in Article 6b of the Paris Convention for the Protection of Industrial Property, or of badges, emblems and escutcheons other than those covered by Article 6b of the said Convention which are of particular public interest in the Member State concerned.

3. The ground provided for in paragraph 1(c) may be invoked solely by the person who is entitled to the design right under the law of the Member State concerned.

4. The grounds provided for in paragraph 1(d) and in paragraph 2(a) and (b) may be invoked solely by the applicant for or the holder of the conflicting right.

5. The ground provided for in paragraph 2(c) may be invoked solely by the person or entity concerned by the use.

6. Paragraphs 4 and 5 shall be without prejudice to the freedom of Member States to provide that the grounds provided for in paragraphs 1(d) and 2(c) may also be invoked by the appropriate authority of the Member State in question on its own initiative.

7. When a design has been refused registration or a design right has been declared invalid pursuant to paragraph 1(b) or to paragraph 2, the design may be registered or the design right maintained in an amended form, if in that form it complies with the requirements for protection and the identity of the design is retained. Registration or maintenance in an amended form may include registration accompanied by a partial disclaimer by the holder of the design right or entry in the design Register of a court decision declaring the partial invalidity of the design right.

8. Any Member State may provide that, by way of derogation from paragraphs 1 to 7, the grounds for refusal of registration or for invalidation in force in that State prior to the date on which the provisions necessary to comply with this Directive enter into force shall apply to design applications which have been made prior to that date and to resulting registrations.

9. A design right may be declared invalid even after it has lapsed or has been surrendered.

Article 12 — Rights conferred by the design right

1. The registration of a design shall confer on its holder the exclusive right to use it and to prevent any third party not having his consent from using it. The aforementioned use shall cover, in particular, the making, offering, putting on the market, importing, exporting or using of a product in which the design is incorporated or to which it is applied, or stocking such a product for those purposes.

2. Where, under the law of a Member State, acts referred to in paragraph 1 could not be prevented before the date on which the provisions necessary to comply with this Directive entered into force, the rights conferred by the design right may not be invoked to prevent continuation of such acts by any person who had begun such acts prior to that date.

Article 13 — Limitation of the rights conferred by the design right

1. The rights conferred by a design right upon registration shall not be exercised in respect of:

(a)   acts done privately and for non-commercial purposes;
(b)   acts done for experimental purposes;
(c)   acts of reproduction for the purposes of making citations or of teaching, provided that such acts are compatible with fair trade practice and do not unduly prejudice the normal exploitation of the design, and that mention is made of the source.

2. In addition, the rights conferred by a design right upon registration shall not be exercised in respect of:

(a)   the equipment on ships and aircraft registered in another country when these temporarily enter the territory of the Member State concerned;
(b)   the importation in the Member State concerned of spare parts and accessories for the purpose of repairing such craft;
(c)   the execution of repairs on such craft.

Article 14 — Transitional provision

Until such time as amendments to this Directive are adopted on a proposal from the Commission in accordance with the provisions of Article 18, Member States shall maintain in force their existing legal provisions relating to the use of the design of a component part used for the purpose of the repair of a complex product so as to restore its original appearance and shall introduce changes to those provisions only if the purpose is to liberalise the market for such parts.

Article 15 — Exhaustion of rights

The rights conferred by a design right upon registration shall not extend to acts relating to a product in which a design included within the scope of protection of the design right is incorporated or to which it is applied, when the product has been put on the market in the Community by the holder of the design right or with his consent.

Article 16 — Relationship to other forms of protection

The provisions of this Directive shall be without prejudice to any provisions of Community law or of the law of the Member State concerned relating to unregistered design rights, trade marks or other distinctive signs, patents and utility models, typefaces, civil liability or unfair competition.

Article 17 — Relationship to copyright

A design protected by a design right registered in or in respect of a Member State in accordance with this Directive shall also be eligible for protection under the law of copyright of that State as from the date on which the design was created or fixed in any form. The extent to which, and the conditions under which, such a protection is conferred, including the level of originality required, shall be determined by each Member State.

Article 18 — Revision

Three years after the implementation date specified in Article 19, the Commission shall submit an analysis of the consequences of the provisions of this Directive for Community industry, in particular the industrial sectors which are most affected, particularly manufacturers of complex products and component parts, for consumers, for competition and for the functioning of the internal market. At the latest one year later the Commission shall propose to the European Parliament and the Council any changes to this Directive needed to complete the internal market in respect of component parts of complex products and any other changes which it considers necessary in light of its consultations with the parties most affected.

Article 19 — Implementation

1. Member States shall bring into force the laws, regulations or administrative provisions necessary to comply with this Directive not later than 28 October 2001.

When Member States adopt these provisions, they shall contain a reference to this Directive or shall be accompanied by such reference on the occasion of their official publication. The methods of making such reference shall be laid down by Member States.

2. Member States shall communicate to the Commission the provisions of national law which they adopt in the field governed by this Directive.

Article 20 — Entry into force

This Directive shall enter into force on the 20th day following its publication in the Official Journal of the European Communities.

Article 21 — Addressees

This Directive is addressed to the Member States.

Done at Luxembourg, 13 October 1998.

For the European Parliament

The President

J. M. GIL-ROBLES

For the Council

The President

C. EINEM

Statement by the Commission

The Commission shares the European Parliament's concern about combating counterfeiting.

The Commission's intention is to present before the end of the year a Green Paper regarding piracy and counterfeiting in the internal market.

The Commission will include in this Green Paper Parliament's idea of creating an obligation for counterfeiters to provide holders of design rights with information on their illegal acts.

Statement by the Commission regarding Article 18

Immediately following the date of adoption of the Directive, and without prejudice to Article 18, the Commission proposes to launch a consultation exercise involving manufacturers of complex products and of component parts in the motor vehicles sector. The aim of this consultation will be to arrive at a voluntary agreement between the parties involved on the protection of designs in cases where the product incorporating the design or to which the design is applied constitutes a component part of a complex product upon whose appearance the protected design is dependent.

The Commission will coordinate the consultation exercise and will report regularly to the Parliament and the Council on its progress. The consulted parties will be invited by the Commission to consider a range of possible options on which to base a voluntary agreement, including a remuneration system and a system based on a limited period of design protection.

Council Directive of 16 December 1986 on the legal protection of topographies of semiconductor products (87/54/EEC)

THE COUNCIL OF THE EUROPEAN COMMUNITIES,

Having regard to the Treaty establishing the European Economic Community and in particular Article 100 thereof,

Having regard to the proposal from the Commission (1),

Having regard to the opinion of the European Parliament (2),

Having regard to the opinion of the Economic and Social Committee (3),

Whereas semiconductor products are playing an increasingly important role in a broad range of industries and semiconductor technology can accordingly be considered as being of fundamental importance for the Community's industrial development;

Whereas the functions of semiconductor products depend in large part on the topographies of such products and whereas the development of such topographies requires the investment of considerable resources, human, technical and financial, while topographies of such products can be copied at a fraction of the cost needed to develop them independently;

Whereas topographies of semiconductor products are at present not clearly protected in all Member States by existing legislation and such protection, where it exists, has different attributes;

Whereas certain existing differences in the legal protection of semiconductor products offered by the laws of the Member States have direct and negative effects on the functioning of the common market as regards semiconductor products and such differences could well become greater as Member States introduce new legislation on this subject;

Whereas existing differences having such effects need to be removed and new ones having a negative effect on the common market prevented from arising;

Whereas, in relation to extension of protection to persons outside the Community, Member States should be free to act on their own behalf in so far as Community decisions have not been taken within a limited period of time;

Whereas the Community's legal framework on the protection of topographies of semiconductor products can, in the first instance, be limited to certain basic principles by provisions specifying whom and what should be protected, the exclusive rights on which protected persons should be able to rely to authorize or prohibit certain acts, exceptions to these rights and for how long the protection should last;

Whereas other matters can for the time being be decided in accordance with national law, in particular, whether registration or deposit is required as a condition for protection and, subject to an exclusion of licences granted for the sole reason that a certain period of time has elapsed, whether and on what conditions non-voluntary licences may be granted in respect of protected topographies;

Whereas protection of topographies of semiconductor products in accordance with this Directive should be without prejudice to the application of some other forms of protection;

Whereas further measures concerning the legal protection of topographies of semiconductor products in the Community can be considered at a later stage, if necessary, while the application of common basic principles by all Member States in accordance with the provisions of this Directive is an urgent necessity,

HAS ADOPTED THIS DIRECTIVE:

Chapter I
Definitions

Article 1

1. For the purposes of this Directive:

   (a)   a 'semiconductor product' shall mean the final or an intermediate form of any product:

       (i)   consisting of a body of material which includes a layer of semiconducting material; and

       (ii) having one or more other layers composed of conducting, insulating or semiconducting material, the layers being arranged in accordance with a predetermined three-dimensional pattern; and

       (iii) intended to perform, exclusively or together with other functions, an electronic function;

   (b)   the 'topography' of a semiconductor product shall mean a series of related images, however fixed or encoded;

       (i)   representing the three-dimensional pattern of the layers of which a semiconductor product is composed; and

       (ii) in which series, each image has the pattern or part of the pattern of a surface of the semiconductor product at any stage of its manufacture;

   (c)   'commercial exploitation' means the sale, rental, leasing or any other method of commercial distribution, or an offer for these purposes. However, for the purposes of Articles 3 (4), 4 (1), 7 (1), (3) and (4) 'commercial exploitation' shall not include exploitation under conditions of confidentiality to the extent that no further distribution to third parties occurs, except where exploitation of a topography takes place under conditions of confidentiality required by a measure taken in conformity with Article 223 (1) (b) of the Treaty.

2. The Council acting by qualified majority on a proposal from the Commission, may amend paragraph 1 (a) (i) and (ii) in order to adapt these provisions in the light of technical progress.

Chapter 2
Protection of topographies of semiconductor products

Article 2

1. Member States shall protect the topographies of semiconductor products by adopting legislative provisions conferring exclusive rights in accordance with the provisions of the Directive.

2. The topography of a semiconductor product shall be protected in so far as it satisfies the conditions that it is the result of its creator's own intellectual effort and is not commonplace in the semiconductor industry. Where the topography of a semiconductor product consists of elements that are commonplace in the semiconductor industry, it shall be protected only to the extent that the combination of such elements, taken as a whole, fulfils the abovementioned conditions.

Article 3

1. Subject to paragraphs 2 to 5, the right to protection shall apply in favour of persons who are the creators of the topographies of semiconductor products.

2. Member States may provide that,

(a) where a topography is created in the course of the creator's employment, the right to protection shall apply in favour of the creator's employer unless the terms of employment provide to the contrary;

(b) where a topography is created under a contract other than a contract of employment, the right to protection shall apply in favour of a party to the contract by whom the topography has been commissioned, unless the contract provides to the contrary.

3.

(a) As regards the persons referred to in paragraph 1, the right to protection shall apply in favour of natural persons who are nationals of a Member State or who have their habitual residence on the territory of a Member State.

(b) Where Member States make provision in accordance with paragraph 2, the right to protection shall apply in favour of:

(i) natural persons who are nationals of a Member State or who have their habitual residence on the territory of a Member State;

(ii) companies or other legal persons which have a real and effective industrial or commercial establishment on the territory of a Member State.

4. Where no right to protection exists in accordance with other provisions of this Article, the right to protection shall also apply in favour of the persons referred to in paragraph 3 (b) (i) and (ii) who:

    (a)   first commercially exploit within a Member State a topography which has not yet been exploited commercially anywhere in the world; and

    (b)   have been exclusively authorized to exploit commercially the topography throughout the Community by the person entitled to dispose of it.

    5. The right to protection shall also apply in favour of the successors in title of the persons mentioned in paragraphs 1 to 4.

6. Subject to paragraph 7, Member States may negotiate and conclude agreements or understandings with third States and multilateral Conventions concerning the legal protection of topographies of semiconductor products whilst respecting Community law and in particular the rules laid down in this Directive.

7. Member States may enter into negotiations which third States with a view to extending the right to protection to persons who do not benefit from the right to protection according to the provisions of this Directive. Member States who enter into such negotiations shall inform the Commission thereof.

When a Member State wishes to extend protection to persons who otherwise do not benefit from the right to protection according to the provisions of this Directive or to conclude an agreement or understanding on the extension of protection with a non-Member State it shall notify the Commission. The Commission shall inform the other Member States thereof. The Member State shall hold the extension of protection or the conclusion of the agreement or understanding in abeyance for one month from the date on which it notifies the Commission. However, if within that period the Commission notifies the Member State concerned of its intention to submit a proposal to the Council for all Member States to extend protection in respect of the persons or non-Member State concerned, the Member State shall hold the extension of protection or the conclusion of the agreement or undestanding in abeyance for a period of two months from the date of the notification by the Member State.

Where, before the end of this two-month period, the Commission submits such a proposal to the Council, the Member State shall hold the extension of protection or the conclusion of the agreement or understanding in abeyance for a further period of four months from the date on which the proposal was submitted.

In the absence of a Commission notification or proposal or a Council decision within the time limits prescribed above, the Member State may extend protection or conclude the agreement or understanding.

A proposal by the Commission to extend protection, whether or not it is made following a notification by a Member State in accordance with the preceding paragraphs shall be adopted by the Council acting by qualified majority.

A Decision of the Council on the basis of a Commission proposal shall not prevent a Member State from extending protection to persons, in addition to those to benefit from protection in all Member States, who were included in the envisaged extension, agreement or understanding as notified, unless the Council acting by qualified majority has decided otherwise.

8. Commission proposals and Council decisions pursuant to paragraph 7 shall be published for information in the Official Journal of the European Communities.

Article 4

1. Member States may provide that the exclusive rights conferred in conformity with Article 2 shall not come into existence or shall no longer apply to the topography of a semiconductor product unless an application for registration in due form has been filed with a public authority within two years of its first commercial exploitation. Member States may require in addition to such registration that material identifying or exemplifying the topography or any combination thereof has been deposited with a public authority, as well as a statement as to the date of first commercial exploitation of the topography where it precedes the date of the applciation for registration.

2. Member States shall ensure that material deposited in conformity with paragraph 1 is not made available to the public where it is a trade secret. This provision shall be without prejudice to the disclosure of such material pursuant to an order of a court or other competent authority to persons involved in litigation concerning the validity or infringement of the excusive rights referred to in Article 2.

3. Member States may require that transfers of rights in protected topographies be registered.

4. Member States may subject registration and deposit in accordance with paragraphs 1 and 3 to the payment of fees not exceeding their administrative costs.

5. Conditions prescribing the fulfilment of additional formalities for obtaining or maintaining protection shall not be admitted.

6. Member States which require registration shall provide for legal remedies in favour of a person having the right to protection in accordance with the provisions of this Directive who can prove that another person has applied for or obtained the registration of a topography without his authorization.

Article 5

1. The exclusive rights referred to in Article 2 shall include the rights to authorize or prohibit any of the following acts:

(a) reproduction of a topography in so far as it is protected under Article 2 (2);

(b) commercial exploitation or the importation for that purpose of a topography or of a semiconductor product manufactured by using the topography.

2. Notwithstanding paragraph 1, a Member State pay permit the reproduction of a topography privately for non commercial aims.

3. The exclusive rights referred to in paragraph 1 (a) shall not apply to reproduction for the purpose of analyzing, evaluating or teaching the concepts, processes, systems or techniques embodied in the topography or the topography itself.

4. The exclusive rights referred to in paragraph 1 shall not extend to any such act in relation to a topography meeting the requirements of Article 2 (2) and created on the basis of an analysis and evaluation of another topography, carried out in conformity with paragraph 3.

5. The exclusive rights to authorize or prohibit the acts specified in paragraph 1 (b) shall not apply to any such act committed after the topography or the semiconductor product has been put on the market in a Member State by the person entitled to authorize its marketing or with his consent. 6. A person who, when he acquires a semiconductor product, does not know, or has no reasonable grounds to believe, that the product is protected by an exclusive right conferred by a Member State in conformity with this Directive shall not be prevented from commercially exploiting that product.

However, for acts committed after that person knows, or has reasonable grounds to believe, that the semiconductor product is so protected, Member States shall ensure that on the demand of the rightholder a tribunal may require, in accordance with the provisions of the national law applicable, the payment of adequate remuneration.

7. The provisions of paragraph 6 shall apply to the successors in title of the person referred to in the first sentence of that paragraph.

Article 6

Member States shall not subject the exclusive rights referred to in Article 2 to licences granted, for the sole reason that a certain period of time has elapsed, automatically, and by operation of law.

Article 7

1. Member States shall provide that the exclusive rights referred to in Article 2 shall come into existence:

    (a)   where registration is the condition for the coming into existence of the exclusive rights in accordance with Article 4, on the earlier of the following dates:

        (i)   the date when the topography is first commercially exploited anywhere in the world;

        (ii)   the date when an application or registration has been filed in due form; or

    (b)   when the topography is first commercially exploited anywhere in the world; or

    (c)   when the topography is first fixed or encoded.

2. Where the exclusive rights come into existence in accordance with paragraph 1 (a) or (b), the Member States shall provide, for the period prior to those rights coming into existence, legal remedies in favour of a person having the

right to protection in accordance with the provisions of this Directive who can prove that another person has fraudulently reproduced or commercially exploited or imported for that purpose a topography. This paragraph shall be without prejudice to legal remedies made available to enforce the exclusive rights conferred in conformity with Article 2.

3. The exclusive rights shall come to an end 10 years from the end of the calendar year in which the topography is first commercially exploited anywhere in the world or, where registration is a condition for the coming into existence or continuing application of the exclusive rights, 10 years from the earlier of the following dates:

(a) the end of the calendar year in which the topography is first commercially exploited anywhere in the world;

(b) the end of the calendar year in which the application for registration has been filed in due form.

4. Where a topography has not been commercially exploited anywhere in the world within a period of 15 years from its first fixation or encoding, any exclusive rights in existence pursuant to paragraph 1 shall come to an end and no new exclusive rights shall come into existence unless an application for registration in due form has been filed within that period in those Member States where registration is a condition for the coming into existence or continuing application of the exclusive rights.

Article 8

The protection granted to the topographies of semiconductor products in accordance with Article 2 shall not extend to any concept, process, system, technique or encoded information embodied in the topography other than the topography itself.

Article 9

Where the legislation of Member States provides that semiconductor products manufactured using protected topographies may carry an indication, the indication to be used shall be a capital T as follows: T, 'T ', [T] , T, T * or T .

Chapter 3
Continued application of other legal provisions

Article 10

1. The provisions of this Directive shall be without prejudice to legal provisions concerning patent and utility model rights.

2. The provisions of this Directive shall be without prejudice:

(a) to rights conferred by the Member States in fulfilment of their obligations under international agreements, including provisions extending such rights to nationals of, or residents in, the territory of the Member State concerned;

(b)   to the law of copyright in Member States, restricting the reproduction of drawing or other artistic representations of topographies by copying them in two dimensions.

3. Protection granted by national law to topographies of semiconductor products fixed or encoded before the entry into force of the national provisions enacting the Directive, but no later than the date set out in Article 11 (1), shall not be affected by the provisions of this Directive.

Final provisions

Article 11

1. Member States shall bring into force the laws, regulations or administrative provisions necessary to comply with this Directive by 7 November 1987.

2. Member States shall ensure that they communicate to the Commission the texts of the main provisions of national law which they adopt in the field covered by this Directive.

Article 12

This Directive is addressed to the Member States.

Done at Brussels, 16 December 1986.

For the Council

The President

G. HOWE

Index

Artistic works 4.08–4.29
  aesthetic appeal 4.12
  artistic appeal 4.10
  craftsmanship 4.15, 4.16
  intention of creator 4.11
  judicial judgment 4.14
  meaning 4.08
  sculpture 4.18–4.29
Available to public 1.33
  European registered design 3.32–3.34

British Leyland exception 2.32–2.34

Coca-Cola
  shape of bottle 5.02–5.04
Commonplace 2.48–2.58
  meaning 2.50–2.58
Community unregistered design
  right 3.68
  criteria 3.69
  duration 3.72
  infringement 3.73, 3.75
  subsistence of 3.69–3.71
Complex products 3.14–3.18
  meaning 3.15
Copyright
  industrially applied artistic
    works 4.01–4.36
Copyright and Design Act 1839 1.01, 1.02

Design
  definition 1.09, 2.06–2.14, 3.09, 3.10
Design Act 1842 1.03
Design documents and models 4.04
Design right 2.01–2.90
  commercial compromise, as 2.03
  commonplace 2.48–2.58
  definition 2.04

Design right – *contd*
  exceptions 2.15–2.41
    British Leyland exception 2.32–2.34
    'must fit' 2.20–2.24
    'must match' 2.25–2.31
    surface decoration 2.35–2.41
  first marketing 2.67, 2.68
  hybrid nature of 2.02
  infringement 2.06–2.14, 2.80–2.90
  licences of right 2.74–2.78
  method or principle of
    construction 2.16–2.19
  originality 2.42–2.47
  property right, as 2.05
  qualification for protection 2.59–2.61
    commissioner 2.59
    designer 2.59
    employer 2.59
    first marketing 2.59
    individuals 2.59
    persons 2.59
  qualifying country 2.65, 2.66
  qualifying designer 2.62–2.64
  recording of design 2.69–2.71
  rights granted by 2.79
  term 2.72, 2.73
  unregistered 2.01–2.90

European Directive 98/71/EC 1.06
European registered design 3.01–3.75
  assignment 3.56
  availability of rights 3.04–3.07
  available to public 3.32–3.34
  complex products 3.14–3.18
  contact lens 3.25
  dealings 3.56
  design, definition 3.09, 3.10
  geographical scope 3.30, 3.31

Index

European registered design – *contd*
grace period 3.43–3.47
  priority, and 3.45–3.47
immaterial differences 3.40–3.42
individual character 3.35–3.39
  operative date
    establishing 3.48–3.52
infringement 3.58–3.67
legislation 3.01–3.03
licensing 3.56
mortgages of 3.56
'must fit' exclusion 3.19–3.25
  Lego bricks clause 3.21
  modular products 3.21
new law after 2001 Regulations 3.08
novelty 3.26–3.29
  operative date establishing 3.48–3.52
product, definition 3.11–3.13
proprietorship 3.53
technically functional features,
  exclusions 3.19–3.25
term of protection 3.54, 3.55
two-dimensional designs 3.24

First marketing 2.67, 2.68

Geographical scope 1.32
European registered design 3.30, 3.31

Immaterial differences
European registered design 3.40–3.42
Individual character 1.15–1.25
European registered design 3.35–3.39
Industrially applied artistic
  works 4.01–4.36
copyright in 4.01–4.36
  exclusions 4.35, 4.36
  limitations 4.33–4.36
  term 4.33, 4.34
design documents and models 4.04
legislation 4.02–4.07
semiconductor topography 6.11, 6.12
surface decoration 4.30–4.32
Infringement 1.49–1.58
community unregistered
  design right 3.74, 3.75
defences 3.65
defences to action 1.56
proof of 1.50, 3.59
registered designs 3.58
remedies 1.55

Infringement – *contd*
UK registered design
  remedies 3.64
  unjustified threats 1.57, 1.58, 3.66–3.67
unregistered Community design
  right 3.74
unregistered design right 2.80–2.90
  remedies 2.86
  secondary 2.85
  test for 2.81
  threats 2.87–2.90
use of design 1.52, 3.61
IPO forms App 1

Lego bricks clause 3.21
Licences of right 2.74–2.78

Method or principle of
  construction 2.16–2.19
Modular products 3.21
Must fit exclusions 1.39–1.41, 2.20–2.24
European registered design 3.19–3.25
Must match exception 2.25–2.31

Novelty 1.13, 1.14
European registered design 3.26–3.29

OHIM
application for registered
  Community design App 2
Originality 2.42–2.47

Passing off 5.21–5.27
fundamentals 5.22
Roho cushion 5.26, 5.27
Jif Lemon 5.22–5.25
Product
definition 3.11–3.13
Proprietorship 1.42–1.44

Qualifying country 2.65, 2.66
Qualifying designer 2.62–2.64

Recording of design 2.64–2.71
Registered Community design
OHIM application App 2
Registered design
application process 1.46–1.48
available to public 1.33
designs connected to one
  another 1.39–1.41
essential elements 1.12

Registered design – *contd*
  exclusions   1.34, 1.35
  geographical scope   1.32
  individual character   1.15–1.25
  infringement   1.49–1.58
  meaning   1.07–1.58
  must fit exclusion   1.39–1.41
  novelty   1.13, 1.14
  parts of products   1.36–1.38
  proprietorship   1.42–1.44
  technical function   1.26–1.31
  term of protection   1.45
Registered Designs Act 1949   1.04
Registered Designs Rules 2006   1.05

Sculpture   4.18–4.29
  Frisbee mould   4.20
  garden gnomes   4.25
  guidelines as to meaning   4.26
  helmet   4.29
  industrially applied work   4.19
  meaning   4.18
  model of dental impression
    tray   4.21, 4.22
  mould of industrial article   4.23, 4.24
Semiconductor topographies   6.01–6.14
  definitions   6.02
  infringement   6.11, 6.12
  layer, protection of   6.04–6.07

Semiconductor topographies – *contd*
  ownership   6.13, 6.14
  patterns   6.06
  patterns in a circuit board   6.07
  qualification   6.13, 6.14
  Regulations   6.01
  term of protection   6.03, 6.08–6.10
Surface decoration   2.35–2.41, 4.30–4.32

Technical function   1.26–1.31
Trade marks   5.01–5.20
  distinctive shapes   5.13
  Philips v Remington   5.09–5.13
    European Court decision   5.12, 5.13
  shape of Coca-Cola bottle   5.02–5.04
  shapes necessary to obtain
    technical result   5.17
  shapes resulting from nature
    of goods   5.14–5.16
  signs consisting exclusively of
    shape giving substantial
    value   5.18–5.20
  'the goods'   5.16
  Trade Marks Act 1994   5.06–5.11
    picture of rotary shaver   5.09–5.13

UK registered design   1.01–1.58
UK unregistered design right
  see Design right
Unjustified threats   1.57, 1.58, 3.66–3.67